THE NATS AND THE GRAYS

THE NATS AND THE GRAYS

HOW BASEBALL IN THE NATION'S CAPITAL SURVIVED WWII AND CHANGED THE GAME FOREVER

David E. Hubler and Joshua H. Drazen

ROWMAN & LITTLEFIELD
Lanham • Boulder • New York • London

Published by Rowman & Littlefield
A wholly owned subsidiary of The Rowman & Littlefield Publishing Group, Inc.
4501 Forbes Boulevard, Suite 200, Lanham, Maryland 20706
www.rowman.com

Unit A, Whitacre Mews, 26-34 Stannary Street, London SE11 4AB

British Library Cataloguing in Publication Information Available

Library of Congress Cataloging-in-Publication Data

Hubler, David, 1941–
The Nats and the Grays : how baseball in the Nation's Capital survived WWII and changed the game forever / David E. Hubler and Joshua H. Drazen.
pages cm
Includes bibliographical references and index.
ISBN 978-1-4422-4574-7 (hardcover : alk. paper) — ISBN 978-1-4422-8190-5 (pbk. : alk. paper) — ISBN 978-1-4422-4575-4 (ebook) 1. Baseball—Washington (D.C.)—History. 2. Washington Senators (Baseball team : 1886-1960)—History. 3. Homestead Grays (Baseball team)—History. 4. Washington Nationals (Baseball team)—History. I. Drazen, Joshua H., 1973– II. Title.
GV863.W18H83 2015
796.357'640975309044--dc23
2014039447

∞™ The paper used in this publication meets the minimum requirements of American National Standard for Information Sciences Permanence of Paper for Printed Library Materials, ANSI/NISO Z39.48-1992.

Printed in the United States of America

To the Hublers, a Murderers Row lineup of sons Geoff and Rob, daughter-in-law Shannon and our talented and beautiful granddaughters Layla and Macie, and of course batting cleanup, my extraordinarily wonderful wife, Rebecca, whose wisdom, patience, and love always bring me home. And to the memory of my parents, Gladys and Nat, who taught me to love baseball, and especially the New York Yankees.

To the memory of my grandfathers, WWII veterans who helped save the world from pure evil: Alvin "Poppy" Lazaroff, a Navy dentist who survived a failed Kamikaze attack while serving on the USS *Cottle*, and Jack "Papa Jack" Drazen, who experienced the Battle of the Bulge first-hand aboard an Army Sherman tank. I miss them both every day. And to my mother Lynne, my father Barrie, and my sister Jennifer. Nothing would have been possible without their incredible encouragement, love, and support, which I appreciate more than they can possibly fathom.

The sounds were the same through the years—the American sounds of summer, the tap of bat against ball, the cries of the infielders, the wooden plumb of the ball into catchers' mitts, the umpires calling "strike three and you're out." The generations circled the bases, the dust rose for forty years as runners slid in from third, dead boys hit doubles, famous men made errors at shortstop, forgotten friends tapped the clay from their spikes with their bats as they stepped into the batter's box, coaches' voices warned, across the decades, "Tag up, tag up!" on fly balls. The distant, mortal innings of boyhood and youth.

Irwin Shaw, Voices of a Summer Day

CONTENTS

Acknowledgments ix

Preface xiii

1 1941: BP—Before Pearl Harbor 1

2 1942: Changing Uniforms 33

3 1943: Coming Up Just Short 87

4 1944: Meet Me in St. Louie, Bluege 137

5 1945: Rounding Third and Heading Home 185

6 1946 and Beyond: Extra Innings 235

Notes 239

Bibliography 279

Index 285

About the Authors 299

ACKNOWLEDGMENTS

The authors could not have undertaken, no less completed, this history without the kind assistance from a group of knowledgeable friends and colleagues. And because we value their contributions equally, we have chosen to acknowledge them alphabetically:

Hal Bock and **Michael Powers**, co-editors of *Willard Mullin's Golden Age of Baseball: Drawings 1934–1972*, for Hal's encouragement and Mike's permission to reprint an example of the great cartoonist's work.

George Case III, son of Washington Nationals great George Case Jr., for correcting many of the print errors in the newspapers of the day. The man we went to for explanations, clarifications, and anecdotes.

Alicia Clark, historian for the city of Sanford, Florida, for helping to clarify some initial confusion as to the location of Tinker Field, spring home of the Nationals before and after the war, and for other local information that proved valuable.

Bob Clark, deputy director of the Franklin D. Roosevelt Presidential Library and Museum in Hyde Park, New York, for his help throughout the process by providing several official White House documents and his expertise.

Stanley Cohen, author of *The Man in the Crowd*, *The Game They Played*, *A Magic Summer*, and other outstanding sports books, whose friendship and guidance have been valued assets during the writing of this book.

Paul Dickson, author of *The Dickson Baseball Dictionary*, *Bill Veeck: Baseball's Greatest Maverick*, *Baseball: The Presidents' Game*, and many other notable volumes, our most knowledgeable guide through the wide world of baseball research.

Dr. Raymond Doswell, vice president of the Negro Leagues Baseball Museum in St. Louis, for his generous permission to reprint the museum's photograph of the Homestead Grays team.

Bill Gilbert, author of *They Also Served: Baseball and the Home Front, 1941–1945*, for permission to quote from his excellent history.

Matthew C. Hanson, archivist at the Franklin D. Roosevelt Presidential Library, for his assistance in providing photographs and answers when we needed them.

Darren R. Jones and the staff of the Library of Congress for their invaluable assistance and remarkable patience in instructing us in the workings of the library's computers and archives and for supplying us with the documentation and photographs without which we could not have written this book.

Christen Karniski, our terrific editor at Rowman & Littlefield who first came up with the idea for the parameters of the book and who wisely shepherded it from gestation to the finished product, all the while providing guidance and encouragement.

Pat Kelly, photo archivist at the Baseball Hall of Fame and Museum at Cooperstown, New York, for his assistance in tracking down and providing us with some excellent photographs.

Ted Leavengood, well-known baseball historian and Clark Griffith biographer, for steering us to a deeper and more accurate understanding of the legendary Washington franchise owner.

William B. Mead, St. Louis native and author of *Even the Browns* and *Baseball Goes to War: Stars Don Khaki, 4-Fs Vie for Pennant*, for permission to quote from his unique history and memoir of the period.

JoAnn Morse, administrative officer of the Franklin D. Roosevelt Presidential Library and Museum, for assistance during our search for photographs and information about the Roosevelt family.

Amanda Rodriguez, of the Minnesota Twins baseball organization, for finding and sending us photos of several Washington Nationals players while simultaneously engaged in the demanding work of assisting the Twins host the 2014 All-Star Game at Target Field.

Mark Schlueb, of the *Orlando Sentinel*, for keeping us apprised of the city's plans for the antiquated and rarely used Tinker Field even as the demolition ball prepares to take down the Nats' old spring-training site.

Brad Snyder, author of *Beyond the Shadow of the Senators*, who kindly allowed us to mine his authoritative history of the Homestead Grays, in which we found nuggets of pure gold.

The Society for American Baseball Research, the font of all baseball history, lore, biographical information and day-by-day schedules and results of all the wartime games.

Charles "Chuck" Taylor, longtime personal friend of Mickey Vernon, who provided us with valuable insight into the Washington first baseman's life and career.

Jim Vankoski, curator of the Mickey Vernon Sports Museum in Media, Pennsylvania, the keeper of the Vernon flame.

Phil Wood, well-known DC-area TV sports commentator and lifelong Washington baseball fan whose encyclopedic memory of the team and personal collection of memorabilia was a great help to us and proof positive that the team's nickname was the Nationals.

Dr. Richard Zamoff, associate professorial lecturer in sociology at the George Washington University and authority on Jackie Robinson and the Brooklyn Dodgers, for steering us in the right direction about Branch Rickey and to Jules Tygiel's classic work *Baseball's Great Experiment: Jackie Robinson and His Legacy*.

PREFACE

Except for a few years in the mid-1920s, Washington's major-league baseball team could hardly be described as a powerhouse before, during, and especially after World War II. But whether they were called the Senators, the Nationals, or simply the Nats, the Washington franchise and its owner experienced the war from a front-row box seat. The close relationship between the prairie-bred entrepreneur Clark Griffith, frequently known as the Old Fox, and the New York patrician President Franklin D. Roosevelt played an important, if often backstage, role in decisions that affected the team but, more importantly, the national pastime itself. Roosevelt's White House door was usually open to the baseball executive because, as author Richard Goldstein writes in his book *Spartan Seasons*, "The seventy-year-old owner of the Senators had built a friendly relationship with the president beginning in 1917 when, as the wartime assistant secretary of the Navy, Roosevelt marched to the flagpole on the opening day of the baseball season in step with the Griffith-managed Washington team. 'The Old Fox' would do some quiet lobbying at the White House."[1] Yet, despite the closeness of the pair, the Washington franchise was not exempt from placing some of its members in harm's way or temporarily losing several key players who actively participated in winning the war and, in one case, shortening an outstanding diamond career.

The ties between Washington baseball and Washington government predated the U.S. entry into World War II when the Empire of Japan attacked Pearl Harbor, Hawaii, on December 7, 1941. Indeed, the nation—and the team in the person of one former Washington backup catcher—had begun preparations for the conflict—emotionally and militarily—much earlier, even before Nazi armies swept into Poland on September 1, 1939. Soon after the 1934 baseball season ended, with Washington in its all-too-familiar place near the bottom of the eight-team American League with a 66–86 record, now with Cleveland, backstop Moe Berg—described by Casey Stengel as "the strangest man ever to play baseball"—joined an all-star team that included Babe Ruth, Lou Gehrig, Jimmie Foxx, and Lefty Gomez for what was Berg's second exhibition tour of Japan. Berg had first visited Japan in the winter of 1932, while with Washington, to teach catching techniques to young Japanese players as a member of a three-player American delegation. Always a good defensive catcher, on April 21, 1934, Berg set an AL record catching 117 consecutive games without an error. That season was a productive one for Berg at the plate. He hit .244 with the Nats, and then .258 for Cleveland.

Now in Japan again in 1934, Berg's familiarity with the Japanese language (but not fluency as some writers have claimed) and his proclivity to "go native" by wearing a kimono in public allowed him to roam freely about the streets. He took photos and panoramic movies of Tokyo and environs, a highly dangerous activity in an insular country that prohibited "spying" of any kind, especially photography, and was growing ever-more suspicious of Westerners. Upon the group's return to the United States, Berg collected his photos along with some taken by his touring teammates and turned them over to U.S. military officials. Within less than a year after the United States went to war against Japan, then Lt. Col. James H. Doolittle's pilots reportedly viewed Berg's photos to help them become familiar with their target areas before taking off on the famous "Doolittle Raid" on Tokyo on April 18, 1942.

During the war, Berg, the former Princeton scholar and graduate of the Sorbonne and Columbia University Law School—described by his teammates as a man who could speak a dozen languages but couldn't hit in any one of them—worked for the Office of Strategic Services (OSS), the forerunner of the Central Intelligence Agency. Among Berg's OSS missions was to parachute into Yugoslavia to ascertain the strength of the anti-Nazi Chetniks loyal to King Peter and the communist partisans led by Josip Broz Tito. On another mission, posing as a German businessman in Switzerland, Berg met Werner Heisenberg, the 1932 Nobel Prize winner in physics and a prominent German scientist suspected of working on designing an atomic bomb for the Nazi regime. If OSS suspicions were correct, Berg's orders were to assassinate the scientist and then take a cyanide capsule to avoid capture. The astute catcher, who was fluent in German, had boned up on atomic physics for his mission. After listening to a lecture given by Heisenberg, Berg concluded that the Germans were not close to developing the atomic bomb. As a result of Berg's scientific assessment, both men survived the war, and each went on to claim fame in their individual fields: Heisenberg became one of the world's most influential figures in nuclear physics, cited in everything from documentaries on television's the History Channel to the acclaimed AMC TV show *Breaking Bad*. Heisenberg died of cancer at his home in Germany on February 1, 1976. Berg, often called the "smartest baseball player ever," never married. He had no close friends or known romantic attachments. Although he attended many major-league games in New York in later life, he remained a virtual recluse and an enigma until his death in Belleville, New Jersey, in 1972. His extramural career in wartime espionage is enshrined in DC's Spy Museum and was also included in an OSS exhibition at CIA headquarters in Langley, Virginia.

Some might say that major-league baseball survived the war unscathed even if the quality of play was somewhat diminished during the approximately three and a half years that the United States was involved in the conflict. Also, of the more than 500^2 major leaguers who served in the U.S. military during the war, only two were killed in action. One of them played, however briefly, for Washington. He was centerfielder Elmer Gedeon. The Cleveland native was born on April 15, 1917, attended the University of Michigan, and played in just five games for Washington in 1939. His 15 at-bats included three hits, one run batted in, no home runs, and a very mediocre .200 batting average. Sent down in 1940 to Washington's Class B affiliate Charlotte of the Piedmont League, Gedeon appeared in 131 games, upping his stats to 127 hits, 11 home runs, and a .271 batting average. He was then drafted into the Army Air Corps and served first as a B-25 navigator before getting his wings as a B-26 pilot. (Due to a high crash rate of early models, the B-26 acquired several negative nicknames, including the Widow Maker, the Flying Prostitute, and One a Day in Tampa Bay.) Gedeon's twin-engine Martin Marauder B-26 bomber was shot down over France on April 20, 1944, killing him along with most of his crew. Gedeon is buried at Arlington National Cemetery, only a few miles from where Griffith Stadium stood, home of the franchise from 1911 through 1960.

Being colocated in the nation's capital along with the Capitol, the White House, and the five-sided U.S. armed forces citadel, the Pentagon, Washington's baseball franchise led by its wily owner Clark Griffith, alone among the then 16 major-league teams, was uniquely positioned to play an important wartime role of influencing top decision makers. The team—almost universally known before and after the war as the Washington Senators—actually had a different name, the Nationals (as in their current namesake, which is now playing in the National League at Nationals Park, which opened in 2008). Here's how that happened:

In its founding years of the late 19th century, the Washington baseball club, like so many other teams, changed names, cities, and leagues with chaotic regularity. Among Washington's 19th-century nicknames were the Washingtons, the Statesmen, the Olympics, the Nationals, and, from 1892 to 1899, the Senators, a National League franchise. In addition, those early Washington teams played in a number of different ballparks. Examples include the Olympic Grounds, capacity 500 and home to the Washington Olympics of the National Association in 1871. Later, as an expansion member of the American Association and when the league grew to 12 teams in 1884 to become the Union Association, the team was called the Washington Nationals. However, the bloated Union Association quickly folded, and the Washington franchise moved into the Eastern League in 1885, winning the pennant with a 72–24 record. The team then jumped to the major National League as the Senators (aka the Statesmen) in 1886, taking one of the spots vacated by the collapse of the Buffalo, New York, and Providence, Rhode Island, franchises. There the Senators remained, playing between 1886 and 1899, first in colorfully named Swampoodle Grounds. But the Washington Senators folded when the National League contracted from 12 teams to 8 after the 1899 season. Little wonder too because between 1892 and 1899 the Senators finished no higher than seventh place.

The next iteration of the Washington Senators came in 1901 as a founding member of the new American League, where they continued their tradition as a perennial second-division team by finishing sixth that inaugural season. The newly formed competitor of the established National League had been the brainchild of three of baseball's iconic figures—Ban Johnson, a former sportswriter who became the American League's first president; Charlie Comiskey, owner of the Chicago White Sox; and Griffith, the only man who has ever played for, managed, and owned a major-league team for 20 years or more in each of those categories. The new Senators played in what was called American League Park I from 1901 to 1903, before the grounds were moved to Florida Avenue and Seventh Street and known as American League Park II, where the outfield included a doghouse near the flagpole, which housed the Stars and Stripes before and after the games but had no actual canine resident. As author Philip J. Lowry recounts in his history of American baseball parks, *Green Cathedrals*, the groundskeeper one day failed to close the doghouse door. "It just so happened that a Washington batter hit a line drive that afternoon over the head of Philadelphia Athletics center fielder Socks Seybold and the ball rolled inside the Dog House. Seybold stuck his head and shoulders inside to get the ball and promptly got stuck in the Dog House. Three minutes later, A's teammates got Socks out, but the batter had long since crossed home plate with the only inside-the-dog-house homer in Major League history."[3]

Through the 1904 American League season, when Washington lost 113 games against only 38 wins, the team's worst record ever, the team nickname was the Senators. But in 1905, the franchise officially changed it to the Nationals, "not wanting to confuse fans with the previous franchise," as the official team website explains.[4] It's more likely, however, that the club wanted to erase for itself (and for its fans) all remembrances of things past. But that was not to be thanks to sportswriter Charles Dryden, whose clever description of the last-place 1909 Senators as "Washington—first in war, first in peace and last in the American League," stuck with the club for decades. From 1905 through the 1911 season, the Nationals never finished higher than seventh in the eight-team league. On March 17, 1911, the team's luck changed when a fire allegedly started by a workman burned down the wooden stands at American League Park II and damaged the field. But the loss of the single-tier structure and the team's perpetual seasons in or near the American League cellar opened the door for Clark Griffith and led to his lifelong association with the team as its owner and as the go-to leader keeping major-league baseball alive during World War II.

Many Washington fans and even many members of the media never knew or truly accepted the team's actual Nationals nickname, although there is a paper trail to prove it. Copies of several historic documents sent to the authors by local TV sportscaster Phil Wood form a timeline that provides proof positive that the Nationals was the true team nickname: a scorecard from a 1914 home game between the Nationals and the Philadelphia Athletics, the front page of the Nationals' 1937 Orlando, Florida, spring-training guide, the official 1945 Nationals roster, and the cover of the 1956 Nationals Press Guide. Yet, even after the club incorporated "Nationals" into its jersey logo in the early 1950s, the name failed to gain traction, perhaps because so many sportswriters and the popular baseball chewing-gum cards insisted on calling them the Senators. (This was before team logos and nicknames were copyrighted items and huge moneymaking commodities, emblazoned on everything from replica team jerseys, jackets, and caps to children's lunch boxes, underwear, and even pet clothing.)

Thus, to most of the baseball world, including the general public and a good portion of the working press, they were the Senators—or just the Nats, a nickname that was conveniently short for headline purposes and that also could refer to either name, Nats as in short for Nationals and also as short for Senators, found in the middle of the word. The official nickname remained the Nationals until 1956, when the team gave up trying to bend the popular will and the franchise officially became the Washington Senators once again. However, according to Phil Wood, the name Senators didn't appear on the jerseys until 1959. But that rebranding effort was short-lived, a true exercise in futility, as the franchise, now with a roster of young talent including Harmon Killebrew and Bob Allison, moved to Minneapolis–St. Paul after the 1960 season and became the Minnesota Twins.

The following season, 1961, the first expansion in American League history added the Los Angeles Angels and the new Washington Senators. Both franchises were stocked with aging or castoff players taken from a list of eligible players from both leagues. The Senators played only their inaugural season at Griffith Stadium—finishing tied for ninth place with the Kansas City Athletics with 61 wins and 100 losses, 47½ games behind the Yankees. In 1962, the Senators moved into their final home in the nation's capital, D.C. Stadium, later renamed Robert F. Kennedy Memorial Stadium. Between 1962 and 1968, the Nats finished tenth, tenth, ninth, eighth, eighth, sixth, and tenth—never reaching even a .500 season.

They did see some daylight in 1969, when they finished with a respectable 86–76 record which was good for fourth in the six-team AL East, the first year of division play, but placed them sixth overall in the 12-team American League. However, in 1970 and 1971 (their last year in DC), they fell to the bottom of the league. They finished dead last in the AL East and ninth out of the 12 AL teams in 1970 with a 70–92 record, and fifth in the AL East in 1971 and 11th out of the 12 AL teams with a terrible 63–96 record. In September, Senators' owner Bob Short received approval from Major League Baseball to move to Arlington, Texas, for the 1972 season and play as the Texas Rangers. Washington fans were so incensed by a second betrayal and loss of their team that they streamed onto the field in the ninth inning of the final home game with the Senators leading the New York Yankees, 7–5, with two men out. The game was thus forfeited to New York, a fitting coda for the short-lived franchise, and the nation's capital was again left without major-league baseball, not to return for more than three decades.

The current Washington Nationals are a Canadian import, formerly the Montreal Expos, a National League expansion team founded in 1969. But unlike its fellow expansion Canadian club, the Toronto Blue Jays, the Expos failed to create a sustaining presence north of the border despite some very good years and a roster that included stellar players, including four future Hall of Famers, catcher Gary Carter, outfielder Andre Dawson, Frank Robinson (who became the new Nationals first manager after also managing the Expos), and former Expos manager Dick Williams. The Expos franchise and all of its baseball records were transferred to the new Lerner ownership group in Washington, DC, in 2005, which—flying in the face of superstition, a baseball staple—again chose the nickname Nationals. So far, the team has outperformed its namesake and, after a poor first few years, has steadily ridded itself of its former image as a perennial loser. Gone forever (it is to be hoped) is the specter of the perennial loser, the Senators. So no matter what other baseball histories may call the team, for the few years under scrutiny in this book, unless within a quoted passage, we will refer to Washington's wartime team by its proper nickname, the Nationals.

1

1941

BP—Before Pearl Harbor

War came to America when major-league baseball was in its winter hibernation and diamonds had given way to gridirons. It came at the hands of a nation that loved baseball almost as much as the United States and whose gift of 3,000 cherry trees in 1912 had become an icon of the nation's capital, also home to Washington's major-league baseball team. Commonly called the Senators but officially the Nationals (although few knew, or used, that nickname), Washington's baseball fortunes for the 1941 season had concluded in September with another losing season in sixth place tied with the St. Louis Browns with identical records of 70 wins against 84 losses. It was a small improvement over the seventh-place finish in 1940, when the Nationals' record was 64–90. Before that, Washington had finished sixth in 1939, with 65 wins against 87 losses; and fifth in 1938, with just under a .500 record at 75 wins against 76 losses. So the Nats were used to winding up in the lower half, or second division, of the eight-team American League.

By December of 1941, the 25 players, coaches, and Bucky Harris, in his second stint as manager (he'd be back for a third try in 1950), had dispersed to the far corners of the United States, for their winter jobs on farms, in factories, and in other pursuits that supplemented the few thousand dollars they'd earned on the playing field. Clark Griffith, the team owner, had retired to his home in suburban Maryland to prepare for the annual owners meeting in Chicago. Because Griffith was an iconic figure in the history of the game and played such an important role during the war years, not just on the diamond but also in the domestic war effort, it is important to know something about the man, who was already in his eighth decade in December of 1941.

Clark Calvin Griffith was a product of America's roiling post–Civil War Kansas–Missouri frontier. No one in the vicinity of Clear Creek, Missouri, who'd seen the small, sickly boy born on November 20, 1869, in his parents' log cabin would have ever dreamed that one day he'd be a star pitcher, manager, club owner, and confidant of presidents. Griffith was the fifth of six children born to Isaiah and Sarah Anne Griffith, who'd moved west from Illinois to Missouri, where Isaiah eked out a modest existence on farmland he bought to support his family. Later, Clark would tell stories about his father having known Jesse James, who he said had spent a night at the Griffith home, and how as a young boy Clark tended to the famous outlaw's horse the next morning. That memory most likely was either an anecdote told to him by his mother or an imagined tale that became part of Griffith's repertoire of frontier stories he spun to amuse his friends years later. What is true, however, is that in February 1872, Isaiah Griffith was shot and killed by a neighbor who mistook him for a deer as he ran into an open field. Clark was just two years old at the time.

But it wasn't the glamour of James's lawless exploits along the wild Kansas–Missouri frontier that captured young Clark's heart, it was playing the new game of baseball that had become popular during the Civil War and which "gave vent to his natural leadership skills and provided his first chance to lead other men," as Griffith biographer Ted Leavengood puts it.[1] "But more than anything, it allowed him to put behind him the rough times about which he seldom spoke except in folksy yarns that romanticized that early life."

As he grew into a young man, albeit a short one who suffered from what was diagnosed at one time as malarial fever, Griffith nevertheless continued to develop into an outstanding ballplayer especially after Sarah Griffith moved the family back to her home of Normal, Illinois, near Bloomington, in 1883. Although the permanent move was primarily aimed at improving the family's finances and helping Clark overcome his recurring illnesses, the "brutal realities of life on the frontier shaped Griffith in important ways that some say explained the 'bewildering paradoxes' of a man who," as Leavengood notes, "would lead labor revolts in his early adult life before becoming a hard-nosed executive whose wealth made him frequent company for presidents of the United States"[2]

Griffith, who never grew taller than five and a half feet or so, honed his love of and skills for baseball in Bloomington, where he came under the tutelage of Charles Radbourn, a professional pitcher who taught the prospective young ballplayer how to throw a deceptive assortment of pitches that would later baffle opposing batters who pinned on him the nickname "the Old Fox." That nickname also later proved appropriate to those who had to deal with him either as a manager or as a wily, hard-nosed baseball executive. Radbourn, or "Old Hoss" as he was known, was a self-taught pitcher who was born in Rochester, New York, and grew up in Bloomington. As a pro, Radbourn toiled mostly for the Boston Beaneaters and the Providence Grays from 1881 to 1891, racking up 309 wins against 194 losses for a winning percentage of .614 and well-deserved election into the Baseball Hall of Fame in 1939.[3] Old Hoss has also been credited with a personal record that most likely never will be topped: in 1884, pitching for the Grays in the National League, Radbourn tossed 678⅔ innings over 75 games, winning an astounding 59 of them against only 12 losses and racking up a 1.38 earned run average. "Years later Griffith would say of his first baseball teacher, 'He was brainy and game to the core,' two hallmarks of Clark Griffith's career as well."[4]

Griffith's first pro pay was $10 as the winning pitcher in an Illinois game between two town semipro teams. He was just 17 when his performance attracted the attention of Jesse Fell, who owned the Bloomington team and enticed Griffith to join the club in 1887. Griffith made his pitching debut as a starter on May 1, 1888, winning the game, 3–2, and driving in the winning run with a double in the sixth inning. After leaving the Bloomington team, Griffith went to the Milwaukee Brewers of the Western Association, where he pitched for three years. In 1891, Charlie Comiskey lured him from Milwaukee to join his American Association St. Louis Browns. Although the Browns released him in mid-season when Griffith developed a sore arm, he and Comiskey became lifetime friends and both were later instrumental in the 1901 founding of the present American League.

When the American Association folded at the end of the 1891 season, the Old Fox went west for two years to hurl for clubs in Tacoma,

Washington; Missoula, Montana; and Oakland, California. He later claimed it was while he was pitching for the Oakland Colonels of the California League that he invented the screwball. In Oakland, he won 30 games against 18 losses while also participating in Wild West shows to earn some extra cash. In early September 1893, the California League folded, and Griffith signed with Cap Anson's Chicago Colts of the National League, finishing the season there with a record of 1–2 in four games. In the eight years between 1894 and 1899, Griffith won more than 20 games each season for the Chicago Colts and then as the renamed Chicago Orphans, where "he found lasting fame as a pitcher, made numerous friends, and learned about showmanship and gamesmanship from the legendary Anson," according to his SABR biography.[5]

Besides being a leader on the field—racking up 152 wins against only 96 losses while pitching for Chicago—Griffith also led the players' fight for better pay and against the reserve clause that bound players to their teams for as long as ownership wished (a battle that long preceded St. Louis Cardinal Curt Flood's 1969 battle for free agency). However, the recession of 1898 hurt the attendance of a league that had expanded from 8 to 12 teams just six years earlier, and as a result, Washington, Baltimore, Cleveland, and Louisville were dropped from the league after the 1899 season. But the battles between owners and players over wages continued and reached their zenith in 1900. By then, Griffith had become an astute baseball businessman with a keen sense of fairness for those on the field. He was named vice president of the National League players association and became "the aggressive voice in group discussions, much as he was on the field."[6]

As a prime mover in the creation of the Ball Players Protective Association (BPPA) in April 1900, Griffith cut his teeth on the politics and economics of the sport, which stood him in good stead for the rest of his life. It was Ban Johnson, a decent amateur ballplayer in college and sportswriter by profession, who became the spark that ignited the American League in 1901. As historian Leavengood notes, "Johnson had crafted, from the old Western League that he had led for six years, a second major league, but he had a talented supporting cast that included many of the best minds in the game at the time, Charlie Comiskey, Clark Griffith, Connie Mack, and financier Charles Somers."[7] With Griffith as the catalyst, convincing players not to sign any NL contracts until they heard from the Ball Players Protective Association, the new American League challenged the established National League.

In December 1900, as the challengers suspected, the National League owners, meeting in New York for their annual session, rejected the BPPA's demand to raise ballplayers' salaries above the league-mandated ceiling of $2,400 per player. The rejection gave Griffith "the ammunition he needed to recruit players," and he "single-handedly convinced many NL stars to sign AL contracts."[8] Much as he had done on the mound as a star pitcher, Griffith's wily maneuvering resulted in his signing 39 of the 40 targeted NL players who would form the nucleus of the new American League. The only autograph he could not get, Griffith later admitted, was that of Honus Wagner, whose outstanding 21-year National League career with Louisville and Pittsburgh earned him a place among the original five inductees in the Baseball Hall of Fame in 1936. (Today, the Pirate shortstop perhaps is equally well known for his extremely rare 1909 baseball card, which sold at auction in New Jersey in 2013 for a little more than $2.1 million. According to legend, when Wagner discovered that a tobacco company had used his likeness on the card without his permission, he feared it might induce children to start smoking and he demanded that it be withdrawn from circulation. The offending company obliged and the card quickly became scarce.)

The signings by the American League of National League stars such as Napoleon Lajoie, who made his major-league debut for the Phillies against Washington on August 12, 1896, and St. Louis Cardinals pitcher Cy Young helped secure the new American League as a legitimate competitor for baseball fans' attention and dollars. In its 1901 inaugural season, the American League was stocked with more than 100 former National Leaguers on the eight AL rosters.

As a result of Griffith's astute tactics and signings, his friend Charlie Comiskey named him player-manager of the AL Chicago White Stockings for the 1901 and 1902 seasons. By then, the two warring leagues had settled most of their disagreements and had even established a season-ending best-of-nine-games series to determine the "World Series" championship that would begin in 1903. "Clark Griffith and his cohorts were among the best players of their day," Leavengood asserts, "men who had achieved stardom on the field and were now leaders on teams that looked increasingly competitive with their National League rivals."[9] In his dual role as pitcher-manager in 1901, Griffith won 24 games, losing just seven with a 2.67 earned run average. In the process, Chicago won the first American League pennant, edging out Boston by four games, with a league-mandated roster limit of just 15 players. Griffith had "willed them to win, getting great defense and pitching from a team that would not be able to duplicate its success" in succeeding seasons. "The most important member of the team was Griffith himself. He was the rock of a strong pitching staff, and without him they would never have stood up to Boston."[10] The following season, the Old Fox won 15 games against nine losses as the White Stockings slipped to fourth place.

That inaugural year of 1901, playing as the Senators under manager Jimmy Manning, Washington finished sixth with a record of 61 wins against 72 losses. It was the first of 11-straight losing seasons, including three (1904, 1907, and 1909) when the club lost 100 games each year. In 1905, out of desperation and in a futile attempt to change its luck, Washington jettisoned its Senators nickname and adopted a new one, the Nationals.

After two years with the White Stockings, Griffith went east to manage the start-up New York Highlanders. Formerly the Baltimore Orioles, playing in what was the fourth of five fields named Oriole Park[11] (before the present Oriole Park at Camden Yards), the franchise was sold in 1902 for $18,000, and its new owners promptly relocated the club to New York City in time for the next season when the team changed its nickname to the Highlanders to reflect the elevated area of Manhattan where their home field, Hilltop Park, was located. After losing the season opener to Washington in DC, 3–1, on April, 22, 1903, the Highlanders unveiled their new $275,000 ballpark, capacity 15,000, by beating Washington, 6–2, on April 30. The Highlanders finished fourth that season with Griffith pitching in 25 games, amassing a 14–11 record and a 2.70 earned run average.

Always looking to better himself and his players financially, Griffith proposed a postseason intraborough series between his Highlanders and their powerful neighbor, the New York Giants, managed by the legendary John McGraw.

The Manhattan ballparks were close to each other: Hilltop Park at 168th Street and the Polo Grounds near 158th Street on a site known as Coogan's Bluff. The idea was that the added gate receipts would give the players some much-needed additional cash, as was happening in St. Louis and Chicago, also cities with two teams. But McGraw would have none of it. (Years later, beginning in 1946, the Highlanders, now the powerful Yankees, played either the Giants or Brooklyn Dodgers in an annual Mayor's Trophy charity game at alternating ballparks. The series was abandoned when the two National League teams left [diehard fans of the two clubs prefer the word "deserted"] New York and went west to California after the 1957 season. However, in 1944, as part of the war-relief fund-raising efforts, the Giants, Yankees, and Dodgers played a unique round-robin game at the Polo Grounds in which each team fielded for six innings, three against each opponent, and each team batted for three innings against each opponent. The final score was Dodgers 5, Yankees 1, Giants 0, and the event raised $5.5 million in war-bond purchases. Because of the bitter rivalry between the Giants and the Dodgers, the Giants shared their home dugout with the Yankees.)[12]

During Griffith's five and a half seasons in New York, the Highlanders finished second twice but never won an American League pennant. He resigned in June of 1908 following a midseason slump when the New Yorkers dropped 12 of 13 games. Despite his waning pitching skills, recognition of his baseball acumen kept Griffith in high demand for another managerial post. That December, he signed on to pilot the Cincinnati Reds, leading them to successive fourth-, fifth- and sixth-place finishes from 1909 through 1911, respectively.

But Griffith's dream had always been to own a team, and on March 17, 1911, his chance came, oddly enough when Washington's wooden stands burned to the ground and the club needed to raise $100,000 in a stock sale to rebuild. When Washington manager Jimmy McAleer jumped to Boston to become president of the Red Sox in September, Griffith saw an opening to buy into the Washington club whose best finish had been sixth place in 1901 and 1902. That's when the Old Fox's business acumen took over. He raised $7,000 by selling the livestock on a ranch in Montana he owned jointly with his brother. Then he mortgaged the ranch to raise another $20,000 and used all $27,000 to buy stock in the club and gain what turned out to be a lifetime association with Washington baseball. Although the investment gave him a minority interest in what by any measure was the poorest team he was ever associated with, ownership in a major-league franchise was what he had his heart set on, and he assumed the role of team manager beginning with the 1912 season. As famed *Washington Post* sports columnist Shirley Povich recalls in his history of the team, "Manager Griffith strode into the Washington scene with his cowpoke gait and lifted the Senators all the way from seventh place to the heights of a second-place finish"[13] in 1912 and again the following year. Between 1914 and 1920, his last year as manager, the team's best finish was third place in 1914 and again in 1918.

But by 1920, the ownership group was growing concerned about Griffith's ability to field manage, and there was front-office talk of replacing him. To prevent that, the Old Fox secured financial backing from William Richardson, a wealthy grain merchant whom Connie Mack had introduced to Griffith. Griffith parlayed Richardson's cash to secure a bank loan of $87,000, and together they bought 85 percent of the team. Griffith, now 48 years old, became owner and president. Richardson became a silent partner in the venture. To put his personal stamp on the franchise, Griffith rechristened the ballpark Griffith Stadium and added a second deck around the infield. "Clark Griffith was finally in a position to bring his little ballclub to unprecedented heights during the course of the free-wheeling decade that lay ahead," team historian Tom Deveaux writes.[14] In many ways, Griffith's initial moves to build a winning team set a pattern that was later emulated by the current Washington Nationals. Griffith got rid of all the players he thought could not produce or who were showing their age—he called them "old timber"—and began a rebuilding effort with young, talented ballplayers around an exceptional pitcher who had joined Washington in 1907 named Walter Johnson.

But complete success and the holy grail of baseball, a World Series championship, did not come quickly, and when it did, it came only once. After finishing fourth in 1923, the 1924 Nationals, led by the great "Big Train" Johnson and now managed by Bucky Harris, won the pennant and then the World Series against John McGraw's powerful Giants four games to three, topped by a 12-inning game-seven victory. With a total gate of more than $1 million, Griffith cut bonus checks of nearly $6,000 for each player, virtually doubling their annual salaries or better. The Old Fox's return on his investment in the team "was something that Griffith had been waiting for his entire baseball career, since he had first seen Charlie Comiskey step off the playing field and into the owner's suite in Chicago," Leavengood says. To date, the 1924 series remains Washington's only World Series triumph, and although the Nats repeated as the American League pennant winner the following season, they fell to the Pittsburgh Pirates in seven games, after squandering a series lead of three games to one. The losers, who committed nine errors in the series, each took home a World Series share of about $3,800. "The golden age of baseball in Washington, D.C. would fill the stadium and the coffers of his team and bestow the magnate status on Clark Griffith in a way he had talked about for years, but only dreamed would come true. He would increasingly become an institution unto himself, important to all segments of the community in the 'little southern town' known as Washington, D.C.," Leavengood writes.[15] (Washington fans would see their team in the World Series only once more, in 1933, when the Nationals lost to the same Giants four games to one. In 2012, the new Nationals won the National League East title for Washington's first postseason appearance in 79 years.)

Now on that cold, blustery Sunday afternoon, December 7, Griffith Stadium (built in 1911 and demolished in 1965), was hosting the final professional football game of the season between the Washington Redskins and the Philadelphia Eagles. Kickoff was set for 2 p.m. Eastern Standard Time, 8:30 a.m. in Hawaii (In 1941, unlike today, Hawaii was in a half-hour time zone so the attack on Pearl Harbor began at 7:55 AM in Hawaii or 1:25 PM in Washington DC). "Bombs had already fallen on the U.S. fleet, men had died, war had come. In the stands no one knew," recalls S. L. Price in a November 1999 *Sports Illustrated* article.[16] "Only the boys in the press box had any idea. Just before kickoff an Associated Press reporter named Pat O'Brien got a message ordering him to keep his story short. When O'Brien complained, another message flashed: 'The Japanese have kicked off. War now!'" But Redskins owner George Preston Marshall refused to allow the public-address (PA) announcer to broadcast the news, claiming it would be a distraction to the fans. "That made Griffith Stadium one of the last outposts of an era that had already slipped away," Price writes.

Soon, however, the crowd of some 27,000—and even the players on the near frozen field—began to wonder what was happening as, one by one, the PA announcer called military officers by name and told them to report for duty immediately. Nearby, in government buildings across DC, personnel officers "burned the telephone wires calling to their decks [*sic*, likely a typo for "desks"] specialized personnel whose services were immediately required by the situation in the Pacific," the *Washington Post* reported the next day.[17] As radios and newspapers across the country blasted out the news, Americans were dumbfounded, angry, and also fearful. CBS radio reporter Eric Sevareid, describing reactions on the streets of Washington, said the crowds had "the same frightened look" he had seen on the faces of Parisians a year earlier when the Nazis marched into the French capital. He reported, too, that his colleague Edward R. Murrow "detected a fear he remembered from the worst days of the London Blitz."[18]

Recalling that Sunday years later, Redskins quarterback Sammy Baugh told *Sports Illustrated*'s Price, "We didn't know what the hell was going on. I had never heard that many announcements one right after another. We felt something was up, but we just kept playing."[19] For Eagles halfback Nick Basca, it was the final game of his career. Basca enlisted in the Army three days later and was killed in action in France on November 11, 1944, when a mortar shell tore through the tank he was driving.

In New York City, a similar scene was unfolding. The pro football New York Giants were hosting the football Brooklyn Dodgers at the Polo Grounds in Manhattan. Early in the first half, the PA announcer intoned, "Attention, please. Here is an urgent message: will Col. William J. Donovan call Operator 19 in Washington immediately," recalled veteran *New York Times* sportswriter Dave Anderson in an article written on the 50th anniversary of the Pearl Harbor attack.[20] Donovan had been a standout running back on Columbia University's football team, where he earned the nickname "Wild Bill" for his freewheeling running style. He'd also been a hero in the Great War, earning promotion to the rank of colonel and awarded the Medal of Honor for leading an assault on an enemy stronghold under heavy fire. Donovan went on to become acting attorney general in the Coolidge administration before going into private law practice on Wall Street.

Donovan had been a classmate of Franklin D. Roosevelt's at Columbia's Law School, class of 1907, and although he was a Republican and a critic of FDR's New Deal, the two men saw eye-to-eye when it came to the growing menace of National Socialism in Germany. President Roosevelt had sent Donovan to London in July 1940 to meet with British leaders, assess the strength of the nation's defenses, and determine Britain's urgent war needs. When he returned to Washington in August, Donovan assured FDR that the British would fight to the last man, but, he said, they desperately needed supplies from the United States, especially at the front. Donovan also urged Roosevelt, unsuccessfully however, to recall the U.S. ambassador in London, Joseph P. Kennedy, who angered the British and many in the Roosevelt administration, including the president himself, by, among other things, his isolationist stand on U.S. entry into the war and prediction of a Nazi victory. One year after Donovan returned from London, FDR named him national coordinator of information, the position he held when he was urgently summoned to the telephone at the Polo Grounds. (In 1942, Donovan formed and then led the Office of Strategic Services, which was responsible for espionage and aiding the resistance movements in occupied Europe. Among Donovan's OSS operatives was former Nats backstop Moe Berg.)

Long before Pearl Harbor, however, the winds of war blowing through Europe were being felt in Washington. On August 31, 1935, Congress passed the first Neutrality Act prohibiting the United States from exporting arms, ammunition, and implements of war to foreign nations at war. To control the spread of weapons, the law also required U.S. arms manufacturers to apply for export licenses. Roosevelt originally opposed the legislation but relented in the face of strong congressional pressure and public opinion. (When Roosevelt later tried to get Congress to ease some of the arms restrictions in the Neutrality Act in the wake of Germany's invasion of Czechoslovakia, Montana Senator Burton K. Wheeler, a fellow Democrat but a prominent and vocal isolationist, charged FDR with trying to push the United States into a European war that would "plow under every fourth American boy.")[21]

On February 29, 1936, Congress renewed the Neutrality Act until May of 1937, and Roosevelt signed it. One year later, FDR authorized a major expansion of the U.S. Navy's Atlantic and Pacific fleets when Congress approved his request for $4 billion to pay for the additional ships. The Neutrality Act of 1937 did contain one important concession to Roosevelt and pro-democracy groups because, under the act, belligerent nations were allowed, at the discretion of the president, to acquire any items except arms from the United States, so long as they immediately paid for such items and carried them on non-American ships—the so-called cash-and-carry provision.

As the State Department explains, "Since vital raw materials such as oil were not considered 'implements of war,' the 'cash-and-carry' clause would be quite valuable to whatever nation could make use of it. Roosevelt had engineered its inclusion as a deliberate way to assist Great Britain and France in any war against the Axis Powers, since he realized that they were the only countries that had both the hard currency and ships to make use of 'cash-and-carry.' Unlike the rest of the Act, which was permanent, this provision was set to expire after two years."[22]

War broke out in Europe on September 1, 1939, when, despite having signed a nonaggression pact with Warsaw in January 1934, Hitler's armies invaded Poland in a blitzkrieg attack. Britain and France promptly declared war on Germany. In November, U.S. lawmakers passed a final Neutrality Act, which lifted the arms embargo and put all trade with belligerent nations under the terms of "cash-and-carry," a move clearly aimed at helping Britain and France. Also, the ban on loans remained in effect, and American ships were barred from transporting goods to belligerent ports.

In May 1940, Congress appropriated $2.5 billion for Roosevelt's program to rebuild military infrastructure, and in mid-August, FDR met with Canadian Prime Minister Mackenzie King in upstate New York, where they created a Permanent Joint Board on Defense to prevent a German or Japanese attack on North America. The United States and the 21-nation Pan American Union had reached a similar mutual-defense accord for Central and South America in July in Havana. That pact called for one or more signatory nations (in effect, the United States) to step in and govern any islands or territories in the Americas belonging to a non-European state should another non-American state (meaning Germany) attempt to take it over, "until it was able to govern itself freely or had been restored to its previous status," according to *Pan-Americanism and the Pan-American Conferences*,[23] published by Portland State University. Among the many possible targets of potential aggression in the Americas, the most important was the U.S.-owned Panama Canal, the key waterway that facilitated shipping between the Atlantic and Pacific Oceans. U.S. defenses kept the canal open to the world's shipping throughout the global conflict.

In mid-June of 1940, as France fell to Nazi control, Roosevelt outlined his program of universal, compulsory government service. Under the plan, some two million young men, ages 19 to 21, would undergo a year's military training in the Army or Navy or in needed industries such as communications, aviation, industrial technology for essential military goods, or agriculture. Had Congress passed the program, few major leaguers would have been affected because a majority of them were older than 21. But the president quietly abandoned the idea when it met strong opposition from lawmakers. Instead, he tacitly backed the Burke–Wadsworth Bill, which created the first peacetime draft in U.S. history.

The bill was written by Senator Edward Burke, a Nebraska Democrat who served just one term from 1935 to 1941, and by Representative James Wadsworth, a New York Republican, who prior to serving in the House had served in the Senate where he had been chairman of the Senate Committee on Military Affairs in the 66th through 69th Congresses. Wadsworth was one of the very few lawmakers ever to go from the Senate to the House, and he also served as chairman of the National Security Training Commission from 1951 until his death in 1952.

Long before coauthoring the draft bill, Wadsworth had developed a passion for national military preparedness due, he claimed, to his having lived through years of complacency and isolationism. Burke and Wadsworth were counseled by Grenville Clark, a New York lawyer and peace activist who had known Roosevelt since 1907 when they were junior associates at the New York City law firm of Carter, Ledyard, and Milburn. Clark is remembered as the architect of the Selective Service Act because of his experience and interest in military preparedness during World War I, when he helped organize what would later become the Military Training Camps Association. Clark testified before the Senate Military Affairs Committee in favor of the bill's passage and later served as chairman of the Citizens Committee for National War Service from 1944 to 1945. In 1985, the U.S. Postal Service posthumously honored Clark with a 39-cent first-class stamp as part of its Great Americans series.

Despite the concurrent fall of France, initial debate in Congress over the draft bill was loud and vociferous. And much like today's Congresses, opposition to the ground-breaking legislation was stiff indeed. On July 11, John Nevin Sayre, an official with the Christian peace group Fellowship of Reconciliation, told the Senate Committee on Military Affairs that "the Burke–Wadsworth bill is a form of Hitlerism being pressed on the American people by high-power propaganda under the label of 'national defense.'" He urged its defeat. Also speaking out that day was journalist Oswald Garrison Villard, who called the bill "un-American, undemocratic, and repugnant to the fundamental American principles."[24] In an incident more appropriate in DC's Uline Arena, once the city's boxing citadel, two House members came to blows over the bill when Ohio Democrat Martin Sweeney denounced it and Beverly Vincent, a fellow Democrat from Kentucky, called Sweeney a traitor and a son of a bitch. At which point, Sweeney swung at Vincent and missed, but Vincent didn't. He "counterpunched with a hard right to Sweeney's head," writes historian Joseph E. Persico in *American Heritage*. "The House doorkeeper called it the best fistfight he had witnessed in his 50 years at his post."[25] And when Florida Democrat Claude Pepper spoke in favor of the proposed legislation in the Senate, he was hanged in effigy outside the Capitol by an organization calling itself the "Congress of American Mothers."

Opposition to the draft was not limited to Capitol Hill. A 1939 poll of Americans found 80 percent were pulling for Britain and its allies, but a solid 90 percent of respondents did not want the United States to get involved. And America First, a gathering of isolationists, swelled its ranks to some 850,000 members under the slogan "The path to war is a false path to freedom."[26] Yet, on September 14, 1940, with the addition of 33 amendments, the Selective Training and Service Act passed by a vote of 232 to 124 in the House and 47 to 25 in the Senate. FDR signed the bill two days later, and all American males between the ages of 21 and 36—that included just about every player in professional baseball, major and minor leagues alike—were required to register for military service.

To appease the isolationists in Congress and elsewhere (even though their numbers were declining rapidly as the war in Europe heated up), the new law restricted draftees to serve only in the Western Hemisphere or in U.S. possessions or territories. They also would be in uniform only for 12 months and no more than 900,000 men would train at any one time.[27] Within two weeks of the draft's October 16 start, 16,316,908 men had registered for the draft.[28] But just four months before Pearl Harbor, the House—by a razor-thin margin of 203 to 202—extended the length of service by one year. (By the end of 1941, 923,842 men had been inducted into the service. That number grew to

3,033,361 and to 3,323,970 in the peak years of 1942 and 1943, respectively, according to the Selective Service System.)[29]

On the final Sunday of 1940, in one of his famous "fireside chats," Roosevelt laid out what *Washington Post* reporter Robert C. Albright called "an all-out appeal for breathless industrial armament and aid to the British 'front line.'" With the election behind him, Roosevelt felt free to propose sending increasing amounts of munitions and supplies to Britain, Greece, and other nations fighting Nazism. He also "summoned the American people to make their greatest effort of all time to increase production so this country might become the 'arsenal of democracy.'"[30]

Reaction to his "chat" was overwhelmingly positive, with telegrams to the White House running 100 to 1 for his plan. Indeed, public opinion overwhelmingly agreed with Roosevelt that the defense and security of the United States was closely dependent on Britain winning the war, which at the time it was not doing. A Gallup poll released just prior to FDR's radio address showed "deep public concern over the Battle of Britain and a belief that the fate of America is closely related to the fate of the English."[31] Of those polled, 68 percent agreed that the safety of the United States depended on a British victory, and 85 percent believed Britain would lose the war if the United States stopped sending the British war materiel. Only 11 percent thought Germany could conquer Britain within a year's time.

Armed with the backing of the American public, Roosevelt then made his case before a joint session of the new 77th Congress on Monday, January 6, in a State of the Union address that contained specific defense recommendations—continue the defense buildup, aid the besieged democracies, and no appeasement to Hitler. Speaking directly to Britain, he pledged, "We shall send you, in ever increasing numbers, ships, planes, tanks, and guns" and to partially pay for them, he urged Congress to join the American people "in putting patriotism above pocketbooks" and create "a new tax program based on the ability to pay."[32]

The isolationists, Charles Lindbergh and Wheeler prominent among them, criticized the president's program, claiming it was using America's allies as this nation's first line of defense. Addressing members of the pacifist organization American Peace Mobilization, who had marched to the White House two days before Roosevelt's State of the

Union address, Wheeler insisted that "there is no such thing as aid to a belligerent short of war." As he explained to an approving audience, "When you lease or loan you're buying an interest in the war. Some people say it is our war. If it is our war, how can we justify loaning them stuff and asking them to pay us back? If it is our war, we ought to have the courage to go over and fight it—but it isn't our war."[33]

The start of the new decade, 1941, began with traditional New Year's Eve revelry. "Washington took a deep breath last night and blew the old year out with an ear-splitting roar," proclaimed the lead sentence on the front page of the *Washington Post.* "The bedlam of sirens and whistles, horns and bells, shouts and songs, echoed over the city from Foggy Bottom to Chevy Chase, from the flats of Anacostia to the hills of Georgetown. It was farewell to a year that brought total war to the world, misery and starvation to millions—farewell with few regrets for its passing."[34] According to the uncredited *Post* writer, "it was one of the most energetic and gigantic celebrations" the nation's capital had ever seen with some extra 100 police on hand to direct traffic and keep order. But if the evening was a cause for celebration, the days to follow were fraught with the ever-growing menace of the war spreading beyond Europe. President Roosevelt, fresh from his third and unprecedented election victory, spent the evening in the White House with family members and a few close friends enjoying a musical performance and singing "Auld Lang Syne." FDR then delivered a toast "to the United States!"

To those who saw him, the chief executive seemed healthier and in a happier mood than he had been recently, when he faced the quick and humiliating fall of France in June, the start of the horrendous German blitz on London in September, and the tiring electoral campaign against Republican presidential-nominee Wendell Willkie in November, during which he promised if he were reelected there would be no U.S. involvement in foreign wars. "France's fall, so sudden and so complete, disappointed the hopes on which his [war assistance] policy had been founded. The surprise and shock seem to have exhausted him mentally," columnists Joseph Alsop and Robert Kintner wrote in their New Year's paean of praise to the president.

However, after he began taking "long afternoon rests for the first time in his life" and "making a real vacation of his cruise aboard the *Tuscaloosa*," Roosevelt "is now his old self, quick, venturesome and bold as ever."[35] In a sidebar article, journalist Ernest K. Lindley supported FDR in opposing the isolationists who were constantly nipping at the presidential heels, especially fellow Democrat Senator Wheeler. Both men, he wrote, want to avoid war. "But Wheeler is more concerned about avoiding the present one, which the President thinks can be won by our aid, than a future war which we might have to fight alone. The President believes that if this one can be won, we will escape a later and more dangerous and more costly war."[36] That was not to be, of course.

Later, during the summer, FDR got an additional patriotic boost for his anti-isolationism stance from an unexpected, but welcomed, source. In July, the biopic *Sergeant York* premiered in New York starring Gary Cooper as the reluctant World War I hero who single-handedly killed two dozen Germans and captured more than 100 others in the Argonne forest in October 1918, a feat that earned him the Congressional Medal of Honor. The real Sergeant Alvin York, who was serving as a district official of the Selective Service System in his home area of Pall Mall, Tennessee, attended the premiere along with Cooper, who was then negotiating to star in another biopic with a not-so-happy ending, *The Pride of the Yankees*, playing Lou Gehrig, who had died one month earlier on June 2. When *Sergeant York* opened in Washington a week later, Roosevelt attended the premiere. "The quiet, dignified, and finally devastating image of American heroism on the screen, a role that won Cooper an Academy Award, was too pertinent for the President to resist," wrote author Michael Seidel.[37] *Sergeant York* instilled a good deal of pride in the citizen Yanks, too, many of whom would soon be on their way to Britain.

During spring training and into the new baseball season, professional ballplayers, most of them young men in their physical prime, wondered what the new military-service law would mean for them and when, or even if, they'd be called to serve. Bob Feller, Joe DiMaggio, and Hank Greenberg, three of the game's greatest stars, signed up the first day of the draft. But the dubious honor of actually being the first called up for military service went to a luckless Philadelphia Phillies pitcher named Hugh Mulcahy, who was inducted on March 8, 1941, and promptly went off to Fort Devens, Massachusetts, for basic training. Mulcahy had earned the dubious nickname of "Losing Pitcher" because during his nine-year major-league career he had 45 wins and

89 losses, including an astonishing, but understandable, 76 losses between 1937 and 1940 on a Phillies team that finished no higher than seventh between 1933 and 1945.

Mulcahy would serve 53 months in the Army, including time in New Guinea and the Philippines, before receiving an honorable discharge as a master sergeant on August 5, 1945. Mulcahy returned to the Phillies in 1945, finishing 1–3 with a 3.81 ERA over 28⅓ innings. He appeared in 16 games in 1946, compiling a 2–4 record and a 4.45 ERA that did nothing to prompt a revision of his nickname. After the Phillies released him at the end of the 1946 season, he signed with the cross-state Pittsburgh Pirates and pitched in just two games without a decision before being released in May 1947. But as Mulcahy told baseball author William B. Mead many years later, he had no regrets about his early call-up. "Bad luck? I don't know. I might have got hit with a line drive if I spent six more months with the Phillies [laughs]. Seriously, I never felt really bad about it. It never shook me up; I never think back on what might have been. I'm very thankful that I came back."[38]

Washington's roster was not immediately affected by the draft in 1941, thanks in good measure to Griffith's self-appointed role as baseball lobbyist and his political connections in town. Small consolation, though, as the team finished in a sixth-place tie with the always bottom-feeding St. Louis Browns, a distant 31 games behind the American League champion New York Yankees. Because of his franchise's location in the federal city and his well-honed business acumen, Griffith's ties to Washington's power brokers were long and strong (today those in power fall under the rubric "inside the Beltway").

Behind the scenes, Griffith "undertook a discreet role as baseball's resident lobbyist"[39] for his club and for major-league baseball's interests in the wake of the draft. Those ties even reached into the White House, whose occupant had a lifelong love of baseball stemming from the days when a young Franklin Roosevelt was the manager of the Groton prep-school team in 1900. FDR admitted he was never a good player, but he loved the action on the field, especially high-scoring games. "I'm the kind of fan who wants to get plenty of action for my money," he explained. "I get the biggest kick out of the biggest score—a game in which the hitters pole the ball into the far corners of the field, the outfielders scramble and men run the bases."[40]

   Griffith had known FDR since 1917, when, as assistant secretary of the Navy during World War I, Roosevelt subbed for President Woodrow Wilson and accompanied then manager Griffith on the traditional march to the outfield flagpole to raise the American flag on opening day.[41] After the United States entered the conflict on April 6, 1917, Secretary of War Newton Baker ruled in July that baseball, then in mid-season play, was not essential to the war effort, so all eligible men were required either to sign up for the service or be engaged in essential defense work. Baseball prepared to shut down within a few days. But the Old Fox had a better idea, a compromise solution. Griffith convinced Baker to permit the sport to continue through Labor Day plus an additional two weeks for the World Series.[42] In essence, the season would be shortened by a couple of weeks, and in the meantime, the major leaguers would engage in military-training exercises on their home ball fields with bats on their shoulders in place of rifles. (Recalling that time in his *Washington Post* column just after Pearl Harbor, Shirley Povich wrote, "Ball players, in spiked shoes, drilling with bats in present-arms poses, presented a laughable picture of military preparedness, as we look back.")[43]

   To add to the legitimacy of the "basic training," Griffith enlisted his friend Roosevelt (not yet stricken with infantile paralysis) to lead some of the drills, which no doubt encouraged Baker to agree to the plan. Griffith further cemented the friendship by organizing successful charity events at ball games to raise funds for baseball equipment to send to the "doughboys" in France. Ballparks around the country held Griffith Days and collected money for the war effort. When the ship that was carrying the initial batch of equipment overseas was sunk by the German navy, Griffith promptly began gathering new funds.

   Years later, as was the custom, Griffith annually presented President Roosevelt with a season's pass to Washington's home games for himself and first lady Eleanor Roosevelt. The Old Fox also was always ready with some pregame inside information whenever FDR would call asking about the day's starting pitchers before placing some friendly wagers with cabinet members or White House aides. FDR reciprocated by throwing out the ceremonial first ball the first eight years of his presidency,[44] a record that, thanks to the 22nd Amendment to the Constitution, can be tied but is very unlikely ever to be broken.[45] Roosevelt also was on hand to watch the 1937 All-Star Game played at Griffith Stadium on July 7. (On May 16, 2014, a rare 8mm home-movie clip taken by Nats pitcher Jimmie DeShong, who was not on the AL All-Star roster, and donated to the Pennsylvania State Archives by his daughter, showed an upright Roosevelt, his legs supported by heavy metal braces under his trousers, slowly making his way up a ramp to the presidential box on an aide's arm and grasping a handrail. FDR threw out the ceremonial first ball. The short piece of film is said to be only the second such clip in existence showing the president walking.)[46]

In a November column previewing the upcoming December 1941 major-league baseball owners' meeting at the Palmer House hotel in Chicago, Shirley Povich revealed that Griffith was "plotting [to unveil] a new piece of legislation for the big leagues." Griffith wanted to expand each club's night-game allotment from the previous year's 7 to 14 and insisted that "it is always folly to laugh [Griffith] off" because at the owners' meetings "he's a man to be reckoned with." (Povich recalled that four years earlier it was Griffith's arm-twisting at the winter meetings that had led to a rule change allowing a pitcher to keep one foot off the rubber as he went into his windup motion.) Povich said Griffith wasn't necessarily being selfish in wanting more night games. The Nats' seven games under the lights in 1941 averaged 18,000 in attendance, far more than the 4,700 spectators on average who trickled through the gates during the day.[47]

Griffith's illumination advocacy was a complete change of heart. For years, he had adamantly insisted there would never be night baseball in the major leagues because the game rightly ought to be played under "the Lord's own sunshine." That had been his position since the first major-league game was played under the lights at Crosley Field in Cincinnati, Ohio, on May 24, 1935. The first evening contest proved to be an instant success as more than 20,000 fans turned out, "ten times above the average weekday attendance of the lowly Reds," according to baseball historian Benjamin G. Rader.[48] It was Griffith's pal, FDR, who symbolically switched on the lights for the game from the White House. Nevertheless, Griffith's verdict was that "the National League has become a burlesque circuit."

However, sometime between that Crosley Field night game and May of 1941, Griffith had a major change of heart and had ended his adamant opposition to night ball. Like just about everything the Old Fox did in his decades-long baseball career, he had a good reason to change his mind, and like so much of what motivated Griffith, the reason was financial. After winning the team's last pennant in 1933, the Nationals quickly fell into the second division. The nation was in the midst of the Great Depression, and few people had the wherewithal to pay their way into baseball games; Babe Ruth, the game's greatest draw, had recently retired; and Griffith owed the bank $125,000, forcing him in 1934 to send his best player and son-in-law, Joe Cronin, to the Red Sox in exchange for a shortstop, Lyn Lary, and $250,000. [49]

On May 28, 1941, the Nationals played their first night game at Griffith Stadium. A near-capacity crowd of 25,000 fans turned out, an initial good omen, as Griffith obviously wanted to make good on his $130,000 investment in a lighting system. The game commenced with Walter Johnson coming out of the dugout to throw a fastball across a beam of light at home plate that triggered the illumination 150 feet above the field. The Yankees prevailed, 6–5, on an eighth-inning grand-slam home run by George Selkirk (years later, he became Washington's general manager), who was pinch-hitting for shortstop Frankie Crosetti, and Joe DiMaggio hit a triple, extending his soon-to-be-legendary con-secutive-hit streak to 13 games. For Griffith, the game was an epiphany even though it marked the Nationals' 10th loss in a row and dropped them into last place. As Frederic J. Frommer writes in *The Washington Nationals 1859 to Today*, "The Senators continued to draw well under the stars, and Griffith became an enthusiastic supporter" of night base-ball. [50] By the end of the 1941 season, more than 1.5 million fans had attended the 77 major-league night games that year, an average of al-most 20,000 a game. [51]

The Old Fox admitted to his change of heart when he wrote years later, "When the National League instituted night competition [in 1935], I hollered plenty. I envisioned the ruination of the game in the major leagues. I regarded baseball after dark as strictly minor league stuff." However, after seeing the turnout for the Nats' inaugural-night game, Griffith admitted, "I realized then that I had been wrong about the innovation." [52]

Griffith had another reason why night baseball made good sense. "We've got a situation to combat," he said, noting that he'd seen the same situation during the Great War. "It's this national defense work that threatens to keep fans from our parks in the daytime," Griffith explained. So now he wanted more night games for his Nats and for other clubs with lights that wanted an increase. The final decision whether to double the number would be decided by baseball Commissioner Kenesaw Mountain Landis, another of Griffith's close friends and no stranger to the other owners. "If any group had to choose a champion to carry a cause to Landis, it could make no better choice than the 71-year-old owner of the Nats," Povich wrote.[53] Although Landis and Griffith differed in many ways, when it came to baseball they were united in their determination to protect the game at all costs.

Landis was born on November 20, 1866 , in Millville, Ohio, one of seven children of Mary Kumler Landis and Abraham Hoch Landis, a prosperous doctor who named him Kenesaw after the location of the Civil War battle in Georgia (although misspelling it) in which he had been wounded. Although he never completed secondary school, young Landis read for the law and then attended law school before opening a practice in Chicago. He left the practice in 1883 when Secretary of State Walter Gresham made him his personal secretary.

In 1905, President Theodore Roosevelt appointed him a federal judge. Two years later, Landis gained national fame when he fined John D. Rockefeller's Standard Oil of Indiana $29 million, a huge sum at the time, for price-fixing practices involving the railroads.[54] During the First World War, Landis added to his notoriety by levying heavy fines and jail sentences on draft resisters and opponents of the war. The baseball owners hand-picked him for their newly created job of commissioner in 1920 primarily because of the judge's sly handling of the 1915 Federal League anti-trust lawsuit against organized baseball for operating an illegal trust and demanding that the major leagues be dissolved and all contracts voided. Rather than rule for either the plaintiff or the defendants, Landis stalled so long in rendering a decision that the faltering Federal League finally reached an agreement with the major league owners after the season. The lawsuit was dropped. In exchange, Chicago Whales owner Charles "Lucky" Weeghman was allowed to purchase the Chicago Cubs and St. Louis Terriers owner Phil Ball bought the Browns. Other Federal League owners received a cash settlement and the Federal League was dissolved, leaving in place the owners' power over professional baseball and its players. Four years later, in the wake of the 1919 Chicago "Black Sox" gambling scandal, the owners turned to Landis to lead baseball back to respectability.

In accepting the job of commissioner, while remaining an active judge, the strong-willed lifelong Republican made several demands, including a $50,000 annual salary (this at a time when associate justices on the U.S. Supreme Court earned $20,000 and the chief justice $20,500). Like them, he also demanded a lifetime appointment, and he insisted on virtual total authority to act under the ill-defined umbrella of being "in the best interests of baseball," a position that at times put him at odds with the owners and the league presidents. Landis's first official act as baseball's overlord was to ban from the game for life the eight Chicago White Sox players, including the famous "Shoeless" Joe Jackson, who were implicated in the 1919 "Black Sox" World Series gambling scandal, despite their having earlier been found not guilty in a court of law. Landis defended his ruling by saying that any player who throws a game or "sits in a conference with a bunch of crooked players and gamblers" will never play professional ball again.[55] And despite their appeals and participation on semipro teams, the eight never again donned major-league uniforms.

When the owners of baseball's 16 teams began gathering at the Palmer House that first Sunday in December 1941, they were prepared to wheel and deal players and to consider some rule changes, including Griffith's plan to double from 7 to 14 the number of night games each team could host, a plan also advocated by Donald Barnes, the always fiscally challenged St. Louis Browns' president. With Griffith's backing, all that remained to seal the deal was formal approval by the other club owners, who were scheduled to hold a vote on it on Monday, December 8, and then an OK from Landis.

But in the aftermath of news of the attack on Pearl Harbor at 1 p.m., Central Time, the owners became "a strangely subdued group, and while the feeling prevailed that the show must go on, all seemed cognizant of the fact that vast changes in the game's general conduct were in prospect," *New York Times* sportswriter John Drebinger reported from Chicago.[56] "Prospective player deals, for one thing, appeared temporarily to have been swept by the board," he added, because it was futile to try to swap players whose immediate future was unknown. Indeed, "the few attempts at trade talks quickly fizzled" as the owners sat in their rooms "with their ears tuned to the radio bulletins or standing in little huddles in the lobbies," wrote Associated Press sportswriter Judson Bailey.[57]

In his first column after Pearl Harbor, on December 9, Povich surmised that "the outbreak of war has probably already disposed of one move by baseball people. Clark Griffith's plan to increase from seven to 14 games the number of night contests for each club at home, is doubtless doomed." As Povich explained, "In peacetime such an increase in baseball's use of electric power might have been countenanced, but with the Nation at war, the Washington owner may not even introduce his resolution. Such a forebearance [*sic*] may be the first sign of baseball's patriotism."[58] Not to be so easily defeated, Griffith bided his time, and his crusade for more night baseball would reemerge soon, this time with the backing of a new powerful ally. Instead, the Old Fox turned his attention to another wartime crusade.

From the owners' vantage point, the Japanese attack on Pearl Harbor was also an attack on baseball. They feared a complete shutdown of the coming 1942 season, as had been threatened when the United States entered the Great War in 1917. Looking ahead to spring training, they pondered how especially the clubs that trained on the West Coast, geographically closest to Japan, would cope. Of more immediate concern, the owners didn't know how many players might be lost to military service, for how long, and who would replace them. But in his December 9 "This Morning" column, Povich reported that Washington "wasn't particularly concerned about the draft status of its best player, Cecil Travis. Because he passed his twenty-eighth birthday, Travis faced no early draft call despite the fact that he had been classified A-1 [*sic*]. But those Japanese bombs put Travis in direct line for military duty. Selective service officials have announced that the 28-year age limit for draftees will no longer be observed." The Nats had "a half dozen key players who now that peace has ended, have faint hope of escaping the draft call," Povich wrote.[59]

Unbeknownst to the other owners and to Landis, Griffith had been lunching about once a month with General Lewis B. Hershey, who served as director of the Selective Service System from 1941 to 1970. As Hershey confided to author William Mead in an interview years later, "Griffith was trying to keep a ball team on the field," and they often discussed the possibility of deferments. "But I don't think it seemed to a lot of us that you could start out deferring people from service to play ball," Hershey said, and he then added that, as the war progressed and more ballplayers were being called up, "there wasn't any reason for

Griff to talk to me."[60] During those lunches, the Old Fox surely was trying to protect his two best players, Buddy Lewis and Cecil Travis, at the price of a few meal checks. With some luck and some lunches, Lewis and Travis received deferments through the end of the 1941 season, at which time they were called up and were lost to the team for three years.

Born John Kelly Lewis Jr., in Gastonia, North Carolina, on August 10, 1916, Buddy Lewis played right field and third base for Washington between 1935 and 1949 and was 19 when he was called up to the big leagues. He had a career batting average of .297 over 11 seasons and appeared in All-Star Games in 1938 and 1947. Despite being the sole source of income for his parents, Lewis was denied a deferment and was among the first group to be called up by his local North Carolina draft board. "What was my attitude? Well, I didn't particularly like it," Lewis told Mead in a separate interview. "At the time there was no war and no real vision of war. Hell, you kind of hated to just leave." Lewis's draft board never did grant him a deferment, but "Clark Griffith got it through General Hershey," Lewis added, attesting to the Old Fox's lobbying skills.[61] Lewis proved to be as adept at flying as he was at baseball.

Piloting a C-47 cargo plane he named "the Old Fox," Lewis became a decorated transport pilot flying "the hump" of the Himalayas in the China–Burma–India (CBI) theater. Lewis flew 368 missions, made many landings in jungle clearings behind Japanese lines, and was awarded the Distinguished Flying Cross. "Everybody agreed he was the best transport pilot in the CBI theater," Luke Sewell, then the manager of the St. Louis Browns, told the *Washington Post*, after flying with Lewis in Burma. "He set his big transport plane down on tiny strips that didn't look big enough for a mosquito to land on. And he did it while he was talking baseball to me," Sewell recalled.[62] (Lewis played two and a half seasons after he returned in 1945, batting .333 in 69 games that year and then .292 in 1946 and .261 the following season. His last game was at Griffith Stadium against the Boston Red Sox on September 30, 1949, ending with a career batting average of .297. He later became an automobile dealer in Lowell, North Carolina. Buddy Lewis died on February 18, 2011.)

Travis, another southern boy, was born in Riverdale, Georgia, on August 8, 1913. A three-time All-Star, he played shortstop, third base, and the outfield for Washington for 12 years. If anyone besides DiMaggio and Williams left a lasting impression on the ballfields before departing for the service after the 1941 season, it was Cecil Travis. Travis went on a season-long hitting tear, batting .359, with a major-league-leading 218 hits, including 39 doubles, 19 triples, 7 home runs, 101 RBIs, and 106 runs scored. But it was his bad luck to set those personal records and perform at his peak the same year that those two all-time great Hall of Famers had record seasons that still have not been topped. Travis's numbers were permanently overshadowed by DiMaggio's still unbroken 56-game hitting streak and Williams's herculean feat of batting .406 that year, the last time the .400 barrier was broken for an entire season.

Sadly, after he returned to Washington in mid-1945, Travis's major-league career lasted only another year and a half because of two frost-bitten toes on his left foot that he suffered during the frigid 1944 winter when his unit was engaging Nazi forces in the Battle of the Bulge. A career .314 hitter, Travis's best postwar batting average was .252 in 1946. He played his final game on September 23, 1947, at age 34, after appearing in just 74 games and batting a career low of .216, with just 44 hits and 1 home run. Griffith, who always was protective and appreciative of his longtime players, a number of whom also became his managers, told Travis that he could stay with the team as long as he wanted. A proud player, Travis thanked Griffith but told him it was indeed time to quit.[63]

The team held "Cecil Travis Night" on August 15, 1947, which was attended by the former Supreme Allied Commander in Europe, General Dwight D. Eisenhower. Travis was showered with gifts, including a DeSoto automobile and a 1,500-pound Hereford bull. He worked as a scout in the Nationals organization until 1956.[64] Although he had a batting average of .314 over a 12-year career, Travis never made it into the Baseball Hall of Fame. Asked years later about his failure to be enshrined, Travis said, "I know some people say the war cost me a chance at the Hall of Fame, but I don't think about that at all." Then he added, "I was a good player, but I wasn't a great one."[65] To this day, some baseball historians insist that Travis was the best player never to be voted into Cooperstown. (Travis was, however, inducted into the Georgia Sports Hall of Fame in 1975 and into the Ring of Stars at Washington's RFK Stadium in 1993.)

On Monday, December 8, the full complement of owners began their meetings at the Palmer House. The baseball moguls—all of whom remembered how their counterparts in World War I voluntarily cut short the 1918 regular season at Labor Day—stalled on making any momentous decisions too quickly. (After the armistice in November 1918, cooler heads in Washington and among the owners agreed that curtailing the season had been a mistake because it deprived fans of a needed morale boost.) A *New York Times* banner headline on December 9 read, "Baseball Men Advised to Move Cautiously in Gearing Game to War Conditions."

So the owners adopted a "wait-and-see" stance with all eyes and ears on Washington for direction. Landis and the two league presidents, Ford C. Frick and Will Harridge, said they expected no immediate changes. However, they "would stand ready to cooperate with the government and the military authorities in whatever measures might be requested." Larry MacPhail, then the Dodgers general manager, suggested "that for the present we go ahead quietly with our affairs. Some clubs are going to be hit harder than others, but we'll all have to take our chances."[66] Nevertheless, before the Palmer House meetings ended, several trades were completed, and Landis dimmed the bright idea of additional night games after the two leagues could not agree on the issue.

Yet in the wake of Pearl Harbor, a United Press (UP) survey[67] on the prospects of sports in wartime was overwhelmingly bullish on the continuation of college and professional football, boxing, tennis, horse racing, and track and field. Owners, managers, and college officials believed that their particular sport would continue despite an expected general draft of millions of young men. However, there was general agreement that baseball—America's national game and passion—would be hit hardest, the UP poll found. Trying to assuage fears of a complete shutdown or a repeat of a shortened wartime season, Commissioner Landis said it was too early for such speculation, and American League President Harridge added that "while the nation's welfare is our first consideration, I am sure baseball will carry on as it always has—completing the 1942 season and those of other years."[68] Then they headed home for the holidays, with their next gathering scheduled for February.

But if baseball was to fall victim to a wartime interregnum, owners, players, and fans could take solace in the fact that the last prewar season had been a historic one. In his *Baseball in '41*, author Robert W. Creamer judges it to be the best baseball season ever. Indeed, 1941 was indelibly written into the record books by Williams's .406 season batting average and DiMaggio's 56-game hit streak. The Yankee star tied George Sisler's old American League record of 41 consecutive games, set in 1922 (during which the Browns first baseman hit an astounding .459), with a hit in game one of a Sunday doubleheader at Griffith Stadium on June 29. After going hitless in his first three at-bats in game two, DiMaggio broke Sisler's AL record hitting successfully in his 42nd consecutive game.

Luck had been on Griffith's side because he "had been ballyhooing the doubleheader for weeks," Creamer wrote,[69] hoping for good weather and a sellout crowd. "Sisler's record streak meant more to [DiMaggio] than that of Wee Willie Keeler," writes Michael Seidel, "the very existence of which he had first heard about only a couple of days before."[70] (To honor the occasion his Yankee teammates later gave DiMaggio a sterling silver humidor with their etched signatures on the lid.) The Yankee Clipper crept to within one game of "Wee" Willie Keeler's major-league record of 44 hits in as many games, set in 1897 (when foul balls did not count as strikes, effectively giving hitters of that era more opportunities to hit safely), at home on July 1 in the first game of a doubleheader against the visiting Red Sox.

He promptly tied Keeler with his 44th hit, a single to center in the first inning in the rain-shortened nightcap. The next day, against the same Red Sox team, DiMaggio almost set a new record in his first at-bat with a shot into the gap in Yankee Stadium's vast right center field only to be robbed by a fine running catch by Stan Spence, who would be traded to Washington in December. DiMaggio broke Keeler's record in his third at-bat with a line drive over Ted Williams's head for a home run. According to Dom DiMaggio, before breaking Keeler's record, the two brothers had joked about where the baseball writers had found that ancient mark. "Hell, I thought they made it up," Dom DiMaggio told Seidel.[71]

The Yankee slugger then went on hitting successfully in another 12 games as the Yankees marched toward another American League pennant and their ninth World Series championship. Although DiMaggio came in third for the American League batting title behind Williams and the Nats' Cecil Travis, he nevertheless carted off the Most Valuable Player trophy in 1941. Travis finished sixth for the MVP award.

Now, in December with U.S. entry into the war no longer in doubt, Griffith especially was concerned about the future of his franchise. To some of his fellow owners, baseball was a sideline, a means to boost advertising and sales of their main business. Such men included beer magnate Jacob Ruppert Jr., of the Yankees, and brothers Powel and Lewis Crosley, of the Cincinnati Reds, also Chicago Cubs owner Philip K. Wrigley, scion of a chewing-gum empire. But for Griffith, baseball was his sole business; he had no other means of making a living. Shutting down baseball for the duration of the war was tantamount to taking away his livelihood.[72] Some advice on how Griffith could possibly remedy his situation came from an unexpected source.

Sam Lacy, a black sports columnist for the AFRO publishing group, which included the *Baltimore Afro-American* and the *Washington Afro-American*, was an outspoken critic of Griffith and his Nationals. To Lacy, a native Washingtonian and longtime advocate of baseball integration, there was no better city to break the color barrier than Washington, DC, with its large black population and a stadium in the midst of the city's largest black neighborhood. Griffith, however, believed otherwise. He publicly called for strengthening the Negro Leagues so that both black and white organizations would prosper. But in reality, his generation of owners, accustomed to the near-complete separation of the races in all aspects of American life, had no intention of integrating. However, he was not averse to renting his ballpark to Negro League teams, especially to the Homestead Grays, "the greatest baseball dynasty that most people have never heard of," who had debuted in Griffith's old American League Park in 1921, against the black Washington Braves.[73]

Like everything in the professional baseball universe, the growth and maturity of the Negro Leagues evolved over time. Teams like the Atlantic City Bacharach Giants, the Baltimore Stars, and the Washington Potomacs rose and fell regularly until a more-or-less stable solar system of clubs—some more powerful and with greater resources than others—formed in the 1920s when Rube Foster, like Griffith a former pitcher and now club owner of the Chicago American Giants, founded what is today referred to as the Negro Leagues by organizing eight teams in the Midwest and calling it the Negro National League. Three years later, an eastern-based league was created.

The Grays, formed in 1910 in Homestead, Pennsylvania, as a recreational activity for black steelworkers in the Pittsburgh area, originally were not part of either league; they played only exhibition games. A year later, Cumberland "Cum" Posey, a former college basketball star at Penn State, joined the club as an outfielder. Later, as manager and then owner, he put together powerful teams buying the best players available, often raiding other teams' stars. By doing so, he "changed the team's fortunes forever." According to Homestead Grays historian Brad Snyder, the 1930 club was one of Posey's greatest teams, featuring future Hall of Famers Josh Gibson, Judy Johnson, and Oscar Charleston, who had power and speed at the plate and "once roamed center field like Willie Mays." Charleston was regarded as the best player of his generation.[74]

Posey began renting Griffith Stadium for some home games in 1940; for the next two seasons, the Grays divided their games equally between Pittsburgh Pirates' home Forbes Field, where they sported an H on their uniforms, and the nation's capital, where they wore a W. Once they began playing regularly at Griffith Stadium, the Grays became the sun around which all other Negro League teams revolved. "For Lacy and many other black residents, Griffith Stadium was an oasis," as Snyder puts it, because "Clark Griffith made blacks feel welcome inside the ballpark" where the right-field pavilion was reserved (but not officially segregated) for them.[75]

Though the games gave Griffith some added revenue, for the first couple of seasons at Griffith Stadium, in the heart of the black community, the Grays failed to build a true following among the city's African American population. For one, Washington's black baseball fans had long rooted for Griffith's Nats. Snyder attributes the failure to create a homegrown fan base mainly to two reasons: the Grays erred by hiring a white sportswriter as their publicity man. Joe Holman couldn't get the mainstream white press to regularly report on the team, and his hiring alienated the black press. In addition, during their inaugural year of 1940 at Griffith Stadium, the Grays' best player and biggest draw, slugging catcher Josh Gibson, played most of the season in Venezuela, earning a good deal more than Posey had been paying him. He was AWOL again in 1941, selling his services to a Mexican League team in

Vera Cruz for the princely sum of $800 a month, $300 more than his Grays' contract called for.[76] But the Grays and the Old Fox would have far-more lucrative days in the war years.

Just before the new year of 1942 was rung in, Griffith stepped forward with a plan to support the GIs similar to the one he had devised a quarter-century earlier, hoping that the goodwill engendered by his actions would be rewarded by the government with an OK for baseball to continue during this latest world war. Having conferred with his league president, Will Harridge, the Army officer in charge of military morale, and the nation's leading sporting-goods manufacturers, Griffith again launched a campaign to raise funds for bats, balls, and equipment for the men in the armed services just as he had during the First World War. The initial order of about $42,000 would pay for 18,000 baseballs and 4,500 bats, the best possible, none of that cheap stuff for our soldiers and sailors, only the best for them, Griffith insisted. Further funding would come from stadium events during the season and especially from receipts at the midseason All-Star Game. The hundreds of so-called A and B kits would consist of three bats, a dozen balls, and a complete catcher's outfit and would be distributed throughout the war by the Joint Army and Navy Committee on Welfare and Recreation.

Griffith's actions were promptly lauded by the *Sporting News*, which on January 8, 1942, recalled his unique role in baseball and war. "As a player, manager and club owner, Clark Griffith has served the game faithfully and well for half a century. It is especially fitting that his name is included among the nominees now being balloted upon the members of the Baseball Writers' Association of America for additions to the Hall of Fame at Cooperstown. . . . But high as that honor may be, even greater luster is added to the career of the snowy-haired Washington club president by his service to his game and to his country in two wars."[77] (Griffith wasn't elected to the Baseball Hall of Fame until 1946, when he was inducted as a pioneer/executive by the Old Timers Committee.)

In a strange twist of fate, the sneak attack on the U.S. Pacific fleet was a double whammy for another of the Nats' American League opponents, the always cash-strapped St. Louis Browns. As sports historian Thomas Gilbert tells it, Browns owner Donald Barnes, "enticed by a sweetheart deal offered by the Pacific Coast League mainstay Los Angeles, put together a deal that would have transferred his team to a new ballpark in Los Angeles."[78] Simply put, there were many years when the Browns couldn't draw flies at Sportsman's Park in St. Louis. From 1932 to 1939, according to the Baseball Almanac, they never reached 150,000 in annual attendance and often were below 100,000. But between 1940 and 1953 (their last year in St. Louis) things improved somewhat when they averaged more than 200,000 fans every year except 1941 when they had only 176,000 admissions. In Los Angeles, Barnes would be guaranteed 500,000 in ticket sales per season, and he'd receive a cash bonus from the Browns' cotenant, the St. Louis Cardinals, for leaving Sportsman's Park solely to the National League team.

The club owners, however, had more pressing issues to attend to after December 7. "Well, we had the meeting the next day, and that killed the whole thing," Barnes told author William B. Mead years later.[79] The vote was unanimous, even Barnes voted down the proposal. Thus, any thoughts of moving a franchise into possible harm's way on the West Coast vanished, leaving California without major-league baseball for another decade and a half when the Dodgers and the Giants relocated to Los Angeles and San Francisco, respectively, at the end of the 1957 season.

2

1942

Changing Uniforms

In the immediate aftermath of the Japanese aerial attack on Pearl Harbor and the U.S. declaration of war, baseball owners, players, and fans wondered what place, if any, the national pastime would have during the conflict. The loss of major-league talent began as a trickle as the 1942 season loomed. Only 50 major leaguers were lost to their teams due to military service during the first wartime season.[1] But a handful of the game's biggest stars—and fan favorites—had either already been called up or would soon enter military service having been classified 1-A. They included four of the top-ten vote-getters in the 1941 American League Most Valuable Player balloting—MVP Joe DiMaggio, Ted Williams, Bob Feller, and the Nats' Cecil Travis.

Although many did not share his position, American League President Will Harridge was enthusiastic about the value of continuing the sport during the war. Less than one month after Pearl Harbor, in a bylined article for the *New York Times*, Harridge insisted that "baseball may be approaching the finest opportunity for service to our country that the game has ever had, providing a recreational outlet for millions of fans who will be working harder than ever to help achieve our common cause of victory." Referring to the players that had already enlisted, he wrote, "I do not believe that the absence of those stars who have answered the call to colors will be in itself a damaging blow to baseball. It is true that fans will miss the performances of such players as Bob Feller, Cecil Travis and Henry Greenberg, to mention just three. But new players will come up, among them many of ability, and baseball fans always have enjoyed watching the progress of newcomers."[2]

President Roosevelt's former postmaster general, James A. Farley, looked across the Atlantic for inspiration at home when he spoke of the 50,000 soccer fans that had jammed into a stadium in England for a key match, unafraid of the German blitz that had done considerable damage to areas of London and other British cities between September of 1940 and May of 1941. (At the same time, Britain's Royal Air Force was heavily bombing the German-held French port cities of Boulogne and Calais.) "Keep 'em playing, keep 'em active, keep the American people entertained and relaxed during whatever periods of play and rest they may find in these times. This is no time for hysteria," counseled Farley, the son of an Irish immigrant brick maker.[3] Yet hysteria is precisely what appeared to be blossoming in some quarters as when Senator Gerald Nye, a North Dakota Republican, accused the United States (i.e., the Roosevelt administration) of "doing its utmost" to instigate a quarrel with Japan, according to a United Press report the day after Pearl Harbor.[4] The isolationist lawmaker blamed the U.S. peace negotiators for denying the Japanese a chance "to save face." As Americans came to the realization that the nation was at war, so too came the realization that hundreds of thousands of young men would be called into combat, and many of them would not return. Thus, as demands for military draftees ballooned in the succeeding years, baseball players increasingly found themselves in a different uniform.

On January 14, with the United States having formally declared war on Japan on December 8 and Germany on December 11, President Roosevelt received a handwritten note from baseball Commissioner Landis asking whether he thought major-league baseball perhaps ought to be suspended for the duration. "Inasmuch as these are not ordinary times, I venture to ask what you have in mind as to whether professional baseball should continue to operate," Landis wrote to FDR.[5] The next day, the commissioner had his answer in what has become known as the "green light" letter.[6]

Citing his deep love and understanding of the game, Roosevelt told Landis, "I honestly feel that it would be best for the country to keep baseball going."[7] In an era long before TV advertising and multimillion-dollar salaries took control of American sports, FDR pointed out that, "baseball provides a recreation which does not last over two hours or two hours and a half, and which can be got for very little cost." Then he added, almost parenthetically, "And, incidentally, I hope that night games can be extended because it gives an opportunity to the day shift to see a game occasionally." FDR's reply was immediately viewed by baseball executives, the press, and the public as akin to a blessing from the Almighty. There it was in print, recognition that baseball was so integral to the American experience and so crucial to citizen morale that even a world war would not stop play.

The so-called green-light letter has been universally—and rightly so—credited to Roosevelt of course (and with it the continuation of baseball throughout the war) if for no other reason than it was written on White House stationery and signed by the president. But, even in peacetime, a vast portion of presidential correspondence is generated by someone other than the chief executive. Whether Roosevelt actually authored the reply to Landis is debatable because it is well known that there was no love lost between the Democrat in the White House and the lifelong Republican commissioner.

Clark Griffith, who was in the best position to know, described Landis as being "not much more welcome at the White House than the Japanese ambassador"[8] because the judge was an outspoken critic of FDR and especially of his New Deal legislation, which was anathema to the GOP. In *Even the Browns*, author William B. Mead relates an incident that *Washington Post* sports columnist Shirley Povich told him happened in Clearwater, Florida, in early 1942, when Povich and fellow sportswriter Bob Considine were there to cover the Washington club in spring training. One day, they went to Landis's hotel for an interview. "He knew who we were, that we were from Washington," Povich recounted. "Landis was almost violent. He grabbed us by the lapels, both of us, and he said, 'Listen, young fellows, don't you let that man in the White House send you to war!' Did he hate FDR? He sure did."[9]

What was Landis's reason for sending the letter in the first place? U.S. involvement in the war was just beginning, and few people in and out of baseball knew what the future would hold. Since Landis initiated the exchange, was he simply acting in his official capacity as commissioner of baseball to get the president to give his blessings to continuing baseball? Or was he trying to trap FDR into agreeing to a shutdown so he could blame his political foe when it happened? (Landis carried the answer and his animosity toward FDR to the grave, dying of respiratory failure in November 1944 and predeceasing Roosevelt by a little less than five months.)

It is also interesting, and certainly not beyond the realm of possibility, to think that Roosevelt, the Hudson Valley patrician, a product of Harvard and Columbia Law School, who was so disdainful of the arch-conservative commissioner, would deign to respond personally. Rather, he would rely on Griffith, his log-cabin–born, college-dropout pal from the wild Kansas–Missouri frontier, to pen the answer or at least to suggest how to respond. The postscript-like presidential plug for more night baseball, which Griffith advocated, would certainly seem to indicate that the Old Fox had a hand in the authorship of the green-light letter. Indeed, with far more urgent correspondence and problems to attend to at the White House, it's quite plausible that FDR handed Landis's query to his trusted friend and, with his customary cock of his head and his jaws clenched around his trademark cigarette holder, said, "Here, Griff, you answer the SOB." All FDR had to do was to sign the typewritten response. (Roosevelt might not even have had to do that; the robot auto pen created in the 1930s was in use in the White House by 1942.)

In any case, Griffith's influence on the president was considerable, never more so than at this time. In an interview with author Richard Goldstein, Washington's outstanding outfielder George Case Jr. recalled that "Clark Griffith was really instrumental in baseball surviving, he was the guy responsible. He spent considerable time imploring Roosevelt to continue baseball. He kept getting assurances from the White House baseball would continue—but there wouldn't be any favors shown to baseball players." Case's view was seconded by Griffith's nephew and successor as franchise owner, Calvin Griffith, who told Goldstein that Roosevelt questioned his uncle "as to what government could do for baseball. Mr. Griffith told him that the best thing would be to just give baseball permission to carry on the game for the recreation of the people in the United States. The president agreed that this was needed at that time."[10] So, whether it was the power of the White House and FDR or the Old Fox's influence with his fellow owners, Griffith chalked up a doubleheader win: (1) he secured White House approval that baseball would continue during the war, and (2) Griffith's fellow owners agreed to increase the number of home-field night games that each team could play, especially in Washington.

Roosevelt, however, soon committed perhaps the worst error of his long presidency when in February he issued Executive Order 9066, authorizing the secretary of war to organize the resettlement of an estimated 127,000 Japanese Americans on the West Coast into 10 internment camps. Despite the lack of proof that any of them had any loyalties to the enemy, they would spend the rest of the war as virtual prisoners. There were also large concentrations of Italian Americans and German Americans in the country, and some of them had even participated in pro-Nazi rallies in New York and elsewhere, yet it was only the Japanese Americans, two-thirds of whom had been born in the United States and many of whom had never even visited Japan, who were widely viewed as a security risk. Even Japanese American veterans of World War I were forced into the camps. "The move has been taken largely for the protection of the Japanese themselves. And I think we are going to have complete cooperation from the Japanese," proclaimed Attorney General Francis Biddle.[11] Roosevelt selected Milton Eisenhower, General Dwight Eisenhower's brother, to direct the forced removal of 60,000 U.S. citizens from their West Coast homes and businesses—and another 38,000 Japanese aliens in California alone. The effects of FDR's order would reverberate for decades. (In 1988, Congress passed, and President Reagan signed into law, an official apology and reparations of $20,000 to each living Japanese American who had been forced into the camps.)

Even before spring training began, the *Sporting News* reported that seven players who had worn Washington uniforms on opening day in 1941 would be out of the Nats lineup in 1942 due to trades or the draft. "The infield will be completely new," the baseball bible said,[12] with Mickey Vernon at first base in place of part-time first sacker George Archie, Frank Croucher at second replacing Jimmy Bloodworth, Bob Repass taking over for Cecil Travis, and Hillis Layne at third instead of Buddy Lewis. Outfielder Ben Chapman had been released during the 1941 season, and Roger Cramer, another outfielder, was traded to Detroit. So the new outfield alignment would be former Red Sox outfielder Stan Spence, Bruce Campbell (who came to Washington in the Cramer trade), and George Case Jr., the only returnee from 1941.

An "unofficial checkup" of the major leagues conducted by the Associated Press toward the end of January 1942 found that the National League had already lost 18 players to military service, and the American League had lost 29. "The Chicago Cubs have lost no players, but the Washington Senators, already weak, have given up seven."[13] By the war's end, however, a total of 40 members of Washington's major- and minor-league rosters had served, and three had died: former Nats centerfielder Elmer Gedeon; Forrest Vernon "Lefty" Brewer, a minor-league pitcher for the Nats' Charlotte Hornets club in 1940 (11 wins, 9 losses), on D-Day, June 6, 1944; and Jim Trimble, killed on Iwo Jima on March 1, 1945.[14] Gedeon was a 22-year-old Cleveland native whose major-league career consisted of just five games in 1939, before he was sent down to Washington's Class B Charlotte Hornets in 1940. Gedeon was one of only two former major leaguers to die in combat. The other was Harry O'Neill, a catcher who played one game for the Philadelphia Athletics in 1939 and was killed on Iwo Jima in March 1945.[15]

Roster changes notwithstanding, the Washington franchise and Griffith personally stood to benefit from the conflict because Washington was at the epicenter of U.S. involvement, which triggered a population explosion in DC to help prosecute the war and at the same time provide an increased source of box office revenue at Griffith Stadium. As one example of the city's swelling ranks, at its peak during the war the Washington Navy Yard, not far from where Nationals Park now stands, employed nearly 25,000 people housed in 188 buildings, virtually a small city unto itself.[16] As for Griffith, in addition to his being the game's ambassador to the White House, "the heightened visibility for the 73-year-old Griffith lent him a role as a patriarch of the game."[17] As such, the Old Fox played the role to perfection, never overlooking even the smallest of on-field incidents that he considered detrimental to the image of the game. Jim Vankoski, who runs the Mickey Vernon Sports Museum in Media, Pennsylvania, recounted a run-in that his gregarious first-baseman friend Vernon had had with Griffith. "Griffith called [Vernon] into his office one day and told Mickey that he did not approve of him talking to runners when they got to first base. Mickey went on to [tell me] that Mr. Griffith—he always called him Mr. Griffith—warned him that if he continued to talk to the runners he was going to have to fine him."[18]

As winter turned into spring and Congress was in a deep debate on an agriculture price-control bill, the visible result of Griffith's influence at the White House was that many able-bodied young men would continue to play professional baseball at some level, at least for a while. Nevertheless, Roosevelt's green light to baseball raised a thorny issue—fairness: even with the presidential imprimatur, many Americans questioned why baseball players should be given exemptions simply because they could play the game well and why a frivolous pastime like baseball should be allowed to continue during the war. The simple answer was: (1) the players were not exempt—although Griffith had wined and dined Selective Service chief Lewis Hershey, his stars Buddy Lewis and Cecil Travis were granted draft extensions, not exemptions; by early 1942, both men were in uniform; and (2) the majority of the country said, "play ball." The finger-pointing by those who were opposed to baseball continuing, and by some who had already been called up—"Why us when those guys, just because they play baseball, don't have to go?"—was muted by numerous public-opinion surveys, including some taken of men in uniform, which showed Americans wanted their favorite game to go on. In *Spartan Seasons*, author Richard Goldstein cites a May 1942 Gallup poll that found that by more than three to one (66 percent to 24 percent) respondents wanted baseball to continue. Also, Goldstein noted that "although hardly a neutral observer, the *Sporting News* reported a 'thundering yes' for baseball in a poll of servicemen which it commissioned four months after Pearl Harbor."[19] By war's end in 1945, more than 500 major-league players had swapped flannels for khakis or navy blue.[20]

When the team owners met with Landis again in Manhattan on February 3, the number-one topic on the agenda was expanding night baseball—still a relatively new concept for the major leagues—prompted in part by FDR's green-light letter. Night baseball had been popular in the minor leagues and among semipro teams for years. It was the only way to draw in crowds of folks whose days were spent working and who wanted an evening's entertainment. The Kansas City Monarchs of the Negro American League was one of the first pro teams to regularly play night baseball by carrying a portable lighting system as they barnstormed the country in 1929. But the major-league owners, conservative businessmen averse to any change unless it was guaranteed to be profitable, had always banned baseball under the lights.

(Adding illumination was costly, and there was no guarantee that fans would show up.) That is, until the Cincinnati Reds, the oldest team in the majors, having been established in 1881, experimented with night baseball out of necessity.

The Crosley brothers, Powel Jr. and Lewis, wealthy manufacturers of radios and other electronic appliances, bought the bankrupt club in 1934 and named Larry MacPhail as their general manager. MacPhail, an astute businessman in his own right and now in desperate need of a greater revenue stream, convinced the National League to let the cash-strapped Reds play seven night games in 1935. A disgusted Griffith, who as a player and manager was known as an innovator of the game but now as an owner had joined his conservative brethren, was adamantly opposed to the idea. Not even the participation of his friend Roosevelt, who remotely turned on the 600 lights at the Reds first night game by pushing a button from the White House,[21] could assuage his anger. "The National League has become a burlesque circuit," he snorted. And although the first night game on May 24, 1935, was a success at the turnstiles with more than 20,000 Cincinnati fans passing into Crosley Field, it "by no means heralded the wholesale conversion of the big leagues to night baseball," baseball historian Benjamin Rader writes.[22] As late as 1941, when all teams could schedule as many as seven night home games, seven major-league ballparks were still without lights, including Yankee Stadium, Boston's Fenway Park and Braves Field, and Detroit's Briggs Stadium. (The last club to succumb to night baseball was the Chicago Cubs when Wrigley Field was finally lit in August 1988. The game, originally scheduled for 8/8/88 between the Cubs and Phillies was called after the fourth inning due to rain. The next day the first complete night game in Wrigley's history was played between the Cubs and Mets.)[23]

During their first day of the February meetings in New York, the owners failed to reach agreement on the night-games question. But on the second day, they agreed to double the voluntary limit to 14 home games under the lights—except at Griffith Stadium, where the Nats could play as many as 21 night contests (and thus offer "two hours or two hours and a half" of inexpensive amusement to the many government employees and men in uniform now working shifts in the city, as FDR had put it). Like St. Paul on the road to Damascus, Griffith had experienced a miraculous conversion the previous season when Griffith

Stadium hosted crowds averaging 18,000 for Washington's inaugural seven games under the stars, beating the average day-game attendance by several thousand. Now for 1942, the wily Old Fox wanted 28 night games for Washington, arguing that because Philadelphia and St. Louis each had two teams with lighted stadiums (although the AL Browns and the NL Cardinals shared Sportsman's Park) those two cities would have a combined 28 night games while Washington would be limited to only 14.

Known for his near-religious commitment to putting whatever he believed was best for the game above all else, as well as for his staunch patriotism especially in wartime, Griffith's argument may have seemed self-serving. Of course, his demand could also have been another of the Old Fox's sly ways from his days on the mound and as manager of four major-league clubs. In this case, he would ask for more than he knew he could expect to receive and perhaps strike a compromise that would nevertheless increase his allotted number of night games and add to his coffers. If Griffith's request for 28 night games was a deception, it worked—to a degree. Despite their friendship, Judge Landis shot down Griffith's argument, pointing out that 28 night games in Washington might mean some visiting teams would play complete three-game series under the lights. "After all, there still must be some fans in Washington who would like to see a ball game in the afternoon," Landis said.[24] But he did grant Griffith an additional seven night contests. "The Senators, of course, are certain to book their full quota of 21, but whether all the others will take advantage of booking their allotment of 14 at home remains to be determined," *New York Times* sportswriter John Drebinger observed.

However, not every team that played in a ballpark with lights planned to expand its night-game schedule. MacPhail, now with the Dodgers, was content with the seven-game limit. As he told his fellow executives, the new limit was not mandatory, and he hadn't made up his mind whether to book even the seven night games. Cleveland Indians owner Alva Bradley took the same conservative stance while the New York Giants leaned toward scheduling all 14 night games at the Polo Grounds. Ed Barrow of the Yankees, without lights at the huge stadium, said the world champions would commit to booking the full quota for their road games.[25]

As it turned out, there would be no night games in New York at all. Army officials and team representatives from Brooklyn's Ebbets Field and the Giants' Polo Grounds on May 12 tested the visibility of the lights at both parks from a vantage point several miles off the Atlantic coast. When they determined that the glare could backlight U.S. vessels and be seen by prowling Nazi U-boats, New York Police Department Commissioner Lewis Valentine ordered the 14 scheduled night games cancelled and the city "dimmed out," darkening Broadway, the Statue of Liberty, and Coney Island among other landmarks. New York was the only major-league city to lose night baseball.[26] (Not to be outmaneuvered by the commissioner, the Old Fox delayed the start of a number of scheduled day games until late afternoon, so what began in daylight became "twi-nighters" when the lights were turned on. The maneuver allowed more workers to get to the ballpark in time for the game.)

In other moves aimed at aiding the nascent war effort, the owners agreed to institute a voluntary, across-the-board 10-percent salary allotment in both leagues for the purchase of war bonds and defense stamps. The plan covered everyone on all 16 franchise payrolls, including the players. Also, each club could decide whether to admit service personnel in uniform free of charge.

The owners also agreed to consider—reluctantly at first because they were moneymen at heart—a suggestion from Brooklyn's ownership that all teams contribute the gate receipts from one home game of their choosing to the war-relief funds.

To add even more to the war-relief pot, they gave the nod to two All-Star games instead of the usual one midseason classic. The idea was back-to-back exhibitions starting with the actual All-Star Game scheduled for Ebbets Field in Brooklyn on July 7 but actually played on July 6 in the larger Polo Grounds to increase attendance. The following day, there would be an exhibition game either in Cleveland's vast Municipal Stadium or Chicago's Comiskey Park because both AL stadiums had lights and were close enough to New York to reach by train overnight. The second game would pit a major-league All-Star team against a team composed of former major leaguers in the service who would be made available to play. The owners also agreed to double regular-season ticket prices for both games to maximize the amount raised for the fund. NL President Ford Frick announced that, for each ticket sold, the purchaser would receive one dollar's worth of defense stamps. "If a fan paid $2.10 for a seat, 10 cents would constitute the [local] tax, $1 would go to the Bat and Ball Fund and the other dollar would be returned to the fan in defense stamps," Drebinger wrote. Higher ticket prices, for box seats, for example, also would include the $1 in defense stamps. To justify the higher prices, Frick told the owners that Griffith's Bat and Ball Fund project "was a far greater one than at first was realized" because there were "something like 776 military camps in the country, which will have to receive equipment, and at present our fund, inaugurated in Chicago [at the December Palmer House meetings] totals only $35,000. This means that right now we couldn't do more than buy one ball and half a bat for each group of 750 men in military service." Frick added with a flourish of patriotism, "So you see a tremendous amount of work remains to be done before we raise a sum sufficient to do the job as it should and must be done."[27]

The first wave of Washington players arrived at the spring-training camp in Orlando, Florida, on February 22. The team stayed at the Angebilt Hotel, which "wasn't a very pretentious place," according to outfielder George Case Jr.[28] The team trained at Tinker Field (The field was named for Hall of Famer Joe Tinker of the Cubs' Tinker-to-Evers-to-Chance double-play combination.[29] After his major-league career, Tinker coached baseball and managed a team in the Florida State League. He died in Orlando on July 27, 1948, and is buried at Greenwood Cemetery there).

Tinker Field was far different from the vast training complexes of today that include several major-league-quality diamonds, top-notch medical facilities, workout gyms, training rooms—all air-conditioned of course—and lighted grandstands to accommodate several thousand fans. The Tinker Field clubhouse was a small wooden building with a screen door that was the "air conditioning." The field, with a Coca-Cola–sponsored manual scoreboard in right field, was little better than today's high-school diamonds. Built in 1914, the stands held 2,548 fans with an additional 769 bleacher seats. Unlike today's hurlers, pitchers threw batting practice and without the aid of any protection in front of them. George Case's films show a group of ballplayers evidently happy to be on the field again (and in the warm sunshine) honing their skills. Today, Tinker Field sits, mostly unused, in the shadow of Orlando's Citrus Bowl, threatened with either demolition to expand the parking area of the football stadium or conversion to a modest venue for public activities. (The old facility cannot easily be altered because it is listed on the National Register of Historic Places.) A baseball-topped monument, erected on March 23, 1968, stands just inside the front gates, and a bronze plaque—stolen in early 2014—paid tribute to Clark Griffith, who "gave the national pastime great dignity and respect."[30]

In 1942, the Nats were looking to improve on their fifth-place tie with the Browns the previous season (Cleveland and Detroit finished in a tie for fourth behind the Yankees, Boston, and Chicago), even though this would be the first time in eight years that Cecil Travis and Buddy Lewis were not in camp. Hopes were high, however, that first baseman Mickey Vernon would equal or better his 1941 batting average of .299 and that rookie shortstop Bob Repass would be an acceptable infield replacement for Travis. Married and with a 3-A deferment, Repass "has been covering more Florida real estate than the orange groves," Shirley Povich gushed.[31] (Repass would appear in just 81 games for Washington that season, his final game coming on August 10, before being sent down to the minors for the rest of the season and into 1943. He was called up for military service in July 1943 and served overseas in the Army for the next two years. He never made it back to the majors.) By mid-March, the roster in camp had lost 13 players to the draft, including a number of minor leaguers.[32]

Also missing from the Tinker Field training camp was the team's leading pitcher, Dutch Leonard, who was holding out for a raise from his 1941 season, when he won 18 games, his second-best season. (The best year of his 20-year career was 1939 when he won 20 games against just 8 losses.) Once an outspoken proponent of better pay for ballplayers, including himself, owner Griffith now held firm to his original offer and gave his star hurler until March 1 to show up in camp. "If he doesn't accept terms by then, the next offer I make him won't be as much as my last one, and I may fine him when he does report," he told Povich.[33] Also, because on February 8, Roosevelt had ordered year-round daylight saving time, called "war time," to save electricity on nighttime illumination, Griffith and manager Bucky Harris agreed to cancel all morning workouts, which, had they taken place at their regular time, could have possibly led to injuries by practicing on a field that was still moist with dew.

The Nats opened the exhibition season on March 14, playing the Boston Braves in nearby Sanford. What the Nationals did not know at the time, of course, was that 1942 would be Harris's last year at the helm (until he returned for a third time in 1950) and that, due to wartime travel restrictions, this was their last spring-training camp in Florida until 1946. By the end of March, Leonard was in camp, driven back to the fold perhaps by what Shirley Povich called "the best-looking young squad of pitchers Harris has ever had in a training camp in his 19 years as a big league manager."[34] Behind those arms, the team ran off 13 wins in 17 exhibition games. No wonder the Old Fox believed his team could finish in the top-four places come September with a quartet of excellent arms in Leonard, Sid Hudson, Early Wynn, and newly acquired Buck (or "Bobo") Newsom, for whom Griffith reportedly paid Detroit an estimated $40,000 with $20,000 of that going for his salary.[35] (Those figures most likely are somewhat exaggerated: for one, throughout his career, Newsom publicly inflated his salary as a way to enhance his reputation as a top-flight pitcher, and two, it's highly unlikely that Griffith, tightfisted and a fine judge of pitching talent, would pay that much for a hurler who had a 12–20 record the previous season.) Griffith, however, was willing to spend "high for a hitting outfielder and a third baseman," Povich reported, "despite a reputation for smugness in the region of the pocketbook."[36]

Unlike several of his fellow owners, Griffith was in a league of his own when it came to finances. For many of his colleagues, baseball was a sideline, an amusement, and a way to gain popular recognition for their main businesses. But for Griffith, baseball was his sole business; he had no other means of making a living. His players were well aware of that and did not harbor ill will toward him for demurring on salary increases and bonuses. They appreciated the fact that, despite his pecuniary habits, the Old Fox cared for them like a litter of kits.

When Case, the fastest player in baseball during his career, sought a promised $500 bonus from the boss, he received a letter from Griffith agreeing to it but telling him that "at the end of the season if we don't make it up at the gate, please return the money."[37] When rookie first baseman Ed Butka was called up from the minors at the end of the 1943 season, he found the cost of living in Washington too high for his meager pay. So he went to Griffith and told him, "I appreciate what you're trying to do for me, but for the money that I'm getting I cannot live in DC. It's too tough."[38] According to Butka, Griffith laughed and said, "Listen, you go out and find a room and your eating places and send me all the bills after you get done and I will pay for them." Griffith was true to his word and reimbursed the young ballplayer on the spot. "He was great. I thought he was a great man," Butka recounted in an interview years later.

By the first week of April, as the Nats headed north, they had won 19 of 26 Grapefruit League games, which surprised even Harris, although he was not ready to predict a pennant for Washington despite having on paper the strongest pitching staff in the American League. "We've got just as good a chance to beat out the Yankees as any other club," the veteran manager said, while also confessing, "I wouldn't have believed that I would be bringing such a good-looking ball team back to Washington, but there it is, and I'm proud of it."[39] Indeed, Washington's chances in April 1942 looked a good deal better than those of the U.S. military. While the Nats were optimistically preparing for their home opener, the Army was taking a beating in the Pacific, where the Japanese had occupied the Philippines' capital of Manila in January and were taking hold of the island chain. Closer to home, Nazi U-boats were sinking merchant vessels along the Atlantic East Coast.

It took only until opening day, April 14, however, to burst Harris's bubble when the Nationals hosted the World Series champions, the New York Yankees. An overflow crowd jammed into Griffith Stadium not only to see the game but also hoping to see President Roosevelt toss out the ceremonial first pitch. It was an activity he looked forward to each spring since he moved into the White House in 1933. Outfielder George Case's 8mm, color home movies of one of those opening days show a smiling FDR arriving in an open-top car as a military band accompanied his arrival. Aides assisted the polio-stricken chief executive to the first-row presidential box where, surrounded by dignitaries, he tossed out the ceremonial first ball.[40] But in 1942, with the U.S. participation in the war just a few months old, Roosevelt was absent from the festivities. As it turned out, 1941 proved to be his last opening-day appearance at Griffith Stadium.

FDR had attended opening day at Griffith Stadium between 1933 and 1941, missing an appearance only in 1939, as war in Europe grew more ominous. In March of that year, Germany broke its agreement with the western powers, after being allowed to annex the Sudetenland in the fall of 1938, by taking over the remainder of Czechoslovakia. As a result, on April 14, 1939, Roosevelt cabled Hitler urging peaceful discussions about the future of the world's nations and asking for an "assurance that your armed forces will not attack or invade the territory or possessions" of some 31 nations, including Poland, Britain, France, Norway, Denmark, the Netherlands, Greece, and Russia, among others.[41] Hitler, rejecting FDR's appeal for talks, declared that Germany had no intention of attacking the United States or any other nation.

At the same time, the German leader announced the abrogation of the nonaggression pact with Poland, the Anglo–German Naval Agreement, and the appeasement "peace in our time" agreement that British Prime Minister Neville Chamberlain had so proudly waved about upon his return from Munich in September 1938. One month later, in May 1939, Germany and Italy announced the "Pact of Steel" military and political alliance. On September 1, Nazi Germany invaded Poland, and the war in Europe began.

"It must have been obvious to the early arrivals," the *Post* reported in its next-day coverage of opening day, "that the President was not coming to the game. In place of the usual hundred-odd camera and newsreel men in front of the Presidential box only about 10 were standing around."[42] In fact, Roosevelt was dealing with a new crisis, in Europe and in the Pacific. The former involved the government of Vichy France, that portion of the country not fully occupied by the Nazi regime but ruled by Frenchmen hand-picked by Berlin and considered collaborators by the Allies.

The Nazi regime was pressuring the head of the Vichy government, Marshal Henri-Philippe Petain, to replace his vice-premier, Jean-Francois Darlan, with Pierre Laval, a proponent of close cooperation and even a military alliance with Berlin. Learning of this, FDR cabled a warning to Petain that "America would cease all cooperation with Vichy if Laval were restored" to the government. When Darlan revealed FDR's cable to the Germans, "Hitler now saw the premiership of France as a contest between himself and Roosevelt. He ordered Petain to choose: America and Darlan or Germany and Laval."[43] Petain on April 13 made his choice, opting for Laval and Hitler over Darlan and Roosevelt. FDR immediately recalled the U.S. ambassador to the Vichy government, William D. Leahy, and ordered the Navy to disarm the French fleet anchored at France's Caribbean colonies.[44]

In a once-classified and very undiplomatic cable exchange on April 15, Harry Hopkins, FDR's close friend and adviser who was in London, suggested to the president, "How about nailing that wood pussy Laval to your barn door?" Roosevelt promptly replied, "Your suggestion being studied but consensus of opinion is that odor still too strong for family of nations."[45] FDR had good reason to be alarmed. Within months of taking office, Laval ordered the roundup of French Jews. In June, Laval conceived a plan to send skilled French laborers to Germany in exchange for French prisoners of war. And in September, he gave the Gestapo free rein to hunt down the French Resistance that was so active in Vichy France. (Just after the war, Laval was tried, found guilty of treason and other war crimes, and was executed by firing squad on October 15, 1945.)

Roosevelt's absence from opening day was due also to the fierce fighting in the Philippines, where Japanese forces were pounding the U.S. territory with aerial attacks and bombardments. Lieutenant General Jonathan Wainwright had replaced General Douglas MacArthur after Roosevelt in February had ordered MacArthur to secretly leave the Philippines for Australia, which he did on March 11. The Battle of Bataan ended on April 9, with the surrender of as many as 76,000 American and Filipino soldiers. (On May 6, Wainwright surrendered Corregidor, the last American stronghold in the Pacific.)

The United States took the war to the Japanese homeland on April 18, when Lieutenant Colonel James "Jimmy" Doolittle and his specially trained crews flew 16 B-25 Mitchell twin-engine bombers, modified for carrier operations, from the deck of the aircraft carrier USS *Hornet*. "The planes began arriving over Japan about noon and bombed military and industrial targets in Tokyo, Yokohama, Kobe, Osaka and Nagoya."[46] American morale soared when news of the raid reached the United States, and although the bombing did little material damage, it had a strategic impact on the war. The Japanese military recalled many units to the home islands for defense. The raid also stunned and frightened the Japanese population because they had had complete faith in the divinity of the emperor and in their military leaders who had promised that the mainland would never be attacked.

Griffith no doubt was disappointed by his friend's absence, but he certainly was aware of the many decisions and duties that FDR had to perform that took precedence over baseball. However, FDR's absence at Griffith Stadium must have been a relief to the security personnel assigned to guard the president. In its next-day coverage, the *Washington Post* reported that about 2,000 seats scattered around the ballpark that had been set aside for the Secret Service, plainclothes police, and other security officials went on sale as soon as it was known that Roosevelt would not be attending, swelling the paid attendance by almost 1,500 over the 29,613 seating capacity.[47]

So it fell to Vice President Henry Wallace to come in and relieve the president by throwing out the ceremonial first pitch under the watchful eyes of Griffith, Harris, Yankees manager Joe McCarthy, other local dignitaries, both teams, and several thousand military officers and enlisted men. In addition to the national anthem, other pregame patriotic music played by the Army Band included "God Bless America," "Stars and Stripes Forever," and, perhaps as an acknowledgment to the native Southerners in the stands, "Swanee River." Despite all the hoopla and the preseason optimism of Griffith, Harris, Povich, and other members of the press, the visiting world champions easily won the opener, 7–0, holding the Nats to just three hits.

The history of baseball is founded on the myth that the game was invented by Abner Doubleday, an Army officer and Union general in the American Civil War, who devised the game in 1839 at Cooperstown, New York, for the amusement of his troops. Another myth erroneously credits Clark Griffith with originating the tradition of the chief executive throwing out the ceremonial first ball on opening day. It is, however, another of the many tales about Griffith akin to his having watered Jesse James's horse at age two. Despite the facts about the presidential toss, Griffith "embraced the custom to the point where he claimed decades later to have started it," authors William B. Mead and Paul Dickson write in *Baseball: The Presidents' Game*, citing a 1955 *This Week* magazine story. In the article, "Presidents Who Have Pitched for Me," Griffith claimed he inaugurated the opening-day presidential toss with President William Howard Taft in 1912, "conveniently forgetting [Taft's first toss was in] 1910, when [Griffith] was managing in faraway Cincinnati."[48]

Taft, who loved the game as much as FDR, went to the ballpark in 1909 at the invitation of Washington's owner at the time, Thomas C. Noyes. Taft attended simply as an avid spectator, arriving late but staying to the end of the game (a rarity for chief executives at sporting events these days). It was opening day the following year, when, at the suggestion of American League President Ban Johnson, the 300-pound chief executive rose from his presidential box prior to the start of the game and tossed a baseball to Nats pitcher Walter Johnson as the photographers snapped away. The Big Train—a nickname given to Walter Johnson by legendary sportswriter Grantland Rice, who said Johnson's size and fastball reminded him of an express train—kept the ball and sent it to the White House for the president's signature. To his great and lasting pleasure, Johnson got the baseball back inscribed "To Walter Johnson, with the hope that he may continue to be as formidable as in yesterday's game. William H. Taft." By all accounts, Taft had a good throwing arm and enjoyed the sport immensely because it "is a clean, straight game," and he showed up again on opening day 1911 to do the honors again.[49]

But in 1912, Griffith's first year in Washington as manager and part owner, Taft was absent from the ballpark because four days earlier the *Titanic* had gone down in the North Atlantic, claiming the life of the president's close friend and military aide Major Archibald Butt. The chaos that immediately ensued, the poor international communications, and the slow arrival in New York of the RMS *Carpathia* (dubbed the "ship of widows") with some of the 705 survivors kept Taft at the White House anxiously awaiting news of Butt's fate. Unlike some of his fellow male passengers in first class who somehow found a way onto lifeboats reserved for women and children (including J. Bruce Ismay, the chairman of the White Star shipping company that owned the *Titanic*), Butt chose to go down with the sinking liner.

The distraught Taft did not go to Griffith Stadium until June 18. He threw out a ceremonial first pitch, much to the delight of the record crowd, some of whom paid scalpers up to $50 for a ticket to what Griffith had billed as an "after-the-fact opening day."[50] Thus, a nascent Washington baseball custom gained virtual permanent status because Griffith convinced American League President Ban Johnson of the importance of opening the American League season at Griffith Stadium with the presidential rite. (Every president since Taft, with the exception of Jimmy Carter, has thrown out an opening-day ceremonial ball, even if he had to travel to do so. During the three-plus decades or so when the nation's capital was without a major-league team, the custom was often observed in nearby Baltimore. In fact, Carter's only appearance at a major-league stadium came when he attended the seventh game of the 1979 World Series in Baltimore when the Pittsburgh Pirates defeated the Orioles, 4–1, at Memorial Stadium. A softball-loving president but perhaps not a gracious guest, Carter told baseball Commissioner Bowie Kuhn at that game "that he was more interested in playing sports than watching them."[51] Although more inclined toward basketball, President Barack Obama threw out the first pitch on opening day in 2010, when the newest iteration of the Washington Nationals hosted the National League champion Philadelphia Phillies at Nationals Park.)

During the first two weeks of the 1942 season, the Nationals won seven games and lost nine and rested in fifth place, ahead of St. Louis, Philadelphia, and Chicago. The big baseball news at the end of April was the 11 and 3 surge by the Indians, which included 10 wins in a row that put Cleveland in first place. War production was in high gear too. Output of war materiel had increased each month since Pearl Harbor with more plants coming on line every day, the War Department's head of production, Lieutenant General William S. Knudsen, told the press after a tour of facilities. "Every machine tool factory I was in was working three shifts seven days a week," he said.[52] On the downside, according to the Treasury Department, sales of war bonds had fallen 50 percent from $1 billion in January to $500 million by April. To revive sales, the Treasury initiated a drive to enlist workers to join a payroll plan pledging 10 percent of their wages to purchase the bonds.

The voluntary loss of discretionary funds might have been ameliorated to some extent when the Roosevelt administration announced on April 28 that commodities prices would be frozen at their March levels for the duration of the war. The stated goal of what the *Washington Post*'s Alfred Friendly called "the most-far-reaching Governmental control over economic processes in the history of the country" was to reduce the cost of living by about 1.5 percent. The order, announced by Leon Henderson, head of the Office of Price Administration (OPA), covered "literally millions" of commodities, "virtually everything that Americans eat, wear and use."[53]

Designed to stop wartime inflation before it could take hold, Roosevelt's order came as no surprise. The previous July, in a message to Congress, FDR had urged passage of price-control legislation by noting the "frighteningly similar" situation between 1941, when prices and the cost of living rose sharply, and the years between 1915 and 1917, when prices reacted in a similar way.[54] Nevertheless, in his widely read column, "Today and Tomorrow," Walter Lippmann explained that "since inflation exists when there is too much money in the hands of those who wish to spend it, price control and wage control, however desirable for other reasons, cannot cure and cannot prevent inflation." FDR won't begin to come to grips with inflation, Lippmann wrote, until he overrules the Treasury Department's tax and savings policy. He conservatively estimated that even if the Treasury's plan to sell more bonds goes "very well indeed, there will still be at least 10 billions [*sic*] excess purchasing power loose in the market during the coming year," which Lippmann called "quite enough to blow the ceiling off" any price and wage controls system.[55]

In a roundup of press criticism published in the *New York Times*,[56] the Republican-leaning *New York Herald Tribune* wrote, "If prices and rents are to be fixed, then wages must be subjected to a ceiling, and a program of taxation must be adopted which is calculated to absorb surplus purchasing power. Mr. Roosevelt has not grappled seriously with either of those two aspects of the question." The *Buffalo Courier Express* noted that Congress still needed to pass the requested legislation and FDR "is depending to a great extent upon persuasion to reach his objectives." And the *Detroit Free Press* pointed out that the "outstanding weaknesses in his message are his oblique approach to wage control and his emphasis on excessive profits taxation. Limiting incomes of the few who get more than $25,000 a year won't do the job."

Price controls had little effect on major-league baseball, however, at least for 1942, because the season had just begun and ticket prices, set earlier, were unaffected. But the price freeze also included rents in areas of the country that were heavy with defense work. So, many renters in the District of Columbia, suburban Maryland, and northern Virginia—ground zero of the nation's defense areas—got something of a bonus because rents there were cut back to their January 1, 1941, levels.[57] All rental units had to be registered with the OPA, and landlords could file petitions for increases only if they made a capital improvement to the premises or provided a great increase in services. About the only things not covered by the freeze were newspapers, magazines, movies, food served in hotels and restaurants, and locally grown fruits, vegetables, and homemade products, such as cider, smoked hams, and preserves as long as such individual sales did not exceed $75 a month. Also, fees paid to doctors, dentists, lawyers, barbers, and beauty shops were exempt from the price ceilings. The big battle on Capitol Hill then turned to subsidies for the farmers and commodities producers who claimed they needed millions in government subsidies to compensate for the cost increases they would not be able to pass on to consumers.

Although the Doolittle raid had boosted homeland morale, at least temporarily, in fact the war effort was not going well in Europe and especially in the Pacific. So the 1942 baseball season "gave us something resembling normality to cling to, beginning with spring training," Bill Gilbert recalled in his wartime memoir, *They Also Served*.[58] The season became an April to September attempt to rouse patriotic fervor with fund-raising and other charitable events aimed at assisting the war effort and boosting morale. Playing the national anthem became a pre-game ritual that today is a permanent fixture before the start of a game, from the major leagues down to Little League. Fans were asked to throw back baseballs hit into the stands so they could be donated to service teams, and night contests started earlier to avoid lighting curfews. Also, radio play-by-play announcers were prohibited from talking about weather conditions at the ballpark, including rain delays, so as not to give any information to enemy agents listening that could be used in a possible aerial attack. (In an oft-repeated anecdote about folksy announcer Dizzy Dean, who broadcast St. Louis Cardinals' games during the war, the former star pitcher for the Cards would get around the ban by telling fans, "If you folks don't know what's holdin' up this game just stick your head out the window.")[59]

The need for such cautionary acts may have been exaggerated, but they were deemed necessary in wartime. Following the fall of Bataan on April 9, Lieutenant General Jonathan Wainwright sent a radiogram to Army Chief of Staff General George C. Marshall to report that since April 29 (the emperor's birthday) "the fire of hostile artillery increased in intensity and has continued at that tempo to present date." Wainwright then added, "Morale difficult to maintain at best because troops have been constantly under or subject to air or artillery attack since December 29 and have been receiving half of poorly balanced ration since January 8. However, morale amazingly good considering conditions under which troops are now operating."[60] The general also warned that Corregidor, an island near the entrance to Manila Bay in the Phi-lippines, could be the site of an amphibious Japanese attack at any time. "The success or failure of such an assault will depend entirely on stead-fastness of beach defense troops. With morale at present level I esti-mate that we have something less than an even chance to beat off an assault."

It was the commander in chief, Roosevelt, who promptly replied in a cable on May 5: IN SPITE OF ALL THE HANDICAPS OF COM-PLETE ISOLATION COMMA LACK OF FOOD AND AMMUNI-TION YOU HAVE GIVEN THE WORLD A SHINING EXAMPLE OF PATRIOTIC FORTITUDE AND SELF-SACRIFICE PERI-OD."[61] Nevertheless, Corregidor fell to the Japanese on May 6. U.S. casualties included 800 killed, 1,000 wounded, and 11,000 captured. Wainwright and his men—many of whom were survivors of the infa-mous 70-mile Bataan death march on the western peninsula of Luzon island—spent the rest of the war imprisoned in prison camps in north-ern Luzon, Formosa, and Manchuria and used as slaves until Russian troops liberated them in August 1945.

Although he was heading for his 73rd birthday that year, Clark Grif-fith had not lost any of his love for the game or the patina of his self-cultivated image as a baseball living legend; at his age, he didn't have to stick his head out the window to know that stormy weather was surely in the forecast. But he may have begun to question his well-honed in-stincts for assessing baseball talent when his costly pitching acquisition Bobo Newsom had dropped five starts in a row by the end of May. Typical of Newsom's less-than-stellar performance was his May 2 start against Cleveland when he was removed after the third inning after giving up five runs including a three-run homer by leftfielder Jeff Heath. The Indians went on to win, 12–3. A critical Shirley Povich wrote: "Clark Griffith can take no bows for the deal that brought him from Detroit. Newsom is the highest paid pitcher on the Washington club and has done nothing to justify his salary. Bucky Harris opposed the purchase of Newsom in the first place and would not be heart-broken if Griffith relieved him of the responsibility of managing the fellow."[62] Newsom's problem wasn't a lack of talent. It was his refusal to train, especially to run wind sprints as all pitchers do to strengthen their legs to push off the mound forcefully and add velocity to their pitches. (Newsom compiled a poor record of 11–17 before Griffith sold him to

Brooklyn at the end of August for $25,000, where he won two games and lost as many. Newsom would return to Washington briefly in 1943, then for two more partial seasons after the war in 1946 and 1947, and for his final stint with Washington in 1952, when Griffith released him for the last time.)

Off the field, Griffith knew that if he wanted his beloved Washington franchise to be his legacy, he had better start now. So he naturally turned to his family. He and his wife, Ann, who was called "Aunt Addie" by just about everyone, had no children of their own, but they had taken in Addie's nephew Calvin and niece Thelma when their parents, Addie's brother James Robertson and his wife, had fallen on hard times. The Robertsons had two girls and five boys to feed—including newborn twin boys—and James was unemployed. In addition, Robertson was an alcoholic and an abusive spouse, and by the time Addie visited the family in Montreal in 1922, James was in failing health, and the family was nearly destitute.

Addie's solution was to take Calvin and Thelma to live with her and Clark in DC. Upon their arrival in the United States, the Griffiths immediately sought to adopt the siblings. Although Calvin was just 11 at the time, the courts ruled that he was too old to be legally adopted. The Griffiths would not adopt one and not the other, so they had Calvin's middle and last names, Griffith Robertson, legally switched to Robertson Griffith, then did the same for Thelma, and raised them as their own.

When James Robertson died a year later in 1923, the Griffiths brought Addie's sister-in-law Jane and her five other children to the United States and bought them a home in nearby suburban Maryland. As adults, Thelma and Calvin joined their uncle in the world of baseball. Thelma married Joe Haynes, a former Washington pitcher who was with the White Sox at the outbreak of the war. In 1935, Griffith sent his nephew to Chattanooga, Tennessee, to oversee the Lookouts, his Double-A team in the Southern Association. There, Calvin was under the tutelage of manager Clyde Milan, who eventually joined the Nationals as a coach in the 1940s. Unlike his uncle and many minor- and major-league managers before and after him, Calvin had no major-league experience. Nevertheless, by the end of 1937, he was managing the team. From 1938 to 1941, Calvin managed the Class-B Charlotte Hornets of the Piedmont League, another minor-league club owned by

Clark Griffith.[63] In 1940, the Hornets moved into a new ballpark on Magnolia Avenue and named it Calvin Griffith Park. Like many of the minor-league clubs that were being stripped of talent by the draft, the 1942 Charlotte franchise was "floundering around in the second division, headed no place in particular," according to *Charlotte News* sportswriter Furman Bisher.[64] By then, Calvin had become the Nationals' traveling secretary, and he moved into a management role when Uncle Clark named him vice president in 1942.

Calvin Griffith succeeded his uncle as president of the franchise upon Clark Griffith's death at age 85 in 1955, perpetuating the Old Fox's pecuniary ways when it came to ballplayer salaries. (Calvin, it was said, "threw nickels around like manhole covers.")[65] Sadly, he did not follow his uncle's moderate stance when it came to race relations, especially when speaking publicly. More than a decade after the major civil-rights legislation of 1964 and 1965, Calvin Griffith in 1978 explained to a Minneapolis Rotary Club why he had moved the franchise to Minneapolis–St. Paul after 1960. "Black people don't go to ball games," he told them bluntly, "but they'll fill up a rassling ring and put up such a chant they'll scare you to death." Then, as if to firmly underscore where he stood with regard to African Americans, he told the Rotarians that he chose their city "because you've got good, hard-working white people here."[66] When Calvin Griffith sold the club to Carl Pohlad in 1984 for $36 million, he ended 65 years of Griffith family ownership, a move that surely would've killed the Old Fox if he had been alive to witness it. Another trait Calvin inherited from his uncle was longevity. Calvin Griffith died in a nursing home in Melbourne, Florida, on October 20, 1999, at the age of 87. And like his uncle, he is buried in the Griffith family mausoleum at Fort Lincoln Cemetery in Brentwood, Maryland.

The 16 major-league owners met again early in May 1942. After tabling a suggestion made during their February meeting in New York, they now agreed that each team would donate the proceeds from one home game to the Army and Navy relief funds. In addition, they could choose the game and designate the military branch of the service they wanted the money to go to, or they could divide the money between the Army and Navy. To the moguls' credit, the schedule they devised, which appeared in the *Sporting News* on May 7, 1942, showed that wherever possible they selected games with their natural rivals or with teams that were strong gate attractions. The Brooklyn Dodgers, by virtue of having made the proposal, would kick off the fund-raising effort against the New York Giants, at Ebbets Field in Brooklyn on May 8. That would be followed by an intrastate contest between the Philadelphia Phillies and the Pittsburgh Pirates on May 19, and Griffith Stadium would host the New York Yankees, always a popular draw in Washington, on May 23. The New Yorkers would return the favor at Yankee Stadium on August 23, when the Nationals visited the Bronx ballpark.[67]

In addition to the two planned midseason fund-raiser All-Star games, the major leagues gave the OK for several exhibition games between servicemen who'd been major leaguers and teams composed of Negro League stars, contests that the barons of baseball refused to consider between their own (white) ball clubs and the Negro League teams. One such exhibition in particular was of some historic significance because it involved a potential showdown between two of the game's best players not named DiMaggio or Williams. During the previous two seasons, Griffith had leased his ballpark to the Homestead Grays of the Negro National League when the Nats went on the road. The Grays, named for their hometown of Homestead in western Pennsylvania, were slowly developing a following among the burgeoning black community in DC, just as other black teams were building a fan base in other northern urban cities. In fact, "Negro League ball reached the apex of its popularity in the war years," according to historian Benjamin G. Rader, who points out that two million fans watched Negro baseball in 1942 when the annual East–West game in Chicago attracted 51,000 spectators.[68]

In May, Cecil Travis was granted leave from Camp Wheeler, Georgia, to play in a pair of biracial exhibition games. In the first game, on May 24, the Kansas City Monarchs of the Negro American League led by itinerant pitcher Satchel Paige beat a service team called Dizzy Dean's All-Stars, 3–1, before almost 30,000 fans at Wrigley Field in Chicago. For the second game a week later, on May 31, at Travis's home ballpark Griffith Stadium, Dean's All-Stars faced the Grays, again headlined by Paige, who was now wearing a Homestead Grays uniform. Paige's scheduled mound opponent was former Cleveland ace Bob Feller, so the game aroused a good deal of interest because of that unique pitching matchup. The front page of the *Washington Afro-American* included the caption "Big Guns Set for All-Star Pitchers" above photos of Grays stars Josh Gibson and Buck Leonard and a small insert showing the distances to the outfield fences at Griffith Stadium.[69] But Feller was unable to get a furlough from his naval station in Newport, Rhode Island, and was replaced by Dean, who had retired as a player the year before and wasn't in the best of condition. Nevertheless, in a preview of the game, the *Washington Afro-American* warned that Paige "will have to be at his best, for Cecil Travis, formerly of the Washington Senators, is listed among the all-stars."[70]

Paige's team routed Dean's All-Stars, 8–1. An estimated 22,000 perspiring fans, far in excess of what the Grays normally drew there, flocked to the ballpark on an unusually hot afternoon. Despite the heat, one hour before the game, police had to subdue 10,000 angry fans waiting in line to buy tickets while scalpers charged the unheard of sum of $3.30 for a choice grandstand seat.[71] Dean lasted just one inning, giving up three hits and two runs. But Paige struck out seven batters in five innings, including Travis, whose single in his first at-bat irked the ageless hurler. Afterward, according to the *Afro-American*, Paige explained the hit to teammate Buck Leonard by saying, "So Cecil Travis got a single, eh? He took advantage [of] that slow curve—it came right past me, too; could have knocked it down but was afraid I might hurt my hand or something."[72] In any event, the Paige–Travis confrontations during that game "have been cited as an important moment in the early stages of integrating the sport."[73]

By the end of 1942, an estimated 2,000 professional ballplayers were in uniform or engaged in defense work, according to Jeff Obermeyer in *Baseball and the Bottom Line in World War II*. Of all the professional leagues, it was the 12 teams in the Negro National and American Leagues that fared best on several fronts. "Attendance climbed steadily during the war years and the Negro Leagues avoided the decreases suffered by the majors in 1942 and 1943. Even more importantly, the teams were profitable, and the annual East–West All-Star Game drew crowds that sold out major league parks," Obermeyer notes.[74] However, attendance at regular-season Negro League games was light (when the Homestead Grays came to Griffith Stadium for their home opener on a chilly Saturday, May 9, the *Afro-American* reported that only 4,253 witnessed the doubleheader loss to the New York Black Yankees).[75] But when big stars of the Negro Leagues—the Paiges, the Leonards, and the Gibsons, among others—were in the lineup, Griffith Stadium was standing room only.

The attendance statistics however did nothing to move the opponents of baseball integration. Commissioner Landis was no fan of even interracial exhibitions, especially when they outdrew all-white contests. From his office in Chicago on June 4, Landis issued a strongly worded memorandum that banned any such contests not specifically designated for the war-relief effort: "The activities of promoters of games allegedly played 'for relief' but actually as commercial enterprises mislead the public into the erroneous belief that such games are for the Army and Navy Relief funds and thereby interfere with games actually played for those funds."[76] Reporting the memo, the Associated Press noted that Landis did not specifically cite the two Dizzy Dean All-Star games but pointed out that the first contest in Chicago drew more than 29,000 fans and a gate of $30,000, whereas three days later, when the Cubs hosted Cincinnati in the scheduled Wrigley Field relief-fund game, the crowd numbered just under 10,000 and raised only $10,455 for the fund. By contrast, the Washington exhibition game featuring the Paige–Travis matchup attracted 22,000, "the biggest crowd ever to watch a non–Major League game in Griffith Stadium."[77]

In fact, Travis's appearance "marked a new chapter in the Grays–Senators' complex history," Grays historian Brad Snyder notes.[78] Although Washington, DC, and all points south were part of segregated Dixie, Griffith permitted the Grays to use his Orlando spring-training facility, and he even supplied baseball equipment to the dollar-hungry black franchise. But the two clubs were never permitted to play one another. In one of Landis's first edicts after assuming the office of commissioner in 1920, he banned virtually all interracial contests with the exception of a rare handful of exhibition games that excluded most active major leaguers. Because the Grays played in Griffith Stadium when the Nationals were on the road, the teams never actually got to watch each other play, so relations between them "ran from cool to indifferent," but "privately, the Grays relished a showdown with the Senators," Snyder writes.[79] But when such a game was suggested with proceeds going to the Army and Navy Relief funds, Griffith's answer was that the major leagues already had scheduled charitable games and the Negro Leagues should create their own war-relief activities.[80] Of course Griffith received a portion of the Grays' gate at Griffith Stadium, and he might have considered an interracial contest or two with his black tenants if he could be sure of great attendance. But he first had to get Landis's OK. Even the wiliest of Griffith's talents were not up to that task.

Like many Americans at the time, Griffith was opposed to integration, but not due to bigotry like many of his fellow owners; for him, it was a monetary decision. He had set aside the right-field pavilion at Griffith Stadium for his black customers who occasionally also sat in the left-field bleachers without incident, there being no "Coloreds Only" signs. Calvin Griffith, always referring to his uncle as "mister," told Snyder that Clark Griffith had set aside the right-field pavilion at the request of some local black pastors. "Mister Griffith gave them practically down from first base to the right-field fence. That's what they wanted. They got what they asked for," he told Snyder.[51]

If you asked African Americans living in Washington, DC, during the war years what they thought of the Nats owner, the word "racist" probably would not have been their first answer or even the second. In their minds, Clark Griffith stacked up as a paragon of race relations compared to his pro-football counterpart and winter tenant, Washington Redskins owner George Preston Marshall, an outspoken, lifelong racist who adamantly and publicly refused to sign any black players, a position he maintained into the civil-rights era and even into the afterlife. (When Marshall died in 1969, the bulk of his estate went to set up a foundation in his name. But there was a proviso that not a single dollar of the foundation should go to "any purpose which supports or employs the principle of racial integration in any form.")[52] Who couldn't look good by comparison?

Although Griffith joined his fellow club owners in opposing racial integration, the Nationals had a Cuban ballplayer who some sports historians credit with having preceded Jackie Robinson as the first black to integrate the game. Roberto Estalella, a five-foot, eight-inch, 180-pound outfielder–third baseman joined the Nationals in September 1935. He was the product of Nats super scout Joe Cambria's stock of Latin ballplayers, a good number of whom found their way out of Cuba and into Nationals uniforms during the war. Between 1935 and 1942, Estalella played four seasons for Washington, where he was deemed a good-hit, no-field player. His best season with Washington was his last, 1942, when he hit .277 in 133 games. Light-skinned Estalella always thought of himself as white and, as long as he spoke only Spanish, so did the segregation sentries of major-league baseball.

Other Latin players from Cambria's stable followed Estalella into Washington flannels, including Venezuelan Alex Carrasquel, who pitched for the Nats from 1939 to 1945. According to Shirley Povich, "The most heralded Cambria product, though, was one Roberto Ortiz, the biggest Cuban he ever lassoed and brought out of the Pearl of the Antilles." Cambria introduced Ortiz, who was six-feet, four inches tall and weighed 200 pounds, to manager Bucky Harris in 1939 as a pitcher "faster than [Walter] Johnson and a longer hitter than Jimmy [*sic*] Foxx." However, in his six years with Washington, 1941–1944, and then again for parts of the 1949 and 1950 seasons, Ortiz was strictly an outfielder. Although Griffith Stadium was open to Latin players throughout the war years, Povich notes that in 1945, "when Griffith envisioned a new flow of American [that is, white] talent he called Cambria off the Cuban beat."[83]

Racial integration was such a touchy issue during the war years that any talk of even possibly bringing blacks into the major leagues either as individuals or as teams was quickly snuffed out by the owners and of course by Landis. As an example of the major leagues' closed-door policy, in March of 1942, when UCLA's famed multiple-sport-star Jackie Robinson and Negro League pitcher Nate Moreland went to the Chicago White Sox's Pasadena, California, spring-training camp seeking a tryout, they were turned down flat.[84] When Washington sportswriter Vincent X. Flaherty suggested in his *Washington Times-Herald* column that Griffith might be the perfect owner to integrate baseball because of the large and growing black population in the federal city, plus the regular attraction of the Homestead Grays, he appealed to Griffith's business sense. He told the Old Fox that if he were to sign Grays' slugging catcher Josh Gibson he would attract larger crowds at the ballpark, and hence realize greater revenue; Griffith replied, "Colored people should develop their own big league baseball and challenge the best of the white major leagues,"[85] which of course could never happen with Landis standing in the doorway barring their entry.

For some still unfathomable reason, Dodgers manager Leo Durocher stirred up a short-lived hornets' nest (neither his first nor his last), when, according to the *Sporting News*, the feisty manager told the Communist Party newspaper *Daily Worker* that he knew several good

Negro ballplayers he would sign if only they were permitted to play in the majors. Landis hit the ceiling. "There is no rule, formal or informal, or any understanding—written, subterranean or sub anything—against the hiring of Negro players by the teams of Organized Ball," he fumed in the *Sporting News* article, reiterating baseball's standard alibi. In fact, there was no such rule, but in practice, every team followed it. When the Dodgers were in Chicago to play the Cubs, the *Sporting News* added that Durocher had gone before Judge Landis to vow that he had made no such statement. "I told Durocher that he could hire 1 Negro ball player or 25 Negro ball players, just the same as whites," Landis said he had replied.[86] It's most likely both men were bending the truth for their own good. In any case, it took almost another four years before such a hiring occurred, of course, when Robinson signed with the Dodgers organization in October 1945, a move that Griffith, among others, criticized. By then, Landis was dead.

It's fair to say that Griffith's opposition to racial integration was not based on any innate prejudices, but on his belief that there was no money in integration. "Griffith believed he could make more money renting his stadium to black baseball teams than he could by increasing attendance from signing black players," Snyder explains. "Griffith wanted the Negro Leagues to survive because he wanted to keep profiting off them and he recognized that integration would mean their demise."

Griffith was defended by an unlikely source, African American sportswriter Ric Roberts of the *Pittsburgh Courier*, who said he wouldn't call the Old Fox's stand "prejudice." "He just had a yen for making money." Also, because the Nationals and Griffith Stadium were located south of the Mason–Dixon Line, Griffith had to consider his "Southern clientele." But years later, when a television executive asked Calvin Griffith why his uncle had not signed Josh Gibson or Buck Leonard, he explained that "Mr. Griffith already had black ballplayers on there, but he couldn't publicize it," referring to Estalella and the other Latin players.[87] It was a lame excuse indeed, for Gibson and Leonard were outstanding players—game changers in today's sports parlance—and they far surpassed in talent any of the Cubans that wore a Washington uniform. It's clear that Calvin Griffith was merely defending the honor of his venerated relative.

Over the years, Griffith had allowed many black teams, not just the Grays, to use his ballpark, including the Eastern Colored League Washington Potomacs in 1924, the Negro National League Washington Elite Giants in 1936–1937, the Negro National League Washington Black Senators in 1938, and of course the Grays from 1937 to 1948.[88] And, as mentioned, Griffith's wartime rosters included several Latin ballplayers—acceptable by virtue of their being foreigners and on the light side in skin tone and therefore not considered black. (Nevertheless, as we shall see, they received the same vitriolic hate-filled reception in certain cities, especially in St. Louis, as if they had come off an Alabama cotton field and crashed a debutante cotillion in Birmingham.)

In keeping with his character, Griffith wanted the Grays, Monarchs, and the other Negro League teams to survive and feed the revenue stream he derived from them, which in actuality was more often a trickle than a stream. Ever the astute businessman, Griffith knew that if the Negro Leagues were to survive they needed their own stars to attract black fans, a notion subscribed to also by Grays' manager Vic Harris. The Old Fox knew too that if the Negro Leagues had any chance of surviving along with integrated major-league baseball, they would need to be financially compensated for the loss of their stars. The other major-league owners—many of whom did not have or need Negro League teams sharing their ballparks and contributing to their bottom line—were less inclined toward that option.

For several years after Jackie Robinson "broke the color barrier," Griffith insisted that if he could find black players with skills equal to Robinson's he would gladly sign them. But as Snyder points out, "Seven years after Robinson made his major league debut, Griffith still could not find an American-born black man to play on his team."[89] And like his wish-list request several years earlier for 28 night games to everyone else's maximum of 14, this time too Griffith's argument was weak and porous because, once Robinson appeared in a Dodgers uniform at the start of the 1947 season, most (but certainly not all) major-league teams recognized the talent they were missing and began to sign black ballplayers.

In a somewhat ironic way, it was one of Griffith's favorite players who had a small role in helping to integrate the American League. When the Cleveland Indians signed Larry Doby three months after Robinson's debut in Brooklyn, Doby promptly called his old Navy buddy Nats first baseman Mickey Vernon to say he was so ill prepared to play for the Indians that he didn't even have a bat to use. Vernon told him not to worry; he would send him a couple of his own. So when the black centerfielder made his major-league debut as a pinch hitter in Chicago on July 5, 1947, Doby was swinging one of Vernon's bats.[90] (Although he struck out, Doby went on to an outstanding career with Cleveland, the White Sox, and briefly with Detroit. He was elected to the Baseball Hall of Fame by the Veterans Committee in 1998. Doby died at his home in Montclair, New Jersey, on June 18, 2003.)

However, many Negro Leaguers—used to the racial slights and discriminatory practices in housing, dining, and transportation that passed for "normal" in the pre–civil-rights era—harbored strong patriotic feelings toward the country in wartime. In one of his *Afro-American* columns, "All Up in Washington," Ric Roberts writes about sitting in Griffith Stadium with Grays' pitcher Roy Partlow before the 1942 home opener. When the American flag caught a breeze and began to flutter, Partlow told the writer, "Boy, ain't that a pretty sight—that flag, it's a beauty. But, boy, you don't know how pretty that flag really is unless you've been away from it a very long time."[91] Partlow had spent 17 months playing ball in Venezuela, Puerto Rico, and Mexico, and then he "came home by way of New York where, seeing that old flag waving at the Statue of Liberty, I almost cried. Gee, it was good to see that old flag. It is the best in the world—I'm telling you."

Beyond wartime patriotism, the major leagues and the Negro Leagues shared one major concern during those years and that was how to find, cultivate, and put talented players on the field and, equally important, put paying fans in the seats. In that contest the Negro Leagues came out on top, according to historian Jeff Obermeyer. "Whereas Organized Baseball saw three out of every four minor leagues go dormant during the war and attendance drop dramatically in 1942 and 1943, the Negro Leagues entered a new era of popularity, stability and financial gain. What the leagues had in common was the desire to put the best product possible on the field, and despite the challenges they generally succeeded in maintaining baseball's popularity and image as the National Pastime."[92] In the end though, the Old Fox was right about one thing: integration did kill the Negro Leagues.

Roosevelt and British Prime Minister Winston Churchill had met several times during 1941, including at a conference in Newfoundland in mid-August, when they formed the Atlantic Charter, a broad statement of U.S. and British war aims. The charter included eight common principles they would support in the postwar world, including a joint commitment to the restoration of self-government for all countries occupied during the war and for all peoples to choose their own form of government. In December, they met again in Washington and agreed to concentrate first on defeating Nazi Germany while engaging in a holding action against Japan in the Pacific. That holding action was now being tested in the Battle of the Coral Sea, which began on May 3–4, 1942, and forced the Japanese to abandon their attempt to capture Port Moresby, New Guinea, where the establishment of a Japanese air base would have threatened Australia and strengthened Japan's military might throughout the South Pacific.[93] Coral Sea was the first engagement in modern naval history in which opposing warships did not exchange a shot.[94] *Chicago Tribune* reporter Stanley Johnston, who witnessed the battle firsthand, called it "the first great naval defeat ever dealt Japanese fleets, and, ironically enough, it was fought entirely in the air. It was a battle of aircraft carriers."[95]

At home, Americans were increasingly curbing their personal travel due to the government's rationing plan for commodities made from materials vitally needed for the war effort. The Office of Price Administration (OPA) placed limits on tire purchases and auto sales to reduce gas consumption. In May, motorists in 17 Eastern states and the District of Columbia became the first to face restrictions at the pumps because oil tankers, the primary means of delivering the crude oil to be processed into gasoline, were needed to supply troops and allies abroad. Of course, legislators on Capitol Hill thought they should be exempt from the restrictions. After the Senate rejected a resolution to give up their special gas privileges by a vote of 66–2 with 28 abstentions, Roosevelt countered by ordering that the names of persons holding the exemption X rationing cards (which included the House and Senate, giving them unlimited gasoline privileges) be made a matter of public record. He explained that the move was intended to save gasoline as well as rubber.

To further embarrass the lawmakers, FDR said one White House car and one Secret Service vehicle were being left at his home in Hyde Park, New York, instead of being brought to Washington.[96] In contrast to most members of the Senate, Roosevelt's friend and close adviser

Bernard Baruch exchanged his X card for an A card, which entitled him to just three gallons of gasoline a week. "The country needs gasoline for vital services. I guess I can hoof it," Baruch said.[97] Like Baruch, OPA Director Leon Henderson and first lady Eleanor Roosevelt also exchanged in their X cards for A cards.

The effects of gas rationing were felt almost immediately in the Washington area. The *Washington Post* on May 16 reported "a considerable decrease in auto traffic and dwindling business for parking lots and filling stations as Washington entered another phase of its gradual but sometimes jerky metamorphosis from peacetime to wartime living."[98] In June, the rationing card was changed into a coupons program, which was deemed more equitable. Gasoline dealers could obtain fresh supplies only by turning in coupons showing that they were observing the ration regulations. A similar system regulated the purchase of home heating oil. (When the gasoline-rationing program went into effect nationwide on December 1, the *New York Times* estimated that it would affect 20 million passenger cars and five million buses and trucks.)[99]

The primary goal, however, was not to save gas, it was to prolong the life of vehicle tires and alleviate the wartime scarcity of rubber. "Simply stated, unless Nation-wide gasoline rationing were put into effect, the precious stockpile of rubber now on automobiles in the form of tires might be greatly reduced during the remaining hot days of the summer when tires wear out considerably faster than they do in cold winter months," Ben W. Gilbert explained in the *Washington Post* at the peak of the summer's heat. "However, if driving were greatly restricted by a comprehensive Nation-wide rationing plan," he added, "coupled with a ban on driving at high speeds much of the rubber stockpile might be saved, thus keeping many more tires in service for longer periods." The tire industry was campaigning for a 40-percent reduction in driving while it set its sights on producing 870,000 tons of synthetic rubber by 1944 through refinements in the manufacture of butadiene, a base material used in the production of synthetic rubber.[100] The rubber shortage and the drive to find an acceptable replacement would soon affect baseball as well.

The Nats meanwhile had also done some traveling of their own but not in the right direction. After a disastrous East Coast swing to Boston, New York, and Philadelphia, during which at one point they lost five games in a row to the Yankees and the Red Sox, the Nationals sank from their fifth-place position one month earlier to near rock-bottom last on June 1, trailing the first-place Yankees by 15 games. The Old Fox was not happy. Already upset by Bobo Newsom's poor performances on the mound, Griffith expressed his "high disgust with the Nats' infield, both offensively and defensively and declared that he was making strong attempts to procure new talent."[101] He noted, too, "The deadline on trades will be June 15 and some of the other clubs may be willing to make a deal before that time."

In hopes of righting the ship, Bucky Harris selected Early Wynn to pitch the series opener against St. Louis at Griffith Stadium. The choice made good baseball sense because Wynn and Sid Hudson had been the Nats' only consistently good pitchers up to that point in the season. Besides, Wynn was one of the toughest competitors in baseball who looked upon anyone who stepped into the batter's box as his mortal enemy. Nats first baseman Ed Butka recalled taking batting practice one day during his rookie year when Wynn was on the mound (recall that teams in that era did not have the luxury of nonroster batting-practice pitchers or protective screens on the mound), and he hit a hard ground ball that nearly hit Wynn. "He gets mad at me because I hit it through the box," Butka later related, referring to the pitcher's mound. "He says, 'pull that ball! What the hell!' Me, I'm just a rookie. So he throws the ball at me and I throw the bat at him. If I had hit him they would've sent me to Oshkosh right then," Butka said laughing many years after the incident.[102]

Griffith's frustration with the Nats' poor play might have been eased somewhat by a June 10 testimonial luncheon in his honor at the Mayflower Hotel, which was attended by some of his former players, including Walter Johnson, Joe Judge, Nick Altrock, and Ossie Bluege. Shirley Povich explained that the affair was a tribute to Griffith as "a humanitarian and a cheerful pushover for a sob story despite a reputation for driving a hard baseball bargain."[103] Had it not been for the war, it's quite possible that Griffith's pal FDR would have put in an appearance, lured there no doubt by the chance to talk baseball with those championship players of two decades earlier.

Griffith would remember that Wednesday for another reason, too, and not a happy one. That evening, his long-time silent partner and team vice president William M. Richardson died suddenly at age 64. Richardson, whose wealth was derived from several successful business ventures—he had been introduced to Griffith by Philadelphia Athletics owner-manager Connie Mack—was the epitome of the silent partner. Although he and Griffith owned 85 percent of the company stock, Richardson never interfered with Griffith's management of the club. "Never in the 23 years since he helped Griffith buy control of the Washington club was there any kind of a brush between the two men. Griffith voted Richardson's stock in the club as if he had power of attorney with no need to consult the half-owner. He had blanket approval [from] Richardson in any deal he chose to make," Povich wrote.[104]

At the White House, FDR's attention during the latter part of June was focused on initiating the "Europe First" policy that he and Churchill had worked out the previous December. As commander in chief, Roosevelt dispatched 51-year-old Major General Dwight D. Eisenhower to England to take command of the newly created European Theater of Operations (ETO). "The first task will be to establish full collaboration with the British Staff in London," the *New York Times* explained in a front-page article. Despite British setbacks in North Africa, especially in Libya and Egypt, the idea was to create a "second front" in Europe, a plan pushed by Soviet dictator Josef Stalin, whose Red Army was struggling against the Germans in western Russia. In announcing the general's previously unreported arrival in London, the *Times* quoted Eisenhower's praise of Roosevelt and Churchill for setting "a more effective pattern for unqualified partnership than has ever before been envisaged by allied nations in pursuit of a common purpose." The front-page story also noted that Eisenhower's appointment was made public "within a few days after the official announcement that American troops were now in East Anglia, England, as well as on Irish soil, and encamped probably within 30 miles of the East Coast of the English Channel, now occupied by German soldiers."[105]

Eisenhower was an unusual choice for the key London post because several other generals outranked him, and the Army was nothing if not hierarchical when it came to assignments and promotions. But Marshall, the Army's chief of staff, had learned to respect Ike's knowledge of military tactics and his willingness to act on his own decisions when the two men had worked together in the immediate aftermath of Pearl Harbor and the subsequent Japanese aggression in the Philippines. Marshall had put Eisenhower in charge of the Philippines and Far Eastern section of the War Plans Division, telling him, "The Department is filled with able men who analyze their problems well but feel compelled always to bring them to me for final solution. I must have assistants who will solve their own problems and tell me later what they have done."[106]

So in the spring of 1942, when Roosevelt was mulling over the dual diplomatic and military roles that the ETO leader would have to play, Marshall recommended Eisenhower, and the president concurred. FDR "felt that Eisenhower had just the kind of personality to master the terrible problems of welding the armed forces of two nations for the first time in history into an efficient and flexible coalition." The British, initially dubious and naturally somewhat resentful of a U.S. general assuming the leadership of the U.S.–British coalition, were soon won over by Eisenhower's modesty (among other things, he turned down a lavish suite at an exclusive London hotel for more modest personal quarters elsewhere) and for his frank and friendly openness, as when he told his British colleagues that solidarity between Americans and Englishmen was his "religion."[107] (After the war, then-president Eisenhower continued the tradition of throwing out the ceremonial first ball on opening day. In 1954, he added his own personal touch to the annual rite when he presented the Nats' Mickey Vernon with the Silver Slugger award for having won the American League batting title the previous season with 205 hits, a league-leading 43 doubles, and a batting average of .337. Vernon, who had the distinction of playing in four decades, said later that it was the first time the award had ever been presented by the president.)[108]

About a month and a half prior to Ike's arrival in London, Congress on May 14 approved the creation of the Women's Army Auxiliary Corps (WAAC) as the need for manpower in and out of uniform was increasing dramatically. Roosevelt signed the bill into law on May 15, and Oveta Culp Hobby was sworn in as the first WAAC director on May 16. A naval arm, the Women Accepted for Voluntary Emergency Service (WAVES), was established in August, and the Women's Auxiliary Ferrying Squadron (WAFS) was formed in September, a cadre of experienced women pilots who would test and shuttle new aircraft to and from U.S. military bases, saving male pilots for combat duty.

Half a world away in the Pacific, the tide was turning in favor of the U.S. Navy. Until the Battle of Midway, fought near the tiny U.S. mid-Pacific atoll between June 4 and 7, the Japanese "possessed general naval superiority over the United States and could usually choose where and when to attack. After Midway, the two opposing fleets were essentially equals, and the United States soon took the offensive," according to the Naval History and Heritage Command.[109] At Midway, the Japanese fleet lost the aircraft carriers *Kaga*, *Akagi*, *Soryu*, and *Hiryu*, which were involved in the Pearl Harbor attack, while the U.S. Navy lost the carrier *Yorktown*, which had been repaired and hurried back into service after being damaged during the Battle of the Coral Sea.[110]

It wasn't only the Nationals and the Homestead Grays that were the headline attractions at Griffith Stadium during the 1942 season. On Sunday, June 21, the ballpark played host to a mammoth field day organized by the Recreation Services of the Metropolitan Civilian Defense, which included a five-hour patriotic pageant featuring flags of 28 United Nations, a softball game involving a women's team from the FBI, and the raising of the colors at centerfield by Griffith and military brass. The highlight of the program was a ball game between Bob Feller's Navy team from the Norfolk Naval Training Station and an Army team from Camp Lee, Virginia, with a roster of several major and minor leaguers including first baseman Jack Sanford, who played in 47 games for Washington in 1940 and 1941 and then briefly again in 1946 after serving in the air force. The two service teams had met twice previously with each club winning once. Feller, called "Rapid Robert" for his exceptional fastball, pitched the entire nine innings for his Navy squad, yielding eight hits and striking out a dozen soldiers as Norfolk won, 5–2, before 11,000 fans.[111] Sam Cozzi, a former college student at West Chester Teachers College, broke through to Feller in the sixth inning with a towering blast to centerfield for an inside-the-park home run (the first of three such rare feats that day, which said something about the lack of defense in the outfield).

The Griffith Stadium festivities, however, were overshadowed by a contest three days earlier featuring the Homestead Grays. On June 18, 28,000 fans—more than double the 11,000 who watched Feller and company—overflowed Griffith Stadium to witness the Grays beat Satchel Paige's Kansas City Monarchs, 2–1, in a 10-inning pitchers' duel that included five perfect innings thrown by Paige and the Grays' flag-loving Roy Partlow. After nine full shutout innings, the Monarchs pushed across one run in the top of the 10th that was promptly matched by the Grays in the bottom of the extra inning. Then Partlow hit a triple to break the 1–1 tie when Jud Wilson scored the winning run. "It took the mob fully 20 minutes to stop shreiking [sic] and screaming," Ric Roberts wrote.[112] "Partlow, the hero, was carried off the field on the shoulders of a hundred admirers; thousands swarmed onto the field to congratulate the champions of the East, the Washington Homestead Grays, for the most beautifully contested baseball game ever seen on Griffith's Stadium's sod. It was simply terrific," Roberts gushed.

"That night, black Washington accepted a Negro League team origi-nating in Pittsburgh as their own; it was the night the Homestead Grays truly became the *Washington* [italics as published] Homestead Grays," Brad Snyder proclaims in his history of the Homestead Grays, *Beyond the Shadow of the Senators*, echoing Roberts's sentiments.[113] Writing one week after that classic contest, an obviously still giddy Ric Roberts compared the game favorably to the earlier exhibition when "with the white press behind him, the celebrated Bobby Feller plus an assort-ment of big league stars could lure only 11,000 fans to the same lot, Griffith Stadium, free of admission charges."[114] And just to ram home his point, Roberts added, "At the same spot, the kingpin New York Yankees and the washed-up Washington Senators could lure only 10,000 to see Joe DiMaggio and his pals strive for a worthy Army–Navy relief cause. How come." Roberts answered his own question, chalking it up to the fact that "colored major league baseball is coming into its own."

As for the Nats, they were again sinking faster than the Japanese carriers at Midway. Griffith's star pitchers Sid Hudson and Bobo News-om both fell victim to shoddy infield play and a lack of hitting. As the team went into the final week of June, Hudson had lost seven straight games in his last eight starts, and Newsom, although having somewhat recovered from his earlier ineffectiveness, had managed to win only one of his previous nine starts. "With a better hitting club or a team that could make double plays, both Hudson and Newsom would be among the league's leading pitchers, but this year the Senators are guilty of being the worst Washington team in modern history," judged Shirley Povich. Early Wynn, in his first full season in the major leagues, was the only bright light on the staff. His record of seven wins and five losses compared favorably to any pitcher in the league, "having been accom-plished with, or despite, the Senators."[115]

In an effort to improve the infield, manager Bucky Harris had given the Nats' shortstop job to rookie John Sullivan with only two years of organized baseball behind him after Bob Repass "laid an oversized egg at the position," Povich wrote (without referring to his own earlier glowing reports on Repass during spring training). Damning Sullivan with faint praise, Harris predicted, "Some day, he's going to be a good big league shortstop," and he assigned former Nats infielder and now coach Ossie Bluege (BLUE–gee) to oversee Sullivan's on-the-job training.[116] (Sullivan went on to a five-year career with the Nats, with a two-year service break in 1945 and 1946. His final year of 1949 was as a member of the St. Louis Browns. He retired a month shy of his 29th birthday.)

One of the Nats' few offensive bright lights was the hitting of George Case Jr., who had returned to the lineup after a bad sinus attack and shoulder injury. Batting leadoff, he opened five consecutive games with a hit that had raised his average from around .250 to close to the .300 mark. (Case was a mainstay with Washington throughout the war. Although he appeared before his local draft board three times, he was deemed ineligible for military service and was given a 4-F classification because of a shoulder separation injury. The conditions outlined in Roosevelt's green-light letter called for ballplayers with 4-F status to work in the defense industry during the off-season. Case's son, George Case III, said his father worked at a defense plant in the Trenton, New Jersey, area that was either assembling bombers or producing parts for the aircraft. "I was really too young to understand what the 'war effort' was all about," he explained.)[117] Between June 29 and July 5, Washington lost six games and won three. After splitting a Fourth of July doubleheader with the Athletics, the last-place Nats were 22½ games behind the Yankees.

Prior to the All-Star Game at the Polo Grounds, Griffith suffered something of a personal defeat at the summer major-league meetings in New York, although the Old Fox managed to snatch one victory from the jaws of Commissioner Landis. Having already secured permission to play more night games than any other club, Griffith now wanted Landis and his fellow owners to allow him to play all remaining home games under the lights with the exception of Sunday games and Labor Day. The Browns asked for the same deal. The American League surprisingly gave Griffith (and Browns president Donald Barnes) an OK, but "when the matter landed in the joint meeting, the National League and Judge Landis gave it the heave-ho."[118] Griffith was angry at the National League's opposition and especially upset by what he viewed as a betrayal by the Cubs, Phillies, and Dodgers. Griffith fumed, "I had written promises from Chicago and Philadelphia that they would vote for my plan and [Brooklyn's] MacPhail told me over the phone that I could count on his vote."[119] Then he added, "They didn't have the courage to go through with it. Those National Leaguers are like sheep. They always vote with the majority." (The Old Fox was still in a foul mood when he voted as a majority of one to ban beer in the Nats' clubhouse and also in the visiting team's facility. Griffith's crackdown against the age-old custom of a postgame brew or two came after he became enraged at reports that some of his players had had a few too many drinks on the train going back to Washington after an exhibition game in Richmond, Virginia.)[120]

However, Griffith did secure one approval at the meetings. Citing a plan the Dodgers had conceived after the Army banned night games at the two lighted National League ballparks in New York because of dim-out restrictions on coastal areas (in Brooklyn's case, its proximity to New York Harbor and the Atlantic Ocean), Griffith got the OK to start Nats' home games at 7 p.m., when it was still light outside, except on Sundays, and to turn on the lights at dusk.[121] As Griffith reportedly told his fellow owners, "Brooklyn doesn't ask any questions when it wants to start a game at 7," he grumbled. "I don't have to ask anybody's permission either."[122]

With the World Series a little more than two months away, the owners mulled over a plan to donate half the gate receipts from the fall classic to the Army–Navy relief fund, a plan that had the backing of Judge Landis. Most of the clubs favored the idea too, especially those that had no chance of winning the league pennant and getting into the series. But to a man the club owners felt compelled to regularly justify playing baseball in wartime, one way to do that was to become advocates for doing whatever they could to support war-relief funds. As a result, the upcoming 1942 World Series spawned some of the weirdest ideas ever proposed at an owners' meeting. One plan, suggested by Brooklyn's Larry MacPhail, would have turned the championship into a barnstorming event with a best-8-of-15-game series played at different venues around the country. An unnamed official, obviously critical of the idea, offered a scenario in which one team clinched the series in 10 games, 8–2. "That would leave five more games to be played out in the wide open spaces. Can you picture the fans breaking down the fences in Los Angeles to see the fifteenth contest? Neither can I," the Associated Press quoted him as saying.[123] Another plan would have created an exhibition tour after the World Series ended. Both ideas were deemed stillborn by the savants of the game.

Looking ahead one year, Detroit general manager Jack Zeller proposed shortening the 1943 season to 140 games with opening day on April 27 and the season finale on September 19. "We would have 146 days, including 20 Saturdays, 20 Sundays and 3 holidays," he explained. "With week-end double-headers we would not be cramped to take care of 140 games." Originally, Zeller had suggested lopping off the first and last months of the season and playing the regulation 154 games within that shortened calendar. He also suggested that the teams hold spring training at home rather than travel to their customary warm-climate facilities because of transportation problems and a shortage of hotel space in Florida. Zeller claimed that, at his Tigers training camp in Lakeland, Florida, "the influx of soldiers already threatens to force withdrawal of the club," and he believed similar conditions prevailed at other teams' training sites.[124] Griffith said Florida hotel accommodations should be adequate because there weren't tourists there anymore, but he sided with Zeller in wanting to shorten the season by two weeks because "I've always wanted to have the World Series over by October 1."[125] Despite being rebuffed on his spring-training idea by his fellow owners, Zeller was both prescient and a little premature. The 1942 season was the last until after the war when the 16 teams held their training camps in Florida and California.

Unlike today's annual All-Star Game, when all play stops for a four-day midsummer festival of home-run hitting, a game between minor leaguers deemed future stars, and the clash between the American and National leagues with the winner gaining home-field advantage in the World Series, the 10th annual All-Star Game took place on Monday, July 6, 1942, at the Polo Grounds, just two days after the Fourth of July. As planned, the proceeds from the All-Star Game were earmarked for the Army–Navy relief fund, and the winning team would then go on to Cleveland to play a second benefit game the next evening against a team composed of players in uniform. Slugger Stan Spence and pitcher Sid Hudson of the Nats joined the heavily favored American League stars, who won the All-Star Game, 3–1, for the AL's seventh victory in the series. The contest, which drew more than 34,000 fans to the horseshoe-shaped stadium, also marked the last All-Star appearances of Ted Williams until 1946 and Joe DiMaggio until 1947 following their return from military service. (Although DiMaggio was back in a Yankees uniform in 1946, in June in a game he caught his spikes sliding into second base. He sprained an ankle, tore cartilage in his knee, and had to be helped off the field. For the first time in his career, he missed the All-Star Game. At the time, DiMaggio was still not up to his usual high standards and was hitting just .266.)[126]

The next evening in Cleveland's Municipal Stadium, a crowd of more than 60,000 saw the victorious American League All-Stars shut out a combined Army–Navy service team, 5–0, which was headed by a battery of Bob Feller and Mickey Cochrane. (Feller, also in subpar shape, gave up three runs and four hits in the first two innings and was replaced before getting one out in the second.) Despite the enthusiasm of the fans and the players, the future of such contests was immediately cast in doubt when Cleveland Indians president Alva Bradley told the press after the game, "It was a tremendous task to put over, but we did, and we'd gladly try it again next year if we thought we could raise $70,000 for the Army and Navy." Bradley said the exhibition, which included a pregame military parade of the service branches and a mechanized tank battalion, grossed $143,571, of which $62,094 went for the purchase of war savings stamps and $7,797 for federal taxes. Added to the pool was $1,475 in scorecard sales and about $2,000 from concessions.[127]

As AP sportswriter Judson Bailey noted, the contest was one-sided and would probably stay so if there were other such exhibitions. The AL All-Stars were in peak condition and too strong for the service team, Bailey noted, a skills gap that was likely only to increase in the coming years because the players in uniform "are not going to become better ball players during another year of training to become better warriors and certainly they are unlikely to ever become a reasonable match for such an array of active major league stars as the American League was able to bring into the game this year."[128]

Also, such contests were not generating as much excitement or as much money as the owners had believed they would. The idea of each team staging one home game with all proceeds going to the Army–Navy relief fund sounded like a winner, but in fact, those games too were not generating much money. Just prior to the All-Star Game, the five teams that had already staged regular-season fund games—the Red Sox, Indians, Nats, Phillies, and Reds—had raised a combined $45,000. From Boston, Shirley Povich noted that "one little dog track near Revere Beach, Wonderland Park, has already contributed $50,000 for relief."[129] He added that the sport of kings, horseracing, had kicked in $1 million with another million expected by the end of the year. (However, on August 3, a Dodgers–Giants game at the Polo Grounds—always a great draw—attracted a crowd of 57,305 and netted an estimated $80,000 for the Army Emergency Relief Fund. The game was called in the bottom of the ninth due to the dim-out regulations with the Giants trailing 7–4, with two runners on base and no outs.)[130]

In Washington, lawmakers and government officials were attending to matters they considered war related and important, even if few outside the nation's capital agreed with that assessment. The Senate Judiciary Committee approved a bill awarding a medal of honor to recognize the "untiring devotion to duty of [FBI Director] J. Edgar Hoover and the officers and public servants under his direction, who collaborated in the apprehension of numerous enemy agents, saboteurs and fifth columnists during the month of June, 1942, thereby affording great protection to his country and its citizens and effecting a telling blow in the prosecution of the war."[131] At the Office of Price Administration (OPA), "tea experts" were warning the tea-drinking public to expect a 50-percent decline in supplies for the year because of blocked imports. Among the suggestions the OPA experts offered to ease the shortage were: buy tea in bulk, forego the "extra spoonful for the pot," and use only one level teaspoon per cup.[132] (Toiling anonymously—and restlessly—in the agency's tire-rationing division was a young California attorney named Richard Milhous Nixon, who after only eight months on the job was named acting chief of interpretations in the sub-branch of the Rubber Branch. Nixon was soon joined by his wife Pat, who found a $2600-a-year job there as an OPA assistant business analysis.)[133]

By the end of July, U.S. and RAF bombers were pounding German and Italian supply bases and vehicles on Crete and in Libya's port city of Tobruk to stall Field Marshal Erwin Rommel's advance toward Alexandria, Egypt. The Red Army was engaged in heavy fighting at the Don River and the Caucasus in the southern Soviet Union. In Paris, elite

Nazi troops marched down the Champs Elysees on their way to the French coast where the German High Command believed the British, and possibly the Americans, would open the second front, a strategic move that Nazi Propaganda Minister Josef Goebbels said would be an act of madness. Convinced of German superiority, Goebbels taunted the British and Americans in a weekly publication boasting that when the Brits and Yanks arrived, German troops would not be carrying golf clubs and tennis rackets, but first-class weapons and "a vast store of war experience collected on all the European battlefields."[134] And, Goebbels added, the German army "would gladly take the opportunity of making it plain to the Yankees that entrance to Europe is forbidden."

At the same time, the war came as close to Griffith Stadium as it ever would[135] when the Supreme Court, in a historic emergency session on July 29, heard a challenge to Roosevelt's emergency orders of July 2, closing the civilian court system to enemy combatants. The challenge came from eight captured German spies who faced the death penalty. The men arrived with arms and explosives after U-boats had dropped several of them at Long Island, New York, on June 13 and the rest at Ponte Vedra Beach, Florida, four days later. By June 27, the FBI had rounded them all up in New York and Chicago, and a military court was convened at the Justice Department to try them. However, their attorney argued that the men were not enemy combatants but were actually defecting, and therefore, they should not be tried by a panel of seven generals, as the emergency powers demanded, but in the civilian court system.[136]

On July 31, the Supreme Court ruled that they could indeed be tried before a military tribunal because "the law of war draws a distinction between the armed forces and the peaceful populations of belligerent nations and also between those who are lawful and unlawful combatants. Lawful combatants are subject to capture and detention as prisoners of war by opposing military forces. Unlawful combatants are likewise subject to capture and detention, but in addition they are subject to trial and punishment by military tribunals for acts which render their belligerency unlawful."[137] On August 3, a military tribunal found the men guilty, and six of them were electrocuted on the morning of August 8. Of the two remaining German would-be saboteurs who had cooperated with U.S. authorities, one received a life sentence and the other 30 years. (In April 1948, President Truman granted them executive clemency, and both were deported.)[138]

If there was anything that Clark Griffith could find pleasure in at this time besides his family, it was the outstanding hitting of his centerfielder Stan Spence, who started the season hitting .300 and hadn't dropped below that mark. By the end of July, he was leading the league with 136 hits including nine triples and 60 runs scored, and his batting average was .331. Asked about his prowess at the plate, Spence said the credit belonged to speedster George Case, who hit ahead of him at the top of the lineup. "That Case is always getting on base and giving pitchers fits," Spence told Shirley Povich. "They're so worried about whether he's going to steal, that they unconsciously let up against me." Griffith had another reason to be happy about the winter trade that brought Spence to Washington from the Boston Red Sox. The contract Spence brought with him set his 1942 salary at $3,500, making him, as Povich noted, "probably the most underpaid ball player in the American League as a result of his feats this season."[139]

By the end of July, Washington had rung up 41 wins against 61 losses and was 28 games behind first-place New York but only four games behind sixth-place Chicago. The Nats had inched out of the cellar and into seventh place, thanks to the hapless Philadelphia A's, who were worse. It was clear to most observers that, going into the last two months of the season, the loss of Cecil Travis and Buddy Lewis was a severe blow to the club's fortunes and had eradicated the optimism engendered during spring training. Indeed, in no uncertain terms, Povich branded the team as having "the worst-throwing infield the major leagues have ever seen." He singled out third baseman Roy Cullenbine, second baseman Ellis Clary, and shortstop Johnny Sullivan for giving Mickey Vernon fits at first base. Vernon, an excellent first baseman, often had to leap in the air for a wild throw, dig the ball out of the dirt, or charge into the runner's path and trust to luck he wasn't injured every time one of the "scatter-arms" throws to him. In the process, Vernon saved a couple of ball games a week "with his fancy saves of errant throws."[140]

But if the Nats were reading their press coverage, the stories had little effect because they soon departed Washington for what turned out to be their best road trip of the season. While they were away, Griffith Stadium hosted upward of 15,000 fans when the Homestead Grays played the Birmingham Black Barons, a powerful Negro American League team, in the annual Colored Elks' Athletic Day. The big draw was the Barons' Ted "Double Duty" Radcliffe, who got his nickname because he often appeared in doubleheaders pitching one game and catching the other. Radcliffe was reputed to be the oldest living Negro League ballplayer at the time of his death in August 2005.

Just two months before he passed away at age 103, Radcliffe was one of 14 Negro League players honored in a ceremony at Washington's RFK Stadium—the successor to Griffith Stadium and predecessor of the current Nationals Park—before the new Washington Nationals franchise played the Chicago Cubs. Sitting in a golf cart behind home plate, Radcliffe handed the ball to Nationals coach Don Buford as the ceremonial "first pitch."[141] One can only surmise what he and his 13 colleagues might have been thinking at that moment. For almost all of his life, like his contemporaries, Radcliffe had been kept off major-league diamonds by prejudicial thinking epitomized in what today would be viewed as an embarrassing editorial in the *Sporting News* on August 6, 1942. The newspaper of record for the baseball world said, "The country has a great Negro major league [*sic*], which draws heavy support from the colored folk," and players like Satchel Paige might not have "blossomed forth" as a great pitcher if they'd been in the whites-only major leagues. The editorial examined the possibility of baseball integration and came down on the side of the status quo, concluding: "It is not difficult to imagine what would happen if a player on a mixed team, performing before a crowd of the opposite color [*sic*], should throw a bean ball, strike out with the bases full or spike a rival. Clear-minded men of tolerance of both races realize the tragic possibilities and have steered clear of such complications, because they realize it is to the benefit of each and also of the game." Besides, the unsigned editorial continued, citing comments by columnist Joe Bostic in the Harlem-based *People's Voice*, "why subject any [black] player to the humiliation and indignities associated with the problems of eating, sleeping and traveling in a layout dominated by prejudice-ridden southern whites?"[142] Why indeed.

Griffith, who agreed with that sentiment because it had long been his position on integration, was nevertheless attacked again by *Afro-American* sportswriter Sam Lacy, who continued to believe that Washington was the ideal venue to integrate the sport. But Lacy's argument was undercut somewhat when Satchel Paige told syndicated columnist Bob Considine that he wanted "no part of the major leagues" because of the treatment he might receive. Lacy, who also disagreed with the idea of pseudo-integration by permitting an all-black team to join the major leagues, fired off an open letter to Considine in which he argued that, unless Negro players were integrated with white players, "the same situation will exist. A separate club for Negroes is no more logical than a separate team for Italians, Irishmen, Germans, Poles, Lithuanians or Jews."[143] Grays historian Brad Snyder contends Griffith's position that African Americans should strengthen their own league "was completely self-serving. His stale solution only padded his wallet." Snyder writes that Griffith received 20 percent of the Grays' gate receipts on the 127,690 paid season attendance in 1942 and a fee for using the new stadium lights, in all adding an estimated $60,000 or more beyond what the Nats brought in that year.[144] Those numbers were bolstered by the Grays' third-straight Negro National League pennant since calling Griffith Stadium their home away from home.

Upon their return to Griffith Stadium on August 4, the Nationals continued to find the dog days of August to their liking, sweeping back-to-back night games from New York before a combined attendance of 27,000 fans. That extended the Nats' winning pace to 14 of 21 games—including a 3-game sweep in St. Louis—and "drawing hefty crowds, and generally amazing the folks of the Capital who knew them through most of July as the eighth-place club of the American League."[145] The winning streak was fueled by good pitching, finally, from Hudson, Newsom, and Carrasquel and the rejuvenated hitting of Jake Early and Mickey Vernon. Spence and Case meanwhile continued to hit at a .300 pace, with Case reaching the .315 mark, on his way to a career-best .320 for the season. (Case was a stellar outfielder with great speed who led the league in stolen bases five years straight, but he never learned how to slide properly. As a result, he suffered leg and wrist sprains that frequently kept him on the Nats' bench.)[146] The only problem was the team failed to make any headway in climbing out of seventh place.

As the Nats approached September, the final month of the season, when the games dwindled down to a precious few, they again reverted to sub-.500 baseball. On September 1, they were 33½ games behind the first-place Yankees but a reasonably safe seven games ahead of the cellar-dwelling Athletics. Now the Old Fox, looking at the situation in the National League, earned his nickname yet again. In the senior circuit, the Brooklyn Dodgers were in the process of blowing what had been an eight-game lead over the Cardinals for the National League pennant. The lead had shrunk to just three games, and the Dodgers management was close to panicking. (Later that month, when the Dodgers did lose the pennant to the Cardinals by just two games, it was deemed the worst collapse in major-league history. But that's only because no one could have predicted that the "Brooklyn Bums" would surpass themselves nine years later when, having squandered a 13½-game lead in August, they lost the pennant to the rival New York Giants on October 3, 1951, in a postseason playoff at the Polo Grounds immortalized by Bobby Thomson's three-run homer in the bottom of the ninth, now universally known as "the shot heard 'round the world" to win the game, 5–4, and the playoff two games to one.)

With little hope of improving his team's standing, Griffith had a plan to ease the pain in his pocketbook. On the morning of August 29, he asked for waivers on Newsom, the much-traveled pitcher who had failed to justify the reported $40,000 purchase price with a record of 11 wins against 17 losses. Griffith hoped none of his American League rivals would put in a claim. When no AL club obliged and all passed on Newsom, Griffith was in a strong bargaining position. He arranged to meet with Brooklyn's Larry MacPhail, who also had been nervously watching for the 72-hour waiver period to expire. Shortly before noon on August 31, less than 12 hours before the deadline for World Series eligibility, MacPhail was in the nation's capital to purchase Newsom. The sale price was not announced, but it was "reliably" reported that the figure was in excess of $25,000.[147] Newsom then again donned another major-league uniform, counting repeat visits to Brooklyn, St. Louis, and Washington.

But Griffith wasn't finished. Noting that Yankees outfielder Tommy Henrich had just been inducted into the Coast Guard, and with DiMaggio scheduled to enter the service before the 1943 season, Griffith knew New York needed outfield help, so he shipped third baseman–outfielder Roy Cullenbine to the Bronx for an undisclosed sum. Pinstripes must have agreed with the Nashville native because Cullenbine wound up hitting .364 in 21 games for New York versus .286 over 64 games for the Nats. Griffith also unloaded nightlife-loving pitcher Jack Wilson to Detroit for $5,000, less the waiver price.[148] And in an attempt to shore up his infield and give some minor leaguers their first taste of the "bigs," Griffith called up pitcher Lou Bevil and third baseman Ray Hoffman from Chattanooga and catcher Donald Odell Barbary from Charlotte. But in the end, Washington could do no better than a seventh-place finish with a record of 62 wins against 89 losses.

The biggest change for the Nats at the end of the season was Griffith's firing (again) of manager Bucky Harris after eight years at the helm. The Old Fox said, "A change in managers seems to be in order," and he offered Harris the managerial post at Buffalo in a very amicable split.[149] Griffith replaced Harris with Ossie Bluege, the long-time outstanding Nats third baseman and one of the team's coaches in recent years. Harris moved on to manage the Phillies the next season before leading the Yankees to a World Series championship win in 1947. (He returned to Washington for a third time in 1950, where he managed the Nats through the 1954 season.)

On Sunday, September 6, the Homestead Grays won the first of two games against the Newark Eagles, 4–2, in Brooklyn, and then again on Labor Day, September 7, in Newark, 14–12. The twin wins coupled with the Baltimore Elite Giants' loss to the Philadelphia Stars in the second game of a Labor Day doubleheader in Philadelphia gave the Grays their third consecutive Negro National League pennant since beginning play at Griffith Stadium. The Grays promptly faced the Negro American League champions, the powerful Kansas City Monarchs, in the Negro Leagues championship series, which Brad Snyder described as being "more like a postseason barnstorming tour than an annual Fall Classic," but it "reinforced that Griffith Stadium had become the Grays' most important venue, their home ballpark above all home ballparks, their principal moneymaker."[150] In fact, the AFRO publishing group in August had begun sponsoring Grays' games on WWDC, a local radio station.

Snyder's assessment was right on the money. A near-capacity crowd of 25,000 attended the opening game of the Negro Leagues championship series at Griffith Stadium on September 8, the only game to be played there. With Paige on the mound, the Monarchs prevailed, 8–0. Kansas City then went on to what ultimately became a four-game sweep by winning successive games at Pittsburgh's Forbes Field, 8–4, on September 11, and at Yankee Stadium, 9–3, on September 13. In New York, the two clubs also played a second seven-inning exhibition game, also won by the Monarchs, 5–0, that was called after seven innings due to darkness (no lights at the stadium). Ironically, the lone game the Grays won, 4–1, came on September 20 in the Monarchs' Kansas City ballpark but was declared void after the Monarchs protested the addition of four players from other teams to fill out the Grays' roster. So on September 29, a day with "the weather more suited for the gridiron,"[151] 15,000 fans saw the Monarchs wrap up the series at Shibe Park in Philadelphia, 9–5.

The Grays' humiliating defeat was due to their aging roster—Buck Leonard played hurt all season, and backstop Josh Gibson had been showing signs of fatigue since the second half of the regular season. In addition to the Monarchs' overall superior pitching, Paige had the slugging catcher's number: Gibson did not get a hit off the great hurler all season. Nevertheless, 1942 "was an unmitigated success for the Grays," Snyder writes, pointing to the 11 games the Grays played at Griffith Stadium that year that drew a total of 127,690 fans for an average of 11,608 per game. By comparison, the Nationals drew 403,493 in 77 home games, a per-game average of 5,240. "With a limited number of games and flexible scheduling in their favor, the Grays outdrew the Senators on many nights," Snyder also notes. Grays co-owner Cum Posey proclaimed 1942 as "the best financial season ever enjoyed by Negro baseball as a whole," with Griffith Stadium as the prime source of that windfall. Only Yankee Stadium, with a seating capacity of 70,000 and a larger black population overall, drew more fans.[152]

As a result, Griffith, too, enjoyed a good season financially. If his team finished seventh in the league standings, it finished third on the all-important profit-and-loss statement. The Nats turned a profit of $42,526 in 1942, behind the AL-pennant-winning Yankees, the only club in the league to hit six figures at $136,567, and the Browns at $80,855.[153] Some of Griffith's profits may have come from his practice (which he shared with his old friend Connie Mack) of not providing the working press with any sandwiches and sodas between doubleheader games. "The lack was noted particularly this season, with so many double-headers," complained sportswriter Dan Daniel.[154]

The biggest change in official Washington that autumn occurred in the November midterm elections when FDR's unpopular price controls came to the fore again. As a result, the Democrats lost 45 seats in the House while the Republicans added 47 seats (including two by beating third-party candidates) for a total of 209 Republicans in the new 78th Congress. Although Democrats retained their majority, under House rules at the time Republicans gained greater membership on all committees. In the Democratic-controlled Senate, Republicans gained 10 seats but also remained the minority party, 58 to 37, with one Progressive. But the election—and particularly the defeat of popular Michigan Democrat Prentiss Brown, who championed the price-controls bill— served as a warning to fellow Democrats of "what might have happened to them if they had been running and what may possibly happen to those who will face reelection in 1944."[155] "It is clear that the Republican Party has won a sweeping victory," the *Washington Evening Star* editorialized. "So far as the war influenced the balloting, the only reasonable inference is that the vote was a vigorous protest against some aspects of the manner in which it has been conducted by the party in power. These electoral verdicts call for an end to the fumbling in Washington which threatens to bog down the whole war effort in a mass of red tape and bureaucratic confusion."[156]

The biggest change on the war front came on November 8, when roughly 125,000 American (as many as 82,600 from the Army alone) and British sailors, soldiers, and airmen participated in simultaneous landings on major North African beachheads and ports from Morocco to Algeria. Their objective was to retake Casablanca, Oran, and Algiers from the Nazi army. Operation Torch, as it was code-named, was the first major combined Anglo–American offensive of the war and the first amphibious operation involving the Army and Navy since the Spanish–American War. In an attempt to convince the Vichy French forces in North Africa not to resist, Roosevelt addressed them in French,[157] a language he spoke fluently, in a recorded speech that was aired on American and British radio stations. FDR promised the French forces that the Allies would "cause you no harm" and asked them to "help where you are able."[158] The Allies refrained from pre-assault bombardment to minimize the possibility of the French returning fire.

In just one example of the many influences of the national pastime during the war, any Allied unit involved in the operation could signal it was in danger of a Vichy French attack by radioing "batter up," which meant it was preparing to return fire in self-defense. However, only task-force or attack-group commanders could initiate a general engagement with the familiar command, "play ball!"[159]

Gasoline rationing, which had been in place since November in 17 East Coast states, became mandatory for the rest of the country on December 1. On that day, too, baseball's owners opened their annual meeting in Chicago, still uncertain about the future of the game as the war entered its second full year. The growing scarcity of rubber was of concern to the owners because the substance that was vitally needed for the war effort literally was at the center of the baseball. But the first order of business was the unanimous decision that, unlike the two All-Star games played during the past season, in 1943 there would be only one game. It would be played at the Philadelphia Athletics' home field, Shibe Park, on July 7, with the proceeds going to the Griffith-originated Bat and Ball Fund. As they had done during the past season, the owners agreed again to set aside the proceeds of one home game each to the branch of the armed services of their choice. The owners then took up, again, the thorny issue of determining the number of home night games each team could play. The National League stuck to its limit of seven per team while the American League also stood pat with the previous season's 14 night games for all but the Nationals. Griffith again played his up-the-ante game, and when the league said no to his proposal to allow each team to set its own limit, he was granted permission to play 28 night games, an increase of seven from 1942.

Now, however, for the first time, baseball faced wartime travel limitations. Joseph Eastman, the director of the Office of Defense Transportation, sent a letter to Landis and the league presidents urging them to "give careful consideration to the problem of how your basic travel requirements can be met without a waste in space or mileage."[160] The owners interpreted Eastman's letter as a quasi "green light" from Washington, once again permitting baseball to continue but within certain new guidelines and restrictions. They agreed to reduce the number of road trips between East Coast and Midwest clubs from four to three during the 154-game season and also to expand the traditional three-game series whenever possible to four or five games. Also the Nats and their geographically closest rivals, the Athletics and the Yankees, would play four-game series.

The question of spring-training sites was left open for the time being, although the idea of shortening the training schedule and banning the popular barnstorming stops as the teams traveled north to open the season seemed like the most viable solutions for reducing train travel.

After the Chicago meeting, Landis, ever mindful of the need to show official Washington that major-league baseball was doing all it could to support the war effort, wrote to all the clubs advising them to abandon Florida and California as their training-camp sites, in fact, "to forget about relocating anywhere in the Southeast."[161] For Griffith, that meant forsaking his favored Tinker Field in Orlando. That was just one of the innovations that would make the 1943 season a most unusual one.

3

1943

Coming Up Just Short

At the end of the 1942 season, major-league owners again faced the prospect of not having a baseball season in 1943—this time because the draft was siphoning off more quality major-league-caliber ballplayers,[1] overall profits were down, and Judge Landis was keeping up the pressure on the owners to put more money into the various war-relief funds, further reducing the owners' already slim profits. In fact, some owners allegedly hoped the War Manpower Commission would order them to cancel the season, which would force Landis to freeze the contracts of all players and their ties to their clubs. If the season was scrubbed without such an official order from Washington, the players would become free agents who would then be able to negotiate with all clubs for their services when the game resumed,[2] anathema to the moneymen (until arbitrator Peter Seitz in 1974 ruled that Oakland Athletics pitcher Jim "Catfish" Hunter was a free agent and could sign with the New York Yankees because A's owner Charles Finley had breached his contract. The Seitz decision opened the era of free agency to any player who had played out his contract and had six years of major-league service.

For his decision, Seitz was fired by the owners,[3] and his ruling effectively ended 80 years of the owners' domination over the players).[4] One owner who continued to believe there would be baseball in 1943 was Clark Griffith, who steadfastly insisted the game would continue "as long as each team can place nine men on the field, even if they are very old men."[5]

The owners should not have been so concerned because the issue had been more or less resolved at their winter meeting in Chicago in December when they were advised by the Office of Defense Transportation (ODT) to shorten the spring-training schedule and to train closer to home. Not to be outdone by official Washington, Landis decreed California and Florida off-limits for spring training. Early in January, the commissioner took it upon himself to meet with ODT director Joseph Eastman in Washington, where they hammered out a program for the forthcoming season. The agreement was seen as solid affirmation—another "green light" so to speak—that baseball would continue. Landis, ever mindful of his carefully established image of baseball as a leader in homeland support for the war effort, told the press, "Nobody needs to enter any orders on us" because the major leagues were happy to cooperate.[6] The *Sporting News*, a faithful fan of the commissioner, explained that "Landis' talk with Eastman was not primarily for the purpose of finding out what the ODT head expected of baseball. It was more with the idea of telling Eastman what baseball wanted to do, of its own volition, in expectation of more perplexing travel problems next summer, and a more tremendous strain on all our railroad facilities."[7]

Landis promptly took the agreement before an emergency meeting of the lords of baseball in Chicago on January 5. The first point, which was adopted without qualification, had the most profound effect on the game for the rest of the war. With Landis's ban on Florida and California training in mind, they delineated an area north of the Potomac and Ohio rivers and east of the Mississippi as the boundary within which spring-training camps were to be held. Because the two St. Louis clubs, the Cardinals and the Browns, were located west of the Mississippi, they were allowed to train in Missouri if they wished. The geographic delineation became known popularly as the Eastman–Landis line.

With the spring-training boundaries set, the owners agreed to shorten the training season, and they modified slightly another point in the pact, which dealt with the season opener and the final day of the regular season. As *New York World Telegram* sportswriter Dan Daniel reported, "The most important decision was a negative one. The club owners adhered to their old 154-game schedule and their pre-war length of playing season. They postponed the opening one week, from

April 13 to April 21. But they added a week scheduling the close on October 3, instead of September 26."[8]

At the same time, the War Manpower Commission clarified its position on baseball with two official decrees: (1) ballplayers were not entitled to deferments on the basis of their summer occupation because sports could not be classified as essential to the support of the war, and (2) the WMC ruled that ballplayers working offseason in the defense industry were free to leave their jobs in March and return to the diamond. Left unsaid in the *Sporting News* report on the WMC decrees was that, depending on personal circumstances, those players could then be subject to the draft. "Baseball is not going to urge these men to return," the newspaper explained. "Quite the contrary, each man must decide his own case for himself and let his own individual situation dictate his action."[9]

Within a week of the owners' agreement on travel and spring-training schedules, three DC-area universities, all of which had excellent athletic facilities—Georgetown, Catholic, and the University of Maryland—made their campuses and facilities available to Griffith as a spring-training venue. Griffith could not have been more pleased by their largesse. In his first year as Nationals manager in 1912, he took the team as far south as the University of Virginia in Charlottesville, which became the team's spring-training camp for the next five seasons. "I like the idea of training at a college," Griffith told the press. "There are no restrictions [as printed: possible misprint for "distractions," perhaps?] for the ball players. They have to think baseball, and we have them under one roof, within easy call. My clubs were never better conditioned than in those years when we trained at the University of Virginia."[10]

For 1943, Griffith chose the University of Maryland, some 15 miles north of the city in rural College Park, where his players would stay in on-campus housing "and have the advantage not only of a spacious playing field, but the big Ritchie Stadium [actually Ritchie Coliseum, home to the Maryland Terrapins men's basketball team from 1931 to 1955], which houses a large gymnasium."[11] The Maryland campus offered another advantage to Griffith: his players, the young single men in particular, could not easily fall prey to the temptations in the nation's capital where both Georgetown and Catholic Universities were located.

In another nod to baseball's war efforts at home, the patriotic Griffith scheduled some spring-training games with no admission charges at area military facilities, including contests against the Marine Corps at Quantico, Virginia, the Army Corps of Engineers at Fort Belvoir, Virginia, and at Fort Myer in Arlington, Virginia. Also on the schedule were three contests at nearby Camp George C. Meade (today Fort Meade, home of the National Security Agency) against the Athletics, Yankees, and Dodgers. In addition, the Nats would play the collegiate teams from Maryland, Georgetown, and Catholic Universities as well as the U.S. Naval Academy at Annapolis, Maryland. The highlight would be a five-day visit in early April to the Norfolk naval base at the southern end of the Chesapeake Bay to play the installation's two outstanding service teams.

Griffith also announced that he'd sent contracts to all but a few players with a personal note reading, "Thus far I haven't made any salary cuts," which he probably assumed would be a morale booster and encourage early signings.[12] The players, knowing their owner, read that to mean no raises either. Griffith had not yet tendered an offer to his highest paid player, pitcher Dutch Leonard, who had broken his leg in the 1942 season and appeared in just six games with a record of 2–2.[13] In any event, Leonard was "expected to make his usual holdout gestures."[14]

Freshman manager Ossie Bluege called for pitchers and catchers to report to the College Park campus on March 15 and for the remainder of the squad to come into camp 10 days later prepared to deal with the new wartime conditions. Despite the Nats' need for a backup catcher and a first baseman if Mickey Vernon were to be called up, Griffith viewed the coming season through rose-colored glasses. Noting that the Nats had already lost several players to the military, including their two best, Cecil Travis and Buddy Lewis, the Old Fox said, "If we don't lose too many more players, we ought to be in contention for a first-division berth," reasoning that Washington had paid its manpower dues and now it was his competitors' turn to be stripped of key players. "They'll be getting the same dose we got last year," he predicted. "The league won't be as fast and we may be better equipped for the competition than a lot of other clubs whose rosters were intact last season."[15]

Once again, Griffith would prove prescient. The 1943 baseball season would be a momentous one at Griffith Stadium not only for his club but also for his tenants, the Homestead Grays. The Office of Defense Transportation's travel restrictions meant "colored baseball is doomed for the duration," the *Washington Afro-American* opined,[16] because the restrictions would kill the black clubs' usual method of travel, the team bus.

Grays' co-owner Cum Posey, acting as executive secretary of the Negro National League, and Dr. J. B. Martin, president of the Negro American League, held an hour-long meeting in early March with ODT's director, Joseph Eastman, to plead for an exemption. Posey and Martin left the meeting believing that prospects were good for a favorable ruling on their request. They were sure they had presented a strong case based on three cogent points: (1) the black teams must play one-day doubleheaders in each city on Sundays plus three night games during the week, (2) the financial returns do not allow for expensive train travel, and (3) the games "furnish the chief relaxation for several million colored people in 11 metropolitan areas in the country and entertain workers engaged in war production." In addition, they "perform a special service" by playing teams in military camps throughout the nation, and they travel there by bus. Moreover, they told Eastman that if the ban were allowed to stand, the annual East–West game in Chicago would have to be cancelled. For the previous two seasons, the Negro Leagues' equivalent of the major leagues' All-Star Game had drawn capacity crowds of 50,000 or more "with other thousands turned away."[17] Originally conceived as a promotional event by Gus Greenlee, who had organized the new Negro National League in 1933, the annual contest was the black leagues' most popular attraction and biggest moneymaker.[18] It was that mid-season classic that propelled the ever-growing national popularity of Negro League baseball during the 1930s and 1940s. Eastman told the envoys that he would consider their case and then issue a statement.

Toward the end of the month, Eastman kept his word. He sent a telegram to Posey and his Grays co-owner, Rufus "Sonnyman" Jackson, rejecting the leagues' request for special consideration. The *Washington Afro-American* wrote that "Eastman was emphatic in that 'special' busses could not be made available, but expressed the hope that the NNL would be able to arrange their transportation difficulties in a fashion similar to the white major leagues." In telegraphese, Eastman said, "Urge your cooperation in utilizing existing transportation of baseball teams during coming season."[19] In effect, he was telling the Negro Leagues to quit complaining and get on board the train.

But railroad fares would be an expensive burden for the always cash-strapped black clubs. Also, the bus ban meant the elimination of the usual midweek barnstorming that the teams did through small towns to raise extra cash and help offset the rents they paid to use the major-league ball fields. So, as *Afro-American* sports columnist Art Carter saw it, "to a great extent [the teams] will be confined to the big league cities where the clubs use major league parks."[20] However, writing a week later, Carter called the ODT bus ban "a blessing in disguise" because "the clubs will be able to concentrate more on the highly profitable promotions in the bigger cities, which should take care of the difference" between the loss of barnstorming revenue and the expected tripling of travel expenses.[21]

Carter also believed the ban would help to end the Negro Leagues' haphazard scheduling and midweek barnstorming that had been standard since the black leagues were founded, and which the major-league owners used as an excuse not to entertain any sort of integration plan. "Now that they must cut mileage, revise schedules to meet train routes, and abandon many of the tank-town games in midweek, it is possible that they will see the error of many of their past experiences," Carter wrote, "and create a methodical scheduling program that would benefit all teams in the league."[22] Carter's colleague, Harold Jackson, also saw some good in Eastman's ruling. Noting that in past years some clubs had to travel 500 miles or more to play a game for a small return, Jackson wrote, "Perhaps, if these games were eliminated the teams will spend more time in making a success of their big games, and the results will show a better financial return. It would mean more rest for the players, and top promotions in the towns where the game is to be played."[23]

Train travel would also be more comfortable for the black players even if it required them to move to "Colored Only" cars when they journeyed below the Mason–Dixon Line. The bus ban also meant the Grays would play fewer games in Homestead and more in Griffith Stadium, about 40 in all in 1943, because Washington's Union Station was a major railroad hub that made it easy for the other clubs to travel to the nation's capital rather than to Pittsburgh. Also, opposing teams looked forward to playing in Washington because its large African

American population made the city a mecca of black entertainment and, although the city was as segregated as any in the Deep South, housing and dining were more available in Washington. And, as luck would have it, Grays' catcher Josh Gibson would have a career year at the plate that even caught the attention of the white press and the major-league owners. "Grays' games had become so lucrative for Griffith by 1943, that he rescheduled one of the Senators' regular season games so the Grays could play a World Series game in his ballpark," Grays historian Brad Snyder notes.[24]

The Negro National League teams—the Grays, Newark Eagles, Philadelphia Stars, New York Cubans, New York Black Yankees (which split into two teams before the season began), and Baltimore Elite Giants—reluctantly agreed to travel by train; they had no other choice if they wanted to have a season. For the players, train travel was indeed an improvement over the long, uncomfortable trips in the aging buses they were used to. But the Negro American League (NAL), also known as the western division, was in jeopardy of folding because of the greater distances and fewer trains between the cities represented in the NAL—the Kansas City Monarchs, Birmingham Black Barons, Chicago American Giants, Cincinnati Clowns, Cleveland Buckeyes, and Memphis Red Sox. In fact, R. S. Simmons, the league secretary, said bluntly, "The NAL will be unable to operate."[25]

Having reached contract agreements with Gibson, Buck Leonard, and other regulars, the Grays prepared for a two-week training camp to begin April 12, in Akron, Ohio, about 120 miles from Homestead, Pennsylvania, before meeting the Newark Eagles in the season opener at Griffith Stadium on May 16. Like the Nationals, the Grays also had a new manager for 1943, Candy Jim Taylor, a five-foot, nine-inch former third baseman (like Bluege) whose best season was 1916, when he starred on the Indianapolis ABCs championship team. As a manager, he had led numerous Negro League clubs, including the pennant-winning St. Louis Stars in 1928.[26] His predecessor, Vic Harris, opted to remain at his defense-industry job but indicated he would be available for weekend games played in the western Pennsylvania area around Homestead.[27]

When the 1943 baseball season was still months away, a rash of new films opening in Washington with the speed of Bob Feller's fastball became a pleasant late-winter amusement for thousands of defense workers there. In one week alone, the Earle (now the Warner) Theater at 13th and E Streets NW featured Bette Davis and Paul Henreid in *Now, Voyager*, followed by Jack Benny and Ann Sheridan in *George Washington Slept Here*. Then came Bing Crosby, Bob Hope, and Dorothy Lamour in *Road to Morocco*. Following a couple more light comedies that quickly came and went, the majestic art deco theater presented the now immortal—and for the Earle box office at least—the fortuitously titled *Casablanca*. For while Humphrey Bogart and Ingrid Bergman were pledging they'd "always have Paris" on a Hollywood back lot in Burbank, FDR and British Prime Minister Winston Churchill were actually in Casablanca pledging to open a second front soon and to end the war with nothing less than Germany's unconditional surrender. In a weak attempt at humor, *Washington Post* film critic Nelson B. Bell wrote, "Of course, by now, you have heard the favorite crack about the President's recent trip, when his whereabouts became known: 'Oh, yes, he flew over to Africa to see a Warner Brothers picture!'"[28] Bell noted too that, although the studio was being called lucky for the "timeliness of the picture," the studio had been releasing films with antifascist themes since 1939.

The Old Fox chose mid-February, when temperatures often fell into the low teens and single digits, to announce that the spring-training exhibition schedule would begin April 1, with two games at the Norfolk Naval Training Station and three at the Norfolk Naval Air Station in the Tidewater region of Virginia. Griffith said the team would journey by boat to obey the travel restrictions. And in an uncharacteristic moment of levity, he added, "Because Judge Landis has ruled that we cannot train south of the Potomac, I have written him that we will hug the Maryland side of the [Potomac] river on the way to Norfolk." The five-game visit, however, would not be a simple pleasure jaunt because both Navy teams were well stocked with former major leaguers, including Yankees shortstop Phil Rizzuto on the training-station team and Dodgers outfielder and 1941 National League batting champion Pete Reiser on the air-base club. "This kind of opposition will be wonderful for us," Griffith said. "We may even get licked. But we are happy to be able to play for the sailors" free of any admission charge.[29]

Just as the relocated spring-training camps were about to open, the American League announced a curtailed travel schedule during the regular season to abide by the Office of Defense Transportation edict to eliminate unnecessary travel. For the first time since 1935, the eight AL teams would make only three road trips around the league rather than the normal four, which it was estimated would save some 35,000 rail miles and more than one million passenger miles.[30]

On March 15, the Nats pitchers and catchers began arriving at the University of Maryland campus to train under their former coach and now manager Ossie Bluege. Bluege was well liked as an individual and was well respected as an outstanding former major leaguer. He had played his entire career with Washington, from 1922 to 1939, covering third base, shortstop, and second base. The Chicago native was a member of the club's only World Series championship in 1924 and all three pennant winning clubs in 1924, 1925, and 1933. From 1928 through 1930, Bluege hit .297, .295, and .290, respectively. In his 1,816 major-league games, he made only 250 errors for a fielding percentage of .961. Shirley Povich, who began covering the team for the *Washington Post* in the Nats' world-championship season of 1924, called him one of the greatest third basemen of all time. "In street clothes he looked like he should be somebody's bookkeeper, but in uniform he looked like a big league ballplayer," the *Post* columnist said in a 1992 interview.[31] In fact, in the offseason, Bluege was an accountant, and he reportedly handled Griffith's books. But he was also a full-time student of the game and well suited to manage.

In 1943, Washington was looking to strengthen its pitching. It was a need that longtime Nats scout Joe Cambria, whose talent-spotting took place mostly in Cuba, sought to remedy almost immediately. He introduced Bluege to semipro pitcher Chester Foreman, a big right-hander, and Richard Arhens, a seven-footer, who, like many of Cambria's can't-miss phenoms, had no organized baseball background. Cambria's stable of hopefuls also included Warren Reid, who'd pitched for Tallahassee in the Georgia–Florida League in 1942, and John Bunnell, a teenager whom Cambria proudly claimed he'd snatched from under the noses of the Detroit Tigers. Apparently willing to keep an open mind so early in the training season, the rookie skipper said, "Let him bring 'em in and I'll look 'em over. This is a year when you can't be too particular. If one out of the lot makes good in even a modest way, we'll appreciate it."[32] Alas, not one of Cambria's young quartet made it past spring training or ever toed a major-league mound.

To give his squad the best possible chance to win a fourth American League pennant, Griffith sought to strengthen the Nats' defense. Before the season began, he sent pitcher Bill Zuber along with $10,000 to the Yankees for Jerry Priddy, an outstanding second baseman who would shore up what had been a terrible infield in 1942. Yankee farmhand Milo Candini, a right-handed hurler from Manteca, California, was thrown into the deal "to sweeten the pot for Griffith."[33] But Priddy was a man with a quick fuse and from the start did not get on well with Bluege, especially when the manager moved him early in spring training from his accustomed spot on the right side of the infield to third base. (The move was a failure as Priddy played only one game at third. He went into the service at the end of the season, returning to Washington for the 1946 and 1947 seasons before being purchased by the Browns in December of 1947.)

Griffith strengthened his outfield by trading Cuban Roberto Estalella (another of Cambria's finds) and Jimmy Pofahl to the Athletics for leftfielder Bob Johnson, who had 80 runs batted in during the 1942 season with the A's, more than anyone on the Nationals. Johnson made himself trade bait when, after the 1942 season, he and A's owner and manager Connie Mack got into a dispute over bonus money that Johnson believed he was owed based on Shibe Park attendance figures. When Mack insisted that the numbers did not merit the bonus, he and Johnson found themselves at loggerheads over a new contract. Johnson, who made $10,000[34] in 1942, refused to sign for the coming season and requested a trade. When he arrived in Washington, DC, after a three-day cross-country train trip from his Pacific Northwest home in Tacoma, Washington, where he'd spent the winter mostly hunting and fishing, he told the Washington press, "Connie Mack was getting to be a hard man to do business with. I was getting tired of holding out every year and asked him to trade me."[35] Griffith boosted his salary to $12,500.[36] Johnson, who had played some first base in the minor leagues and with the A's, brought along his first-baseman's mitt, insurance if regular Mickey Vernon were lost to the service.

In explaining the Mack–Johnson falling out, sportswriter Red Smith, then with the *Philadelphia Record*, said both were stubborn and proud men. Nevertheless, "the A's lost the finest ball player they have had since championship days [the last of Mack's five World Series wins was in 1930], one of the grandest competitors that ever played for any team and as thoroughly right and level a guy as ever dignified the term major leaguer," Smith wrote.[37] Johnson, he said, had been proud to play for Mack, "proud of the fact that he'd learned Connie's game so well that it had been years since the Old Man had to wave him into position with that scorecard [which he always carried rolled up in the dugout], proud of the confidence the Skipper showed in him many times by seeking his judgment about his young players." And Smith surmised, "It was the same pride, I suppose, which wouldn't let him give in on his argument with Connie. Maybe this is a fault. I wouldn't know. I only know he's still my ball player." A great accolade indeed from a Pulitzer Prize–winning journalist and one of the finest sportswriters of all time.[38]

Griffith, who always acted as his own general manager, had thus constructed an outfield of Johnson, Stan Spence, and George Case, which Griffith and Bluege believed was the best in the American League. "Where are you going to find an outfield in this league to top that one? Look at the record," Bluege crowed before departing for the Norfolk exhibition games. Indeed, Bluege had reason to brag. The previous season, Case hit .320, and Spence batted .323, the only two American League outfield pair to hit over .300, and Johnson hit .291 with the A's. "Put those figures together with the fact that Case is the best base stealer in the league; that the throwing arms of all three are good; that defensively they're all right too, and I like my outfield better than any one in the league," Bluege said.[39]

For additional help, Griffith called up Bill Prout, a first baseman for the Nats' Chattanooga farm team, as insurance to replace Vernon and Johnson if necessary. Vernon, who was married with no children, was classified 3-A but was facing a 1-A reclassification.[40] Seeking a modest pay hike, Vernon hadn't signed his 1943 contract yet[41] and was also rumored to be considering remaining at his defense job rather than playing ball. "It's just a question of money," Griffith assured the press. "Vernon may be able to play ball several months before he is called to the Army."[42]

Just as the nation needed to limit its use of gasoline to save rubber, supplies of which had been cut off by the Japanese occupation of Malaya and the Dutch East Indies, even before the season began, the sport found itself in need of a new baseball. And again, it was Landis who was a prime mover to find an acceptable substitute ball and make a public show of how well the sport was making due amid wartime restrictions. He, American League President Will Harridge, and Cincinnati Reds General Manager Warren Giles (later National League president) conferred with the experts at A. G. Spalding and Brothers, the company that made the baseballs for both leagues, to find a new substance for the ball's cork and tightly wound rubber core. After testing more than a dozen different cores, they settled on a granulated cork and balata center to replace the normal rubber wrapping. "Instead, to give it a little pop, there were two hard shells of balata, a rubberlike substance inside the horsehide cover. One shell was red and the other black," writes *Sports Illustrated*'s Noel Hynd. Balata, a milky substance found in certain tropical trees, was used primarily in the manufacture of industrial gaskets, telephone-line insulation, and golf-ball covers.[43] But it did not have the elasticity of rubber. Nevertheless, everyone associated with the game, especially the players, hoped that the new balata ball would prove to be a worthy wartime substitute.

"The selection of a ball, which, it is hoped, will be livelier, rather than deader, was prompted by the fact that the 16 clubs of the big leagues will be minus many of their batting heroes," the *Sporting News* wrote in a short, lofty editorial, which also warned, "Managers will be called upon to display more ingenuity than in any season for many years. With a shorter training period, more double-headers, restricted manpower [the baseball journal counted 250 former major leaguers serving in the military by early 1943][44] and a changed ball calling for new strategy, every pilot will be compelled to use all of his resources to the fullest extent."[45]

However, the new ball immediately proved to be anything but satisfactory and was dead on the field and off, literally and figuratively. Spalding technicians quickly went back to the drawing board and replaced it with a new and improved balata ball whose center consisted of rubber cement that remained soft and sticky. Tested on the floor of National League president Ford Frick's office, the new ball bounced twice as high as the original balata ball and "turned out to be even 50 percent livelier than the '42 baseballs."[46]

But it wasn't only the ball that required a wartime makeover. The demand for wood pulp and the shortage of lumberjacks to fell trees in the Pacific Northwest created a dearth of the ash wood needed to make bats. According to Nats outfielder George Case, his friend Glenn Martin, airplane manufacturer of the Martin B-26 Marauder and avid base-ball fan, told his aerodynamic engineers to devise a new bat that could stand in for the ash models. When the engineers found a good substitute, Martin sent a few dozen to Case. "Where he got the wood I don't know," Case later recalled for journalist Richard Goldstein.[47] "It wasn't good wood, but it was tapered a little on the end like an airplane wing. It had good wind resistance. Their theory was there's wind resistance when you're using a bat, just like an airplane wing." Martin had sold his Cleveland, Ohio, factory in 1929 and built a new aircraft plant in Middle River, Maryland, northeast of Baltimore, which employed some 53,000 workers during the war. Besides baseball, Martin and Case shared a love of duck hunting. George Case III says his father and Martin hunted together during the offseason in Maryland and New Jersey, both popular duck-hunting states.[48] That would help explain why Martin was quick to put his engineers to work finding a substitute for Case's lumber.

The 16 major-league clubs got down to serious spring training in the fourth week of March, about two weeks later than normal. But, as the *Sporting News* editorialized, "this training season is a strange one. In normal times, most of the clubs already would have had more than a fortnight's action to their credit, and the *Sporting News* would show box scores of the early exhibition games." The editorial noted that "for the first time in almost half a century . . . the home fans are in a position to see their favorites train without being forced to make long trips." Concluding, the baseball publication made an eerily prescient prediction even if it took several decades to come to fruition: "When this war is over, baseball will see a boom, the like of which man cannot now picture. And with that boom will come a fresh start in Florida and California training, and a keener appreciation of those semi-tropical locales."[49] Had the newspaper had a little more foresight, it might have added Arizona to the boom. But the baseball journal could never have imagined the multimillion-dollar spring-training complexes to come, each with multiple major-league-dimension ball fields, gyms, weight and whirlpool rooms, indoor batting cages all comfortably air conditioned, and grandstands packed with spring-season ticket holders.

For as long as there has been baseball, spring training has had an almost mystic aura of suspense, unbounded hope, improvement, and redemption. Before television and routine air travel, fans avidly followed the formation of their favorite clubs with the help of only radio and their hometown newspapers. They looked forward eagerly to opening day and to a long season of endless possibilities. But spring training in 1943 (and the following two seasons) was different, an interregnum of sorts from the warmth of faraway camps. As Shirley Povich accurately put it, "with the teams training virtually in their own back yards, much of the romance has gone out of spring training."

Gone, too, was the early financial windfall of pre–season-ticket purchases by fans hungry to see games in person and especially on opening day. At this point in previous springs, Griffith Stadium was always virtually sold out for the opener in part because those attending would have the rare opportunity to see the president in person, even if he was seated across the field and they were in the last row of the upper deck. "This year, seat sales for the opener are lagging, plenty," Povich reported. The Nats' potential loss of preseason ticket sales was balanced to a degree, however, by the considerable savings in travel and lodgings by training at the University of Maryland rather than at Tinker Field in Orlando, a cost further ameliorated by the generosity of the school's president, Dr. Harry Clifton Byrd, who told Griffith, "The charge [for use of the campus facilities] will be not a penny more than the cost to Maryland. We appreciate those days when you permitted our teams to use your stadium at the lowest possible rates when we were a small and struggling university. We're glad to repay your kindness."[50]

March, a notoriously fickle month for weather, seemed to be planning to go out like the proverbial lamb. From March 18 to 20, temperatures were in the mid- to upper 60s, reaching 78 degrees for the warmest day of the month on March 19. But the first day of spring, just two days later, brought snow and temperatures in the low 30s, curtailing the Nats' practices on campus. (Even with gas restrictions in place and fewer autos on the roads, Washington was—and still is—a city whose residents find driving in even a veneer of snow a skill beyond their ability to master. Between 3:45 p.m. and midnight, there were more than 30 "storm"-related traffic accidents even though by 10 p.m. the snowfall still measured less than one inch.)[51]

Inclement weather, mostly in the form of cold rain, plagued the team for most of the first full week of practice. The infield was too wet to use, so workouts were confined to the university's large gymnasium. The rain cleared enough by the weekend of March 26 to permit full outdoor workouts and even a short intrasquad game on the chilly, windy Sunday. A second five-inning affair Monday in springlike temperatures helped the Nats prepare for their first tests against the service teams in Norfolk. Compared to his rivals, however, the Old Fox did well with the weather. Training in the New York area, the Yankees, Giants, and Dodgers encountered the New York and New Jersey area's coldest and windiest spring in a decade.[52] Chicago's Cubs and White Sox shared training facilities in French Lick, Indiana, where they "argued over use of a golf course that turned out to be the only available playing field in sight" after heavy rains caused the Lost River to overflow and flood their ball fields.[53] And when it wasn't raining in Indiana, it was snowing.

African American sportswriter Art Carter used the Negro Leagues' truncated schedule and restricted travel to again press his case for baseball integration. Writing with an acerbic pen in the *Baltimore Afro-American* newspaper, Carter noted, "Spring is here and with it another baseball season, yet there are no colored players among the varied assortment of washed-up has-beens, teen-aged kids and draft-exempt family men battling for positions on the major league teams." He then recalled the unfulfilled "solemn promise" made the previous fall by the Pittsburgh Pirates and Cleveland Indians to grant tryouts to colored ballplayers. "And what has happened to all the pressure that was to be exerted this spring when the tryouts started in the northern training camps, where the magnates are deprived of their age-old excuse of southern prejudice and jim-crow laws preventing them an opportunity to invite colored candidates for trials?" he asked rhetorically. "Now is the time to urge the magnates to give colored players tryouts! Not midsummer after the teams have been well established and business is booming at the turnstiles!"[54] There was silence from the white owners.

Griffith viewed the five scheduled exhibition games in Tidewater Virginia as an early test of Washington's potential because Norfolk had two near-major-league-caliber outfits, the Naval Training Station team and the Naval Air Station team. Besides shortstop Phil Rizzuto of the Yankees, the Naval Training Station lineup included such former major leaguers as Eddie Collins, pitchers Freddy Hutchinson, Walter Masterson, formerly of the Nats, and Boston's Charlie Wagner, who had won 14 games for the Red Sox in 1942. Such was the power of the base commanding officer, Captain H. A. McClure, and his staff that a recent addition to the Naval Training Station club was Wagner's former team-

mate, Dom DiMaggio, who had been transferred from the Treasure
Island Training Station in San Francisco Bay when the Norfolk Naval
Training Station team needed another outfielder. In fact, the Naval
Training Station team was so loaded with talent that Pee Wee Reese,
once and future Dodgers star and Hall of Famer, couldn't crack the
lineup and was sent over to the Naval Air Station team to join another
former and future Dodgers pitcher Hugh Casey, Tigers infielder Murray Franklin, and former Nats catcher Al Evans who also would later
rejoin Washington. If Bob Feller, who was on the 1942 Naval Training
Station team, hadn't shipped out already, he would have anchored the
team's pitching staff.

After a day's cruise down the Chesapeake Bay, the Nationals arrived
at the vast Navy complex appropriately enough on Thursday, April
Fools' Day, ready for their first game the next afternoon and for a taste
of military life. "Here the Nats, who previously haven't hesitated to
bellow when waiters or chambermaids failed to present service rapidly
enough, are standing in line with sailors, picking up their own trays and
generally making themselves more useful. If they want breakfast they
must be in line by 7 o'clock," wrote Burton Hawkins, one of the scribes
who accompanied the club to Norfolk.[55]

On Friday, in front of 6,000 sailors and officers, including Captain
McClure, the Naval Training Station's Freddie Hutchison limited
Washington to just seven hits and outpitched Dutch Leonard for a 10–5
victory, highlighted by a Rizzuto home run. Washington rebounded to
win the Saturday game, 9–6, with homers by Johnny Sullivan and
George Case. The pros also won the following game on Sunday against
the slightly weaker Naval Air Station club, 6–4, with Leonard redeem-
ing himself by pitching the final three innings in relief and yielding just
one hit. The Nats won again on Monday, 10–4, in a game that was
halted in the eighth inning so the visitors could catch a boat back to
Washington one day earlier than planned because no vessel would be
available on Tuesday. The Tuesday exhibition game, again against the
Naval Air Station, was cancelled.

The Nats sailed north with three wins against one loss and prepared
to meet their next opponent, also a team in military uniform, the U.S.
Naval Academy at Annapolis. (They would see the powerful Norfolk
Naval Training Station team again in May when the Nats' hosted them
for a war-bond exhibition game.) Besides providing the Nationals with

their first decent competition, the games in Norfolk convinced Bluege to install Ellis Clary at third base, move Jerry Priddy to his normal second base, and bench George Myatt, who had not played well there. Bluege, an outstanding third baseman in his day, explained the moves by saying, "Priddy is the second baseman. Second base is more important on any club than third."[56]

Back home, Washingtonians found several things more important at the moment than who would anchor the hot corner for the Nats. The U.S. Department of Agriculture (USDA) announced that a scheduled 43-cent-per-hundredweight increase in the price of milk paid to producers—from $3.57 to $4.00—would take effect on April 8, forcing the Office of Price Administration to push up the retail price of a quart by a penny, to 15 cents. The *Washington Post*, citing the USDA, said the adjustment would bring the city in line with others on the Eastern Seaboard.[57] Also, the new meat-rationing order had just gone in effect at the end of March, further reducing each family's weekly allowance and creating what the *Washington Afro-American* called "an enormous demand for smoked or cured ham . . . but there were very few hams available." The newspaper also printed a variety of citizens' responses to the meat order, which ranged from, "There are five in the family. Really, I think we eat too much meat, and I think this cut will be something I have been trying to bring about for the past ten years," to "I need a lot of meat to do my work at the Navy Yard."[58]

But higher dairy prices and less meat for the table weren't the only problems facing Washingtonians. The influx of service personnel and government workers—including 280,000 women working as "government girls, or "G-girls" for short[59] —created a serious housing shortage. Author Bill Gilbert, who grew up in Washington during the war years (and served as a batboy for the Nats), recalled that "the wartime atmosphere was unmistakable and becoming more pronounced amid the sea of military uniforms, the daily hardships caused by the scarce housing, and the constant complaints about buses and streetcars that ran too late as they groaned under the burdens of too many passengers." He recalled also how the severe shortage of office space was resolved by so-called tempos. Twenty-seven such eyesores that marred the DC landscape, including semicircular galvanized steel and wood Quonset huts that were placed on the National Mall, were built in less than a year at a cost of $850,000, "providing more than three million square feet of critically needed office space but lacking air-conditioning for Washington's hot and sticky summers."[60] (The U.S. military reportedly modeled and developed the portable structures after using the British-designed Nissan hut during World War I. The U.S. buildings were initially manufactured in Quonset Point, Rhode Island, hence the name.)[61]

On a happier note, but only for some local residents, on Saturday, April 10, the gates of Glen Echo Park, just across the DC line in Maryland, "will spring open for the fun-loving multitudes at 1 p.m. Its more than 50 amusement features, including the wide variety of thrill rides and a large swimming pool, will be in operation every day until midnight."[62] Left unsaid was that "the fun-loving multitudes" would all be white. Glen Echo Park and its pool were strictly segregated and would remain a whites-only enclave until 1961. (That's when park owners Abram and Samuel Baker quietly dropped their public opposition to integration and instead introduced an admission fee for the first time—clearly an effort to deter blacks from entering.)[63]

As the new season grew near, demands to end segregation in baseball, especially in Washington, flared once again. Griffith's oft-stated position, build up your own league first, "was completely self-serving," author Brad Snyder insists, and he had the numbers to prove it. Twenty percent of the Grays' 127,690 paid admissions at Griffith Stadium in 1942, plus a utility fee for using Clark Griffith's lighting system, a total of some $60,000, went directly into Griffith's coffers. No wonder "Griffith preferred that the Thunder Twins [Josh Gibson and Buck Leonard] stayed in their own league," Snyder says.[64] As opening day approached, black college students from nearby Howard University, frustrated by the same old story line and no action toward integration, began a four-day campaign of nonviolent protests, including sit-ins at two area restaurants that would not serve them (17 years before the historic February 1960 sit-in at a Woolworth's lunch counter in Greensboro, North Carolina). Washington's black press joined the movement and urged its readers to abandon the Nats in favor of the Grays as a matter of racial pride.

African Americans also were nowhere to be seen at an April 14 luncheon by 500 white members of the Washington Board of Trade who "honored the Washington Baseball Club,"[65] that is, Griffith's club, at the Mayflower Hotel. The Old Fox thanked the crowd for the "boost baseball" theme of the midday event and promised an improved team that season. Then, in a cryptic comment, he remarked, "Baseball is wanted by our Government officials from the top on down and maybe soon something will be worked out to help keep us going." *Washington Star* sportswriter Burton Hawkins reported that Griffith didn't expand on his comment but noted how it dovetailed with Griffith's remarks earlier in the week after his visit to the White House when he presented FDR with his annual season's pass to the ballpark.

"The President was very solicitous about our problems," Griffith had told the press afterward, adding, "No, I can't tell you what he said—I don't dare—but he was interested to know if I thought we could keep going." Hawkins suggested that the Old Fox perhaps had some plan up his sleeve to stem the drain of major-league players into the military. "The talent has been spreading thin for a long time and while the sport is expected to survive the 1943 season Griffith undoubtedly is scanning the future," Hawkins reported. In either case, he warned, Griffith was exposing himself to considerable criticism by even suggesting that something might happen to assist the game.[66]

Among the other luncheon speakers was Kentucky senator Albert "Happy" Chandler, who ingratiated himself to Griffith and the baseball-loving crowd when he said it would be a tragedy if baseball were to stop. "It seems to me that it would be entirely logical to spare as few as 400 men to play baseball during the war," he said. "That number is all that would be required to man the two major leagues."[67] Chandler also regaled his audience with talk of his youthful desire to be a big-league ballplayer, an unfulfilled dream that many in the audience no doubt shared with him.

After cancelling an exhibition game against the Fort Belvoir Army team because of cold weather on April 13, the Nats left Thursday morning, April 15, on a short exhibition swing that began with an afternoon game in Trenton, New Jersey, against the Phillies now led by former Nats manager Bucky Harris. They then moved north to Newark for a contest against the minor-league Bears, capping the trip with games against the Giants at the Polo Grounds on Saturday and Sunday. Bluege's team completed spring training with 9 wins in 11 games. Although the exhibition season was shorter than in previous years and the Nats' opponents were mostly service teams and the then-minor-league Baltimore Orioles, the usual air of optimism that precedes every opening day was further strengthened by Washington's strong pitching staff and by the addition of outfielder Bob Johnson and infielder Jerry Prid-dy. Griffith, Bluege, and the Nats themselves believed they had a good chance to reverse four successive years of opening-day losses—if for no other reason than their opponent this year was the lowly Philadelphia Athletics, the only team to finish lower than the Nats in 1942.

Thanks to the almost regular appearance of the residents of the White House since Taft, it was now a tradition to open the baseball season at Griffith Stadium. It was the curtain raiser for all of major-league baseball. Even veteran players felt a bit of a knot in their stom-achs as they took the field for the first time in April. Nats pitcher Early Wynn, a man not given to lofty praise about most things on the diamond and who was no stranger to season openers during his four decades in uniform and 300 wins, said opening day was like no other game. "There's that little extra excitement, a faster beating of the heart. You have that anxiety to get off to a good start, for yourself and for the team. You know that when you win the first one, you can't lose 'em all."[68]

The weather on Tuesday, April 20, was obliging, providing bright sun and mild spring temperatures for the overflow crowd of 25,000 spectators. But the day failed to include the usual high-powered not-ables in the pregame festivities. Roosevelt was in Mexico City confer-ring with his Mexican counterpart, and Vice President Wallace was on an official visit to South America—a rare moment when the president and vice president were out of the country simultaneously, especially in wartime. Paul V. McNutt, chairman of the War Manpower Commis-sion, represented Roosevelt in the presidential box and threw out the ceremonial first ball. McNutt, a former college pitcher at Indiana Uni-versity, shared the front-row box with several local officials and Senator Alben W. Barkley of Kentucky (who in 1948 would become Harry S. Truman's vice president). Unlike today's instant news fed live around the world, Roosevelt's and Wallace's trips abroad weren't reported until both men were both safely at their destinations (a practice that has been repeated in recent years when chief executives or other high-ranking U.S. officials journey into dangerous war zones), prompting inquiries as to whether the country had an acting president. The Associated Press, citing Justice Department lawyers, explained that FDR had not given up his presidential powers while abroad and was carrying out the duties of his office as he had done earlier in the year while conferring with Churchill in Casablanca.[69]

At the same time, the War Department finally released details of the Doolittle raid on Japan one year earlier. None of the 16 B-25 bombers landed safely at their unidentified home landing fields after successful raids on Tokyo, Yokohama, Nagoya, Kobe, and Osaka. "Five of the 80 American participants in the historic raid are interned in Russia," the War Department reported. "Eight are prisoners or presumed to be prisoners of the Japanese government. Two are missing. One was killed. Although several were long-delayed, the other 64 participants made their way to the camps of our Chinese allies and then back to American authority. Seven of those who escaped in this manner were injured but survived."[70]

When the venerable 80-year-old Connie Mack, still at the helm of the Athletics, joined his old friend Clark Griffith at the railing of the presidential box for the pregame ceremonies, they represented a total of 109 years of baseball experience. Among the many ties that bound the two men was a belief that baseball was a business and, as such, required fiscal constraint. Mack even had an unusual theory that it was more profitable for a team to start out hot and ultimately finish fourth than to play in the middle of the pack all season. "A team like that will draw well enough during the first part of the season to show a profit for the year, and you don't have to give the players raises when they don't win [at the end]," he said. Indeed, Mack often practiced what he preached: in his 53 seasons as a manager (a record unlikely to ever be broken), Mack won nine pennants and five World Series. Also, Mack's teams finished last 17 times. (He also was the last manager in major-league baseball allowed to wear street clothes in the dugout.)[71]

Mack constructed his 1943 team based on his assumption—later proved correct—that married men with children would be deferred from military service. So if it came down to a choice between two equally competent players, Mack opted for the married man and the assurance that he would last the full season. Despite the much-improved Washington ball club that he saw across the field in the home-team dugout, Mack predicted another pennant for the Yankees because of their strong pitching.

Bluege's new lineup was indeed impressive with Ellis Clary, 3B, leading off; followed by Case, RF; Spence, CF; Johnson, LF; Vernon, 1B; Priddy, 2B; Early, C (who led the team in hitting all spring); Sullivan, SS; and knuckleballer Dutch Leonard in the traditional pitcher's ninth spot and facing "Lum" Harris, the A's starter, who also relied on a knuckleball to balance his fastball. The Nats won the opener, 7–5, with a 12-hit attack, including 3 by Case. The victory ended Washington's opening-day drought, although by "beating the Athletics, the Nats weren't exactly dazzling, but the customers whooped it up loudly," Povich wrote.[72]

With the customary next day off, the Nats went up to New York for a pair, where reality quickly set in: they lost both games, 5–4 and 1–0. Then it was down to Philadelphia for two games against the A's then a three-game set against their favorite patsies at Griffith Stadium, all in all, winning four of five games against the A's. Between their opening-day victory and May 9, the Nats played 18 games, 11 at home and 7 on the road, including three doubleheaders. As a result of the mandated curtailed travel schedule, all of the contests were against their East Coast rivals, the A's, Yankees, and Red Sox. As the Pennsylvania Railroad shuttled the Nats up and down the northeast corridor, on the field they just spun their wheels, winning 10 (5 of them at the hands of Mack's A's) and losing 8 to trail the Yankees and Indians in the American League standings by one game.

Although the scores were typical of any season, to the professionals on the field the new balata core baseball was a failure. The ball had no bounce to it; hitting it was like hitting a rock. Just three days into the season, Lou Coleman, who was in charge of baseball production for A. G. Spalding and Brothers, acknowledged that the balata ball was indeed an inferior product and did not meet major-league standards, but a new and improved ball was on the way.[73] The balata core at the center of the ball was the problem. The Associated Press explained that the only difference "between the corrected ball and the dismally dead model" was that the rubber cement used to form the balata core in the "clunk" ball was made from a poor grade of reclaimed rubber that soaked into the many yards of woolen yarn wound around the core, hardening and making the wool brittle. "The new ball contains fresh cement that remains soft and sticky," Coleman said.[74] (True to its word, Spalding began circulating the new and improved baseballs the first week in May.)

When Roosevelt returned from his Mexico trip and went on a tour of domestic defense installations, he also faced serious domestic unrest on several fronts. On April 22, FDR received a letter from Milton Eisenhower, the associate director of the Office of War Information, urging the president to support the War Relocation Authority's planned closing of some of the Japanese American internment camps on the West Coast and to allow loyal internees to be absorbed back into U.S. communities. "They have suffered heavily in property losses; they have lost their businesses and their means of support," Milton Eisenhower pleaded. "Under the circumstances it would be amazing if extreme bitterness [among the internees] did not develop." In addition, Eisenhower warned that "it will be unsafe to wait until the war is over to attempt to reestablish them because acceptance by the American public cannot be expected after the war if they are denied the privilege of serving their country now."[75] Whether Roosevelt agreed with the plan or not, he had a more immediate domestic problem to deal with much closer to home—and of greater national importance at the moment—than the Japanese American internees on the other side of the country.

Less than a week later, on April 28, 480,000 soft-coal miners in Pennsylvania and West Virginia, including about 40,000 black miners (most of them in West Virginia, Alabama, and Kentucky), went on strike, seeking a $2-a-day pay hike.[76] In an effort to quickly resolve the dispute, FDR sent a telegram to United Mine Workers of America president John L. Lewis, announcing that he'd ordered the Office of Price Administration to examine the union's claim that price controls were disproportionately harming the mining industry. FDR also told Lewis, whose union had ignored a call for negotiations with the National War Labor Board, that the work stoppages in effect were strikes against the federal government itself and "a direct interference with the prosecution of the war."[77] Also, the president threatened to invoke the War Powers Act if Lewis did not direct his miners to return to work by 10 a.m. the following morning. On May 1 (May Day, ironically, a holiday in many countries to pay tribute to workers), Roosevelt made good on his threat and placed the mines under federal control. Lewis promptly ordered the men back to work the following day.

While the work stoppage drama was playing out across the coal fields of Appalachia, the Homestead Grays, training in Akron, Ohio, were hard at work preparing for the May 21 season opener at Griffith Stadium against the Newark Eagles. At the same time, another group of baseball-minded folks gathered in Chicago at the invitation of Cubs owner Philip K. Wrigley, the son of the chewing-gum magnate. Like his fellow owners, Wrigley wanted to find a way to keep fans enthusiastic about the sport and perhaps put paying customers into the Wrigley Field seats when his Cubs were on the road. Wrigley was aware that the loss of major leaguers caused by the draft was having an increasingly negative effect on the quality of play on the field and that the dearth of talent was not conducive to maintaining fan interest. Worst of all, the increasingly weak product on the field would perhaps eventually lead to a complete shutdown of the game.

Wrigley's brainchild was the All-American Girls Professional Softball League. (By midseason, the word "Baseball" replaced "Softball" in the name because the women were indeed playing baseball, and it would also distinguish the league from the other women's softball leagues. The distaff league was popularized on the big screen in the 1992 film, *A League of Their Own*.) For the duration, Wrigley believed, the women could replace the men on the baseball diamonds, just as Rosie the Riveter and her distaff army were subbing for the men in America's war plants. However, Wrigley's idea did not go over well with the other owners, including Griffith. The Old Fox, who once had been an innovator of the game and had demonstrated his flexibility when he reversed his stand against night baseball, might have been more amenable to the idea if the Grays weren't providing him with an extra $700 to $1,000 in net revenue from each Grays' game at Griffith Stadium. (Pittsburgh Pirates president William Benswanger, who was married to the daughter of team owner Barney Dreyfuss, sided with Griffith because he and his in-laws were also benefitting from Grays' home games at Forbes Field.)[78] Despite the opposition, Wrigley's staff held tryouts, and after making the final cuts, the management group created four 15-woman teams to represent South Bend, Indiana; Rockford, Illinois; and Kenosha and Racine, Wisconsin—all venues close to Chicago that, with any luck, would keep the home fires burning until the war was over and peace and profits would return to Wrigley Field. The new league's 150-game season officially began on May 30.[79]

The Nats were in Cleveland May 12–14, taking two of three games from the Indians on the first leg of their initial western swing, when word came of the Allies' resounding victory in the North Africa campaign. The Germans and Italians lost 756,000 troops combined, not including the 50,000 captured when the Germans surrendered unconditionally in Tunis and the Tunisian port city of Bizerte. The news was a welcome coda to British Prime Minister Winston Churchill's arrival in Washington on May 11 to confer again with FDR on preparations for a second front. They also would discuss "the next moves necessary to achieve [Germany's] 'unconditional surrender' goal they set at their last meeting in Casablanca in January."[80] The two leaders agreed to postpone opening the second front in Western Europe (Operation Overlord) until the spring of 1944, a bilateral decision that did not sit well with Stalin. "This decision creates exceptional difficulties for the Soviet Union, which has already been fighting for two years," the Soviet leader wrote to FDR on June 11, pointing out that the invasion of France had already been postponed from 1942 to 1943. This latest "decision may result in grave consequences for the future progress of the war," Stalin warned,[81] without explaining what those consequences might be. Later in the week, in an address to an approving joint session of Congress and broadcast nationally, the British leader promised that once Hitler was defeated, Britain would join in "the unstinting and relentless waging of war against Japan."[82]

The Nats routed the Chicago White Sox, 11–0 in the first game of a scheduled doubleheader on Sunday, May 23. Perhaps with an eye on the threatening weather, Washington scored seven runs in the top of the first inning, aided by three White Sox errors. The early outburst gave starting pitcher Early Wynn enough of a cushion to cruise to an easy six-hit victory in which he faced only 31 batters. The second game was rained out, so Washington's lone win against the White Sox gave the Nats a mediocre 5–4 record during their stops in Cleveland, Detroit, and Chicago. Their overall record now was 15–13, good enough to regain the third-place standing they'd lost earlier, but they still trailed the Indians and the Yankees, who'd swapped places at the top of the standings during the month.

The home stand began with an exhibition game on Monday, May 24, against the same powerful Naval Training Station team that had split two spring-training contests with the Nats in Norfolk in April. To draw as many fans as possible, the game was scheduled as a night contest, which required the American League to lift the energy-saving ban on night exhibition games. As early as April 30, the *Washington Post* was promoting the war-bonds fund-raiser with a carnival barker-like call: "Griffith Stadium fans will see the best-conditioned set of athletes in existence" and a team that includes "approximately a half-million dollars worth of former big league baseball talent." Indeed, Norfolk's top pitcher, former Detroit Tiger star Fred Hutchinson, was quoted as saying that his Navy squad was "good enough to win the pennant," all it needed was a few more pitchers to compete in a 154-game season.[83] Hutchinson, who years later became a beloved manager with the Tigers, Cardinals, and the pennant-winning Reds in 1961,[84] may well have been right because his Navy squad beat the Nats, 4–3, shutting out Washington until the bottom of the ninth inning.

But the final score was of no real consequence to the more than 29,000 fans—including many soldiers and sailors—who raised almost $2 million in war-bond sales during what was by any measure a special evening. Lieutenant Jacob Chester Shively, an airman who had been wounded while piloting his B-17 Flying Fortress over Nazi-held territory in Europe, threw out the ceremonial first pitch. Babe Ruth made a surprise appearance and trotted around the bases, popular radio singer Kate Smith[85] sang the national anthem, and with a pause in the game between the sixth and seventh innings, Bing Crosby came out to sing a medley of popular songs including his classic version of "White Christmas" surrounded by the Nats infielders. Also on hand and introduced to the crowd were British field marshal Sir Archibald Wavell (whose troops were the first to score an Allied victory against Axis partner Italy in North Africa in 1940–1941), presidential advisor Bernard Baruch, Navy Secretary Frank Knox, and the *Post*'s own Shirley Povich, who was lauded for having conceived the idea of the charity game. Griffith—who picked up the electricity tab for the lighting and shelled out $2,500 on war bonds for himself and his guests—told the crowd that Povich "deserves a world of credit for his untiring efforts in making [the evening] a huge success," and Griffith urged all clubs in the major and minor leagues to hold a similar event to contribute to the war effort.[86]

Two days later, on May 26, the Nats promptly started a three-game winning streak, two against the St. Louis Browns and the opener of a three-game set against Chicago, which briefly elevated Washington into first place—an unfamiliar spot indeed for the club, especially one that wasn't getting much hitting. Case was leading the Nats with a modest .265 batting average, Johnson was at .246, and Vernon and Spence were hovering at the .200 mark. After losing the Sunday doubleheader to White Sox on May 30, they promptly fell out of first place. They then won three of four against the Indians, including a 13–1 Cleveland send-off rout on June 2. The Nats concluded the home stand with a five-game series against Detroit by losing the first two games and then bouncing back to take the final three, including a Sunday doubleheader sweep, 5–1 and 8–4. Washington arrived in Boston in second place with a record of 24–18. And as May ended, the Nats were just one game behind the Yankees and seemingly headed for their best season in a decade. Good starting pitching, led by Wynn, Leonard, Alex Carrasquel, and Milo Candini, had kept the club competitive.

Still, like every baseball general manager or owner before and since, Griffith was constantly on the lookout to improve his pitching staff, especially the bullpen, which was not performing well. Two days before the war-bonds benefit exhibition against the Norfolk club, the Old Fox signed free agent Lefty Gomez, a great pitcher with the Yankees whose record was 189 wins and 101 losses (his final loss for a career total of 102 came with the Nats). But now, the future Hall of Famer's best days were clearly behind him, as evidenced by his having been let go by the lowly Boston Braves. Griffith justified signing the left-hander by saying, "At least Gomez isn't going to throw away a ball game with a base on balls or a wild pitch like some of our green kids."

Gomez had spent 13 years in Yankee pinstripes and had a perfect 6–0 record in the World Series, which might explain why he was no fan of the National League or of the Braves for that matter. Since being acquired by Boston prior to the start of the season, he had not taken the mound once. "I wasn't pitching because their pitchers were going so good apparently they didn't need me," he told Povich. "But I did try to show some hustle on the bench by talking it up. Those Braves were a lot of dead fish and I couldn't work up much enthusiasm on that Boston bench."

Gomez had a couple of offers after the Braves released him unconditionally on May 19, "but they were in the National League. I'm not a National Leaguer. You don't spend 11 [sic] seasons with the Yankees and then become a National Leaguer overnight," he said. So he jumped at Griffith's offer to rejoin the American League. The always verbose and usually humorous Gomez took one final shot at his former teammates. "Finally I had to tell 'em, 'listen you guys, no wonder Stengel is in the hospital. You mummies would drive anybody to the hospital.'"[87] Braves manager Casey Stengel was in a Boston hospital recuperating from a severe leg injury suffered in an auto accident prior to the start of the season and had not managed the team at all so far.[88] Although Griffith signed Gomez to be a reliever, he started the second game of the May 30 Sunday doubleheader against the White Sox. He lasted only four and two-thirds innings, giving up four hits, four runs, and five walks without a strikeout in a 5–1 Nats' loss. (It was Gomez's last major-league appearance. Griffith released him in July.)

As May turned into June, Griffith's mood grew brighter. Not only had he experienced the overwhelming success at the war-bonds exhibition game, but also his Nationals were playing well enough to remain in the unfamiliar position of nipping at the heels of the first-place Yankees, just one game behind the American League champions on June 8. Also, Griffith's coffers were growing. Through June 5, 241,000 fans had pushed through his turnstiles, an average of more than 10,000 per game. The 10 night contests had attracted an average of 13,000 spectators, and with 14 more such games remaining, Griffith could envision breaking the team's all-time attendance record of 817,000 paying customers during the pennant-winning season of 1925.[89] "Small wonder, then, that Griffith is incessantly beseeching Commissioner Landis to lift the limit and permit him to play at night on all days except Sundays and holidays," Povich commented. (Had he been successful, Griffith later might have been credited, or blamed, for turning the sport he once insisted should only be played "under the Lord's own sunshine" into the nocturnal spectacle it has become. So give credit to FDR for the idea of expanding night baseball.)

The Homestead Grays also contributed to Griffith's happiness. The Grays opened their Negro National League season on May 16, with an immediate claim on first place. In front of a Griffith Stadium crowd of 8,000, they won both games of the Sunday doubleheader against the Baltimore Elite Giants, 2–1 and 7–0. Gibson pounded out five hits in six at-bats, including four doubles, and he drove in three runs and scored as many.

The Grays and the Elite Giants then went on the road to Portsmouth, Virginia, where the Grays won the Monday game, 8–3, before the two clubs tied, 5–5, on Wednesday. The next evening, in their inaugural night game of the season back at Griffith Stadium, the Grays shut out the Newark Eagles, 6–0. On Saturday, the Grays beat the Philadelphia Stars, 7–1, to remain undefeated. Reprising their twin win of the previous week, the Grays swept another Sunday doubleheader at

Griffith Stadium on May 23, beating the Stars, 9–3 and 8–2, to lead the league with a 7–0 record. Again Gibson was the hero. In eight official at-bats, the Grays' power-hitting catcher collected five hits, drove in seven runs, and scored five. The highlight was Gibson's prodigious 440-foot home run into the left-field stands in the sixth inning of the second game with Leonard aboard. And despite losing their first two games when the Baltimore Elite Giants beat the Grays on Sunday, May 30, 11–8 and 2–0, Gibson continued his hitting binge into early June, when his batting average reached an astounding .580, with 19 RBIs and three home runs in eight official league games. As a team, the Grays were hitting .348.

The Old Fox attended almost every Grays' game at Griffith Stadium because they piqued his curiosity due to the tremendous talent in his ballpark when the Senators were out of town. Griffith's appearances at Grays' games no doubt also raised hopes and assumptions—as well as fears and possibly even anger from some club owners, black and white—that he might be planning to sign the Grays' two biggest stars, Buck Leonard and Josh Gibson. Grays historian Brad Snyder writes that sometime either in the 1943 season or during the previous year—there are conflicting accounts about the date of the incident—Griffith called both players to his office following a Grays' doubleheader and told them that several black sportswriters, including Sam Lacy and Ric Roberts, were talking up the idea of "you fellows" joining his club. (From the context of Griffith's remarks, as Snyder reports them, it's likely he was not referring specifically to Leonard and Gibson but to black players in general.) "Well, let me tell you something: if we get you boys, we're going to get the best ones," Griffith was quoted as telling the two super-stars. "It's going to break up your league. Now what do you think of that?" The two could only reply that, if given the chance, they believed they could play in the major leagues but they weren't about to campaign for it.

How serious was Griffith about integrating his team? Although no one can say for sure, even if Griffith wanted to do so—and that's a big if—his chances were slim to none. Meeting with Leonard and Gibson was just another move by the Old Fox "to mollify the Senators' black fans while protecting his business interests in the Grays," Snyder sug-gests. Snyder also cites Buck Leonard's later conversation with John Holway in which Leonard told the black baseball historian, "I always thought the Senators might be the first to take a Negro, because Washington was about half Negro then. I figured that if half the city boycotted the games, the other half would come. But Griffith was always looking for Cuban ballplayers."[90] In any event, nothing came of the postgame conversation, although Griffith probably could have signed them both for not much more than he was paying his Cuban players.[91] One anonymous angry letter writer told the *Baltimore Afro-American* in May that "global war or no war, I'm amazed to know that throughout the length and breadth of America there wasn't a single club magnate who possessed the courage of his convictions" by signing Negro League players.[92] "Fine effrontery our national pastime has in employing (for untold years) foreigners of all colors and allegiances but frowning upon the swarthy face of the ex-slave," the writer added.

The magnates had no interest in such a drastic move as integrating the game, not then or ever and especially not while the war raged on. They did not want to do anything that might rock the baseball boat or perhaps sink it, their perennial fear. Besides, they knew it would take more courage than that group of aging autocrats possessed to deal with the haphazardly regulated Negro Leagues. In Griffith's case, he was 74 years old, comfortable in the status quo and perhaps feeling he was beyond the age of tilting at windmills, particularly those that blew ill winds among his band of brothers. As Griffith biographer Leavengood points out, "The Grays helped to create new popularity for the Nationals as well, who drew extremely well in the African American community in 1943, contributing to the upsurge in attendance for the Nationals."[93]

The black teams weren't easy to deal with, even among themselves. Operating without an overall leader a la Landis, the two Negro Leagues were not constrained by the same kind of binding regulations that governed the 16 major-league clubs. Negro League players were continually jumping from one team to another when a few more dollars than they were currently making was promised to them. The owners too did whatever they pleased to attract fans and pad their bottom line. Without fear of league sanctions or legal action, they had no qualms about raiding each other's players, relocating their franchises whenever the grass looked greener elsewhere, or playing against any team that could field nine men and offer a decent box-office return.

Just before their season got under way, a public spat erupted over which Negro League, National or American, had broken their joint agreement that prohibited raiding teams and signing each other's players. The leagues were "locked in a do or die dispute over player ownership," Art Carter wrote, because the NAL had accused the NNL of "snatching" players.[94] "Of all times to engage in an inter-league squabble, this appears to be the worst. Baseball is in enough trouble, with manpower shortages, transportation difficulties and equipment reductions," he noted while also suggesting that if the leagues had proper organization, including a commissioner, the dispute "would never reach the silly stage that it has." Carter also acknowledged that there was "probably some merit to the charges of both circuits," but "what the controversy does bring out, however, is the need for a neutral party as commissioner of the two leagues."

Grays co-owner Cum Posey, acting in his role as Negro National League executive secretary, insisted that it was the rival Negro American League that had abrogated their August 1942 agreement by permitting its teams to play the Miami Ethiopian Clowns, a nomadic and comedic independent team[95] that both leagues had blackballed.

The owners had taken that step because they believed—and Posey was one of the strongest voices for the ban—that the diamond antics of the Clowns, such as painting their faces white and playing the game for laughs, were an embarrassment to the race and detrimental to Negro League baseball. "Clowning around on the ball field, it was argued, played to the negative and offensive stereotypes about Blacks common at the time," explains Raymond A. Mohl, distinguished professor of urban history, postwar America, and race and ethnicity at the University of Alabama Birmingham.[96] Also, the Negro League owners were envious of the Clowns' ability to routinely draw larger crowds than their own teams did.

Clowns owner Syd Pollock, a close associate of Harlem Globetrotters basketball team founder Abe Saperstein, had tried to resolve the dispute. Pollock dropped the name Ethiopian because it had become a proud rallying cry among American blacks after Mussolini's forces brutally took over that African nation (then known as Abyssinia) in 1935. Pollock also banned the Clowns' offensive whiteface makeup, wigs, grass skirts, and clown suits that Posey and his colleagues found so offensive. And Pollock limited the Clowns' comedy routines to barnstorming tours, pregame activities, and between games of doubleheaders. In return, the newly renamed Cincinnati Clowns were admitted to the Negro American League for the 1943 season, and the NAL's Cincinnati Buckeyes were relocated to Cleveland. (The Clowns competed in the league until integration forced the Negro Leagues to disband in the 1950s, just as Griffith had warned. Ironically, the defunct Clowns bequeathed to the major leagues one of baseball's all-time greats, Henry Aaron, who had signed with the team in 1952 while still a teenager. Pollack sold Aaron's contract to the Boston Braves for $10,000.)[97]

No "satisfactory explanation of the NAL's action in breaking the agreement by playing [against] the Clowns was ever given," Posey claimed, reviewing the origins of the disagreement as his league saw it.[98] He was responding to NAL countercharges that it was the NNL teams, his Grays and the other league clubs, that had broken the agreement by signing several NAL ballplayers for a so-called All-Star Game the previous year without their original clubs' consent. (Specifically cited was catcher Roy Campanella's jumping from the Baltimore Elite Giants to play for the Cleveland Buckeyes in that 1942 game, which earned the future Brooklyn Dodgers star and Hall of Famer a fine of $250 and a suspension. He then jumped to the Mexican League, signed with the Monterrey Industriales, and hit .296 for the season.)[99]

Posey also stated that the Grays and the Philadelphia Stars would not return any players to their former NAL teams "until the Kansas City Monarchs return Satchel Paige to the Newark Eagles along with other 'stolen players' to NNL clubs" and until the NAL president publicly apologized.[100] Apparently, the Negro Leagues did make an attempt to correct the poaching problem when team owners from both leagues met again in early June, this time in virtual secrecy, and agreed to discontinue player raids. A majority of the owners also indicated they favored having a commissioner to oversee the leagues. "Nothing could be more pleasing to this chronic critic of the organizational policy of the sport as there has never been greater need for sound, unbiased leadership in the leagues than during these perilous times," Carter wrote.[101] But he simultaneously wondered "if the action is to be interpreted as a forward step, or just a paper agreement which will disappear in thin air when the dollars are considered."

Spring 1943, however, was anything but a good time for Griffith's friend in the White House. About the only good news reaching Roosevelt toward the end of May was the death of Japanese admiral Isoroku Yamamoto, who once had boasted that he would dictate the terms of peace from the White House.[102] In addition to overseeing the war in the Pacific and North Africa, Roosevelt was battling growing domestic unrest from consumers and producers alike over the unpopular price and wage restrictions. He also faced new labor disputes among leaders of vital war-production programs and strikes in the all-important rubber and coal (again) industries, all of which posed a serious threat to the precarious wartime economy.

So FDR put together a lineup of top-flight executives from business and his administration to consolidate the handling of these issues and other domestic problems. Dubbed his "war cabinet," the group included future Supreme Court justice Fred M. Vinson, Secretary of War Henry L. Stimson, Navy Secretary Frank Knox, and James F. Byrnes, director of the Office of War Mobilization.[103] FDR's action came none too soon because on Saturday, May 22, an estimated 40,000 rubber workers, members of the Congress of Industrial Organizations (CIO), struck the Goodyear, Goodrich, and Firestone plants in Akron, Ohio, after the War Labor Board and the workers' union could not agree on a wage hike. The stoppage affected the production of gas masks, life belts, airplane deicers, and tank treads, among other war materiel.

In Detroit, fewer than 2,000 of the 29,000 striking Chrysler workers returned to work for their Saturday shift, and an additional 2,900 Chrysler tank-arsenal workers were sent home for lack of parts from strike-bound plants.[104] Then on June 1, coal miners in 25 states stopped work when their contract expired, initially idling an estimated 450,000 workers.[105] And when all workers also walked off the job at Chrysler plants in Detroit, the action prompted the War Labor Board to issue an injunction ordering them back to work immediately. The Labor Department—which had calculated the previous month's (April) man-days lost at a record 675,000—called the actions the "most serious outbreak of strikes since Pearl Harbor."[106]

The War Production Board made plans to save coal stockpiles at coal-firing electric power plants by ordering unnecessary lighting, such as on theater marquees and outdoor advertising, to be turned off. The plan also included a drastic cut in railroad service by eliminating nonessential travel, the aim of which was to save the fuel needed to power coal-fired locomotives. Whether that travel restriction would affect the baseball schedules quickly became moot when FDR, wearing his hat as commander in chief, ordered the coal miners to return to work no later than June 7. His executive order, issued on June 3, told the striking miners—now numbering 530,000—in no uncertain terms that they were working "for the government on essential war work and it is their duty no less than that of their sons and brothers in the armed forces to fulfill their war duties."[107] John L. Lewis's United Mine Workers union complied, and more than half a million coal miners went back to work the following Monday, June 7.

Had the strikes continued and the War Production Board's plans been implemented, millions more Americans would have been subjected to new financial hardships and perhaps swelled the ranks of those who objected to the continuation of baseball on grounds that it was nothing more than a frivolous pursuit for the lucky few who played it well and for the already-rich owners. The Bureau of Labor Statistics' initial May assessment of the coal strike estimated that more than two million man-days had been lost that month, more than three times the loss caused by all strikes the previous month. (Actually, the coal miners were doing quite well compared with other sectors of the workforce. Their average weekly wages had risen in March to $42.97 for a 38-hour workweek compared to $41.84 for an average 44.8-hour workweek for workers in all manufacturing industries.)[108]

On a happier note for the president and the American people—although FDR surely knew the news before it became public—on June 5, the Army revealed that FDR's second son, Colonel Elliott Roosevelt, had survived the crash of his B-17 Flying Fortress "somewhere in Africa months before the American invasion of Vichy-held French territory." According to the press account from Lowry Field in Denver, Colorado, Roosevelt, a navigation officer, was participating in a historic preinvasion "mission to North Africa" that "paved the way for later landing of American troops under command of Lieut. Gen. Dwight Eisenhower and for driving the Axis out of Africa." When the plane, a photo-equipped aircraft known as the Blue Goose, developed engine trouble, the pilot was forced to make a crash landing. Roosevelt and two other crewmen were not injured, and they made their way on foot to their base at an undisclosed location. A quartet of noncommissioned photographers on board received commissions as a reward for their work. The precise date of the mission was not given, but it did produce "the first complete photographs and maps of Northern African expanses" months before U.S. and British forces launched Operation Torch, the amphibious invasion of French North Africa, on November 8, 1942.[109]

Within weeks of resolving the coal miners' strike, Roosevelt faced another unsettling domestic disturbance. On Sunday, June 20, a 90-degree-plus day, "thousands of white and Negro war workers on their day off from the Motor City's humming armament plants" gathered on Belle Isle, a city-owned recreational site in the Detroit River. Toward the end of the day as crowds headed home, a fistfight broke out between a white man and an African American on the Belle Isle Bridge. The fight touched off two nights and a day of racial violence that included burning and overturning cars and torching homes and other buildings. Authorities blamed the rioting on "racial antagonisms that had been intensified by wartime conditions."[110]

When Michigan Governor Harry F. Kelly appealed to Roosevelt for help, Secretary of War Henry L. Stimson mobilized a reported 3,000 troops, deploying one-third of them to Detroit to assist civilian authorities restore order. The rioting left as many as 34 people killed, including about 25 African Americans,[111] at least 700 injured, and 1,300 arrested, of whom about 85 percent were African Americans.[112]

At about the same time, other cities, including Los Angeles; Mobile, Alabama; and Beaumont, Texas, also experienced racial unrest. A *New York Times* account blamed the unrest on wartime conditions and migration. "Large numbers of rural Southerners, both Negro and white, have been drawn to war-production centers—North and South. Skilled Negro workers have competed with whites for higher-paid jobs in armament plants. Bad housing has complicated conditions."[113]

In a letter to Roosevelt dated June 26, Reverend Anson Phelps Stokes, chairman of the Committee on the Negro American in Defense Industries and president of the Phelps Stokes Fund in New York, wrote of his concern about the "tragic series of events." He suggested that the president go on the radio and propose a three-point plan to examine the "threatening interracial tension," including "an impartial local study of conditions by strong interracial groups in every large industrial community."[114] Roosevelt's prompt response was vague and noncommittal.[115] He told Stokes that all citizens "interested in the success of the war effort must be concerned about racial tensions and the violence growing from them which in too many cases have interrupted the production program at home and given comfort to our enemies abroad."[116] Then FDR went on to add, "Where needed, as in Detroit, the full Federal power will be available to put a prompt end to violence immediately upon request from State and local authorities. Certainly, however, we shall not limit ourselves to the repression of violence. In the National Government, as in groups like yours, we are determined upon effective preventative procedures based upon justice for all in the productive unity of America."

(Although FDR did not refer to the riots in his July 28 fireside chat, he did stress the importance of bearing up to the hardships on the battlefield as well as those in the defense industries, warning that, in either case, complacency, indifference, or slacking off "could sacrifice the lives of American soldiers and contribute to the loss of an important battle."[117] Vice President Wallace was less hesitant to directly address the race issue. Speaking to a gathering of labor and civic organizations in Detroit on July 18, the lifelong liberal, who also supported universal health care in America, said, "We cannot fight to crush Nazi brutality abroad and condone race riots at home."[118] Then, looking ahead to the end of the war, Wallace remarked, "In that tomorrow when peace comes, education for tolerance will be just as important as the production of television [sets].")

Ennui plagued the Nats throughout June. For most of the month, it was win one and lose one, win two and lose three, win three and lose two. They were unable to string together more than three victories in succession. And they did that only twice—first at home when they won the final three games of the home stand against Detroit, including a Sunday doubleheader sweep on June 6, and then winning two games in Philadelphia and the opener of a three-game set in New York between June 18 and 20. Nevertheless, Washington remained close to league-leading New York. The Nats' pinnacle came on June 27, when they beat their favorite patsies, the A's, 9–0, in the first game of a doubleheader at Shibe Park, where the annual All-Star Game would be played in just a few weeks. The Nats were now seven games over .500. However, they lost the nightcap, 5–4, and the following two games in Chicago when their hitting all but disappeared, 7–1 and 2–0. Leading up to the All-Star break, Washington lost two of three in St. Louis, three of four in Detroit, and then managed to win three of five in Cleveland. At the break, the Nats' record was a feeble 40–37.

The 1943 annual midsummer classic on July 13 was notable for several "firsts." It was the first All-Star Game played under the lights and the first play-by-play radio account to have a sponsor. According to a report, the Gillette Safety Razor Company, which had been sponsoring the World Series broadcasts for four years, paid $25,000[119] for the exclusive rights to air the game over the Columbia Broadcasting System (now simply CBS) to 200 of its affiliate stations in the United States and Canada and to the armed forces overseas via shortwave. Griffith could not help but be pleased that a consensus of the managers had selected four of his Nats to the 26-man AL squad: outfielders George Case and Bob Johnson (both men were selected unanimously) and the battery of catcher Jake Early and pitcher Dutch Leonard. The quartet represented the largest contingent of Washington ballplayers ever to take part in the event. (Only the Yankees and Indians, with six players each, had greater representation.)

The only sour note was the omission of Milo Candini who, with a 7–0 record, led the league in victories. The *Post*'s Shirley Povich criticized the managers for their omission (as well as leaving off Brooklyn's Bobo Newsom, the second-leading pitcher in wins in the National League). In Candini's case, Povich said, the oversight might be excused because he was a rookie with a 5–0 record at the time of the balloting.[120] The right-hander had arrived in Washington with a sore arm. At Griffith's instructions, trainer Mike Martin worked with Candini daily, and he didn't take the mound until June. Candini's first two wins came as a relief pitcher before he reeled off three wins as a starter.[121]

Candini's failure to be named to the AL All-Star team was logical for the time because pitchers consigned to relief duty were often those who couldn't cut it as a starter or were past their prime and usually did spot starting, as in Lefty Gomez's singular start for Washington, or mop-up duty in games that were considered no longer winnable. Relievers did not have the star status they gained in the latter decades of the 20th century when innings specialists, especially outstanding ninth-inning closers such as Mariano Rivera and Trevor Hoffman, became a far more important—and highly paid—strategic element of the game. Still, the selection process itself came in for criticism. Povich, for one, said, "The trouble with the whole system of letting the managers name the All-Star teams is they don't name the fans' [favorite] players. They go for the old standbys while the fans clamor to see the better rookies."[122]

In making out his AL lineup for the All-Star Game, Yankees manager Joe McCarthy might have been thinking of another recent criticism of the annual contest. In a nod to those critics, he chose to keep his entire New York contingent—Bill Dickey, Joe Gordon, Johnny Lindell, Charlie Keller, and pitchers Spud Chandler and Ernie "Tiny" Bonham—on the bench or in the bullpen for the entire game. "We didn't need them," was McCarthy's excuse after his AL All-Stars won the game, 5–3. "We got out there in front early enough. Besides, these other boys deserved a chance to shine. The Yankees have had enough of the limelight."[123] *New York Times* sportswriter John Drebinger explained that McCarthy was pragmatically answering National League fans who claimed that the American League's annual roster was always composed of "one great ball club, the Yankees, and that the rest of the circuit is composed of extremely mediocre material."[124]

Without a Yankee taking the field or coming to bat, the American League nevertheless prevailed for the eighth time in the 11 All-Star Games played since its inception in 1933. Even if the Yankees had played, McCarthy might have been able to counter the critics because the 1943 Yankees were without Joe DiMaggio, Tommy Henrich, Phil Rizzuto, and pitchers Red Ruffing and Marius Russo. (Dickey, a member of the AL All-Star team that year, was drafted in 1944 when he was 37.)[125] The bottom line, however, was that the Shibe Park exhibition proved to be an outstanding evening and a showcase for the Washington contingent. George Case led off, Dutch Leonard got the win, and Jake Early walked and scored a run, made three putouts, and caught the entire game (proof perhaps that Dickey wasn't needed); in addition, Griffith saw his Bat and Ball Fund grow by $115,174, which included $65,174 in admissions from the 31,938 paying fans.[126]

If he had had the time to listen to the game, baseball-loving FDR would have enjoyed the broadcast. But he was dealing not only with prosecuting the war but also refereeing a very public (and embarrassing) spat between his commerce secretary, Jesse H. Jones, and the vice president. Wallace had accused Jones of obstructing the war effort by mishandling the financing of foreign defense-related contracts mostly in Latin America. On July 15, an angry Roosevelt sent a letter to both men notifying them that he was abolishing the defense committee they were serving on, effectively relieving them of their duties.[127] "In the midst of waging a war so critical to our national security and to the future of all civilization, there is not sufficient time to investigate and determine where the truth lies in your conflicting versions as to transactions which took place over a year and a half ago," Roosevelt wrote. "My action today is not intended to decide that question. The important thing is to clear the decks and to get on with the war at once. To do this requires a fresh start with new men, unencumbered by interagency dissension and bitterness." With that, the president issued Executive Order 9361,[128] abolishing the Bureau of Economic Warfare and transferring its duties to the newly created Office of Economic Warfare within the Office for Emergency Management, whose new director was former Supreme Court justice James Byrnes.

The regular season resumed on Thursday, July 15, with the Nationals hosting the Red Sox for a five-game series that began a long 23-game home stand. Washington went into the Boston series with a mediocre but winning record of 40 wins and 37 losses. After the two clubs split the first two games, the Nats slipped into third place by two percentage points. The Yankees were five and a half games in front with Detroit in second at 38–35, and Washington was at 41–38. By winning the next three games against Boston, Washington boosted its record to 44–38 for a winning percentage of .537. The Nats won the next game too, beating the visiting Tigers, 6–5, in the first game of a doubleheader to stretch their record to 45 wins and 38 losses and tying their previous high for the season of seven games above .500 on June 27.

Then, almost as rapidly as the Sicilian capital of Palermo fell to General Patton's Seventh Army after an 18-hour blitz on July 22–23,[129] the Nats fell into a five-game losing streak—three against Detroit and two against Cleveland, including a loss in the first game of a Sunday doubleheader on July 25. After winning the nightcap, their record stood at 46–43, a fall from grace that coincided with another and far more noteworthy tumble—Benito Mussolini's fall from power in Rome and his prompt arrest. After losing their ninth game in 10 to the White Sox, 5–4, on July 29, before the smallest night crowd of the season, 3,500 fans, the Nationals fell below .500 for the first time since May 8. At 46–47, they found themselves wedged between Cleveland and St. Louis in fifth place, 10½ games off the lead. Then suddenly from those depths—as Eisenhower publicly called for Italy's unconditional surrender and pledging that all "ancient liberties and traditions" would be restored if Allied prisoners there were turned over to the United States and not to the Germans[130]—the Nationals began a blitz of their own.

The surge began with a 4–1 win against the White Sox when Wynn pitched a five-hitter on July 30, the final contest of the four-game set in which the Nats lost the first three games. That brought them back to .500, with a 47–47 record. Bluege, desperate to bolster the offense, benched Stan Spence for the first time in his two years with the club and played infielder Alex Kampouris in right field. Gene Moore moved to center, and George Case was in left. Kampouris went hitless in the game but made three fine running catches, and the speedy Case stole second in the one time he reached base, which put him in a tie with the White Sox's Wally Moses for the league base-stealing lead. The win moved Washington into third place, 10½ games behind the Yankees and 10 behind Chicago and Detroit, which were tied for second with 45–44 records.

Griffith again sought to bolster his pitching staff by purchasing left-hander Bill LeFebvre from the minor-league Minneapolis Millers, where his record at the time was 10–7. Washington promptly reeled off seven more wins in a row, six against the St. Louis Browns, including a 20–6 walloping to start off August and both games of an unusual Tuesday doubleheader, 7–4 and 3–0, to close out the home stand. The Nats won the opener at Fenway Park, where they beat the Red Sox, 4–2, for their eighth-straight victory and a record of 54–47. They were now in second place, seven games behind New York and two games ahead of third-place Chicago. The other five AL clubs all trailed the Yankees by double digits.

In another move to improve his team, this one highly controversial, Griffith added outfielder Jake Powell to the Washington lineup from the minor-league St. Paul Saints, where he was hitting .283. The always-scrappy native of Silver Spring, Maryland, had first played for Griffith in 1930 and then again between 1934 and 1936, when he was traded to the Yankees. Powell met the team in Boston sporting a black eye from a barroom brawl the night before he was sold to Washington.[131] In reporting the acquisition, Nats beat writer Povich called Powell a character and "the enemy of the dull moment."[132]

What the sportswriter failed to mention was that Powell was also a blatant racist, more an enemy of African Americans and other minorities than of dullness. While playing for the Yankees in 1938, Powell was asked by a Chicago radio interviewer how he stayed in shape in the offseason. Powell replied that he was a Dayton, Ohio, policeman[133] in the winter and he wielded his billy club "cracking niggers over the head."[134] Blacks were incensed (probably more by Powell's blatant admission of his actions than by his use of the derogatory word that was quite common, but no less offensive, in the years prior to the civil-rights movement). Landis promptly suspended Powell for 10 days. When the Yankees outfielder appeared in Griffith Stadium in the first game following his suspension, on August 16, 1938, African American anger erupted. Powell was greeted by a salvo of glass soda bottles that began in the second inning and lasted into the seventh, causing delays in the game so the field crew could clean up the field.[135]

Powell was no fan of Jews either. In May 1936, he hit a routine grounder and ran so hard into first baseman Hank Greenberg that the great Tigers star and future Hall of Famer dropped the ball and broke his wrist in the collision, putting him out of action for the remainder of the season. According to Povich, an unapologetic Powell growled at Greenberg, "Learn how to play the position before you come up to the big leagues."[136] Povich no doubt deleted Powell's anti-Semitic expletives for the family newspaper just as he had edited out the racial epithet in reporting Powell's Chicago interview. Now, in the middle of the 1943 campaign, Powell was again wearing a W on his uniform and would do so for the next three years.

The move by Griffith was typical of his management of the organization. He had a well-known penchant for favoring former Nats and, when possible, for returning them to the fold. In this case, Griffith was remembering Powell's bat and banking on black fans forgetting Powell's past because he hadn't played in the major leagues since 1940. But Homestead Grays historian Brad Snyder believes "Griffith showed a total disregard for the Senators' black fans."[137] (In the end, Powell had little impact on the club's performance in 1943, appearing in 37 games with 35 hits, no home runs, 10 doubles, 14 runs scored, and a .265 batting average.)

On August 1, it was the Negro Leagues' turn to showcase their best in the annual East–West game between all-star squads from the NAL and NNL at Chicago's Comiskey Park. The game was so popular that it traditionally attracted more fans than the Negro Leagues' World Series at the end of the season. In 1943, the East–West game drew a record crowd of 51,723,[138] outdrawing the major-league All-Star Game by more than 20,000, one of the 10 times the black classic had attracted more fans than the major-league midsummer classic. "The event is the game of the year," wrote Harold Jackson, a *Baltimore Afro-American* sportswriter, on his way to covering the game.

Unlike the major leagues' All-Star Game for which the managers chose the two teams, it was the black voting public that elected the Negro teams and placed six Grays on the 1943 NNL squad. That balloting system led Jackson—perhaps with the criticism of the major leagues' having one great squad dominate the classic each year in mind—to write: "To me, [the East–West game] represents the Homestead Grays (the greatest colored team in baseball) against the Western stars."[139] Although Josh Gibson, the Grays' star of stars, was expected to provide the clout at the plate that would give the NNL squad its seventh-straight victory in the series, the game turned out to be a 2–1 pitchers' duel between Kansas City's Satchel Paige for the Negro American Leaguers and the New York Cubans' Dave Barnhill for the Negro National Leaguers with the two sides amassing 10 hits between them. The Negro American League scored its two runs in the second and fourth innings while the National squad mustered its lone run in the top of the ninth.

Gibson, a man of erratic moods and plagued by bouts of alcoholism, drug use, and mental demons, nevertheless continued his season-long torrid hitting (by August 21 he was hitting an amazing .518). And although he had just eight home runs thus far in the season, all were of the tape-measure variety, including a 435-foot blast on August 14, in the first game of a doubleheader against the Newark Eagles at Griffith Stadium.[140] He followed that home run with a 480-foot triple to the centerfield wall in the nightcap. (Typical of catchers, black or white, Gibson was no speedster, which probably kept him from turning the triple into an inside-the-park home run.)

The Nats' longest road trip of the season, 24 games, and their final swing through the western circuit, began with the 4–2 win in Boston on Friday, August 6, and ended in St. Louis on August 26. Concluding the trip, the Nats played a rare eight-game series with the Browns, each team winning four, and Washington returned home having won 13 games and losing 11. Stan Spence returned to the lineup in St. Louis, where he'd always hit well and continued to do so. He raised his batting average at Sportsman's Park to .621 with 18 hits in 29 at bats there, 7 of them home runs. However, his good hitting this time didn't do much for his overall average, which sat at the .260 mark. While in St. Louis, Griffith reacquired Browns' pitcher Bobo Newsom, who had pitched well enough for the Dodgers earlier in the season (nine wins and four losses) to be considered for the All-Star Game, but he was 1–6 as a Brown following his trade from Brooklyn on July 15. When no other American League team claimed Newsom, Griffith purchased the itinerant pitcher for the third time for the bargain waiver price of $7,500, a sharp reduction from the $40,000 the Old Fox reportedly paid to get Newsom from the same Browns in 1935.[141] As a former pitcher himself, the Old Fox figured he knew what was ailing Newsom. "There's nothing the matter with his arm," Griffith insisted. "He can't work with only three days' rest, though. We've got enough pitchers to give Newsom plenty of rest, and I think he'll win."[142]

The Nationals boosted their record quickly at home with three straight wins against their obliging neighbors to the north, the Philadelphia A's. So, going into the final month of the season, Washington's record of 69–58 was good enough to remain in second place, albeit a distant nine and a half games behind New York. Although they promptly had a chance to narrow that gap when they traveled to New York to play the Yankees, the clubs split the four games there, and the Nationals dropped two more in Boston.

The president too was on the road in August. Three months after Churchill's visit to FDR in Washington, Roosevelt journeyed north to Quebec City on August 14, for 10 days of further discussions—labeled the Quadrant Conference—on opening a second front. The two leaders were joined by their host, Canadian Prime Minister Mackenzie King. With the Allies having made decisive inroads in Sicily, Churchill pushed for completing the job by taking a weakened Italy out of the war altogether. FDR favored planning for the invasion of France, which was to be directed by Eisenhower. The British also put forth a plan to defeat Japan by 1948, including an invasion of South East Asia and taking control of Chinese airfields and ports for a total blockade of the Japanese islands. The U.S. position was to defeat Japan within a year of Germany's surrender. In the end, Churchill agreed to accelerate the Pacific campaign and British admiral Lord Louis Mountbatten was named the supreme allied commander of the Southeast Asia Command that was formed at the Quebec meetings.[143]

Meanwhile, after a doubleheader loss on September 6 in their final visit to Boston, the Nats headed to Philadelphia once again where they smothered the Athletics in a four-game sweep. A pumped-up Nats squad then returned to Griffith Stadium, where they added another six wins in a row, two against Boston, three against New York, and the opener of the final series against St. Louis. The win streak brought the Nats' record to 81–62, but they'd managed to lop off only two games from the Yankees' comfortable lead. Although Washington won only 3 of its remaining 10 games during the final two weeks of the season, the Nationals still finished in second place, a distant 13½ games behind the Yankees and 2 games ahead of third-place Cleveland. Their record of 84–69, and winning percentage of .549, produced Washington's best finish since 1933, the year the Nats won their third and final pennant. And despite losing the season finale to Detroit, 4–1, the 5,000 home-town fans witnessed George Case steal three bases to run his season total to 61 and beat out Chicago's Wally Moses's 56. It was the only one of Case's five straight years as stolen-base champion when he was seriously challenged for the title.[144]

It was a good year for Griffith financially as well. Season attendance at Griffith Stadium was 574,694, third best in the league.[145] Also, the bottom-line profit of $46,631, some $4,000 more than the previous season, was the AL's second highest.[146] Griffith also profited from the record 225,000 fans that paid to see the Grays play. Their fans were rewarded by Josh Gibson's outstanding season in which he batted .503 and hit 10 tape-measure home runs. September 6 was "Josh Gibson Night" at Griffith Stadium, and between the sixth and seventh innings, the slugging catcher received a giant replica bat with the words "Josh the Basher" on it that was filled with cash. He also received luggage from team co-owner Cum Posey, who had journeyed to Washington from his home in Pittsburgh for the occasion. Gibson's teammate Buck Leonard also had a terrific year, batting .326 with 11 doubles, six triples, two homers, and 38 RBIs.[147]

After the season, Gibson and Leonard joined a Satchel Paige–led touring club in California and competed against a major-league All-Star exhibition team that included the ever-present Bobo Newsom. Although Gibson did not play in the West Coast series (Snyder suggests he may have sat out "because of his erratic behavior and mental prob-lems"), Leonard hit safely in seven of the eight exhibition games and finished with a .333 batting average, evidence that if given the chance, the 35-year-old veteran would hold his own in the major leagues. (Leo-nard and Gibson were voted into the Baseball Hall of Fame by the Negro Leagues Committee in 1972.)

Perhaps best of all for Grays' fans, the team won the first of two consecutive Negro League world championships (during a string of nine straight league championships between 1937 and 1945), beating the Birmingham Black Barons four games to three with one tie. Despite Griffith's rigid stance against integration, he went out of his way to accommodate the Grays and their fans in the championship by com-pressing the Nats' final 13 home games into five doubleheaders and three single games so Griffith Stadium was free to host the first and third games of the championship series, both of which the Grays unfor-tunately lost (the second game, played in Baltimore, ended in a 5–5 tie). The Black Barons, however, played only once at home in Montgomery, and it was the deciding game won by the Grays, 8–4. (In between, the Grays and Black Barons took the series on the road to Chicago; Colum-bus, Ohio; and Indianapolis.) Also, following the series, Griffith Sta-dium hosted a show called the "Cavalcade of Negro Music," which included performances by Billy Eckstein and Art Tatum.

The growing popularity of the Negro Leagues coupled with the de-cline in the quality of play in the major leagues prompted some observ-ers to believe that integration was rapidly approaching. In early Sep-tember, an unattributed article in the *New York Amsterdam News*, one of America's largest circulation African American newspapers, pre-dicted that black ballplayers would be in the major leagues by 1944 or 1945. The article noted that baseball was due to play an increasing role in wartime recreation, and it uncharacteristically took to task the Negro Leagues' owners for their resistance to integration. "The selfish attitude expressed by the operators of colored clubs in coming out at a crucial time (as in 1942) and stating for public information that they were not interested in nor sympathetic with the program to put some of their players in major league uniforms shows the short-sightedness with which the colored variety of the [game] has to contend." The article singled out for special criticism the lack of a Negro Leagues' commis-sioner, not establishing regular schedules, and avoiding playing in certain cities. "Such is the situation that finds the Homestead Grays sticking to Washington and Pittsburgh; the Newark Eagles confining most of their appearances to Newark; both of which clubs have had little to do in the way of appearing in New York." The article concluded by predicting that despite "this situation in Negro baseball, it is felt that the majors will make up their minds this Winter on the colored question once and for all and that in the Spring they'll start shopping around for Negro talent."[148]

In late November, President Roosevelt flew to Tehran to confer with Churchill and Stalin. And again, the main topic was opening the second front in France with an estimated date of May 1944. Journalist and historian Jon Meacham calls the Tehran conference Roosevelt's "hour of decision" because Stalin "pressed and pressed for a cross-Channel operation" and FDR finally sided with the Soviet leader, rejecting Churchill's call for further delay.[149] The Allied leaders also discussed the fate of Germany and Eastern Europe in the postwar period. Stalin insisted on redrawing Poland's borders and promised to enter the war against Japan 90 days after Germany's surrender. When FDR returned to Washington early in December, he faced another potentially crippling work stoppage, this one involving the railroad workers. To prevent any disruptions in crucial transportation, three days before the end of the year, the president issued Executive Order 9412, seizing the nation's railroads and directing the secretary of war "to manage and operate or arrange for the management and operation of the carriers" until a labor agreement could be reached.[150]

Also in December, for the first time in 24 years, the owners' winter baseball meeting was held in New York. The yearly gathering was unusual for another reason. With Judge Landis's consent and participation, the owners and the two league presidents agreed to hold a closed-door meeting with an eight-man African American delegation organized by Sam Lacy and led by three black newspaper publishers at the Roosevelt Hotel on December 3. The group was led by John Herman Henry Sengstacke, president of the Negro Publishers Association and publisher of the *Chicago Defender*. Although Lacy had organized the meeting and had been a voice for integration as far back as the 1930s, Sengstacke, Lacy's former boss at the *Chicago Defender*, barred him from the meeting because the two men had had a serious falling-out that prompted Lacy to quit Chicago and return to Washington. Sengstacke's colleagues were Howard H. Murphy, the association secretary and business manager of the *Afro-American* newspapers, and Dr. C. B. Powell, publisher of the *Amsterdam News*. The publishing group was strengthened by the inclusion of several other black newspaper executives.

But the biggest bat in the lineup was Paul Robeson, former All-American football player at Rutgers University, Columbia Law School graduate, actor, and noted baritone, whom Landis had invited to the meeting. In an impassioned speech, Robeson (at the time starring on Broadway in Shakespeare's *Othello*) used his own experiences in football and on the stage to illustrate that black men could rise above racial prejudice to achieve national acclaim if given the opportunity. In urging the baseball men to give Negro ballplayers the same opportunity on the diamond that he had been given in his own endeavors, he passionately appealed to their patriotism: "We live in times when the world is changing very fast and when you might be able to make a great contribution to not only the advance of our own country, but the whole world, because a thing like this—Negro ballplayers becoming a part of the great national pastime of America—could make a great difference in what peoples all over the world would feel toward us as a country in a time when we need their help."[151]

The baseball magnates greeted Robeson's remarks with polite applause, but his plea for fair play, tolerance, and inclusion in the American pastime was tainted by his well-known leftist, some said communist, sympathies that only hardened the baseball moguls against taking concrete action (which might have been the raison d'être why an avowed segregationist like Landis had received Robeson in the first place). As Snyder notes, "After Robeson spoke, it didn't matter what the three publishers said. [To the baseball men, the black delegation] was just a group of Communist agitators."[152] The publishers ended their presentation by offering a four-point resolution: (1) that immediate steps be taken to accept qualified Negroes into organized baseball, (2) that upward movement within the minor leagues be the same for all players, (3) that the selection process for signing ballplayers at all levels—schools, sandlot, semipro—be the same for Negro players, and (4) that a statement be issued by the meeting declaring Negroes eligible for baseball tryouts and permanent places on the teams.[153] With that, Landis thanked the group, sent the guests off, and immediately turned to the next item on the agenda without any discussion of the resolution.

And because Landis had so ordered it beforehand, neither he nor the owners asked their guests any questions. There was also no immediate public statement issued afterward.

A week later, wrapping himself in the twin flags of American patriotism and anticommunism, Griffith again stated his opposition to African Americans playing in the major leagues when he told a group of black journalists: "The question of the use of colored baseball players in the ranks of organized professional baseball clubs is no different now than it has been for the last fifty years. Why should propagandists [i.e., Robeson, the black press, and the communist tabloids] be bringing it up at this time just when we are in a total war, and when everyone, both colored and white, should be cemented together in the common cause of winning the war?"[154] Sam Lacy quickly tore the cover off that ruse, writing that "the major league club owners are almost fanatical in their dislike for Communism. . . . By this clever little maneuver, Landis told the gullible colored folks, 'This is your chance to put it squarely up to the men who control the purse-strings of the game. I'm with you, now go to it.' But on the other hand, he said to the owners, 'Use your own judgment in this matter, but remember here's a Communist influence [Robeson] along with these people.'"[155]

Just as the year was ending, Brooklyn Dodgers president Branch Rickey, always a visionary, issued a prescient warning to the 16 major-league baseball clubs. Baseball could lose its long-held position as America's favorite sport, he said, if the 75 or so minor leagues that had been crippled or shut down by the loss of players were not back in operation as soon as possible after the war. "In order to preserve our hold as the [nation's] No. 1 sport, we must have it played everywhere," he said, and added, "Baseball must take heed, or football will become our national sport."[156] At the same time, he envisioned that football's "pro season will [last] six months. There will be bigger player limits, bigger salaries, bigger crowds." Interest in college football also would wane, "against the drive of the pros, with their finer skills and more thrills." About the only things Rickey did not foresee for the National Football League were its tax-exempt status,[157] giant Jumbotron TV screens in every pro stadium, a two-week bacchanalia leading up to the Super Bowl championship during which advertisers pay millions of dollars for 30-second TV ads, and a halftime show that rivals a Broadway production. Rickey also had a vision for major-league baseball integration, one that he personally would bring to fruition.

Cecil Travis spent his entire 12-year major-league career with Washington, with the exception of 1942 through most of 1945, when he was in the Army. During the Battle of the Bulge Travis developed frostbite on two toes of his left foot, which shortened his baseball career. Travis retired in 1947 at age 34. His best year was 1941 when he set career highs in batting average (.359), doubles (39), triples (19), home runs (7), RBIs (101), and runs scored (106). He also led all of baseball with 218 hits and 153 singles. Travis has been called the best player not to have been inducted into the Hall of Fame. *National Baseball Hall of Fame and Museum, Cooperstown, NY.*

Infielder George Myatt joined the Nats in 1943 after two seasons with the NY Giants. During his five years with Washington, he played second, short, and third base, often filling in for Buddy Lewis and Cecil Travis while they were in the service. His best all-around season was 1945 when he batted .296, had 145 hits, stole 30 bases, and finished fifth in the MVP balloting. *Courtesy of the Minnesota Twins.*

The Washington Nationals finished second in the American League in 1943 with an excellent starting lineup: (l to r) Ellis Clary, third base; George Case, right field; Stan Spence, center field; Bob Johnson, left field; Mickey Vernon, first base; Jerry

The 1944 Homestead Grays, who won their second consecutive Negro Leagues world series that year, line up at the dugout in Griffith Stadium. Cool Papa Bell (far right), Josh Gibson (fifth from right holding catcher's mitt), and Buck Leonard (to Gibson's left) were the stars. Also in the photo are pitcher/outfielder Dave Hoskins (third from right) and outfielder Jerry Benjamin (second from right). *Courtesy of the Negro Leagues Baseball Museum, Kansas City, MO.*

Walter Johnson was Washington's greatest pitcher and one of the original five players elected to the Hall of Fame in 1936. During his 21-year major-league career, all with Washington (1907–1927), "The Big Train" won 417 games and lost 279. He also managed to collect autographed baseballs (shown here) from six American presidents, Theodore Roosevelt, Taft, Wilson, Harding, Coolidge, and Hoover. Johnson's son donated the collection to Cooperstown in 1968. The signed baseballs were stolen in 1973 and recovered by the FBI in 2001. *Library of Congress*

John Kelly "Buddy" Lewis played infield and outfield for Washington for his entire 11-year career (1935 to 1949), with three years off for military duty. As an Army Air Corps pilot he flew more than 300 missions in the China–Burma–India Theater and won the Distinguished Flying Cross. He did not play in 1948 due to an injury. Lewis had a lifetime batting average of .297 in 1,349 games and played in two All-Star Games, at third base in 1938 and in right field in 1947. *Courtesy of the Minnesota Twins*

Emil John "Dutch" Leonard joined the Washington Nationals in 1938 and pitched for them until 1946. Predominantly a knuckleball pitcher, Leonard's best years were 1939, when he had a record of 20–8 and a 3.54 ERA, and 1945 when his record was 17–7 with a 2.13 ERA. His last appearance on the mound came on September 25, 1953, pitching for the Chicago Cubs when he was 44. *Courtesy of the Minnesota Twins*

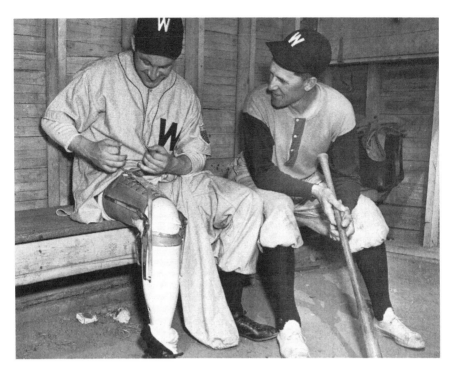

Shot down and captured near Berlin on May 21, 1944, Army Air Corps pilot Bert Shepard's severely wounded right leg was amputated in a German POW camp. After returning home in 1945 at a tryout he impressed Clark Griffith with his abilities on the mound and at the plate and was signed by Washington. Shepard appeared in just one regular season game, pitching five and a third innings in relief on August 4, 1945. He gave up three hits and one run for a career ERA of 1.69. Here he shows manager Ossie Bluege how he straps on his artificial leg. *Library of Congress*

George Washington Case Jr. joined the Washington Nationals in 1937 and played with the team until 1947, with the exception of one season with Cleveland. Case was named to three All-Star teams and was considered the fastest runner in the game during his career, winning five major-league and six American League stolen base titles for a career total of 349 steals. In a wartime charity race Case was narrowly beaten by Jesse Owens, the "world's fastest man." *Courtesy of George Case III*

With Woodrow Wilson occupied with the recent U.S. entry into World War I, then-assistant secretary of the Navy Franklin D. Roosevelt stood in for the president and helped Washington Nationals manager Clark Griffith raise the American flag to open the 1917 season at National Park, later renamed Griffith Stadium. The two formed a friendship there that lasted until President Roosevelt died in office on April 12, 1945. *Courtesy of the Franklin D. Roosevelt Library and Museum, Hyde Park, New York*

Vice President Harry S. Truman became president upon the sudden death of FDR in 1945, a mere six months after the pair won the 1944 presidential election. Within the first four days of his administration, Truman addressed a joint session of Congress and made a nationwide radio address to reassure America, its allies, and the Axis powers that he would prosecute the war as vigorously as FDR had and also to work for world peace when the war ended. *Library of Congress*

Clark Griffith's baseball career spanned nearly 70 years, during which time he was a pitcher, manager, and team owner. His Washington teams played in three World Series, winning just one. Known as the "Old Fox" for his many innovations to the game, Griffith played an important role in the formation of the American League in 1901. As owner–general manager of the Washington franchise he was baseball's unofficial, but important link to the White House during the war as well as a close friend of Presidents Roosevelt and Truman. *Courtesy of the Minnesota Twins*

Joe Kuhel broke into the major leagues with Washington in 1930 and played first base for the Nationals until he was traded to the Chicago White Sox in March of 1938. He returned to Washington in 1944 for a little more than two seasons, before ending his playing career as a member of the 1947 White Sox. As a member of the Nationals Kuhel had career batting average of .288 with 56 home runs and 667 RBIs in 1205 games. He played in all five World Series games in 1933 when Washington lost to the New York Giants, four games to one. *Courtesy of the Minnesota Twins*

Oswald Louis "Ossie" Bluege played his entire 18-year career with Washington, mostly at third base, from 1922 through 1939. He had a career batting average of .272 with 43 home runs and 848 RBIs in 1867 games. Bluege played in one All-Star Game and all three Nationals' World Series appearances in 1924, '25, and '33. A favorite of Clark Griffith's, Bluege managed the Nationals from 1943 to 1947, leading them to second-place finishes in 1943 and 1945. *Courtesy of the Minnesota Twins*

Josh Gibson, known as "the Black Babe Ruth," was a prodigious home run hitter and a Negro League crowd favorite at Griffith Stadium. A catcher, he broke in with the Homestead Grays in 1930 and played with them sporadically until 1946. His career was marred by bouts of alcoholism, possible drug use, and several nervous breakdowns. During the 1943 season, he spent time in a Washington, DC, sanitarium. Gibson died of a stroke on January 20, 1947, at just 35 years of age. He was inducted into the Baseball Hall of Fame by the Negro Leagues Committee in 1972. *National Baseball Hall of Fame and Museum, Cooperstown, NY.*

Walter "Buck" Leonard, who played first base for the Homestead Grays from 1934 through 1950, was a superb line drive hitter. He led the Grays into four consecutive Negro Leagues' world championships, winning two of them. In 15 official seasons, Leonard had a batting average of .320 with 476 hits, 57 home runs, and 352 runs scored. Leonard was elected to the Baseball Hall of Fame by the Negro Leagues Committee in 1972. *National Baseball Hall of Fame and Museum, Cooperstown, NY.*

Each year, just prior to the start of the baseball season, Clark Griffith went to the White House to present his friend Franklin D. Roosevelt with a season's pass to Griffith Stadium. FDR, a lifelong baseball enthusiast, participated in the opening day tradition of throwing out the ceremonial first pitch for the first eight years of his presidency. Once the United States entered World War II in 1941, he was too preoccupied and did not attend another opening day. *Library of Congress*

Clark Griffith and Addie Robertson Griffith, who were married in December 1900, had no children. But when the family of Addie's alcoholic brother, James Robertson, fell on hard times, the Griffiths brought the two oldest Robertson children, Calvin and Thelma, to DC and raised them as their own. Two years after James Robertson died in 1923, the Griffiths brought the rest of his family to live with them. When Clark Griffith died in 1955, Calvin and Thelma inherited the Washington franchise. *Library of Congress*

The legendary Leroy Robert "Satchel" Paige was the biggest drawing card in Negro League baseball history. He led the Kansas City Monarchs to pennants from 1939 to 1942. Paige finally made it to the major leagues when he was signed by Cleveland in 1948 at age 42. Helping the Indians win their first pennant in 28 years and only their second World Series, Paige became the first African American to pitch in the fall classic when he came in to relieve Bob Feller in the fifth game of the series. In 1971, Paige became the first player to be elected to the Baseball Hall of Fame by the Negro Leagues Committee. Paige died in 1982 in Kansas City, MO, one month before his 76th birthday. *Courtesy of the Negro Leagues Baseball Museum, Kansas City, MO.*

Mickey Vernon, shown here in a publicity shot taken at Washington's spring training camp at Tinker Field in Orlando, FL, broke in with Washington in 1939 and was
a Nats stalwart through 1948, with two years off in the service in 1944 and 1945.
After playing for Cleveland in 1949 and part of 1950, he was reacquired by the Nats
and played for Washington until 1955. He ended his career with the Pirates in
1960, having played major-league baseball over four decades. *Courtesy of Charles
Taylor and Jim Vankoski of the Mickey Vernon Sports Museum, Media, PA.*

That Long Shortstop Debate in St. Louis

By beating Detroit in the final game of the 1944 season, the Nats helped their hated rivals, the St. Louis Browns, to their one and only pennant, setting up a World Series played entirely in St. Louis and on the same baseball diamond. The fall classic also featured the two best shortstops in the game, the Browns' Vern Stephens and the Cardinals' Marty Marion, as illustrated by the great sports cartoonist Willard Mullin. *Courtesy of Hal Bock and Michael Powers, attorney for the Willard Mullin estate.*

President Roosevelt on April 14, 1936, launches one of the eight opening day ceremonial first pitches he made during his presidency, a record unlikely ever to be broken. Looking on are Yankees manager Joe McCarthy, Nats skipper Bucky Harris, Clark Griffith, and American League President Will Harridge. FDR's son Elliott and his wife, Ruth Googins Roosevelt, are to the right of the president. *Library of Congress*

CLARK C. GRIFFITH
1869 - 1955

THIS MEMORIAL IS DEDICATED TO THE
MEMORY OF THE LATE CLARK C. GRIFFITH
WHO BROUGHT THE WASHINGTON
SENATORS TO SPRING TRAINING IN
ORLANDO, FLORIDA IN 1936.
HE DEVOTED MORE THAN 65 YEARS
OF HIS LIFE TO BASEBALL.
A DISTINGUISHED MEMBER OF BASEBALL'S
IMMORTAL HALL OF FAME, HE WON
237 GAMES AS A PITCHER; HE HELPED
FOUND THE AMERICAN LEAGUE IN 1900;
WAS PRESIDENT OF THE SENATORS' PENNANT
WINNING TEAMS OF 1924, '25 AND '33. CLARK
GRIFFITH GAVE THE NATIONAL PASTIME GREAT
DIGNITY AND RESPECT...TRULY ONE OF ITS
FINEST BENEFACTORS. THE IMAGE OF
BASEBALL IS EXEMPLIFIED BY THE
IMMORTAL "OLD FOX."

This plaque was affixed to the Clark Griffith monument erected by the city of Orlando inside the front gates of Tinker Field, spring training home of the Washington Nationals from 1936 to 1942, and then again from 1946 to 1960. The plaque was stolen from the monument sometime in early 2014 and as of this writing has not been recovered. *Courtesy of Rob N. Hubler*

4

1944

Meet Me in St. Louie, Bluege

With the war now increasingly turning in the Allies' favor, January was a busy month for Roosevelt and the second session of the 78th Congress. Legislators faced "a plethora of nettlesome issues in this climactic year," according to a preview piece in the *Washington Post*.[1] Those issues included "higher taxes, aid for servicemen and women, the soldier vote, food subsidies, national service legislation, renegotiation of war contracts to siphon back excess profits to the Treasury, provisions for industrial conversion from war to peace production, and poll tax repeal." With the advantage of hindsight from the Great War, America's lawmakers knew they would face the return of millions of young men who would want to resume their interrupted education, marry, buy homes, and start delayed careers. Twenty-five years earlier, veterans returning from the First World War received nothing more than $20 for a bus or train ticket home.

One of the WWI "doughboys" was Harry W. Colmery, a Kansas attorney and a past national commander of the American Legion. When the United States entered World War I, he served stateside as an Army Air Service instructor and pursuit pilot. In 1919, he resumed his law career in Topeka while also serving on the American Legion's national legislative committee, an important lobby that was seeking to change regulations and allow veterans to be treated at VA hospitals for non-service-related illnesses. Recalling his own return to civilian life and carfare home, Colmery moved into the Mayflower Hotel sometime around the middle of 1943, determined to improve the transition for the new wave of veterans.

Working in the hotel for five months, he produced a draft piece of legislation, the Servicemen's Readjustment Act of 1944, commonly known today as the GI Bill of Rights. The historic legislation reached the House on January 10 and the Senate a day later. Both bodies promptly passed their versions of the bill, agreeing on two of three key provisions—government home loans for veterans and funding for their education. But the 14 lawmakers who formed the House–Senate conference committee were unable to agree on the third provision—the cost, duration, and administration of unemployment insurance for the GIs. (The Capitol Hill deadlock continued into late May when a little-known congressman, Georgia Democrat John Gibson, cast the tie-breaking vote after a strange, and perhaps embellished, search to locate him.[2] Having secured a final agreement, which became unanimous when the three dissenting committee members changed their votes from nay to yea, the compromise bill went to the White House for FDR's signature on June 12.) In practice, the deadlock over unemployment insurance proved to be a nonissue because most returning servicemen quickly found work or went back to school; in the end, less than 20 percent of the unemployment funds were distributed.[3]

Still ailing from a flu-like illness that had sent him to bed on New Year's Eve, Roosevelt was scheduled to deliver his State of the Union address on January 11, one day after the lawmakers reconvened. The president also was feeling the ill effects of severe criticism from an unlikely source. Army General George C. Marshall, the nation's top-ranking military officer, had publicly accused Roosevelt of doing little to stem the rash of labor strikes—such as those by the United Mine Workers and the railroad brotherhoods—plaguing the nation. Marshall claimed FDR was "prolonging the war and causing unnecessary loss—in part because knowledge of these American strikes encourages the peoples of Germany and the satellite nations to keep on fighting, beyond a time when the Army had reason to expect a Nazi crackup might come."[4] Strangely enough, Roosevelt agreed with the criticism; in fact, he had used the same argument in private talks with labor leaders at the end of 1943, hoping to promptly end the work stoppages. But when that argument failed, Roosevelt had seized the vital transportation system by executive order at the end of December and ordered the War Department to keep the trains running. Utmost in his mind was to prevent crippling the defense industry's flow of manufacturing materials and products and to maintain the vital movement of troops across the nation. So Roosevelt could not have been too pleased by Marshall's outspoken critique.

FDR was not thinking about the effects of the strikes on baseball when he took control of the railroads, but had the work stoppages continued for any length of time, baseball's moguls might again have faced the prospect of a shortened season, one that perhaps would have limited diamond contests to nearby clubs and maybe one western swing or even no season at all. With the strike settled after the rail workers won a small pay hike, Roosevelt returned the nation's railroads to their rightful owners, and the workers went back on the job. The trains would operate properly once again and so would the baseball season.

In the State of the Union address he sent up to Congress, FDR warned of overconfidence and complacency, calling them "our deadliest enemies." As he noted, "Last spring—after notable victories at Stalingrad and in Tunisia and against the U-boats on the high seas—overconfidence became so pronounced that war production fell off. In two months, June and July, 1943, more than a thousand airplanes that could have been made and should have been made were not made. Those who failed to make them were not on strike. They were merely saying, 'The war's in the bag—so let's relax.'"[5] In looking ahead to the return of peacetime prosperity and security, Roosevelt called on Congress to pass a "second Bill of Rights" that would include: the right to a useful and remunerative job in the industries, shops, farms, or mines of the nation; the right to earn enough to provide adequate food and clothing and recreation; the right of every farmer to raise and sell his products at a return that will give him and his family a decent living; the right of every businessman, large and small, to trade in an atmosphere of freedom from unfair competition and domination by monopolies at home or abroad; and the right of every family to a decent home and health care.

Toward the end of the month, FDR took action to assist another segment of humanity profoundly affected by the war, European Jewry. (Roosevelt and the Allies knew of Hitler's "Final Solution" as early as 1942, when the United States and 10 allied governments condemned

Nazi Germany's "Bestial policy of cold-blooded extermination of the Jews.")[6] Upon hearing charges by Treasury Secretary Henry Morgenthau Jr. that the State Department was obstructing relief efforts, FDR on January 22 announced the creation of a War Refugee Board, consisting of the secretaries of war, state, and Treasury, to join other like-minded groups for the rescue and relief of "all civilian victims of enemy savagery," as his presidential statement put it.[7] "It is the policy of this Government to take all measures within its power to rescue the victims of enemy oppression who are in imminent danger of death and otherwise to afford such victims all possible relief and assistance consistent with the successful prosecution of the war." At the same time, the Democratic National Committee met and unanimously adopted a resolution calling on Roosevelt to run for a fourth term and to continue "as our great world humanitarian leader."[8]

Black baseball and its supporters, including the press, was another segment of the population that felt in need of relief and assistance following the stinging rebuff in December when the delegation of black publishers starring Paul Robeson met with major-league baseball's top echelon and came away empty handed. Anyone who was entertaining thoughts of integration in the 1944 season should "dismiss them from your mind," advised *Washington Afro-American* columnist Harold Jackson, "because, brother, the battle is still ahead and the opposition has shown no weakness, no matter what you may have read."[9] Jackson said Robeson was not the right man to lead the delegation. "We needed someone who is well-versed on the subject of baseball, colored ball players, and with ideas to offer the non-receptive audience that woud [sic] make them feel that they, too, could be sure of double benefit [as published] by making such a drastic change in their baseball world," the column explained. Although Jackson would not name that person, he described his candidate as "the fellow who I am told gained the audience for the group [and] should have been there." That person was his colleague Sam Lacy, who had been barred from the meeting. Jackson naively believed that the well-known barriers to integration could be overcome, including how to house black players on the road. "This, I feel can be worked out," he wrote without saying how, "and the idea that no harmony can exist on these ball clubs because of the many Southerners on the rosters is another joke because they can be educated, too."

At the same time, Lacy took the black owners to task for barring the press and for the secrecy that surrounded the annual meeting of the Negro National Baseball League at Harlem's Theresa Hotel. As Lacy wrote from New York, "Aside from an estimate by Mrs. Effa Manley, [owner] of the Newark Eagles, that colored baseball did $500,000 worth of business in its biggest season last year, reporters were stalemated as to what else went on behind the closed doors of the conference."[10] Lacy no doubt was particularly irked because the league "refrained from discussing the campaign for inclusion of qualified colored players in major league baseball."[11]

For Clark Griffith and his Washington Nationals, the early months of 1944 were a time of optimism based on the club's outstanding and profitable second-place finish in 1943. Just after the New Year's holiday, the club's few stockholders met. To no one's surprise, they reelected Griffith as president for the 24th consecutive year. Likewise, Edward B. Eynon, who had joined Griffith in 1920, was reelected to begin his 24th year as secretary treasurer. And George Richardson, who two years earlier had succeeded his late brother William Richardson, was retained as the club's vice president. Also kept on was Nats trainer Mike Martin, who had been with Griffith ever since Griffith managed the old New York Highlanders starting in 1903, and ticket manager John Morrissey, who also had two decades of service to the organization. Manager Ossie Bluege was likewise retained. He first became a Nats employee in 1921 when Griffith bought him from the minor-league Peoria ball club and sent him to Double A Minneapolis before becoming a Nats' fixture at third base.[12]

With the business functions completed, management was eager for the season to start. However, Griffith knew that on paper at least the Nationals of 1944 were not as good as the team that had done so well the preceding season. For one, soon after the World Series, first-base stalwart Mickey Vernon was inducted into the Navy and promptly joined the wartime baseball powerhouse at the Norfolk Naval Air Station. From there, Vernon shipped out to the Pacific theater and didn't return to the Nationals until 1946. Also lost for the new campaign was catcher Jake Early, infielder Jerry Priddy, and pitcher Ray Scarborough. In addition, Early Wynn was now expecting to be called up.

With America's participation in the war now in its third full year and the threat of Nazi submarines reaching U.S. shores virtually eliminated, government restrictions on night baseball in coastal cities were eased, and baseball under the lights was encouraged to provide entertainment, especially to workers in defense industries. As a result, the Brooklyn Dodgers and New York Giants received permission to each play 14 home night games.[13] At the same time, several thorny issues sprang to the fore just as spring training loomed. One was the question of whether ballplayers working in defense-industry jobs "should remain in their industrial jobs and retain their 2-B classifications, or return to the diamond and take their chances with the draft," as the *Sporting News* posed it in an editorial. "It is a decision that cannot be delayed any longer, and which may prove to be the most momentous of their careers." Acknowledging that "nobody can supply the answers but [the affected players] themselves," the editorial also recalled "the criticism that was heaped upon the young men who took the easy way out and flocked to shipyards and other bomb proof jobs" during the First World War. "Among them were some prominent athletes who, for years afterwards, found themselves the target of barbs directed at them for their wartime course. It was an embittering experience, causing them to regret they had not been better counseled."[14]

A second issue involved an internal dispute among the owners over whether the clubs could use players who were working in defense industries in a part-time role. That controversy arose when the perennial second-division St. Louis Browns and Philadelphia Athletics announced at the start of spring training that they intended to use some players who were defense workers with 2-B classifications and other players with draft deferments in home games on weekends and holidays. (Among those who balked at the plan was Yankees President Ed Barrow; his Dodgers counterpart, iconoclast Branch Rickey, defended the idea.) For the Browns at least, the idea had merit. They entered the 1944 season with the oldest and most 4-F–laden team in the American League—13 players and catcher Frank Mancuso, who had already been honorably discharged.[15] (Regardless what the other clubs thought, St. Louis went ahead with its plan. As a result, pitcher Denny Galehouse won nine games for the Browns in 1944 while working weekdays at a Goodyear aircraft plant in Akron, Ohio. Another part-timer was outfielder Chet Laabs, who had worked at a Dodge factory in Detroit making jeeps for the Army before getting a transfer to a St. Louis plant so he also could play for the Browns on weekends and holidays.)[16]

The third issue—and one that had arisen every year since 1942 and probably should have been moot by now—was whether baseball should even be played as long as the war continued, especially now with so many major-league players in the service and the quality of the game diluted by less-talented replacements. Paul McNutt, head of the War Manpower Commission, relit the spark of that controversy when he publicly expressed doubt about baseball's place during wartime. When a reporter asked Yankees President Ed Barrow whether he'd heard about McNutt saying baseball wasn't essential, Barrow replied, "Whoever said it was?"[17]

Even famed sportswriter Grantland Rice, writing about the upcoming season in the *Washington Evening Star*, had his doubts about the sport's immediate future. "Whatever happens to baseball through 1944," he wrote, "you can write it down in advance as the game's greatest all-around gamble since Abner Doubleday had his fantastic dream."[18] Rice was referring to the question of how the military draft, "now working busily and effectively day by day," would change the game as the season progressed because "no one can possibly tell what will happen from week to week or from month to month." Nevertheless, Rice came down in favor of the game. "It may seem to be a rather futile matter and a minor argument to bring in baseball at such a vital point in this Nation's history, but the fact remains that millions still are following what is left of baseball, including a large per cent of the 11,000,000 Americans now in Army or Navy service. Only pay a visit to any camp or talk with the returning wounded."

Rice may have been prompted to defend the sport after seeing a widely reported story by columnist Corporal Bill McElwain in the Mediterranean issue of the military newspaper *Stars and Stripes* and picked up by the *Washington Post*. "We think we speak for most GIs when we say that the average serviceman, at home or overseas, would feel rather let down if the big leagues shut up shop," McElwain wrote.[19] "Baseball still has a strong hold on Americans and when they can't see it, they like to talk about it. This goes for the soldier, the sailor, the Marine—the civilian. Suppose the teams do have to use old men and youngsters to keep going? It won't wreck the game." McElwain ended, however, with a stern warning to the athletes. "The boys on this side of the pond aren't over-enthused by any form of strikes, no matter how important they may be to the men involved. And for a baseball player who isn't exactly a key production figure to moan over his salary comes as a bit of a pain. There isn't a major leaguer playing who makes as little as the average serviceman," McElain wrote. "Keep baseball alive, but don't put up with any fancy holdouts. A lot of guys in other uniforms won't like it."

The one issue that the owners did not broach, and that would not go away, was the growing demand by members of the black press for integration. Among the leaders was a rejuvenated Sam Lacy, who had left his onerous position at the *Chicago Defender* and by 1944 was again writing for the Baltimore-based *Afro-American* newspapers, a chain that included Washington, Philadelphia, and Newark and whose flagship Maryland newspaper was exceeded in circulation only by that of the *Pittsburgh Courier*.[20] Lacy again found Clark Griffith's position that integration would destroy the Negro Leagues an easy target to condemn, especially because of the large African American population in the nation's capital who would support integration wholeheartedly, especially if the Nats were to be in the forefront of signing black players.

In a series of open letters addressed to fellow journalist Art Carter, who was then a war correspondent attached to the 99th Fighter Squadron, part of the now famous Tuskegee Airmen, whose exploits in aerial combat matched or exceeded those of the white aviators, Lacy continued his written salvos against Griffith[21] and his propensity for signing Latin ballplayers. In one typical column published on March 4, Lacy told Carter, "Just threw a rock at Clark Griffith for his latest trick of scouring Cuban bush leagues to make up his quota of 'ball players' for the coming season." Then, in the next sentence—one that was tinged with a bit of racism—Lacy added that Griffith "had [Latin scout] Joe Cambria wash the mud out of the ears of a lot of unknowns and guide their hands across the dotted line of Washington Senator contracts so that he wouldn't have to face the dilemma of using colored players or no players at all."[22] Lacy remained unrelenting throughout the season, especially when the Nats failed to win many games. Weighed against other more widespread issues, baseball integration took a backseat to racial integration in society again in general. For example, when the Supreme Court ruled in early April that Negroes could not be barred from voting in Democratic primaries in Texas, Southern legislators, fearing the ruling could destroy state sovereignty, insisted that the Deep South would not open its polls to Negroes.

Again away from their customary Tinker Field in Orlando, the Nationals began to gather in mid-March for their second spring-training camp at the University of Maryland. Among those to arrive early was newly reacquired catcher Rick Ferrell as well as pitchers Dutch Leonard, Mickey Haefner (the only left-hander in the starting rotation), Johnny Niggeling, Roger Wolff, and Bill LeFebvre, all knuckleball hurlers, a rarity in the history of the sport; also in camp was Early Wynn, who had stayed in good shape over the winter because of his expected call-up to the service. A snowstorm the night before the official opening of camp on March 19 delayed the arrival of some players, including outfielders Case and Spence, and put a layer of snow on the field and a damper on the usual first-day reunions and gabfests.

Then, after a few warm, summerlike days, March turned unseasonably rainy and cold, particularly for the dozen or so Latin players that Griffith brought into camp from tropical Cuba, Puerto Rico, Venezuela, and Mexico. Several successive days of cold forced the team to practice indoors in the Ritchie Coliseum field house, which limited workouts to infield tosses, bunting practice, calisthenics, and pitching sessions, all of them boring, especially to the veterans. The indoor sessions could not replace the Florida sun and the long, sweaty workouts that helped the players get their timing down as well as their weight after a winter of working in factories and shops, on farms, and even in mines and graveyards. Everyone waited for a break in the weather to get outdoors onto the college diamond and experience actual batting practice against live pitching. Now in his second year as manager, Ossie Bluege devised a plan that called for his starters to throw against his planned starting lineup with the reserves hitting against the bullpen pitchers. But that was no substitute for practice on the diamond. He predicted that if the bad weather continued, "there isn't going to be any good baseball in the league until mid-May." The constant inclement weather got to Clark Griffith, too, who promised a return to Florida the first spring after the war ended. "You bet we're going South just as soon as the travel restrictions are lifted," he said. "The idea that a team can be trained in the North is absurd. It won't work. I thought it could be done, but now I'm a convert to Southern training."[23]

With former backstop Jake Early in the service, Griffith in February had reacquired Rick Ferrell,[24] a Nats backstop from 1937 to mid-1941, after a two-and-a-half-year stint with the St. Louis Browns. Griffith needed Ferrell's expertise in catching the always-erratic knuckleball, which Ferrell said "was the toughest job in baseball."[25] Not only was it impossible to know just how and when the ball would break, but base runners were always trying to steal on the slow pitch because "you had to wait until the last break of the ball before you could start to make your throw to second, Ferrell explained." (He mastered the task well enough, using just a standard catcher's mitt years before catcher and later manager and Hall of Fame inductee Paul Richards introduced the oversized glove to improve catching the knuckler.)

Now with five practitioners of that art in camp, Ferrell had his work cut out for him from day one. Griffith sent catcher Angelo "Tony" Giuliani and cash to the Browns for Ferrell. But soon after training camp opened, Landis threatened to void the trade when Giuliani, rather than report to St. Louis, chose to retire from baseball and remain at his defense job because of back problems. So the Old Fox reluctantly sent outfielder Gene Moore to the Browns to keep the deal from collapsing. Griffith claimed that "the Browns put the squeeze on us by demanding Moore" and admitted he offered a pitcher and "a lot of cash but they insisted on Moore. We couldn't give up Ferrell, so I had to let Moore go, even though it weakened our own outfield."[26] (Moore played the final two years of his 14-year major-league career with the Browns, retiring at age 36 following the 1945 season.)

One of the early highlights of the training camp was the impressive work behind the plate of backup catcher Mike Guerra, who also impressed Bluege with his bat and his speed on the base paths. Like many players of that era, the Cuban native had paid his dues, spending seven years in the minor leagues with Nationals' affiliates in Greenville, South Carolina; Springfield, Massachusetts; Trenton, New Jersey; Charlotte, North Carolina; and Chattanooga, Tennessee. He also played for minor-league clubs in Salisbury, Maryland; York, Pennsylvania; and Albany, New York. "With Ferrell and Guerra on the club, I'm not worried a bit about my pitching staff," Bluege was able to say thanks to Griffith's swift action in dealing Moore.[27]

The Nats began play with six-inning intrasquad games on Saturday, March 25, and then expanded to nine-inning contests the following Wednesday. On a gloomy April Fools' Day, before a sparse crowd of 700 with rain threatening all afternoon, the Nationals played their first exhibition game at Maryland's Byrd Stadium, beating the Martin

Bombers, 7–2, the defense-plant team from Baltimore. Over the next few days, despite continuing rain that shortened several of the games, the Nationals played in-state contests against teams from the Army, Navy, Coast Guard, and the minor-league Baltimore Orioles. The Nats finally traveled across the Maryland state line to Wilmington, Delaware, where they played their first game against a major-league team, losing, 5–4, to the Philadelphia Phillies. Griffith, Bluege, and the Nats must have issued a sigh of relief when, with the war going well in the Pacific and with the Red Army advancing against Nazi positions in Eastern Europe, Selective Service Director Hershey in early April told local draft boards they could stop drafting men over age 30, especially those with children. On the opening-day roster, 8 of the 23 Nats qualified for the new exemption: pitchers Alex Carrasquel, 30; Mickey Haefner, 31; Leonard, 34; Niggeling, 39; and Wolff, 30; as well as catcher Ferrell, 38; first baseman Joe Kuhel, 37; and outfielder Jake Powell, 33. Hershey's order provided the roster stability the team needed, at least for the moment.

On March 2, the champion Homestead Grays held their annual pre-season banquet at an Elks Lodge in Washington. Perhaps because the Negro Leagues had enjoyed such a profitable season in 1943, league executives, like their white counterparts, did not want to do anything to rock the baseball boat. So they gave the 100 or so banquet guests, including the press, the go-slow sign on pushing integration despite the latest rebuff still ringing in their ears—the icy silence that greeted Paul Robeson and the black press delegation when it met with the major-league owners and Landis in December. Although Robeson's soaring oratory had attracted some national press attention and reenergized the advocates of swift integration, the black owners were more immediately concerned about a threat from south of the border, which they interpreted as a harbinger of things to come if baseball integrated.

The culprit was money—dollars and pesos—in the form of player contracts. Top Mexican teams were competing for the services of the best players in the Negro Leagues, and they were paying above-market salaries to import the talent. Catcher Roy Campanella and shortstop Tommy Butts had played in Mexico the previous baseball season, and "both had been made flattering offers to return this year."[28] A *Washington Afro-American* preview for an exhibition game to be played between the Grays and the Newark Eagles at Griffith Stadium on Sunday,

April 23, acknowledged the inherent threat to black baseball. "What with the major leagues promising an inferior brand of baseball during the coming campaign, the Negro National League teams appear to be on the road to one of their best seasons. While flattering Mexican offers have cut inroads into the colored game, owners and fans alike are pleased at the prospect of a brilliant season." The Negro Leagues fought back. In April while training in Hot Springs, Arkansas, the Baltimore Elite Giants re-signed both Campanella and Butts. In addition, Willie Wells and Ray Dandridge, "two men whom the Mexican League wanted badly,"[29] were back in Newark Eagles uniforms for the year.

Now with the major-league season opener just a few days away, Griffith stopped by the White House on April 15 to make his traditional presentation of a season pass to FDR. The fact that Roosevelt was away on a brief vacation did not deter the Old Fox nor did the fact that FDR had not been to an opening day at Griffith Stadium since 1941. Griffith was certainly happy, however, to hear from White House aide Steve Early that "the President is pleased to see baseball continuing."[30]

Opening day at Griffith Stadium arrived on a cloudy and cool Tuesday, April 18. Vice President Henry Wallace again threw out the ceremonial first pitch before 27,000 hometown fans and a large contingent of prominent legislators. *Post* columnist Shirley Povich humorously wrote the next day: "Griffith Stadium is one place where the Democrats have a clear majority. If they were smart, they'd make the next vote here instead of in the Halls of Congress. Democratic Senators O'Mahoney, Truman [who almost one year later to the day would be in the White House], Lucas, McKellar, Gillette, Barkley, Jackson, Thomas and Meade [*sic*] outnumber Republicans Shipstead, Nye, Taft, Vandenberg and White who are also at the game."[31] Structuring his column in short, tweet-like bursts of sentences decades before the word was used for anything other than describing noise from a bird, Povich reported the festivities as the action was unfolding. Wallace's toss from the front-row presidential box, Povich wrote, was "the longest White House pitch in history, and it looks as if Wallace is out to get Roosevelt's regular job." The ball flew halfway across the diamond to where the players had gathered to try to catch it. The ball was caught by Alex Carrasquel, just the man Wallace had promised to throw it to when the Venezuelan had visited the vice president on Capitol Hill the previous week.[32]

When the festivities ended, the Nationals disappointed their 27,000 fans by losing to the Athletics, 3–2, in 12 innings, wasting Niggeling's excellent six-hitter over 11 innings before reliever Milo Candini gave up the winning run in the top of the 12th. The Nats blanked the A's, 5–0, to win the second game on April 20 for Wynn's first win of the season, a complete-game shutout. The inclement weather that kept the second-day's crowd down to a mere 1,500 followed the team to New York, where, after a rainout on Friday, Mayor Fiorello La Guardia did the honors of throwing out the first ball on Saturday, April 22, opening the home season at Yankee Stadium. But "the Little Flower" (English translation of Fiorello) did not stay to see the world champions win, 6–3. The Nats then returned to Washington for a five-game home stand during which they split two games with the Red Sox and lost two of three games to the Yankees, both losses coming in the season's first Sunday doubleheader, 2–1 and 3–2. The Nats ended April with three wins and five losses, in a two-way tie for fourth place, five games behind the league-leading Browns, who sprang from the gate with a 10–2 start. Although few baseball fans, especially those in St. Louis, would have believed it then, the early season standings were an omen.

In the May Day opener in Boston, the Nats beat the Red Sox, 11–4, collecting 20 hits, including second baseman George Myatt's six hits in six consecutive at-bats, a hitting feat not done in six years. The following day, the Nats evened their season record at 5–5 by again beating Boston, 5–2, for Niggeling's first win of the season and 15th of his career against the Red Sox. Coincidently, while the Red Sox were losing the game, former Red Sox outfielder Ted Williams was receiving his wings as a second lieutenant in the Marine Corps Reserves at Pensacola, Florida. (As his mother's sole source of income, Williams initially received a hardship classification of 3-A, but that was changed to 1-A when the United States entered the war. He enlisted in the Navy on May 22, 1942. Williams became a flight instructor at Bronson Field in Pensacola, where he also played baseball for the Bronson Bombers, who not surprisingly won the Training Command championship that year.) Boston won the final game of the three-game set at Fenway, 11–10, when 38-year-old Sox player-manager Joe Cronin wrote himself into the starting lineup at first base and drove in the tying run in the sixth inning and homered in the eighth to put the Sox ahead for good. The Nats then headed south by train, stopping in New Jersey to play an exhibition game at Fort Dix before going on to Philadelphia. Wynn, however, continued straight on to Washington to check on his draft status before rejoining the team in Philadelphia, where the Nats won three of four games at Shibe Park.

With the Nationals in Philadelphia, the Homestead Grays opened their championship defense on May 7 with a Sunday doubleheader at Griffith Stadium against the New York Black Yankees. The *Washington Afro-American* predicted "an inferior brand of baseball during the coming [major leagues'] campaign [while] the Negro National League teams appear to be on the road to one of their best seasons."[33] A crowd of 15,000 was on hand to see the Grays sweep, 5–4 and 7–3. Unlike opening day for the Nats and Griffith, who enjoyed staging pregame festivities and reveled being in the spotlight with presidents and dignitaries, Grays owners Cum Posey and Rufus "Sunnyman" Jackson, for reasons unknown, opted "to do away with the moss-covered practice of beseeching some big muckety-muck to do the highly unnecessary job of tossing out the first ball," wrote Lacy, clearly in favor of their decision.[34]

The owners, who lived in Homestead, Pennsylvania, instructed their three DC representatives not to invite any well-known politicians, judges, or other local big shots to perform the task. "Get a guy everybody knows," they instructed the trio, someone "who comes out to the ball game occasionally during the summer months and doesn't wait for the next season to begin before he remembers there is any such a thing as colored baseball." The "honor" went to John T. Rhines, a well-liked DC undertaker "who has long been considered a friend of athletes from the high schools to the professional ranks."[35] However, in their quest to find precisely the right person, the three organizers forgot to arrange for a marching band, and so there was no music. "As a consequence," Lacy concluded, "the march to the flagpole was done in the cadence to the paddle-footed marching of Candy Jim Taylor, Gray[s] manager." Lacy's column was so critical of all traditional opening-day ceremonies, black or white—including the presidential ceremonial toss and even the playing of the national anthem—that not a few readers might have taken his comments as a mean-spirited riposte to the Grays owners and their committee for not selecting him to do the honors.

Returning to Griffith Stadium, the Nationals played their initial night game of the season on Wednesday, May 10, by beating the Browns, 5–1, without the services of George Case, who was out indefinitely after dislocating a shoulder while pulling on his overcoat after the Sunday doubleheader in Philadelphia. It was the first of about 45 games under the lights for Washington, including those that began as "twi-nighters" in the late afternoon. Again in 1944, no team would play more night games than the Nationals. Recalling those contests years later, Povich said, "Night baseball in Washington was big business during the war, although it was widely believed that once the war was over the game would revert to its normal day schedule."[36] In fact, when the Nationals completed the home stand on Sunday, May 21, by dropping a doubleheader to Detroit for a mediocre season record of 15–14, they nevertheless led the major leagues in home attendance with 229,821, about half of that figure coming from so-called owl games.[37] The Grays also benefitted from the lights at Griffith Stadium. When the Grays hosted the Philadelphia Stars on May 25 in their inaugural night game at Griffith Stadium, they had four, and possibly five, more games sched-uled under the lights before the Fourth of July, "the nocturnal sport having proved so popular hereabouts last year," the *Washington Afro-American* commented.[38]

The numbers, current and projected, certainly pleased Griffith, who had journeyed to Pittsburgh on May 20 for an owners meeting to plan for the upcoming All-Star Game to be hosted by the Pirates. He promptly returned to Washington on May 23, to appear as the guest of honor at the weekly Tuesday luncheon at the Touchdown Club. The club had recently nominated him for enshrinement in the Baseball Hall of Fame, an honor that "has gained nation wide [sic] impetus recently," according to the *Washington Post*.[39]

On Monday, May 22, the Nationals and their press entourage boarded a train packed with service personnel for their first western road trip, a counterclockwise loop of Cleveland, Detroit, St. Louis, Chi-cago, and Philadelphia. A long-standing rule that the Nationals and the other clubs maintained was that if the team had a game on the first day following a long train ride, the scheduled starting pitcher automatically got a lower berth in the Pullman cars. But during the war, like the other teams, the Nats were forced to take a backseat—or no seat at all—to the many traveling servicemen. Rick Ferrell said he and his teammates would be lucky if they got even an upper berth in the sleeping cars. One time traveling the 300 miles or so from St. Louis to Chicago, Ferrell years later recalled, "We never got a seat and had to stand in the aisle or sit on our suitcases. There was discomfort, sure, but they [the servicemen] had priority."[40]

After numerous stops along the way, the Nats arrived in Cleveland on Tuesday, an offday, before Wednesday's opener against the Indians in vast Municipal Stadium. In winning the first three of the four-game set against the Indians, including Cleveland's first night game of the season, the star was George Case, who'd returned to the lineup with a vengeance. He stole two bases in three games, and his single with two out in the top of the 13th inning off pitcher Allie Reynolds gave Washington the go-ahead runs needed to win the Friday night contest, 5–3. In completing the extra-inning contest, Wynn set down the Indians in order in the home half of the 13th inning, to secure a complete-game win. Before the game, the Indians honored their star pitcher Mel Harder for his recently won 200th game and for his 17 years with the club. Harder received a $1,000 war bond, an extraordinarily generous gift for the time.

From Cleveland, the Nationals went to Detroit via the overnight ferry across Lake Erie, not often a smooth crossing but a pleasant break from the congested rail travel. The Nats lost two of three games in the Motor City and ended the month by extending their losing streak to five games while in St. Louis, where Washington dropped both ends of the Memorial Day doubleheader, 6–4 and 4–2, on Tuesday.[41] They also lost the following day, 4–3, in 11 innings, before winning the finale of the four-game set, 11–5, on June 1. The win evened the Nats' season record at 20 and 20. Browns fans, accustomed to their team dwelling at or near the bottom of the American League, were in shock by the rarity of the Browns' sudden surge into first place, a half game ahead of the Yankees. And although the 15,488[42] St. Louis fans who witnessed the four-game series was the highest attendance at Sportsman's Park in recent years, the average attendance for the three days of play was only 5,163, an indication of just how few fans the Browns had been drawing until then. By comparison, the Grays and Elites drew 8,000 fans for a Mother's Day doubleheader in Baltimore on May 14.[43]

Despite winning the final game in St. Louis, the Nats' slide continued into June, when they lost all four contests against the White Sox to fall into a last-place tie with Cleveland, five and a half games off the lead. Their futility was most evident during the Sunday, June 4, doubleheader loss to Chicago. In the opener, behind starter Johnny Niggeling who went eight innings before giving way to reliever Roger Wolff, the Nats battled into the 10th inning when Rick Ferrell dropped the ball at the plate as the White Sox pushed across the winning run, to end it at 6–5. In the nightcap, Mickey Haefner gave up 10 hits, but it was poor defense that did the Nats in. Spence and Case let a ball drop between them in the sixth inning for a double as the Sox put up three runs. One inning later, George Myatt let a ball scoot between his legs, and the next two batters got hits, leading to four more runs, giving Chicago's Eddie Lopat an easy 9–1 win.

While the team was en route to Philadelphia and expecting a change of luck, the U.S. Fifth Army, moving northward from Sicily, took control of Rome on June 4. Even better news came on Wednesday, June 7, with the first reports that Allied forces had landed on the beaches of Normandy, France, the day before, June 6, in Operation Overlord, now universally known as D-Day. Eisenhower had been named Supreme Allied Commander the previous December, and in a radio address to the U.S., British, and Canadian troops, he told them, "You will bring about the destruction of the German war machine, the elimination of Nazi tyranny over the oppressed peoples of Europe, and security for ourselves in a free world. Your task will not be an easy one. Your enemy is well trained, well equipped, and battle-hardened. He will fight savagely. . . . The free men of the world are marching together to victory. I have full confidence in your courage, devotion to duty, and skill in battle. We will accept nothing less than full victory."[44] Over the next several days and despite heavy losses, the troops continued to press inland and toward Paris. The success of the invasion was aided by the Nazi High Command's obstinate refusal to bring up reserve Panzer divisions, believing that the Allies would also attack at Pas de Calais because it was the closest point to Britain across the English Channel.

Beginning their final series of the long 19-game road trip in Philadelphia at always-accommodating Shibe Park on June 8, the Nats won the first two games before again losing a Sunday doubleheader, this time by scores of 6–1 and 6–5. Their first western swing ended with seven wins and 12 losses for a record of 22–26, leaving the Nats alone in last place. Manager Ossie Bluege perhaps could have used Ike's words of encouragement as he tried to rally the Nationals out of their torpor, exemplified by poor outfield play, a lack of hitting, and injuries: Joe Kuhel was manning first base with pain from torn rib muscles; George

Case, his shoulder better now, was running on two injured knees; second baseman George Myatt had a fractured finger but continued to play; and Jake Powell had a sprained ankle. Griffith, aching for help, had been pressing former third baseman Harlond Clift to leave his ranch in Yakima, Washington, and return to the Nats. Although Clift had a 3-A classification as an agricultural worker, he had refused to report to spring training because he thought that by doing so he might jeopardize his exemption. Griffith, aware of Clift's position, nevertheless continued to pursue him.

After being on the road since May 22, the Nats won the first two games of a four-game set against the Yankees on June 12 and 13 to run New York's losing streak to seven games and move Washington into sixth place. On the following day, June 14, which was designated "New Yorkers Night" at the ballpark, the Nats lost, 6–2, before a contingent of legislators from the Empire State. Washington won the next two games, 3–2 and 4–0, against the Yankees and Red Sox, respectively, and advanced into a three-way tie for fourth place with Chicago and New York, four and a half games behind the still surprising St. Louis Browns.[45] With Spence and Ferrell sidelined with stomach pains, the Saturday "Ladies Night" resulted in an easy 11–4 win for the Red Sox. On a sweltering Sunday, Washington and Boston split a doubleheader with Wynn, shutting out Boston in the nightcap, 1–0, after the Nats dropped the opener, 9–6. Now in fifth place, the Nats caught the Pennsylvania Railroad at Union Station for a return to New York, where Washington lost three of four. When the June 19 game against the Yankees was rained out, a frustrated Bluege recapped the recent Boston series for the press. "We won two games on pitching alone. Otherwise we got the daylights beaten out of us. We're still not hitting with men on base," he said.[46]

In an attempt to improve the team's weak hitting, Griffith had sent backup third baseman Luis Suarez to his Chattanooga farm club after Suarez played in only one game, and he called up Joe Vosmik from Minneapolis. The 34-year-old outfielder with a .300 career batting average had played a dozen years in the majors with Cleveland, St. Louis, Boston, and Brooklyn. In addition, his military service was behind him. Although he was in fine shape when he arrived in New York to join the Nats for the Boston series, like Lefty Gomez before him, Vosmik's best years as a ballplayer were also behind him. However, in desperation,

Bluege promptly named Vosmik as his regular right fielder, saying, "He has been meeting the ball solidly and moving the [opposing] outfielders back even when he has not hit safely."[47]

Vosmik replaced Roberto Ortiz, a capable right fielder who had the strongest arm on the team but was reluctant to make the longer throws to second and third because he feared throwing wild. Povich was being kind when he assessed Ortiz as having "speed on the bases and in the outfield, but is shaky on both fly balls and ground balls."[48] Vosmik promptly got hits against Boston in the first two games he played, including a long double that drove in two runs on June 17, making Griffith and Bluege look particularly astute. After winning the June 23 opener in Boston, 7–1, with Wynn again getting another victory and taking the first game of a split doubleheader, 5–4, on June 25 after a rainout the previous day, the Nats record was still below .500 at 30–33. Nevertheless, a suddenly optimistic Bluege summed up the team's play by saying, "We have our faults but look at the other clubs. They're suffering too, but not in as good a spot to improve. One hot man in our batting order, and most of our troubles would be over."[49] But those troubles were big ones—Case was in a deep slump, Powell wasn't doing the job in the outfield, and Ortiz, a good hitter, was now riding the bench. Only the pitching was holding up with Candini's two recent stellar outings and Wynn having won three of his last four starts.

The Nats' mediocre play and rash of injuries prompted Negro League historian Brad Snyder to suggest that, had Griffith been more amenable to integration, he might have solved some of his on-field problems by signing several Homestead Grays, a team loaded with excellent players whom the Old Fox knew well from watching them play at Griffith Stadium when the Nats were on the road. Why didn't Griffith add players like Jerry Benjamin, a speedy outfielder, or James "Cool Papa" Bell, an outfielder with exceptional speed and base-running skills,[50] or ace pitcher and outfielder Ray Brown? Snyder asked, asserting that "Benjamin, Bell, or Brown—not to mention Gibson and Leonard—could have helped the Senators out of the American League cellar."[51]

In a frank assessment years later, Bell remembered Gibson as "a good catcher, but not outstanding. He didn't have good hands."[52] But at the plate instead of behind it, he was "one of the greatest hitters you ever saw," Bell added. "The most powerful. Never swung hard at the ball either. Just a short swing. Never swung all the way around." The blatantly obvious snubs to integration prompted Lacy and other black sportswriters to continue their jihad against baseball's—and in particular the Nats'—discriminatory practices.

But, in fairness to Griffith, Gibson was an emotional train wreck. The previous year he'd again battled alcoholism and was beset by psychiatric problems that landed him in a couple of mental hospitals. Toward the end of May, according to the *Washington Afro-American*, Gibson again got into hot water with management over his inability to obey team rules. For several weeks, he had been breaking training, and "shortly after leaving Washington following the opening day doubleheader, [he] was given what was supposed to be his 'final' admonition." When Gibson again disregarded the warning, he was ruled unfit to play in an exhibition game in New Jersey on May 20. Although the precise nature of Gibson's condition was not reported, he was known to suffer from alcoholism and drug use, two problems that no doubt contributed to his erratic behavior on and off the field. The ban was almost immediately rescinded so Gibson could play in a doubleheader against the Newark Eagles on May 21 because "management felt an obligation to the large number of fans who had made the trip to Ebbets Field from Newark."[53] This was another instance when Negro League management altered its own already-weak rules in favor of a bigger payday. Today, the Grays management would be labeled "an enabler" by not sticking to its punishment of their star catcher, but at the time, Gibson was truly a terrific gate attraction who also was needed in the lineup.

In a lengthy article praising Gibson's abilities, *Afro-American* sports editor Art Carter wrote that "he hits more homers than any player in baseball annually, and has hit for distances unequalled by the great Babe Ruth and Jimmy [*sic*] Foxx of the big league majors." When Carter's column was published on July 24, in the middle of the 1943 season, Gibson had already hit seven home runs "into the faraway left and centerfield bleachers at massive Griffith Stadium. He is the uncrowned Home Run King of Baseball."[54] (Gibson has been credited by some historians—but without conclusive proof because of the sporadic press coverage of Negro League baseball—with once hitting a home run clear out of Yankee Stadium, a feat never performed by any major-league player in the 85-year history of the original ballpark.)

If Griffith didn't pay much attention to the Grays' baseball talents, he surely took note of their pugilistic abilities when the Grays got into a donnybrook with the Black Barons during a Sunday doubleheader at Griffith Stadium on June 11.[55] In this particular incident, both benches were cleared in the seventh and scheduled last inning of the nightcap (due to Sunday restrictions) after Buck Leonard tripled in the tying run and the Black Barons chose to walk Gibson intentionally. According to the *Washington Afro-American* write-up of the incident, when a frustrated Gibson lunged wildly at a pitch, he may have stepped across home plate to reach the ball, an automatic out according to the rules. Barons manager Winfield Welch demanded that umpire Eggie Greenfield call Gibson out, which Greenfield refused to do. Birmingham first baseman Slats Davis then ran in and pushed Greenfield in the face. When Grays outfielder Jerry Benjamin tried to calm Davis, Davis took a swing at him, which led to the bench-clearing fracas that was finally quelled by the police. No one was hurt or ejected, and the Grays went on to win the game in the eighth, or "extra," inning on a base hit by Cool Papa Bell.

Although there always have been on-field brawls between teams in every league from the majors down to the lowliest of the minor leagues, such incidents by Negro League players, however, only reinforced the racist views about blacks that were prevalent during the era and added to the white owners' perception that African American players were too rough and undisciplined to play with whites. Worse still was the image of the Negro Leagues as undisciplined and devoid of proper regulation, as exemplified by Gibson's quick return to the diamond after a ban that amounted only to a one-day suspension.

Another example was the so-called war that broke out at the end of June when the Negro National League pitted itself against Chicago sports promoter Abe Saperstein and the Negro American League. Saperstein (who gained fame and fortune as the founder, owner, and longtime "coach" of the Harlem Globetrotters basketball team) was a part owner of the Birmingham Black Barons and the official booking agent of the Cincinnati Clowns, both NAL clubs (something of a conflict of interest in itself). Cum Posey, in his capacity as NNL executive secretary, and the other NNL owners had banned Saperstein from any promotional activities because he was "guilty of defying the ruling of organized colored baseball by demanding in excess of 40 per cent of the gross receipts as his (promoter's) share for games put on by him."[56] As an example, Posey said, Saperstein offers each club in a game in Indianapolis 25 percent of the gate. "This leaves him 50 per cent to take care of park expenses, cost of baseballs, umpires and publicity." But of the "individual clubs in Indianapolis, Columbus, Ohio, and other cities now under the wing of Saperstein, none ever received less than 30 per cent from the parks." In addition, Posey charged, games under their own promotion "drew better crowds and larger receipts than now, despite the current boom" in black baseball popularity. After condemning Saperstein's practices, the NNL voted to send its president, Tom Wilson, and Posey to the various ballparks where Saperstein was doing the bookings and advise the owners of what Saperstein was doing. In addition, the NNL owners sent a letter to the president of the Negro American League, J. B. Martin, condemning the NAL teams for continuing to play against the St. Louis Stars, a team that was under suspension for having joined the NNL in 1943 only to quit later that spring to barnstorm with an all-star team led by Dizzy Dean. "Martin was also told [that] the NNL club owners expect all players of the St. Louis Stars, now playing with teams in the NAL, to be returned to the Eastern loop without delay." (The Stars disbanded after the tour with Dean.)[57]

While at Fenway Park for the June 23–25 three-game set, the Nats learned that Elmer Gedeon, a Washington rookie in 1939, had been listed as missing in action. As a 22-year-old Nats outfielder, Gedeon appeared in five games that September, getting three hits and scoring one run. In the service, he had earned a promotion to captain in the Air Corps and was cited for heroism after rescuing a downed pilot from a burning plane. (It was later learned that the three-sport star at the University of Michigan actually had died on April 20, when his bomber was shot down over Saint Pol, France.)[58] The Cleveland native was the only Washington ballplayer to die in combat and just one of two former major leaguers to be killed in the war. (The other was Harry O'Neill, who caught one game for the Philadelphia Athletics, also in 1939, and died a Marine first lieutenant on Iwo Jima on March 6, 1945.)[59]

Washington opened a long home stand on June 28 by winning two of three games against the Tigers to end the month with a record of 32–34, good for fifth place, six games off the lead. They then promptly lost two of three to the visiting Indians and also again lost George Case, who fell on his shoulder lunging for a fly ball hit by third baseman Ken Keltner in the opening game of the Sunday doubleheader. As Case rolled in pain, Keltner scored on an inside-the-park home run. The injury was especially painful to the fleet-footed Nats outfielder because it would keep Case out of action for at least two weeks, ending his chances to play in the upcoming All-Star Game, after Bluege had named him to the squad only the day before. The Nats lost the game, 4–3, when player-manager Lou Boudreau doubled in the 10th inning, and after an intentional walk, Keltner singled, scoring Boudreau with the winning run. Washington also lost the nightcap, 6–3.

Sunday and holiday doubleheaders were a regular feature on every team's schedule during the war and throughout the postwar era of the 154-game season, often drawing some of the largest crowds of the year. So when the Nationals split their Fourth of July twinbill with the Chicago White Sox—winning game one, 2–0, before losing the second game, 3–2 in 12 innings, for Wynn's second successive loss, it marked the 13th time that season that Washington had failed to sweep a doubleheader. The only good news for the Nats was Griffith's announcement that Harlond Clift—after failing to answer several of the Old Fox's follow-up pleas—was about to fly to Washington and join the team. The Nats won the next three games, two against the White Sox and the opening game against the still-first-place St. Louis Browns, 7–0, on July 7, War Relief Night, to even their record at 37–37, good for fourth place, five games behind the first-place Browns.

To assist in the fund-raising effort, everyone at Griffith Stadium that Friday evening paid their way in. In addition to the 17,983 fans, all reporters, ushers, concessionaires, even the players, coaches, and management had to buy a ticket. So all in all, paid attendance topped 20,000, and more than $17,000 was earmarked for the wartime charities. Pregame activities featured popular "skill contests" among the players, including a 50-yard dash between Nationals' number-two catcher Mike Guerra and the Browns' backup backstop, Frank Mancuso. Guerra won a $100 war bond for his victory. Other events included tossing baseballs from home plate into the mouth of an open barrel facing them on second base and a fun race in which seven players from each team placed their spikes in a pile at home plate. Then they had to run from second base to home, find their own pair, lace them up, and then run back to second.

The main highlight of the festivities was the appearance of Walter Johnson, Washington's greatest pitcher and one of the original five men elected to the Baseball Hall of Fame at Cooperstown, New York, in 1936. Now almost 57 years old, the former Nationals' manager from 1929 to 1932 tossed a few balls to Muddy Ruel, his battery mate on their World Series championship team of 1924.[60] The crowd also gave a rousing hero's welcome to Charles "Commando" Kelly, a Pittsburgh native who that spring had become the war's first enlisted recipient of the Medal of Honor. Kelly, dubbed a one-man army for his heroics in the European theater, was part of a service team of about three dozen GIs who toured the country spurring war-bond sales under the rubric "Here's Your Infantry."

Clift finally made it to Washington on Sunday, July 9, as the Nats were splitting a doubleheader against the Browns, with Wynn absorbing his third-straight loss, a 10 0 laugher, before the Nats took the night-cap, 4–0, the final two games before the All-Star break. Clift had been due several days earlier, but as he explained to Griffith and Bluege, he was bumped off his flight in Billings, Montana, by servicemen who had priority and then had trouble getting train reservations to Washington.

Taking advantage of the All-Star Game in Pittsburgh in July 11, the owners held a three-hour session there with Commissioner Landis and approved a plan that would allow those clubs with illuminated ballparks to play as many night games as they wished, except of course on Sundays. Up to that point in the season, only the Nationals were playing their weekday games under the lights (many of them as "twi-nighters") and would continue to do so. The only proviso in the new plan was that the visiting team had to agree to the time change, a condition columnist Shirley Povich called "laughable" because the visiting club's share of the gate was "so much greater at night, eight times greater in St. Louis for example." Povich went on to predict, correctly, that "night ball won't go out after the war. The work-a-day public has already made known its preference for the night games."[61]

Although Bluege had selected Case for the AL All-Star squad, three other Nats—Dutch Leonard, Rick Ferrell, and Stan Spence—were also tapped for the honor. But only Spence got into the game, which was won by the National League, 7–1, the most lopsided of the 12 midsummer classics played to date and only the fourth win by the senior circuit. Upon resuming play on July 14, the Nationals promptly won three of five games against the Athletics, including their first doubleheader sweep, 8–4 and 4–3, on Sunday, July 16, the 16th twinbill they'd played that season. Washington was now in fourth place, five and a half games behind the Browns, but with a mediocre 41–41 record. Sadly, that was to be the team's high-water mark; the Nats would not reach .500 for the rest of the season.

The Nats' fine showing in the All-Star Game and their first double-header sweep were greatly diminished, however, by unsettling news that had reached Griffith just after the All-Star Game and put the team in a new precarious position. The Selective Service System informed Griffith that four of his Cuban citizens—Mike Guerra, Roberto Ortiz, Gilberto "Gil" Torres, and 21-year-old rookie shortstop Preston Go-mez—had to register for the draft within 10 days or return to Cuba. The Cubans had been playing under a rule that exempted them from the draft for six months following receipt of their State Department nonresident visa certificates, which meant they could remain in the country until November, well after the season ended. But the Selective Service System—still under the leadership of Griffith's sometimes lunch companion, General Lewis Hershey—had changed that rule; the six-month pass was no longer in force, and they were now considered resident aliens and subject to military call-up. (The new ruling was curious. The draft agency had exempted men who'd reached the age of 30 because the war was seen as being on track for an Allied victory within a year, but almost at the same time, it extended its reach to aliens in the United States whose numbers and availability to serve could not come close to replacing the men over 30.)

Guerra and Ortiz immediately began packing. Torres told the press, "I may decide to register and stick it out in this country" (he was hitting .272 at the time), but Torres's wife and young son were already on their way back to Cuba, as were Guerra's wife and two-year-old daughter.[62] The backup catcher was torn between options. "My wife wants me to return to Cuba," Guerra said, "but I am undecided. I do not like to give up my baseball career in this country. It took me 11 years of playing American baseball to get into the big leagues, and I do not want to quit now."[63] Torres, too, faced a hard choice. He would consider returning to Cuba after the season but only if he didn't have to then join the Cuban army. "I could not live on the $11 a month they pay the Cuban soldiers," Torres said. Besides, he was hitting .270, followed closely by

Guerra's .269. The loss of Torres, Guerra, and Ortiz would have further weakened the Nats' already modest offense. In the end, the four parted company with their teammates and prepared to leave for Cuba, and the Nats departed for Detroit, the beginning of a western road trip that would seal the Nats' fate for the year.

After losing all four games against the Tigers in Detroit, Washington won the opener in Cleveland, 9–6. The Nats then proceeded to drop the following three games against the Indians that put them on a skid of 11 straight losses in Cleveland, Chicago, and St. Louis, including a Sunday doubleheader at Sportsman's Park that attracted 12,170 fans, the largest crowd of the season and also the largest to see a Browns–Nationals game in 22 years. On Monday, July 31, now with only 5,831 Browns' fans in attendance, the Nationals lost, 3–2, burying themselves in the cellar with a record of 42–55.

Desperate to strengthen the outfield and the team's hitting, at the end of the month, Bluege orchestrated the purchase of Tom Hafey, an outfielder who'd appeared in 70 games with the New York Giants in 1939 before disappearing into the maw of the minor leagues. Hafey, who was resurrected by the Browns in 1944, was to go to the Nats for the waiver price of $7,500. Hafey, 31, had appeared in just eight games for the Browns but had an outstanding batting average of .357. Griffith liked the deal because (1) the price was right, and (2) he saw good bloodlines in Hafey, who was the cousin of 1931 National League batting champion Chick Hafey, who played with the Reds and the Cardinals from 1924 to 1937. (Chick Hafey was elected to the Hall of Fame by the Veterans Committee in 1971.) But Tom Hafey, who had preferred to stay on the job at a California shipyard rather than report to the Toledo Mud Hens minor-league club in 1943, now opted to retire rather than report to the Nats. After all, he was with the first-place Browns and was heading for the last-place Nats. Hafey's final appearance on the field came as a pinch hitter in the first game of the Sunday, July 30, doubleheader against the Nats and won by the Browns, 2–1. (The cash-hungry Browns tried unsuccessfully to collect the $7,500 waiver price for Tom Hafey, further exacerbating the off-field feud between the two clubs that began when, after Griffith paid the Browns $35,000 for Harlond Clift in 1943, Clift arrived in Washington with a bad shoulder.)[64] About the only good thing to happen while the Nats were collapsing on the road was the change of heart by the self-exiled

Cubans. Torres wired Griffith that he was returning and would promptly register with the draft. Ortiz and Guerra also signaled their intention
to return and sign up also. Infielder Preston Gomez also returned and
appeared in just eight games for the Nats in 1944. He played his final
game on August 12.

Torres met the Nats in St. Louis after a wartime travel odyssey. He
caught a flight in Havana that landed in Miami on Monday, July 24.
After he was twice bumped off flights to Washington, he opted to go by
train to DC and then fly to St. Louis. When the train reached Fort
Lauderdale, he received word by telegraph to return to Miami because
there was a seat waiting for him on another flight. Minutes before
takeoff, he was bumped again. After finally reaching Washington by
plane, his flight to St. Louis was grounded for three hours in Pittsburgh
for an undisclosed Army priority. Torres reached the Nats' dressing
room minutes before the scheduled start of the game, but he had plenty
of time to catch up with his teammates because the game was rained
out by a hurricane-like downpour.

The Nats' disastrous road trip culminated with three loses in five
games at Boston to complete the 21-game trip with a grand total of just
three victories. Washington was in free fall not just because it was losing
games faster than the German army was losing ground in France; going
into the final two months of the season, many of the players were in
poor shape. An unproductive Ed Butka was gone, sent to the minor-
league team in Buffalo, New York, when the Nats were in Cleveland;
new arrival Harlond Clift, after finally completing his cross-country
journey from the rainy Northwest, was exhibiting a good deal of rust on
the diamond; without Guerra to spell him, Rick Ferrell was just about
out of gas from too many games behind the plate, although backup
catcher Al Evans was back after receiving a discharge from the Navy;
Case was in a terrible hitting slump; and coach George Uhle's chroni-
cally ill back had become so bad that, to end the suffering—on the field
and off—he retired.

So desperate were the Nats for help that they literally searched
through the garbage. While in Detroit, Griffith sought to entice Ed
Boland to join the team. The 36-year-old former Philadelphia Phillies
utility outfielder and pinch hitter was now a full-time employee of the
New York City Sanitation Department. But Boland said thanks but no
thanks, fearing that, if he left even temporarily, he would jeopardize his

municipal pension. Griffith would not be deterred, and he always knew just whom to turn to for help, from the president of the United States on down. In this case, Griffith enlisted the aid of City Hall. New York Mayor La Guardia arranged for the Sanitation Department to grant Boland a one-month leave to join the Nationals. Soon after, however, sanitation officials—perhaps eyeing the American League standings—decided the Nationals needed Boland more than New York City's streets did, and they extended his leave of absence to September 1.

Meanwhile, the Negro Leagues' champion Homestead Grays were faring well in their title defense. Between April 18 and July 15, the halfway mark in the season, the Grays played 69 games, winning 55, losing 12, and tying 2. Only 21 of those games counted in the official standings, of which the Grays won 17 and lost just 4, "with no other co-member club anywhere close," the *Washington Afro-American* trumpeted.[65] At Griffith Stadium, the Grays were almost unbeatable. Of the 20 games played there, the hometown club was 18–2. "This record accounts for the extraordinary popularity of the club in the park where all Sunday games are played," the newspaper also noted. Kicking off the second half of the season, the Grays split a Sunday doubleheader against the Newark Eagles on July 23 with 7,200 fans looking on.

With the war now on course for victory perhaps as early as next year, the baseball bosses, white and black, could breathe a little easier about the future of their game. Some, like the venerable Connie Mack, even began to make optimistic predictions. In an article written for the *Philadelphia Inquirer* and reported in other journals, Mack played Janus and looked back and ahead, and what he saw in the future especially was to his liking. When he first led Pittsburgh in 1894, he recalled that the players of that era were rough, tough, and uncouth and "were not welcome in first or second class hotels. Third class hostelries received us only when we promised not to eat with other guests." Now, though, as "players have progressed in sociability just so has baseball advanced in speed, cleverness and appeal," and "as a group today's players are faster, smarter and more skillful," he said, adding, "I am speaking of baseball before the war." Then came a little crystal-ball gazing. He predicted that postwar attendance would soar. "[Even] now baseball is making millions of new friends, young friends and women friends. . . . Night games have done much to popularize baseball. . . . Whether night games will be increased after the war I don't know," he admitted, stating his belief that no team should play more than 14 home night games. Though, in the end, of course, he added, "I believe baseball will give the fans what they want."[66]

What black baseball fans wanted at the moment was to see the annual East–West game at Chicago's Comiskey Park. Like white critics of the All-Star Game who decried the dominance of the New York Yankees, black critics were equally adamant about the lopsided representation of the Homestead Grays. Harold Jackson, writing about the six-member Grays' roster on the 1943 East club, said the game "represents the Homestead Grays (the greatest colored team in baseball) against the Western stars."[67] But this year, the pregame focus was not on the Grays' representation (five players, still a dominating number). Rather, it was on the threatened no-show of the game's brightest star, Satchel Paige, and his accompanying threat.

Paige was adamant that there would be no East–West game unless the proceeds went to the war charities. To force the issue, he claimed he would lead 16 players in a walkout protest if the promoters did not comply with his demand. Criticizing the black owners as greedy and shortsighted, Paige said, "I'd like to play in this twelfth game, since I've played in all but three. Last year's game took in 51,777 fans at $1.50 per head, which is real money. And those big boys know it. It should go to those fightin' lads, but some greedy folks want to line their pockets." The president of the Negro American League, Dr. J. B. Martin, however, revealed another aspect of Paige's vocal patriotism. According to Martin, Paige did make the war-fund proposal. "But only after he had been refused a sizable cut off the top for himself."

Although Martin would not say just how much Paige wanted in order to appear, the NAL president admitted that "the crack pitcher received 10 per cent of the gate whenever he plays in games for the Kansas City Monarchs during the regular season." Cum Posey, who was also in on the negotiations as NNL executive secretary, added, "Satchel is a little late with his patriotism. We promoted a game similar to the East–West classic in Cleveland in 1942. At that time, players, club owners and all the participants donated their services to the extent that the armed forces benefited by $8,000. It would have been more had not Satchel refused to play for nothing."[68] Also implicated in the story was Abe Saperstein, who allegedly took Paige to the *Chicago Daily News* to break the story, which was carried by four other local dailies before the

Afro-American reported it. Martin, Posey, and other black officials accused Saperstein of meddling in the affair as retaliation for their refusal to allow him to handle the publicity for the game.

In the end, the West beat the East, 7–4, without Paige's services. "The huge turnout, aproximately [*sic*] 50,000 in all, braved sun and heat and inadequate transportation facilities in order to view the affair; and in so doing proved to Satchel Paige, beyond the shadow of a doubt, that he is no more to them than another baseball player," Jackson wrote.[69] Gibson, who caught the entire game, contributed a run scored and two hits, one of them an eighth-inning leadoff double that struck the public address amplifiers 440 feet away in centerfield.

The Nats returned to Griffith Stadium to begin a 20-game home stand against Detroit on August 9. Their record of 44–59 put them 17½ games behind St. Louis, which at the same time was running off 10 consecutive wins, including the four that Washington had contributed. *Evening Star* sportswriter John B. Keller summed up the disastrous road trip by proclaiming that after 18 losses in 21 games Washington's pennant prospects were gone. "The Nats now are as bad a ball club as their record for the dismal western swing and the final invasion of Boston indicates," he wrote. He specifically cited the team's inability to turn a double play and the "woefully inadequate" hitting by the Nats' bench with the exception of Bill LeFebvre, a pinch hitter when not on the mound, and "Eddie Boland, the vacationing New York City employee,"[70] who had hit safely in 10 of 11 games since being called up. (Boland did prove to be something of a bargain and a help during his brief stay. He appeared in 19 games, hit .271, and made his 16 hits count by driving in an outstanding 14 runs.

Boland's last major-league appearance came on August 14, in a win against Cleveland when he unsuccessfully pinch-hit for starter Roger Wolff. All in all, Griffith couldn't have been too displeased with the sanitation worker. He'd only paid Boland $4,200 for his services.)[71] Although the team batting average was among the league leaders, most of the Nats' hits were puny, Keller wrote. "They have outhit five of their rivals, but outscored only three of them over the season."[72] A porous defense was also hampering the Nats' on-field efforts.

Washington began its home stand by losing all four games to the Tigers and falling to 44–63, 20½ games off the pace. Somehow they managed to rebound and take three straight from Cleveland before losing another four in a row, the Indians' season finale at Griffith Stadium and the first three of four to Chicago, during which span the Nats managed to score just three runs. They equaled that run production in the finale, beating the White Sox, 3–2.

Another black cloud came when Early Wynn received his induction notice, telling him he had three weeks to report to the service. Wynn probably was not too unhappy to change uniforms because on August 13 his record stood at 7 wins against 17 losses. (It was hardly a harbinger of a career that would end in 1963 when Wynn was 43 and had amassed exactly 300 victories, worthy of election to the Hall of Fame in 1972. He died in 1999 at age 79.)

Despite his losing record at the time, Wynn was always a shrewd, confident hurler who rarely gave up many runs and kept the team competitive in games even when they failed to score for him. Wynn was also confident of his quick return to the diamond because the U.S. 4th Infantry Division and the French 2nd Armored Division were massed outside Paris ready to retake the French capital. Wynn's going away gift to his teammates before leaving for the Army was an easy 12–1 rout of the Browns and their star pitcher Jack Kramer on Sunday, August 20, the nightcap of only the third doubleheader sweep by Washington that season. Wynn was inducted into the Army at Fort Myer, Virginia, just across the Potomac River from DC, and after basic training was sent to the Philippines. There he played baseball on the Base 30 Manila Dodgers, which had such a large and potent pitching staff that Wynn, a good hitter, often played shortstop.[73]

The three home victories against the Browns were particularly sweet for Griffith and his minions. The Nats not only slowed the Browns' pennant chase, but also they gave Washington some revenge against the despised rival. In visiting Sportsman's Park, the Nats were routinely subjected to an unending barrage of the vilest of racial slurs aimed at the Nats' dark-skinned Cuban contingent.[74] At the time, St. Louis was as notoriously segregated and bigoted as any town in the Deep South. As St. Louis native Bill Mead recalled, "At Sportsman's Park in St. Louis, blacks sat in the right-field pavilion, a distant vantage point from which they viewed the game through a screen that stretched from the outfield wall to the roof above."[75] The taunting and verbal assaults came to a head on Sunday, July 30, when a fight broke out between the two teams. The brawl ended quickly, but it only further stoked the bitter rivalry—particularly acidic for Washington in last place looking up at first-place St. Louis.

Fists flew again during the Nats' August 22 home-game blanking of the Browns, 3–0. According to Shirley Povich's account,[76] the Browns were already in a foul mood, having lost five of the past seven games to the A's and the Nats, the two clubs at the bottom of the AL standings. To further incite the Browns, it was the Nats' Cubans who ruined the Browns in their doubleheader loss to Washington, 4–2 and 12–1 on Sunday, August 20, while the second-place Red Sox were sweeping their doubleheader. Ortiz and Torres both went two for four in game one, with Torres driving in one run. In the nightcap, Ortiz went three for three, including a double and an RBI. Torres went three for four, including a triple and an RBI, and Guerra's two hits included a triple and three RBIs.[77]

So in the series finale on August 22, when Washington got five straight hits off Nelson Potter, the Browns pitcher was angered because three of the hits came on bunts. The lid blew off in the seventh inning when Nats second baseman Fred Vaughn led off with a bunt single and was sacrificed to second by another bunt. Potter made his feelings known, ridiculing the Nats for relying on bunting because they couldn't hit his screwball. Later, when he and George Case met along the first-base line as Potter was fielding Case's foul bunt, more words were exchanged, and Case, who'd been called "a nasty name" by Potter,[78] got in the first punch, on Potter's chin. Teammates separated the two but not before Ed Butka charged out of the dugout and slugged infielder Don Gutteridge. Case, Potter, and Butka were ejected. But that was far from the end of the teams' personal war. Povich criticized St. Louis manager Luke Sewell and the team for not playing smart baseball. "The Yankees, when they were holding longer leads than the 4½–game margins the Browns boast, never aroused the opposition to a fighting pitch. They were always content to let sleeping dogs lie, metaphorically speaking. The Yanks tried to be nice to everybody when they were on top."[79] No one could say that of the Browns' treatment of the Nats and their Cubans.

The Allies ended the Nazi occupation of Paris on August 25, with little resistance from the Germans. Indeed, Nazi garrison commander General Dietrich von Choltitz signed a formal surrender that afternoon, after defying Hitler's orders to blow up landmarks and burn the City of

Light. A day later, General Charles de Gaulle's Free French forces marched down the Champs Elysees. On August 29, de Gaulle's army joined the U.S. 28th Infantry Division in a second historic celebratory march down the famed boulevard. The Allied victory in Paris buoyed spirits on both sides of the Atlantic but did nothing to raise the Nationals' level of play. They remained league patsy, dropping three of four games to the Yankees, who were now 3½ games behind the Browns with the Tigers four games back. After the Nats lost two of three games in Philadelphia, they went on to New York, where between August 31 and September 3, the Yankees won five of the six games, including a sweep in two doubleheaders. At the end of August, with a record of 53–75, the Nationals were so deep in the cellar that they headed into the final month of the season 18½ games behind league-leading St. Louis. Splitting a Labor Day doubleheader at home against Boston and then taking three of four games from Philadelphia, the Nats failed to gain any ground or move out of the cellar.

In the nation's capital, the final month of the baseball season went mostly unnoticed to all but the few remaining die-hard Nats fans as the big news was the Allies' important victories in both the European and Pacific theaters. On September 2, Allied forces entered Belgium, liberating most of the country within seven days. By mid-month, the U.S. 1st Army had taken its first steps into Germany, crossing the Siegfried line, and was less than 30 miles from the outskirts of Cologne. In the South Pacific, U.S. naval forces began a strategic assault to retake the Philippines, which were providing Japan with sea lanes to import petroleum. Liberating the Philippines of course was a special priority of General MacArthur, who some two and a half years earlier had been forced to leave the U.S. protectorate, famously vowing, "I shall return." From September to early October 1944, the U.S. 3rd Fleet under Admiral William F. "Bull" Halsey carried out a series of successful missions, destroying 500 enemy aircraft and 180 seagoing merchant ships during the island campaigns on Palau and Morotai.[80]

On September 9, President Roosevelt quietly slipped out of the White House at 10:10 p.m. and headed for his special train awaiting him at the railroad yards near the Bureau of Engraving and Printing. From there, he headed north for the Canadian border to meet Churchill again. Having learned earlier that Churchill was bringing his wife, Clementine, to Quebec, Roosevelt cabled the prime minister: "Perfectly delighted that Clemmie will be with you. Eleanor will go with me."[81] FDR was accompanied by his personal physician and other government officials including Admiral William D. Leahy and Treasury Secretary Henry Morgenthau Jr., author of a draconian plan to strip postwar Germany of its heavy industry. The controversial plan was supposed to be secret, but when it found its way into the press, it angered FDR, became fodder for Germany's propaganda machine, and was a convenient campaign cudgel for Republican presidential candidate Thomas E. Dewey to use against FDR. The president and the British prime minister opened their Second Quebec Conference at the Citadel castle on September 11, within days of the Nazis launching their first V-2 rocket attacks on London and Antwerp.[82] The 11-day conference was the 11th such meeting between the wartime allies since 1941. So confident were they of an approaching defeat of Hitler—despite the last-gasp V-2 attacks—that their attention was focused mainly on postwar control of Germany and the war in the Pacific.

While the two leaders were planning a victorious conclusion to World War II, Griffith, Bluege, and the Nationals were wrapping up a disastrous baseball season. They played their final home game on September 17, beating Boston, 7–6, on the only Sunday when they did not play a doubleheader. The game virtually eliminated the Red Sox from the pennant race and allowed the Nats to board an early train for their final western road trip that would begin in St. Louis, where the now-slumping Browns had ceded first place to the Tigers by a half game. Griffith viewed the 13 games on the road as one last chance to overtake seventh-place Chicago, and he urged Bluege to try to win as many as possible at all costs.

After a long train ride, the Nationals checked into the King's Highway Hotel in St. Louis on Monday, September 18. There, they promptly found themselves in the midst of a local brouhaha that was causing a good deal of angst among the long-suffering Browns fans. On his NBC radio program the previous Friday, popular sportscaster Bill Stern had predicted "a national baseball scandal" involving the Browns would appear in the next day's edition of an obscure magazine called *Collyer's Eye and the Baseball World*.[83] (The Chicago publication, originally a horse-racing tip sheet, reportedly was the first magazine to reveal the infamous 1919 World Series scandal that left eight White Sox players banned from the game for life.) Stern told his listeners that the magazine was going to claim that the Browns were slumping at the behest of unnamed league officials. Although not stated in so many words, the alleged goal of these anonymous officials was for either New York or Detroit to overtake the Browns and win the American League pennant because a World Series in either Yankee Stadium, capacity 70,000, or Briggs Stadium, capacity 58,000,[84] would perhaps more than double World Series revenue than if the series were held in tiny Sportsman's Park, capacity 33,000. The story, Stern said, "may produce the 'greatest scandal in baseball' since the World Series of 1919."[85]

Browns officials called the story "ridiculous," according to the *Sporting News*, which concluded, "The best answer [to the story] seemed to come in the fact that the very day the article appeared in print, the Browns regained first place." In fact, the story was almost immediately killed by Stern himself in a locally broadcast mea culpa on New York radio on September 18 and again on his NBC nationally broadcast show four days later (quite appropriately too as the Browns promptly won three of four games against the White Sox). Accordingly, Stern told his listeners, "Last Friday night, I stated that a story was appearing the following day which threw doubt upon the integrity of the St. Louis Browns. I would like it very clearly understood that I was quoting from a story and in no wise [sic] inferred that I believed the story to be true. The story shocked me so that I immediately began a careful investigation and have been able to find, to the best of my ability, that there is absolutely no basis for such an accusation. In fact, all evidence proves exactly the opposite. The St. Louis Browns are doing their utmost to win the American League pennant, as are all the other teams in the very close American League race. I cannot state too strongly my feeling that baseball is run in a thoroughly honest and dignified manner." (Some might say that Stern's expression of shock would place Bill, not Howard, first among the pioneers of shock radio.)

The Nats opened their final visit of the year to Sportsman's Park with a 6–0 win on September 19, all of the runs coming in the top of the 11th inning. The bad blood between the clubs spilled out when Nats reliever Roger Wolff hit shortstop Vern Stephens with a pitch. Browns manager Luke Sewell "had to be restrained by the umpires from mixing with the hurler. Luke, as if to emphasize his anger, waved a bat, as you or I would a toothpick," wrote Red Smith in a *Sporting News* story that epitomized the great sportswriter's wit and way with words.[86] Smith recounted how "the Senators and Browns have been exchanging compliments all summer, using language distinguished more for candor than for tact." He then cited an incident during Nats' batting practice on September 21 at Sportsman's Park when Browns backup catcher Tom Turner unleashed a wicked racial assault aimed at reserve catcher Mike Guerra and outfielder Roberto Ortiz.

"Turner sat on the bench and sought to calm his nerves by playing a word game," Smith wrote. "This consisted of digging interesting words with a Biblical flavor out of his vocabulary and flinging them at the Senators." Ortiz, the much bigger of the two targets of the assault, stepped in literally to pinch-hit. Smith described Ortiz as a "student of Pan-American diplomacy," who armed himself with one of George Case's bats (perhaps because hitters have always been very protective about their own lumber), strode over to the Browns' dugout, "and spoke briefly for the defense." Accepting Turner's dare to "discard the shilla-lah, they could do the rest of their talking with their hands." Ortiz dropped the bat and the two squared off in a makeshift ring created by Turner's teammates who were eager to see the Cuban beaten. Ortiz broke a thumb in the melee, and Turner suffered a bloody nose. "Unnoticed in the confusion was the fact that the Browns' [fiery Ellis] Clary set a new American League record by speaking before punching. It was the first time in his career this forthright character ever did that," Smith noted.

When tempers cooled some and Bluege met Sewell at home plate to exchange batting lineups, the Nats skipper shook his fist and warned Sewell to "lay off my Cubans or you and I are going to fight."[87] Bluege yelled, "Any manager who would sit on the bench and let his ball players call another team the kind of names they called us tonight is as contemptible as his players. Luke, you and I are finished." The Nats skipper accused Sewell of encouraging the abuse from the very start of the season and especially of egging on Turner, a bench player, to pick a fight with Ortiz, usually a starter, Sewell's goal being to get them both thrown out of the game before it began, and thus give the Browns an advantage. The two managers then almost came to blows and had to be separated by umpire Ed Rommel. In an era when racial and religious slurs and vicious taunts were part and parcel of the game, Turner's vitriol (coupled with a season of similar abuse) must have been particularly offensive to provoke "the most explosive moment of [Bluege's] 24-

year career in the majors." Bluege returned to the Nats dugout where he told his players, "If these guys want to fight, we'll fight 'em. But if any of us get thrown out of the game, make sure we take a couple of the Browns out with us."[88] Perhaps the worst outcome of the brawl was the hostility it engendered between the two managers who had been room-mates and close friends when they played together on Washington's last pennant-winning team in 1933. The rift was irreparable, and a long-standing friendship ended.

Now, in their final series of the season, the Browns won the second game, 5–2, and the finale, 9–4. Moving eastward, Washington dropped three games in Chicago and two of three in Cleveland. The Nationals fell to 62–88, 24 games off the pace and any chance of rising from the cellar long gone. About the only thing left that could bring the Nats any kind of satisfaction, and a bit of revenge, was to play spoilers in the Browns–Tigers race for a ticket to the World Series. And there wasn't a National who didn't know which team he wanted to win.

From Cleveland, the Nats headed across Lake Erie for the final four games of the season in Detroit, where a scenario right out of a Damon Runyon short story awaited them. Following a rainout on Thursday, the Nationals and Tigers—with Detroit now leading the league by one game over the Browns—split their Friday doubleheader. Washington lost the first game, 5–2, but came back to win the nightcap, 9–2. At the same time, St. Louis was sweeping a doubleheader from visiting New York, 4–1 and 1–0, eliminating the Yankees from the pennant race. On Saturday, the Tigers beat the Nats again, 7–3, behind ace pitcher Hal Newhouser, who won his 29th game of the season, and the Browns again beat the Yankees, 2–0. With the Browns and Tigers now tied atop the American League at 88–65, the entire season came down to Sun-day's finales in St. Louis and Detroit. It was the first time since 1908 that the American League pennant would be decided on the final day— or perhaps not. What transpired that Sunday, even before the games began, was indeed a tale of two cities—the best of times for one munici-pality and the worst of endings for the other.

In St. Louis, the Browns prepared for the game by moving into the Melbourne Hotel the night before to get some undisturbed rest. Their hopes for the pennant rested on the announced starter, Sigmund "Sig" Jakucki, whose record was an acceptable 12–9 with an earned run aver-age of 3.67.[89] But he was the least reliable hurler on the club because, like many players of that era, Jakucki's right arm was more reliable hoisting a bottle than throwing a baseball. And for this—the most crucial game in the Browns' 51-year history—Jakucki definitely needed liquid courage, despite the pleading by fellow pitcher Jack Kramer. "This could mean the pennant to us. Can't you, one night, lay off the stuff and come in shape. Because we really need you," Kramer begged Jakucki, according to teammate and fellow pitcher Denny Galehouse's account. But late that evening, Browns coach Zack Taylor encountered Jakucki in the hotel lobby bringing in a whiskey bottle in a big paper bag. Taylor confronted the pitcher and made him promise not to drink that night, and Jakucki solemnly promised that he would not. But the next day at the ballpark prior to the game, trainer Bob Bauman could see that Jakucki had been drinking and Bauman confronted him. Jakucki's excuse: "I told [Taylor] I wouldn't take a drink last night but I didn't promise I wouldn't take one this morning."[90]

Meanwhile, in his room at the Book-Cadillac Hotel in Detroit, Dutch Leonard got a morning "wake-up" call of sorts. Detroit in those days was known as a gamblers' haven, as personified by Damon Runyon's character Nathan Detroit. The unknown caller asked Leonard if he was pitching that afternoon. As Leonard later recounted for the press, when he confirmed that he indeed was starting that day, the caller said, "Good. You have a chance to make a lot of money," and then added, "I'm authorized to offer you better than $20,000 if you don't have a good day."[91] The amount was a veritable fortune in those days, more by far than the top salary on the club. As soon as Leonard realized what the caller meant, he told him to go to hell and hung up. But the call left Leonard frightened. Recalling the event 32 years later, Leonard (who won 191 ball games in his 20-year career), told author William B. Mead, "I'll tell you the truth, I was scared. I was just a small-town boy and I didn't know what to do. But George Case was my buddy, and on the way to the ball park I told him about the call. He said, 'Dutch, somebody might have heard that conversation. You'd better tell somebody about it, Ossie or someone.'" Reaching the ballpark, Leonard promptly told coach Clyde Milan. "He went over and told Ossie, then came back with a new ball, handed it to me, and said, 'You're still the pitcher.'"[92]

Because he reported the call promptly and Bluege in turn promptly notified league officials, no action was taken against Leonard. But had he agreed to throw the game in favor of the Tigers, the Nationals would have had their revenge against the hated St. Louis club by denying the Browns their first World Series appearance, at least temporarily. (If Detroit won—whether by fair or foul means—the Browns would have had to prevail again against the Yankees and force a one-game playoff with the Tigers on Monday to decide the AL championship.) The anonymous caller, presumably a gambler, might not have been so quick to offer Leonard the bribe if he had first checked the baseball stats: Leonard hadn't beaten the Tigers in three years and was about to face Detroit's best pitcher, Dizzy Trout, who was looking for his 28th win of the season and was sporting an ERA of 2.07. So the odds clearly favored the Motor City club. But the unknown caller, like all gamblers, wanted to put his money on a sure thing and was willing to pay for it.

It was the Nationals who struck first, scoring three runs in the top of the fourth inning, led by Stan Spence's two-run homer into the upper deck in right field, quickly dampening the hopes of the 45,565 fans jammed into Briggs Stadium, who then shouted for Detroit manager Steve O'Neill to bring in a reliever. O'Neill stayed with Trout, who then gave up successive singles to second baseman Fred Vaughn and outfielder Jake Powell. Rick Ferrell's long fly out scored Vaughn. Leonard's knuckleball, coupled with a surprising fastball, kept the Tigers off stride all game, as he tossed a four-hit complete game. The Nats added one more run in the top of the eighth. The Tigers rallied in their last at-bat, scoring one run on a sacrifice fly that scored Charlie Hostetler, who'd led off the ninth with a single. But it was too little too late. Final score: Nats 4, Tigers 1. Winning pitcher: Dutch Leonard. Thousands of heartbroken Tigers fans remained in their seats for another hour or so, their eyes glued to the out-of-town scoreboard praying for a Yankees' victory at Sportsman's Park. Most stayed in their seats until the final St. Louis score was posted.

In St. Louis, despite their importance, the Friday doubleheader and Saturday day game against the defending world champions drew a combined paid attendance of only 19,154.[93] But by early Sunday morning, the historic significance of the day finally dawned on Browns fans, and long lines began to form at the ballpark gates. A lucky 35,518, almost 2,000 over capacity, jammed through the turnstiles, and another 15,000 were turned away. It was the first time the Browns had filled Sportsman's Park since their appropriately named owner at the time, Philip

Ball, expanded the seating capacity in 1925.[94] The rare overflow crowd did not intimidate the Browns, however. "We were loose and cool," infielder Don Gutteridge recalled.[95] So loose that before the game teammate Al Zarilla was chipping golf balls out of a sandbox in the clubhouse. When manager Luke Sewell went out to the coaching lines during the game,[96] Ellis Clary turned on a radio in the dugout to listen to a football game, Gutteridge said. "The Chicago Bears were playing Green Bay, as I remember, and he [Clary] had some money on it."[97]

Libation-fortified Sig Jakucki did not disappoint the fans. He pitched the best complete game of his three-year major-league career (he played for the Browns in 1936 and 1944–1945 and amassed a modest 25–22 record), earning his season salary of $4,200 in one afternoon. Jakucki gave up six hits, struck out four batters, allowed just one earned run, and permitted only one Yankee to reach third base over the final six innings. The Yankees went out meekly in the top half of the ninth, passing on their 1943 American League championship to St. Louis. Final score: Browns 5, Yankees 2. The hitting star of the game turned out to be former weekender Chet Laabs, who had finally quit his defense job to play full-time for St. Louis. Laabs contributed four RBIs by hitting two homers to bring his season total to five. The Browns had won their first—and, as it turned out, their only—American League pennant and set up the only World Series played exclusively in St. Louis with all games played on the Sportsman's Park diamond.

The Browns went on to lose the World Series to the more powerful Cardinals, four games to two. Among the series highlights was the matchup between the two best shortstops in the game, the Browns' Vern Stephens and the Cardinals' Marty Marion. Over the season, Stephens amassed 164 hits, scored 91 runs, and drove in 109 runs, and he had a fielding average of .954 to finish third in the American League Most Valuable Player balloting. Marion, who won the National League MVP award that year, had 135 hits, scored 50 runs, and drove in 63, with a fielding average of .972. Years later, Marion told Mead, "We thought we were going to just walk through them. Who the hell's the Browns, you know. By the time we got in that first game, we found out they were a pretty good ballclub."[98]

As so often happens in such championships, the hitting star of the series was a player no one would have picked beforehand. Normally light-hitting Cardinal second baseman Emil Verban finished the series with a .412 batting average with seven hits in the six games. In a seven-year major-league career in which he hit just one home run and never batted .300 except in the World Series, Verban "won the respect and fond memories of important people who thought his maximum effort every day represented the best in all of us," baseball historian and author Bill Gilbert writes.[99] "That's why some high-powered baseball fans in Washington, including President Reagan, Presidential Press Secretary Jim Brady, columnist George Will, Senator Alan Dixon of Illinois, and Lobbyist Bruce Ladd, formed the Emil Verban Memorial Society, so named even though Verban was still very much among the living." The group gathered for dinner every two years, and Verban was the guest of honor each time. Verban, whose other claim to fame was he shared a nickname with the former president, "Dutch," died in 1989 at age 73.

The Nationals' final victory didn't mean much in the end, of course; win or lose, they would've finished far down in last place in either event. With a record of 64–90, a winning percentage of .416, they finished seven games behind the seventh-place Chicago White Sox and 25 games behind the Browns. For Griffith, the season was a personal humiliation, alleviated only in the ledgers. The Nationals finished another year in the black with a profit of $90,429, behind Detroit ($207,043) and New York ($151,043) and ahead of Cleveland ($86,803), Chicago ($61,295), Philadelphia (-$6,133), and Boston (-$43,131).[100] Although history has branded Griffith's clubs as perennial losers, Washington's last-place finish in 1944 was its first since 1909, three years before Griffith signed on to manage the team. In fact, it wasn't until after the war ended that sportswriter Charles Dryden's well-known epithet, inspired by that '09 finish, was affixed to Griffith's teams: "First in war, first in peace, and last in the American League." That catchphrase remained with Washington baseball (which officially returned to its pre-1905 nickname, the Senators, in 1956) until Calvin Griffith moved the franchise to Minnesota for the 1961 season. Dryden was simply being prescient.[101]

The Homestead Grays fared much better in their league than their stadium hosts did in theirs. The Grays again won the Negro National League pennant, finishing five and a half games ahead of the Baltimore Elite Giants, and would face their 1943 opponents, the Birmingham Black Barons. For this series, however, the Black Barons would be without three of their starting infielders and two other players as the result of a bad auto accident. Following a night game on September 9, the five were about 20 miles outside Birmingham early Saturday morning when they were involved in a head-on collision. The team lost second baseman Tommy Sampson, who suffered a broken leg, a hip fracture, and multiple fractures in one hand; veteran third baseman Johnny Britton, who sustained cuts to his face and knees; and shortstop Art Wilson, who suffered a strained wrist. Also injured were second-string catcher Lloyd "Pepper" Bassett, who sustained two broken ribs, and utility outfielder Leandy Young, who received body injuries and leg fractures. Despite the loss of key players, the Black Barons voted to go ahead with the playoff.[102]

In the absence of an overall commissioner, a three-member commission was created to handle any protests or disputes during the series: black sports editors Frank A. Young, of the *Chicago Defender*; Wendell Smith, of the *Pittsburgh Courier*; and Sam Lacy, of the AFRO group. The Negro World Series began on September 17 and ended with the Grays winning four games to one. Whereas in 1943 Birmingham was the site of only one series game, in 1944 the city played host to the first and third games. Only the series finale on September 24 was played at Griffith Stadium. There, the Grays scored three runs in the home first en route to a 4–2 victory. Josh Gibson, old at 32 due to his years of abusing alcohol and drugs, finished the season sixth in the league in hitting with a very respectable .365 batting average and nine home runs. (Roy Campanella, a young catcher destined for the Hall of Fame who split his season between the Baltimore Elite Giants and the Philadelphia Stars, batted .440 to finish second behind batting champion Bob Harvey of the Newark Eagles with a .453 average.)

Just prior to the start of the Grays–Black Barons series, a Steel City magnate named Gus Greenlee who had the innovative talents of a Bill Veeck was setting the stage that would threaten the survival of the two Negro Leagues. As black players gained a measure of stardom beyond their leagues during the war years, the meager salaries they received— with the few exceptions of the "super" stars such as Satchel Paige, who commanded $1,000 a game plus a percentage of the gate—became a bone of contention. Some players were making as little at $45 a game with the average player earning about $200 a month. Greenlee, one of the organizers of the Negro National League and originator of the an-

nual East–West classic in Chicago, had owned the Pittsburgh Crawfords (the 1935 Crawfords are considered by many to be the greatest
Negro League team of all time)[103] until he went bankrupt and was
henceforth blackballed by his once fellow club owners.

Greenlee saw the players' paltry pay as a way to get back into baseball by organizing a new Negro League and luring the stars of the
established leagues with better pay, just as the Mexican leagues were
doing somewhat successfully. The new league's teams would play in
major-league ballparks and adhere to regular schedules, a facet of Negro baseball that had yet to be remedied. Greenlee's proposed league
would include a revived Crawfords, who would play in the Pirates'
Forbes Field. In addition, Greenlee was expecting to add teams in
Cleveland and in New York, where the nascent team would play at one
of that city's three major-league ballparks.

Greenlee found an ally and, more importantly, a financial backer in
Abe Saperstein. After losing his PR gig for the East–West game due to
"an anti-Semitic viewpoint in a hectic session of the promoters several
months ago," according to *Afro-American* writer Don De Leighbur,
Saperstein had become Paige's advisor when the great pitcher threatened a strike and was a no-show at the most recent Chicago classic. If
the reappearance of Saperstein and his deep pockets weren't enough to
scare the established league owners, Greenlee had another arrow in his
quiver. He would gather the best colored players for a team "that will
oppose in a season or two a picked club of white players from the major
leagues in an annual test of who can play the better brand of baseball."[104] Although this was a most unlikely occurrence considering the
white owners' views, and especially those of their segregationist commissioner who held veto power over any black–white baseball, nevertheless Greenlee went ahead with his plans to bring the new league to
fruition the following year.

As the baseball season was winding down, delegates from the United
States, Great Britain, China, and the Soviet Union arrived in Washington to meet at the Dumbarton Oaks estate in Georgetown between
August 21 and October 7, across town from Griffith Stadium. There
they worked to hammer out a postwar framework for the United Nations, a new world organization designed to correct many of the problems of the defunct League of Nations and to work to maintain international peace and security.

Back home at Hyde Park, after the Quebec Conference ended on September 16, Roosevelt turned his attention to the rapidly approaching presidential election and his new running mate. In July, just before the vice presidential nominating process at the Democratic Party Convention in Chicago, Vice President Henry Wallace had overwhelming public approval for a second term. Few Democrats gave much thought to Missouri Senator Harry S. Truman for the post. Both as a man and as a politician, Wallace surely would have felt more at home in today's Nationals Park than in old quasi-segregated Griffith Stadium because in many ways Wallace was far ahead of his time, especially when it came to race relations. A liberal with religious and social views that were unorthodox for the time (his advocacy of universal health care for all Americans, for example), Wallace often angered politicians in his own party, particularly Southern Democrats.[105] Though Wallace outpolled Truman on the first ballot 429.5 to 319.5, convention delegates rallied behind Truman for an overwhelming second ballot victory, 1,100 to 66. In keeping with his character, Truman "was sitting on the platform eating a sandwich when the result was announced."[106]

On November 7, FDR won a fourth term by defeating 42-year-old New York Republican Governor Thomas E. Dewey. Although his margin of victory in the Electoral College was wide, 432 to 99, FDR's popular vote tally was the closest in any presidential election since 1912. Fewer than three million votes separated the two candidates.[107] Democrats gained 27 seats in the House to retain control of Congress with a 49-seat majority. And while losing one seat in the Senate, they still held a large majority there as well, 57–38, with one Progressive.

At his estate in Hyde Park, Roosevelt released a statement noting that the election was the first in 80 years held during wartime (the previous was the 1864 reelection of Abraham Lincoln during the Civil War) and which "again demonstrated to the world that democracy is a living vital force; that our faith in American institutions is unshaken, that conscience and not force is the source of power in the government of man."[108] Although the election was over, Roosevelt would not have much time to celebrate because he would soon leave for Europe even before his inauguration on January 20, 1945, for meetings with Churchill, Stalin, and General de Gaulle to discuss war planning and postwar peace.

Baseball, though dormant on the playing field, reemerged in the news two days after Thanksgiving when Kenesaw Mountain Landis died at age 78 in Chicago, following a coronary thrombosis. Landis had entered the hospital on October 2, suffering from a severe cold. Just one week before his death, a joint committee of the two leagues had recommended reelecting Landis to another seven-year term beginning in January 1946. "His death left the major leagues without a guiding genius and placed tremendous importance on the National and American League winter meeting here on Dec. 11, 12 and 13," the *New York Times* noted.[109] In keeping with his wishes, the judge's body was cremated, and there was no funeral service. Landis "was sincere in his thought that his friends would have brighter memories of him if there was no funeral," explained American League president Will Harridge, who added that it was "unlikely" organized baseball would hold a memorial service.[110] However, within two weeks, Landis was elected to the Baseball Hall of Fame by an induction committee he himself had appointed in April to select "old-timers" who had played in earlier eras.

Having had time to mull over their horrendous season and just before traveling to New York for the owners meetings in mid-December, Griffith and Bluege announced that they were "solidly in the trading market this winter, willing to deal for infielders and outfielders with any teams," the *Sporting News* reported.[111] Their list of untouchables was a short one indeed: pitchers Leonard, Niggeling, and Haefner; outfielders Spence and Case; and catcher Guerra. What they left unsaid was that the entire infield—Kuhel, Myatt, Sullivan, and Torres—which had been the bane of Bluege's season, was on the trading block. "The last-place finish of his team in 1944 displeased Griffith considerably and he is expected to make a grand attempt to show the fans that he is not idle in his efforts to improve the club," the same *Sporting News* article noted.

With Landis dead and the 1921 agreement that created the office of commissioner having expired, the owners were more concerned about possible new military draft rules than they were about picking Landis's successor. They unanimously agreed to create a three-member council—composed of the two league presidents, Will Harridge and Ford Frick, and the secretary to the commissioner's office, Leslie M. O'Connor—to oversee the game until a new major-league agreement could be reached and a new commissioner appointed. In cancelling the old pact, the owners also eliminated an original provision that allowed the president of the United States to name a baseball commissioner if they were unable to do so. Despite Griffith and Bluege's hopes and plans to strengthen the Nats by wheeling and dealing with their colleagues, the meetings did not become the usual player swap shop because the owners had a more immediate concern. They were worried about a request James F. Byrnes, the director of the War Mobilization Commission, had sent to Selective Service chief Lewis Hershey. Byrnes had a problem understanding how professional athletes could be in the fine physical shape needed to play baseball at its highest levels while at the same time physically unfit for military service. So he wanted Hershey to amend the existing draft regulations to include men ages 26 to 37 who were not working in defense industries. Such a change, baseball officials feared, would likely keep men in that age bracket who normally worked in defense industries in the winter at their industrial jobs year-round and further drain the 16 teams of veteran ballplayers. "The chief concern was over what effect the order would have on limited-service-men, who, in addition to 4-F's, form the bulk of the older players in the majors," explained the *Sporting News*.[112]

Baseball also made a cameo appearance in the Ardennes forest of Belgium, site of the crucial Battle of the Bulge, which began on December 16.[113] There, U.S. forces—which included former Washington National, now Army sergeant Cecil Travis—fought stubborn Nazi troops in horrendous winter conditions. To create confusion within the U.S. ranks, special English-speaking Nazi commando groups, wearing captured American uniforms in some cases, shouted out bogus orders to upset communications in the freezing fog and near-zero visibility. When word got around that the Germans were impersonating Americans, anyone sighted who in any way looked suspicious or who couldn't immediately identify himself satisfactorily was grilled with questions only Americans could answer, such as "Who are the players on the Brooklyn Dodgers?" The method wasn't foolproof, however. GIs held one U.S. brigadier general at gunpoint for several hours after he erroneously put the Chicago Cubs in the American League. (History does not record whether anyone was asked to name the last time the Nationals finished in last place.)

With Christmas and the New Year at hand, Roosevelt was in good humor and full of the holiday spirit. According to a brief Associated

Press item in the *Sporting News*, when FDR, whose family fortune had made him a wealthy man, learned that the chairman of the House Foreign Affairs Committee, Sol Bloom, had purchased a baseball signed by Calvin Coolidge for $700 at a charity auction, FDR instructed the New York Democrat, "You get a lot of baseballs. I'll do the autographing and you do the selling. We ought to make ourselves a piece of change."[114]

5

1945

Rounding Third and Heading Home

Despite Allied gains in the European and Pacific campaigns, January 1945 proved to be the most costly month of the war in terms of baseball-related deaths in the military. Twelve former minor leaguers were either killed in action or died as a result of their battle wounds.[1] The Negro Leagues were embroiled in a different sort of battle even before the first week of January was over. Gus Greenlee was planning to make good on his promise to form a new league (with the assistance of Branch Rickey), the United States Negro Baseball League, but with some major changes from his original plan. Of the four member clubs he had announced the previous September, only the resuscitated Pittsburgh Crawfords remained, ready to give the Homestead Grays new competition in the Pittsburgh area. The revised roster of teams included the Chicago Brown Bombers, St. Louis Stars (which would operate as a traveling team), Atlanta Black Crackers (which would move to Buffalo, New York), and also teams in Detroit and Philadelphia.

The newly elected league president, John Shackelford, a former ballplayer and now a Cleveland lawyer, promptly sought a meeting with the heads of the Negro American League and the Negro National League, Dr. J. B. Martin and Tom Wilson, respectively, in an attempt to reassure them of the new league's strict hands-off policy. (According to reports, Greenlee had allegedly tampered with the existing teams when he tried to sign some players during the 1944 East–West game and several had accepted money from him, for which he was censured by Martin and Wilson.) No doubt Grays' co-owner Cum Posey, who never liked Greenlee, also expressed his displeasure. As owner of the champion Grays playing in the nation's capital with its large black population, Posey was the de facto Negro Leagues commissioner. With an enigmatic introductory clause, the *Chicago Defender* said of Greenlee's plan: "As far as the public is concerned, the new league started with its hands clean. No attempt was made to tamper with any club in either the Negro National or the Negro American League."[2]

President Roosevelt and his new vice president, former Missouri Senator Harry S. Truman, were sworn into office on Saturday, January 20. The ceremony was moved to the south portico of the White House instead of the customary Capitol Hill site because of inclement weather and Roosevelt's ill health. Accompanied by his son, Marine Corps Colonel James Roosevelt, FDR took the oath of office from Chief Justice Harlan Stone. The entire ceremony was one of the shortest on record, lasting just 15 minutes, 6 of them taken up by Roosevelt's 551-word inaugural address,[3] the second shortest in history (after Washington's second inaugural address of just 135 words on March 4, 1793). Ten days after being sworn in for the fourth time, FDR celebrated his 63rd birthday on January 30, with a traditional round of birthday balls in his honor that each year raised millions of dollars for the charity he had established in 1938, the National Foundation for Infantile Paralysis, a disease better known as polio. The charitable organization, renamed the March of Dimes (after comic and singer Eddie Cantor's call for "a march of dimes" into the charity to raise money to combat the disease) in 1945, helped finance and support the Warm Springs, Georgia, facility FDR had purchased in 1926 and converted into a therapeutic center a year later, after having contracted the disease in 1921 at age 39.

Three days after his inauguration and visibly ill, Roosevelt left for Malta, where he would hold talks with Churchill between January 30 and February 2 to prepare for their upcoming meetings with Stalin at Yalta from February 4–11. Also in attendance at Yalta were the three Allied powers' foreign ministers, U.S. Secretary of State Edward Stettinius, British Foreign Secretary Anthony Eden, and Soviet Foreign Minister Vyacheslav Molotov. The Yalta agreement established the foundations for postwar Europe, specifically the borders of Poland and the reestablishment of the original, prewar governments in the liberated countries. The Big Three also agreed on the establishment of the UN Security Council and its composition, including the Soviet Union as a permanent member. After another stop in Malta and then on to Egypt, FDR headed home.[4]

Less than a month after what was to be FDR's final birthday ball, a former minor-league pitcher with gritty determination to make it to the majors was being fitted with a prosthetic leg and undergoing a rehab regimen at Walter Reed Army Hospital, just north of Washington in Bethesda, Maryland. Army Air Corps pilot and Lieutenant Bert Shepard's fighter plane had been shot down while strafing a Nazi convoy near Berlin on May 21, 1944, and the 24-year-old Indiana native was severely injured.[5] The unconscious airman was pulled from the wreckage, and when Shepard awoke, he was in a prisoner-of-war camp. His right leg had been amputated just below the knee by a German military doctor. Shepard returned home in a POW exchange in February 1945 with a makeshift artificial leg fashioned by a fellow prisoner. While rehabbing at Walter Reed, the self-taught left-hander met Robert Patterson, undersecretary of war, who had asked to meet some GI patients. The meeting would soon play an important role in Shepard's brief major-league career.

The Nats were about to open their spring-training camp in College Park, Maryland, when Griffith showed up at the White House at 11:30 a.m. on March 12 to present the president with his annual season's pass. Griffith was always glad to have an opportunity to thank FDR for promoting night baseball in his 1942 "green light" letter, which had benefitted baseball in general and the Old Fox in particular. The two old friends chatted and posed for photos during what turned out to be their last public meeting. According to Griffith, FDR said he still favored night baseball and then added, "You've got to give me credit for night baseball." The president also told Griffith that "it isn't beyond possibility" that he would attend opening day for the first time since 1941.[6]

When the Nationals opened camp at the University of Maryland for the third consecutive year, they were determined not to repeat their disastrous season of 1944. As has long been the custom among the major-league clubs, pitchers and catchers reported a few days before the rest of the squad, so Dutch Leonard's battery mates were the first to learn of his unusual off-season. Leonard had seen the war in Europe firsthand as a member of a USO baseball tour along with Cincinnati pitcher Bucky Walters, Giants player-manager Mel Ott, and Pirates skipper Frankie Frisch. Speaking at the Touchdown Club's weekly Tuesday luncheon on March 13, Leonard said the winter tour had been "terrific" despite often having to stage their shows on makeshift stages and in precarious conditions—sometimes on rickety platforms, in roofless bombed-out buildings, or in terrible weather and usually close to the dangerous front lines. The ballplayers even entertained GIs in Belgium just as the German army opened its winter offensive in the Battle of the Bulge. "I've gone through some bad winters around my home in Illinois," Leonard said, "but what we had on the trip around the front beat anything I'd ever experienced. No matter how much I put on, I never felt warm."[7] In some cases, the shows were staged within 1,000 yards of the front lines, Leonard recalled, "and the boys who listened to us at night would be in action the next morning."

The tour through Holland, Germany, Belgium, and France drew a combined audience of about 300,000, and the baseball-hungry GIs hung around after each performance to quiz the pros on all aspects of the game until the MPs had to break up the gabfest. Leonard also told the Touchdown Club audience how, after one show in Belgium, he decided to stroll around a recently bombed town to see the damage firsthand. "I didn't get far," Leonard related. "A sentry challenged me and I had forgotten the password. I yanked out my flashlight, played it on my face and told the boy who I was. He had a rifle pointed smack at me and was wearing a mean look. But he had seen me in the show. 'Better get back and learn that password if you want to live outside,' he growled. I got back to quarters right away and stayed there. And I was lucky. Those boys have itchy fingers when they're holding a gun."[8] The incident might have ended sooner if, instead of a password, the sentry had asked Leonard to name the players on the Brooklyn Dodgers.[9]

In training camp, the players spoke of their latent ability and their determination for the Nats to rise in the standings this season. The Old Fox, however, always a great judge of baseball talent, was not so optimistic. The infield, which failed miserably the previous season, again was a big question mark. Early Wynn was lost to military service, and outfielder Stan Spence was due to be called up any day soon. Catcher Rick Ferrell was a holdout and not expected into camp for at least another week. Also, Griffith's veterans were a year older and some were plagued by injuries. Speedy George Case's prolonged shoulder injury from the previous season was still on the mend following delicate off-season surgery. Physicians at Johns Hopkins Hospital had transplanted fascia, fibrous tissue that surrounds muscles, from his thigh into his shoulder to strengthen it. As a result, Case's throwing was initially restricted, and he also wore a cast on his leg for two months, so he was not at 100 percent when he arrived in camp.

The "star" of the camp—who attracted more reporters, photographers, and movie cameramen than anyone else—was Bert Shepard, the hurler and former POW with the artificial leg. Robert Patterson, soon to be named secretary of war, was so impressed by the young flier's grit and determination that he had urged Griffith to give Shepard a tryout, and Griffith agreed. On March 14, Shepard also impressed on the ball field. As *Washington Post* sportswriter Walter Haight noted, "Yesterday, eyes that were sympathizing with the 24-year-old, sturdy built fellow the day before saw that he not only means business but that he has a chance to make the grade." Having worn his new prosthetic leg for only four days, Shepard pitched batting practice with "exceptional control" and "plenty of speed on the ball," Haight reported. Haight added that Shepard also banged out two straight balls over second base, "hits in any league," ran the bases well, and even cleanly fielded some bunts. Afterward, when Haight accompanied Shepard back to Walter Reed Hospital, where he was still rehabbing, Shepard told Haight that if he made the team he would visit hospitals during and after the season. "I want all the fellows to get going. If I make it, they're going to make it too," Shepard said.[10] In an interview years later with author and one-time Nats batboy Bill Gilbert, Shepard said he always considered himself lucky. "I could have lost my left leg [instead]," he said, explaining to Gilbert, "You need the back leg for balance and since I'm a southpaw, I would drive off my left leg." Coming down on an artificial front leg in the pitching motion, Shepard added, "doesn't hurt a thing. There's very little handicap as far as throwing is concerned."[11]

By March 15, some 23 Nationals were in camp, including nine Cubans, and spring training went into high gear under a warm sun. It was crucial to take advantage of every practice session because, once again, the two leagues had shortened their exhibition season by approximately 60 percent to meet the latest wartime travel restrictions. The new limitations came from a meeting in Washington on that Ides of March involving the director of the Office of Defense Transportation, Colonel

J. Monroe Johnson, NL president Ford Frick, AL president Will Harridge, and Clark Griffith. "The particular type of game ruled out is that which calls for a trip from one camp to another camp in a different town," explained Bus Ham writing for the Associated Press.[12] "Thus the Nats, training here, won't go to Baltimore, Md., about 40 miles, to meet the [minor league] Baltimore Orioles." But teams whose camps were in relatively close proximity to one another, such as the Yankees and Red Sox, who both trained in the Atlantic City, New Jersey, area, could play as many games against each other as they liked. For the Nats, the ruling meant dropping five scheduled away games against the Phillies, Giants, and Baltimore, but Washington was able to add games with the Boston Braves, who were training on the Georgetown University campus.

As spring training began in earnest, the 16 clubs had another vexing war-related issue to deal with: the status of players with deferments who wished to leave their defense-industry jobs and return to the baseball diamond for the season. Since the latter part of the previous year, the War Manpower Commission (WMC) had been mulling over whether such players could go back to the game and then return to their defense jobs when the season ended without jeopardizing their draft-exempt status, in many cases 4-F. Roosevelt had roiled the waters on March 14, when he said he "favored baseball as long as it did not require perfectly healthy people who could be doing more useful war work."[13] The Negro Leagues were also concerned. Writing in the *New York Amsterdam News*, Dan Burley argued, "If the weight of [WMC head] Byrnes' decision hits everywhere as it is obviously intended to do, Negro baseball would be in a precarious position in its [1945] program."[14] The black columnist noted that the game already had its share of "old men," players 35 and older. "Whether the fans will be willing to support clubs made up of these ancients is a game which I wouldn't want to venture a prediction upon here."

Opponents of the commission's thinking pointed out that many ballplayers had draft exemptions because of chronic conditions or injuries that required regular treatment, such as whirlpool baths and taped ankles or knees, which would defer them from military service but not from playing a sport; others likened ballplayers to schoolteachers who worked in the defense industry during the summer and returned to teaching in the fall. One of the strongest proponents of the exemption was Cleveland Indians third baseman Ken Keltner, who had already left his defense job to report to the Indians' training camp just as he had done the year before, saying, "Baseball is my business. If the Army wants me, it will find me working at it."[15] The War Department began reexamining—and, in some cases, drafting—the formerly deferred men, including Keltner.[16]

The issue weighed on the minds of owners, managers, and players into the opening of the baseball season. Many players in the defense plants stayed on the job awaiting a final decision and did not report to their respective spring-training camps. Then Congress weighed in, led by Kentucky senator A. B. "Happy" Chandler and others (including FBI director J. Edgar Hoover) to oppose the proposed regulation change. Finally on March 21, McNutt intervened to kill the proposal, saying he was satisfied that there was overwhelming support for the sport among civilians and service personnel alike. "There is considerable evidence that [baseball] adds to the morale on the home front in wartime and that, therefore, there is real justification for this action," McNutt said.[17] The new ruling specifically stated that ballplayers who had played in 1944 and had contractual obligations to their teams, including an option for the 1945 season, now could go back to their primary occupation of baseball without having to get permission from the U.S. Employment Service. They were no longer in jeopardy of being referred to their respective draft boards as "job jumpers." The WMC ruling was broad enough to allow Jake Powell to leave his job as a Montgomery County, Maryland, police safety officer[18] and return to the Nats. The ruling also spared Powell's teammates Dutch Leonard and Mickey Haefner from military service. But Stan Spence was inducted into the service and missed the entire season, and 24-year-old shortstop John Sullivan, who played in 138 games in 1944, entered the Army on March 27 and would be lost to the team for the next two seasons.

One player in the Nats' camp who was not affected, no matter what the WMC ultimately ruled, was of course Bert Shepard. On March 18, Bluege slotted the amputee war hero to come in as a reliever sometime during a scheduled seven-inning intrasquad game. Instead of taking the mound, however, the former pilot took to the air and went AWOL, thus precipitating a small war of his own. Larry MacPhail, newly named Yankees president, flew Shepard from Bolling Field (now known as Joint Base Anacostia-Bolling) in southeast Washington to the Yankees'

Bader Field training camp in Atlantic City, New Jersey. Griffith, who had gone to the camp specifically to watch Shepard pitch, was outraged, calling MacPhail's action brazen piracy. Griffith acknowledged that Shepard, a former minor leaguer, was a free agent and could negotiate with any club, but Griffith charged, "If MacPhail is trying to sign Shepard, he is using unethical methods." Bluege, too, was upset. "When they come right into your camp and snatch them, something's wrong," he said.[19] Shepard's argument was, "I want a job in baseball. So far no one around the Washington club has talked business. If Mr. MacPhail wants me, I'll go to the Yankees."[20] As for missing his turn on the Nats' mound, Shepard pleaded ignorance, saying he was unaware of the assignment. After also impressing the Yankees with his pitching and hitting skills, and even showing some good defensive work covering first base, Shepard flew back to Washington to continue his rehabilitation and recovery, especially for the skull fracture over his right eye that he suffered when his plane was shot down.

Shepard explained his desire to be a big leaguer at a sold-out March 20 Touchdown Club luncheon with the Old Fox in attendance. Even Griffith, ever the ardent patriot, must have been moved when Shepard spoke of his eight-month confinement in a German prisoner-of-war camp and how happy he was when a fellow prisoner, a Canadian POW, fashioned an artificial leg for him that allowed him to walk more normally again. Though both the Nats and Yankees thought of him as a potential batting-practice pitcher and morale booster, Shepard primarily thought of himself as a future major leaguer who also would help the War Department's efforts at morale building on the side (which he did after Griffith beat out MacPhail and signed him to a contract). Shepard became one of the 10 pitchers on the Washington Nats roster just prior to the opening of the season.

Looking at the Shepard story some seven decades later, it's hard to imagine two major-league teams squabbling over the signing of a one-legged batting-practice pitcher.[21] But in 1945, owners were eager to fill the seats left empty by the exodus of the stars, and major-league baseball had reached the nadir of talent with 79.2 percent of players in the opening day lineups in 1941 were now serving in the armed forces or were defense workers. "Of the 144 performers who helped open the prewar season, only 30 remain on major league rosters, several [of them] on borrowed time, as some have already been accepted for military duty while others are awaiting reclassification," according to the Associated Press survey. "Excluding the pitchers, there are more than 50 new starters, including 22 playing their first big league game. And no club was expected to have as many as four prewar regulars on the field for the start of the 1945 season." (Washington had only George Case, Joe Kuhel, and Dutch Leonard.)[22]

In fact, the *Sporting News* counted 37 Washington franchise players serving in the military.[23] Shepard and one-armed Pete Gray, who played in the Browns outfield that year, certainly had exceptional abilities on the baseball field, but cynics might say they were signed primarily for their crowd-drawing and morale-building value. In any case, neither Shepard nor Gray found a place on a major-league roster after 1945, when the leagues began to restock their clubs with returning veterans and promising youngsters.

The Nats' spring-training exhibition games began on March 24 against a team from the Curtis Bay Naval Station, south of Baltimore in Anne Arundel County, Maryland. The tightly packed schedule called for the Nats to play some 21 games with only two off days, including a week of games at the Norfolk Naval Training Station again, five against the Boston Braves, and only one against an opponent from their own American League, the Philadelphia A's, at nearby Fort Meade, Maryland, on April 12. As it stood, the curtailed schedule would provide Washington with major-league opposition in only six games.

As Allied forces were knocking on the gates of Berlin and massing on the shores of the Japanese home islands, on March 29, the president left on an overnight train for the "Little White House" at Warm Springs, Georgia, seeking to regain his health for the final push to defeat Germany and Japan. On Thursday afternoon, April 12, while sitting for a portrait, Roosevelt collapsed and died suddenly. An autopsy determined that he died of a cerebral hemorrhage with arteriosclerosis as a contributing factor.

In Washington, Vice President Truman was enjoying his usual afternoon libation and card game with his Capitol Hill pals in House Speaker Sam Rayburn's private hideaway in the bowels of the building when he learned of FDR's death by returning a call from FDR's press secretary, Steve Early.[24] According to witnesses as reported in David McCullough's Pulitzer Prize–winning eponymous biography, Truman turned pale as he listened to Early's instructions, and when he put down the phone, he muttered, "Jesus Christ and General Jackson." Without further explanation, Truman ran through the Capitol and was then sped in the VP's car to the White House, where he was met by Eleanor Roosevelt. She put her arm on Truman's shoulder and said, "The President is dead." When a stunned Truman asked, "Is there anything I can do for you?" she famously replied, "Is there anything we can do for you? For you are the one in trouble now."[25]

After gathering a bevy of witnesses, including Bess Truman, now First Lady, and their daughter Margaret, as well as most members of FDR's cabinet and other wartime officials, Chief Justice Stone administered the oath of office to Truman in the West Wing at seven in the evening. McCullough vividly recalls the scene at the White House: "The West Wing throbbed with activity and tension. Reporters, photographers, White House staff people, the Secret Service, and a few of Truman's own staff converged from several directions, crowding corridors and offices. Voices were hushed and tense. Telephones kept ringing. In the twilight outside, across Pennsylvania Avenue, in Lafayette Square, thousands of people gathered in silence."[26]

The following day, Truman addressed a joint session of Congress which also including the cabinet, the Supreme Court justices, and foreign dignitaries such as British Foreign Secretary Anthony Eden. Truman—a man who never had aspirations to be president—pledged to carry out FDR's war and peace policies. For many in the national radio audience, it was the first time they heard a chief executive other than Roosevelt speak. Although Truman had been a U.S. senator since 1935 and had established a well-regarded reputation among his colleagues, he was almost a complete stranger to the American public. Truman's flat Midwestern tones and cadence were in sharp contrast to the mellifluent, well-enunciated diction of the patrician president he had just succeeded. In calling for continued unity among the Allies to win the war, Truman acknowledged FDR's death by saying that "no man could possibly fill the tremendous void left by the passing of that noble soul," and he noted that the world was looking to America for enlightened leadership that could only come from a country that was itself united. He pledged that "America will never become a party to any plan for partial victory."[27] Truman's plain-spoken address evoked frequent rounds of loud applause, and he received standing ovations when he entered and left the chamber.

Both as a courtesy and as a hedge against the less than 50–50 chance that Roosevelt would actually appear at the ballpark on opening day, Griffith earlier had sent Truman box-seat tickets to the game. The Nats owner received a remarkable typed thank-you note from Truman, written on his official vice-presidential stationery and dated April 12, the very day he became the seventh vice president to succeed to the presidency upon the death of the chief executive. The typed portion (no doubt dictated by Truman to a secretary earlier) read: "Appreciated very much the tickets for the opening game. We will have a carload on deck. Hope the weather is fine and everything goes off all right." Then below his signature, in a handwritten postscript that leaves no doubt that the former Missouri haberdasher was now the president of the United States, Truman wrote: "We must postpone it now. I'm in up to my neck and must think of my terrible responsibilities for some days to come."[28] How Truman found the time—or the inclination—to respond personally within hours of the heavy burden of the presidency falling onto his shoulders remains a mystery. Then again, the Truman presidency would be full of surprises.

Major-league baseball also got a new chief executive in April. Ever since the death of Kenesaw Mountain Landis the previous November, the Office of Commissioner had been run by a troika composed of the two league presidents and the office secretary. "For years, Landis had served as Griffith and [Connie] Mack's front man in keeping major league baseball all-white," wrote author Brad Snyder, and the death "of baseball's segregationist-in-chief sent the black press into overdrive."[29] Even before a new commissioner was elected, as early as the start of the year, *Afro-American* sports editor Sam Lacy was calling for a Fourth of July black boycott of major-league baseball. "As I have pointed out in 'Looking 'Em Over' on numerous occasions in the past, the major leagues have given baseball jobs to athletes of every race of people on earth with the exception of our own," Lacy wrote.[30] Under the mistaken impression that Griffith had even signed a Chinese ballplayer, Lacy added, "Why then, all other methods having failed, should we not agree that July 4, 1945 will be honored (?) [as published] as 'lily white day' in baseball as a means of expressing our contempt for the flaunted prejudices of our so-called 'national pastime'?" Lacy also urged cabbies and stadium vendors to join the planned boycott, and he ended by saying, "Major league operators don't want us. They should be able to do without us." Later, under advisement from his AFRO publisher, he moderated his call for a boycott, but Lacy and other black leaders had valid complaints against Griffith. On a roster that already included overt racist Jake Powell, the Old Fox had now added a one-legged pitcher. African Americans could only wonder what it would take for Griffith to sign a black baseball player.

But if Griffith stood pat in refusing to sign black ballplayers, Brooklyn Dodgers President Branch Rickey, a deeply religious man fond of quoting the Bible, had charted his own path to integration. Rickey, whose full name was Wesley Branch Rickey, was born 12 years after Clark Griffith, on December 20, 1881, in Stockdale, Ohio, a tiny community about 80 miles south of Columbus. Like Griffith, Rickey was a gifted athlete who played semiprofessional baseball and football to pay his way through Ohio Wesleyan University. Although he was drafted by the Cincinnati Reds in August 1904 from a minor league team in Texas, his refusal to play on Sundays led the Reds to return him to Texas one month later. Nevertheless, he managed to play in the major leagues for parts of four seasons, catching for the St. Louis Browns briefly in 1905 and then catching and playing outfield for them in 1906. The following season, the Browns traded him to the New York Highlanders (later renamed the Yankees) managed by Clark Griffith for pitcher-infielder Joe Yeager. With a weak career batting average of .239, Rickey decided that his baseball career was over, and he enrolled in the University of Michigan Law School and got his degree in 1911. He returned to manage the Browns at the end of the 1913 season, through 1915, before moving on to the St. Louis Cardinals, first as president of the club, then back into the dugout again for a seven-year stint as the Cards' manager between 1919 and 1925, and then finally in the front office again as general manager.

It was during his 25-year association with the Cardinals that Rickey created the first minor-league farm system by convincing the owner to buy an interest in two minor-league teams to have a leg up on selecting players for the major-league squad. The results proved the wisdom of his idea. As a result of organizing the first farm system, the Cardinals won nine league championships with rosters filled from the Cardinals' minor-league system. Rickey also relied on the use of statistics—another of his innovations to the game—to judge performance on the field. Of course, his most famous innovation was integration. As one

Rickey biography put it: "While he was criticized for encouraging continued segregation in sports, Rickey's overriding idea was to scout black
ballplayers until he found just the right one to bring about desegrega-
tion of the major leagues."[31] So when former Pittsburgh Crawfords
owner Gus Greenlee unveiled his plan to form the U.S. Negro Baseball
League, also known as the U.S. League, in February 1945, Rickey not
only was the only major-league official to publicly support it, but also he
participated in its short-lived existence.

Talk of a new league, however, did not assuage the frustration of the
black press over the decided lack of progress toward integration; neither did it create a united front among black journalists, even as Sam
Lacy kept up his campaign to bring blacks into the majors. In April,
Lacy took issue with comments by the city editor of the *Amsterdam
News*, S. W. Garlington. Lacy's "Looking 'Em Over" column took the
form of an open letter to Dan Burley, one of Garlington's staff writers
on the Harlem periodical. Lacy said Garlington had correctly noted, as
had their peers in the black press, that a "one-legged vet [and] a one-
armed player," Bert Shepard and Pete Gray, respectively, were on major-league rosters "while Negroes, including those in excellent shape for
[the] big leagues are given the old runaround."[32] Then Lacy quoted
Garlington's own words, which were the source of Lacy's ire: "I only
wish Negro sports writers [Garlington wrote] were as expressive in their
interest to get Negroes in the majors. Seemingly their [*sic*] are sabotag-
ing the project with their silence. I wonder why?" Lacy was so angered
by the New York editor's claim that he produced a list of a dozen or so
black journalists who had written "reams upon reams of copy in support
of the battle." Lacy concluded by suggesting to Burley that Garlington
"would know a lot more about what's going on if he read the colored
papers once in a while."

Black sportswriters were also embittered by two sham tryouts of
Negro League players in April, which were intended to mollify the
proponents of integration, at least temporarily. Sportswriter Joe Bostic
of the *People's Voice*, another New York–based African American news-
paper that was founded in 1942 by local politician Adam Clayton Powell
Jr., showed up unannounced at the Dodgers training camp in Bear
Mountain, New York, on April 6, demanding a tryout for two Negro
Leaguers, Terris "the Great" McDuffie of the Newark Eagles and Dave
"Showboat" Thomas of the New York Cubans.[33] Branch Rickey, put off

by the blindside maneuver, gave the pair a short look and sent them packing.

On April 14, Wendell Smith, sports editor of the *Pittsburgh Courier*, backed by a couple of Boston politicians, brought Jackie Robinson (then with the Kansas City Monarchs), Sam Jethroe (an outfielder on the Cleveland Buckeyes), and infielder Marvin Williams (of the Philadelphia Stars) to Fenway Park for a tryout. (The Red Sox were not the best choice of a franchise to attempt to integrate the sport because the Red Sox were the last major-league team to sign an African American, infielder Pumpsie Green, in 1959, 12 years after Robinson joined the Dodgers.) After waiting around for two days, the trio batted and fielded for about an hour and a half in front of coaches Hugh Duffy and Larry Woodall. No Red Sox players or representatives from the front office were present but according to a brief, unsubstantiated article with a Boston dateline that appeared in the *Baltimore Afro-American* a week later, Red Sox manager Joe Cronin watched the workout.[34]

Smith and his three players left with barely a thank you and never heard from the Red Sox again. (Jethroe, signed by the Dodgers in 1948, one year after Robinson debuted in Brooklyn, played for the Boston Braves and the Pittsburgh Pirates between 1950 and 1954; Williams played for the Philadelphia Stars for 3 of his 19-year Negro Leagues career, never making it to the majors.) The black press also wanted to press Clark Griffith to agree to such a tryout using two keys points in their argument: (1) that Griffith was employing Latin ballplayers so why not Negroes? and (2) Washington's large black population would become avid supporters of a Nationals team that was improved by the addition of outstanding Negro ballplayers, and that, in turn, would improve Griffith's revenue stream. But Roosevelt's recent death monopolized the press and "destroyed any national publicity value" such a tryout might have had.[35]

Concerned about the dearth of true major-league talent taking the field in 1945, American League president Will Harridge penned an article for the Associated Press on the eve of the new season that was intended to prevent fan apathy and stoke greater interest in the sport. Harridge predicted that the season would "rank as one of the most notable in the history of the game" despite the fact that "most of the game's greatest stars have left the playing field." He said almost 260 major leaguers were now in the service, and more would soon follow.

Just the fact that baseball was opening a fourth consecutive wartime season was "a remarkable tribute to the fans of our national sport, both at home and abroad." Then, recalling the hard-fought pennant race in 1944 and the "remarkable increase" in attendance over the previous season, Harridge said, "I have every reason to believe that we will have an equally close fight for the pennant in 1945."[36]

On April 24, one week after the new season began, the 16 team owners unanimously selected Albert B. "Happy" Chandler as their new commissioner, in part as a reward for his work on Capitol Hill to quash the WMC's planned reexamination of exempt ballplayers that threatened many of them with the draft.[37] When he was first approached about the job, Chandler demurred, saying he couldn't leave the Senate. But he later changed his mind and agreed to the offer of a seven-year term at $50,000 a year, explaining, "Now that the war with Germany is virtually over I can conscientiously leave my other duties" and would be "immediately available."[38] Considering how little—if anything—a lone legislator could do to help end the war and that a senator's pay in 1945 was just $10,000 a year, one-fifth of what he would earn from baseball, Chandler's reasoning for accepting the job strikes a false chord as self-serving. .

However, in recalling Landis's total control over baseball, how he had freely spent the leagues' money, and how helpless they had been to rein him in, the owners did not give Chandler a contract immediately. When the moguls met in July to draft one for him, Shirley Povich explained that "the big league owners don't want Chandler to have the same authority over the funds of the baseball commissioner's office that Landis had. They're trying to clip Chandler's wings before the fledgling commissioner begins to fly too high."[39] Chandler remained in the Senate until October 29, several weeks after the baseball season and the World Series were over, before officially resigning his Senate seat to take his new job. Chandler's postwar years in the office, like those of Truman, would be marked by high drama and controversy, but unlike Truman, he would have no second act.

The Nationals opened the 1945 season on April 17 on the road in Philadelphia beating Connie Mack's A's, 14–8. After taking two of three games at Shibe Park, they came home for an April 20 home opener at Griffith Stadium against the Yankees. The Nats dedicated the afternoon to the memory of Franklin Roosevelt with a full minute of silent prayer.

But there were no other changes in the day's program because, according to unnamed officials, "Mr. Roosevelt would have wanted things to go on as usual."[40] The opening-day ceremonies were notably muted, however, as when the band, along with managers Bluege and Joe McCarthy and other officials, marched to the flagpole in centerfield at funereal cadence. According to protocol, the Stars and Stripes was raised to the top of the pole and then lowered to half-staff as a trumpeter played taps.

Just as he had intimated in his note to Griffith eight days earlier, Truman did not attend. With no vice president,[41] the ceremonial task of throwing out the first ball went to House Speaker Sam Rayburn. His toss from the front-row box seats landed well into the infield. "It unquestionably was a new record," wrote Lewis F. Atchison in the *Evening Star*.[42] In the dugout, the great Walter "Big Train" Johnson, the Nats Hall of Fame pitcher, sat talking with former teammates Bluege and coach Clyde Milan while the rest of the team looked at the legend in awe. The biggest ovation from the crowd of 24,494 (the smallest opening-day attendance in several years) was for three of the GIs who'd become famous for the photos of them raising the Stars and Stripes atop Mount Suribachi on Iwo Jima, John Bradley, Rene Gagnon, and Ira Hayes, who were making public appearances at Victory Bond rallies around the country.

The visitors won the opener handily, 6–3, with 11 hits, 4 of them for extra bases. Washington's offense was led by George "Bingo" Binks[43] who doubled and scored one run. Binks had been acquired from the minor-league Milwaukee Brewers late in the 1944 season when the 30-year-old outfielder was batting close to .400. Binks had been out of baseball and working as a machinist in 1942 and 1943 but had a 4-F classification because of a mastoid operation when he was a youngster that left him deaf in his left ear. Batting cleanup for the Nats, Binks started the season on a tear, going four for five in the opener at Philadelphia, with a walk, two RBIs, and a run scored. Although his fielding was spotty at best, he proved his value to the team with speed on the base paths, and he even subbed adequately for Joe Kuhel when the first baseman was injured later in the season. Nevertheless, the Nationals' season began much like the previous one had ended. Of the 11 games they played in April, the Nats won 6 and lost 5, including a 14–3 blowout in the first game of a doubleheader at Yankee Stadium on April 29.

Yet, before the beginning of play on May 1, Washington was holding its own, in second place just a game behind Chicago, Detroit, and New York, all tied for the lead.

Still concerned about baseball's relevance in wartime and with a new chief executive, one of Chandler's first acts as commissioner was to visit his old Senate colleague now residing at the White House on April 28. Talking to the press afterward, Chandler said he and Truman both had a difficult task. "He and I inherited two difficult jobs simultaneously. I know my man (Judge Kenesaw Mountain Landis) [as published] had a big pair of shoes, and I think it is generally conceded that the man he succeeded (Franklin Delano Roosevelt) had a big pair of shoes too." Chandler called Truman a great baseball fan who understood the sport's problems. "I think he's anxious for the game to continue," Chandler said, adding that he gained the impression the president thought baseball has justified that right, having "made the maximum contribution to the war effort." Chandler also spoke of his own commitment to allowing "legitimate 4-Fs" to play baseball, estimating about 400 to 500 of the estimated four million 4-Fs "ought to be available to the game."[44] He also told the press that before he accepted the job he, like Landis before him, insisted on "absolute power to stop anything that is detrimental to baseball."

He then headed west on his first trip as commissioner (although he had not yet signed a contract and still held his seat in the Senate), visiting Louisville and his home in Versailles, Kentucky, before going on to St. Louis to attend the Browns' American League pennant-raising ceremony at Sportsman's Park. While in St. Louis, Chandler again spoke out against targeting 4-Fs for the draft. Without mentioning James F. Byrnes by name, the administration official who had suggested that the Selective Service System ought to expand the draft to include 4-Fs who'd been ballplayers, Chandler told the press he feared "that somebody has abused his authority when physically unfit men are inducted into the Army simply because they happen to be ball players" and "that President Truman will look into the matter."[45] He also announced he was planning to move the commissioner's office from Chicago to Cincinnati because of its central location and closeness to Kentucky.

From there, he went to Chicago to confer with members of the baseball advisory committee, including Will Harridge and Leslie

O'Connor. Chandler formally announced the move to Cincinnati two days later at his first—and last—news conference at the commissioner's Chicago headquarters, ending the Windy City's 24-year reign as the capital of baseball. He also announced that the war would keep him in Washington longer than he had expected. To ward off any possible criticism, he pointed out that his predecessor did not resign from the federal bench until he'd been commissioner for a year and a half. Moreover, Chandler said, "I won't draw salaries for both jobs,"[46] leaving unsaid whether he'd opt for the Senate's $10,000 or baseball's $50,000. In a separate meeting with the press on May 5, when a *Chicago Defender* reporter raised the question of integration, Chandler's reply was noncommittal. He simply said he would invite Negro leaders to "sit across the table and talk this problem over." Chandler sent a mixed message to African Americans when he said he planned "no startling changes or innovations but has already said he will 'fully consider' the pressing question of Negroes playing in organized baseball."[47]

Truman's April 28 meeting with Chandler was one item on a busy morning for the new president. He met with four other visitors and then spent more than an hour posing at his desk for photographers. He finally called it a day at 1 p.m. As he walked across Pennsylvania Avenue to his temporary residence at Blair House (to allow Eleanor Roosevelt and FDR's staffers time to pack and leave the White House living quarters and offices), the new president had many urgent things to occupy his mind. Among them was the need to quash widespread rumors of an imminent German surrender to only the United States and Britain, despite a White House statement insisting that any offer of an unconditional surrender must be addressed also to the Soviet Union.[48]

The Nats began May by losing two games in Boston and giving Bluege cause for concern about the lack of depth of his starting pitching. The Homestead Grays opened their season on May 6 at Yankee Stadium with a scheduled doubleheader against the Black Yankees. The defending Negro League champions were seeking their fourth-straight pennant and a chance to win their third consecutive world championship. And like the Nationals, the Grays also were relying on a veteran corps. The pitching was still led by Ray Brown, Roy Welmaker, and John Wright, if he could get leave from the Navy's Great Lakes base. Sluggers Josh Gibson and Buck Leonard were a year older, and the left side of the infield was porous. Nevertheless, the Grays prevailed, rout-ing the Black Yankees, 13–3, on a rainy Sunday that held the crowd down to about 4,000 and led to the cancellation of the second game with the Grays ahead, 4–1. However, the fans did get their money's worth when Gibson hit one of his prodigious home runs, a 430-foot, three-run blast in the top of the first inning.

The first week of May wasn't over before Grays co-owner Cum Posey and his colleagues had something else to worry about other than their teams' performances on the field. On May 7, Dodgers boss Branch Rickey formally announced the formation of Greenlee's United States League, a new Negro League with Cleveland attorney John Shackelford as its president. The latest plan was for the USL to have teams in Brooklyn, Detroit, Pittsburgh, Chicago–Toledo, and Philadelphia, all cities with major-league ballparks.[49] Play would begin on May 24 with an inaugural game between Brooklyn and Philadelphia. As the late historian and self-described baseball fanatic Jules Tygiel noted: "The institution of a new Negro League hardly seemed the answer to baseball's racial dilemma. Some commentators accused [Rickey] of aspiring to the 'dictatorship' of black baseball."[50].

Afro-American columnist Sam Lacy admitted he was confused and wondered, "How is it that Rickey last week was credited with 'organizing,' a league that was already set up, named, officered [*sic*] and franchised four months previously. Don't tell me this is a case of 'It's true now' cause Mistah Charlie says so."[51] Lacy, with the endorsement of his AFRO chain of newspapers and even the major leagues, quickly opened a campaign to abolish racial discrimination in baseball by creating a committee of black and white executives, including Rickey and the Yankees' Larry MacPhail. The committee's goals were: to create a closer relationship between the black leagues and the major leagues, to gain major-league baseball's recognition of the Negro Leagues and find ways for qualified black players to play on white teams, and "to set up, in time, a player pool from which competent colored players may be drafted."[52] A few weeks later, Posey, in his alter ego as secretary of the Negro National League, announced that the NNL and NAL had declined the committee's invitation to appoint representatives. The effort died for the moment, only to be resuscitated later in New York.

Rickey's involvement in the USL was multilayered and controversial, including his partial ownership of the new league's Brooklyn Brown Dodgers. For a start, he named Oscar Charleston as manager of the

Brown Dodgers, one of the greatest Negro League ballplayers of all time and one of the feistiest, whose short fuse and eagerness to duke it out with anyone, on the field or off, was likened to that of Ty Cobb. In an article about the legendary Charleston, author Paul Dickson cites longtime Giants manager John McGraw, who saw Charleston play, as saying, "If Oscar Charleston isn't the greatest baseball player in the world, then I'm no judge of baseball talent." Sports columnist Grant-land Rice echoed McGraw when he said, "It's impossible for anybody to be a better ballplayer than Oscar Charleston." And Ted "Double Duty" Radcliffe, who played with Charleston, called him "Willie Mays before there was a Willie Mays except that he was a better base runner, a better center fielder and a better hitter."[53]

Rickey 's involvement would also aid his Brooklyn Dodgers financial-ly by renting Ebbets Field to the nascent Brown Dodgers for five games during the season just as Griffith was doing with the Grays. Also Rickey saw the new league as a way to spot talent as he moved closer to signing a black player for his Dodgers organization. Although the fledgling league failed to fly, lasting fewer than two seasons, Rickey's backing of the USL—which also included a financial stake in the Brooklyn Brown Dodgers—caused a sharp rift between Rickey and his old New York Highlanders manager. Even members of the black press doubted the wisdom of adding a third Negro League. In his column in the *Chicago Defender*, Fay Young advised Shackelford to change his plans to oper-ate the USL "as a full-fledged organization even in the face of all the difficulties the new league will run into."[54] Instead, Young suggested that Shackelford's clubs operate as independent teams, one reason be-ing "there aren't enough ball players at present for the three leagues" and wouldn't be until the war ends.

The white owners, as well as many black journalists, had long cited the lack of central leadership as the reason why the two established Negro Leagues operated so haphazardly and therefore—to the white owners at least—weren't worthy of being considered for integration. Indeed, in unveiling the new league and its structure, Rickey criticized the existing leagues as "no leagues at all," and defended the upstart as a "dependable and permanent league." The prompt selection of a USL president was a clear signal to all that, right from the start, the upstart league would be different. Shackelford said he hoped the USL would be "accepted as a regularly constituted member of organized baseball" by the end of the 1946 season.[55] Rickey added that the USL would also include its players in major league baseball's annual draft (a step toward eventual integration) and would not attempt to poach players under contract in the existing leagues. But by its second year, the USL was moribund, reduced from six teams to four with only Greenlee's Pittsburgh Crawfords remaining from the original group.[56]

As it became clear in the lens of hindsight, Rickey was a white executive who quietly favored integration and had given considerable thought to the best way to bring it about. "The United States League was indeed a subterfuge, though not of the kind Rickey's detractors suspected," historian Tygiel explained. "The Brooklyn Dodger [sic] president was not camouflaging his attempt to perpetuate baseball's color line, but rather his intention to eliminate it. Behind the façade of looking for talent for the strange new league, Rickey, in reality, was seeking Black athletes for the Dodger organization. Though none of those present [at Rickey's announcement] knew it, they had witnessed the first act in the drama of baseball integration."[57]

Whatever his true motives—and he kept them well hidden—Rickey's involvement in the nascent league did not sit well with the black press. If the USL was the opening act of integration, Lacy ought to be credited with having warmed up the audience, albeit in an unusual way. The longtime *Afro-American* crusader for integration was quick to ridicule the new league, Rickey's remarks about it, and Griffith's reaction, calling them all "good for a laugh"[58] and an attempt by Rickey to set himself up as a Negro League dictator. Lacy included the Old Fox among the white owners whom he called the Fraternity of Ebullient Double-Talkers. "First thing I'd like to know in connection with Griffith's reprimand of Rickey, is how come he thinks Rickey CAN [as published] set himself up as any 'dictator' of colored baseball, such as he charges the Brooklyn Dodger boss is trying to do?"[59] The columnist cleverly contrasted Griffith's defense of the existing two Negro Leagues as being well-organized, in existence for some time, and "in which colored people . . . have faith and confidence" with what Lacy called "the tripe he has been handing [me] for the past six years, to wit: The first step toward getting colored players into the major leagues is for the colored people to set up their own leagues, not the kind they have now, but good strong organizations in which the public will have faith and confidence." As for the USL, Lacy dismissed it as having no more than four "topline ball players" with teams set to play in stadiums, especially in Chicago and Detroit, that were "out-of-the-way for colored patronage." Lacy took a final—and familiar—swipe at Griffith when he then asked, "Why does Griff begrudge Rickey his one little 'sideline' when he has one of his own in that nondescript flock he's brought up from the Cuban bushes?" Fay Young, in his *Chicago Defender* column, charged Rickey with "trying to assume the role of an Abraham Lincoln in Negro baseball" while in actuality "wearing the black hood of one who seeks to form or sponsor a Negro organization in order to stave off the clamor of the white and Negro fans to have Negroes integrated into the major leagues."[60]

Buoyed by taking three of four games from the A's to complete their home stand, an optimistic group of Nationals went on the road to begin their first western swing with three night games against the AL champions in St. Louis. Nats' hitting and fielding was improving, especially the surprising play of outfielders Bingo Binks and Cuban newcomer Jose Zardon, who joined stalwart George Case. In fact, the speedy 21-year-old Havana native was giving Case a run for his money in beating out grounders and chasing down balls in left field. The May 8 opener at Sportsman's Park had every reason to be a joyous occasion and a day of pride for fans, players, and Browns officials. But the franchise's first pennant wasn't the only reason for jubilation. The banner headline on page 1 of the Washington *Evening Star* (with a similar extra-large-type headline in just about every American newspaper) said it all: TRUMAN PROCLAIMS V-E DAY; CALLS FOR JAP SURRENDER. The war in Europe finally was over. In his V-E Day proclamation, which coincided with the president's 61st birthday (now a state holiday in Missouri), Truman cautioned: "Much remains to be done. The victory won in the west must now be won in the east." Then the chief executive of less than one month said, "I call on the people of the United States, whatever their faith, to unite in joyful thanks to God for the victory we have won and to pray that He will support us to the end of our present struggle and guide us into the way of peace." Then he added, "I also call upon my countrymen to dedicate this day of prayer to the memory of those who have given their lives to make possible our victory."[61]

But old customs die hard and prejudices sometimes even harder. Despite the long-awaited peace in Europe, Truman's call for a day of prayer and remembrance, to say nothing of the Browns being the

American League champions for the first (and only) time, the team and their fans failed to display a kinder and more fraternal mind-set. The opener, won by St. Louis 7–1, was marked by nonstop bigotry—catcalls, racist slurs, jeering, and booing, even missiles thrown from the stands at Washington's five Cubans. As an unnamed Nats reporter put it, "The St. Louis players and everyone on the bench, for that matter, seems allergic to our Cuban players and are said to be riding and heckling them in a manner unsportsmanshiplike [sic] even in professional ball and the habit has spread to the stands,"[62] where rookie Jose Zardon[63] in left field was pelted with debris and small stones, at least one of them striking him in the back.

After losing two of three games in St. Louis (one game ended in a 1–1 tie due to inclement weather), the Nats moved on to Chicago, where they managed to win only the opener of a three-game set. The scheduled four-game series against the Indians was postponed due to frigid temperatures, not uncommon weather in Cleveland at that time of the year, so the Nats moved on to Detroit, where they split four games in two doubleheaders before heading home. The Nats began the road trip with a record of 9–8 and returned to Griffith Stadium in fifth place with 12 wins, 14 losses, and one tie. Like Cleveland's weather, the Nats' bats were cold, and they were hitting a combined .201 against a league filled with pitchers who wouldn't have been in the majors except for the war. To underscore how weak they were at the plate, the Nats' leading hitter was pitcher Dutch Leonard.

The Nats opened their home stand by promptly losing three games to Cleveland, scoring a total of just two runs. Their fourth consecutive loss came in the opener against Detroit, 3–1, the preseason favorite to win the pennant. Washington then bounced back to win the following game when Detroit could muster just one run to the Nats' two. (Detroit's fortunes would soon brighten when Hank Greenberg, who'd been among the first to enlist in May 1941, was discharged from the Army on June 14, after almost four years in the service. His return would also have a direct effect on the Nationals' season.)

Rallying at home against the despised Browns, the Nats took two of three games and ended May with a record of 15–19–1, slipping into seventh place. Hitting—or the lack of it—remained anemic into June. Among the most frustrated was Jake Powell, whose 11 hits in 60 at bats gave him a batting average of .172 and a ride on the Nats bench, which prompted the always-volatile Powell to quit the team. When he cooled down, he ended his retirement a day later, but it cost him about $50 because Griffith docked him a day's pay.

If the baseball moguls remained concerned about the status of the game even after the war in Europe had ended, those concerns were justified in early June by a North Dakota Republican senator with a checkered political past that included being removed as governor following a felony conviction and then, after his exoneration, winning another term as governor. William "Wild Bill" Langer introduced an unusual piece of legislation ostensibly designed to assist returning veterans rehabilitate and find employment by requiring the major leagues to set aside at least 10 percent of each team's roster for men who had lost "one or more" arms, legs, or hands in the war.[64] The *Post*'s Shirley Povich quickly debunked the idea, pointing out that baseball cannot be legislated from Capitol Hill. Besides, "Langer's bill would be putting the war wounded on a ridiculous and unnecessary spot," Povich wrote.[65] Such a requirement would do little to alleviate the GIs' rehabilitation because 10 percent "would mean 40 men at the most, and the Nation's rehabilitation problem must deal in millions of men," Povich calculated. Wild Bill's wild bill promptly died.

Of greater concern on the labor front, however, was an announcement by the federal Budget Bureau that a quarter of a million workers would be dropped from the federal payroll during the next year.[66] In a letter to the House Civil Service Committee, F. J. Lawson, the bureau's administrative assistant, calculated that if the war continued to progress as it was, approximately 20,000 federal employees would lose their jobs, beginning with workers at field offices before affecting the 250,000 or so federal workers in Washington. Ironically, the announcement came as the committee met to consider a bill that would raise federal pay by about 15 percent.

The Nats continued to play .500 ball the first two weeks of June with a record of 7–7–1, until the middle of June when they swept the always-accommodating Philadelphia A's, winning a doubleheader on Tuesday and then a single game, 7–5, on Wednesday, June 20. Then they left for Boston and a 19-game road trip during which they won 13 games—including a Fourth of July doubleheader sweep of the Chicago White Sox—while losing just six contests, two of them the final pair of a four-game set in St. Louis. So on July 13, after winning both games of a two-game set against the visiting White Sox, 4–2 and 3–2, the Nats' record was 40–32–2 (they'd picked up a second tie, 4–4, on June 15, at home against the Red Sox), and they were in second place two and a half games behind league-leading Detroit.

For the first time since its inception in 1933, there was no All-Star Game in 1945. Originally scheduled for Boston's Fenway Park, the more restrictive government travel requirements announced earlier in the year forced the cancellation of the annual event even as attendance across both leagues was approaching prewar numbers.[67] (The dearth of true "All-Star" talent no doubt influenced the decision.) Instead, the owners dreamed up a series of seven interleague exhibitions over two days to help raise money for war relief, whose coffers had amassed $2.62 million since the program began.[68] The "marquee game" featured the second-place Washington Nationals hosting the second-place Brooklyn Dodgers at Griffith Stadium, while the Giants and Yankees would meet at the Polo Grounds. The other scheduled exhibitions were the Phillies and A's at Shibe Park, the White Sox and Cubs at Comiskey Park, and the Indians and Reds at Cleveland's Municipal Stadium; the two St. Louis teams would reprise their 1944 World Series clash at Sportsman's Park, and the Red Sox and Braves would play at Fenway Park (the lone day game because of the ballpark's lack of lights). Only Pittsburgh and Detroit fell victim to the travel restrictions and would have two days off.

For the Nats, the 23,791 fans who witnessed the July 10 exhibition and festivities, and especially for Griffith, everything about the evening was special. How could it be anything but? His oft-struggling team was in the thick of the battle hoping for another pennant, he'd heard that his former star third baseman Buddy Lewis would soon be discharged from the service and rejoin the team, the stands were filled once again with joyous fans, and there, on the field evoking memories of some two decades ago, was Ossie Bluege manning the hot corner as he had when Washington won its only World Series in 1924. In the spirit of friendly competition, before the game, Bluege had challenged his counterpart, Dodgers manager Leo Durocher, to join him and play an inning, and the Dodgers skipper had promptly agreed. (Both men walked in their only plate appearance in the first inning, and Bluege was credited with a pop-fly putout.)

If there was one person at Griffith Stadium who was even happier than Griffith, it was Bert Shepard, the war hero with the artificial leg whom Griffith had signed in spring training as a batting-practice hurler. Shepard received the loudest ovation of the evening when he walked to the mound in the bottom of the first inning, ball in hand, ready to pitch to the Dodgers lineup. Just a little more than a year ago, the prewar minor leaguer had been an amputee in a German POW camp. Now, although it was only an exhibition game that had no real importance (except to Shepard of course), he was making his first appearance on a major-league mound and as a starter to boot. And, just as he had in spring training, he again did not disappoint. Relying on his excellent curve ball, Shepard allowed just one hit over three scoreless innings before giving up two runs on four hits in the Dodgers' fourth when he was relieved by Roger Wolff. Washington won the game, 4–2. (Ten days later, on July 19, Griffith placed Shepard on the active roster. "We'll work him in relief roles to start with," Ossie Bluege told the media, "and we'll all be rooting for Shepard to be a starting pitcher. With that curve, he has a chance.")[69]

One week after Shepard made his first start, Harry Truman began his first overseas visit as president when he, Churchill,[70] and Stalin began meetings in Potsdam, a suburb of Berlin that had been spared Allied bombing, from July 17 to August 2. They met to try to cobble together agreements on how to treat postwar Germany, war-crimes issues, the question of Poland's borders, and a postwar balance of power between the Allies and the Soviet Union. By this time, Truman was fully aware of the top-secret Manhattan Project that had produced the newly developed but unproven atomic bomb. In a handwritten memo for himself dated July 18, 1945, one day after the conference began, Truman wrote that he had "discussed Manhattan (if it is a success)" with Churchill and was sure that the Japanese "will fold up" when "Manhattan appears over their homeland."[71] (Midway through the conference, Truman lost his close ally when Churchill was forced to depart for home after his Tory Party was defeated in national elections and Labour's Clement Attlee became prime minister.)

Washington's Mayflower Hotel played host to a conference of a different sort when the baseball magnates gathered in mid-July to discuss the parameters of commissioner-elect Chandler's yet-to-be-agreed-upon contract. To a man, they did not want Landis's successor to have the same unlimited powers that they had so eagerly granted to the judge in 1920 in the wake of the Black Sox scandal that had threatened to destroy the game. They also did not want to perpetuate the practice Landis had instituted of writing his own contract renewals, which he literally forced upon his employers, "who were so intimidated by the forcefulness of Landis' personality and his iron rule that they could scarcely object." [72].

In separate league meetings on Wednesday and then in a joint session on Thursday, the moguls hammered out an agreement. But in the end, the owners gave the Kentucky senator everything he wanted after Chandler met with them for less than two hours and overwhelmed them with his outsized personality choking off any dissent. Under Chandler's threat of immediately resigning, he was given the power to determine, as he saw fit, anything he thought detrimental to the interests of baseball, control of the commissioner's office funds (derived primarily from the World Series), approval to move the commissioner's headquarters from Chicago to Cincinnati, and acknowledgment that his office could hire or fire employees at will. Chandler and the owners tabled for later discussion the question of signing teenage players while they were in high school or college. [73] "It was the most harmonious meeting which I have ever attended," Chandler announced afterward. [74] "All of the gentlemen saw eye-to-eye with me," he added, living up to his apt nickname "Happy."

Any disappointment or regrets Griffith might have had regarding the outcome of the meetings were quickly assuaged when he received a telegram on July 11 from Buddy Lewis saying that he would be discharged in about a week and would promptly rejoin the team. Lewis, who entered the Army in 1942 as an air cadet, had risen to the rank of captain and had flown 368 missions as a transport pilot on the dangerous China–India–Burma route, known simply as the hump. [75] He came home with the Distinguished Flying Cross, the Air Medal with Oak Leaf Clusters, and the Distinguished Unit Citation Badge. The always-dangerous left-handed hitter had spent the previous three months manning the outfield for the Stout Field Air Force team near Indianapolis and had honed his hitting skills.

During the last two weeks in July, the Nats' fortunes ebbed and flowed. Immediately after the exhibition game against the Dodgers and two wins against the White Sox, the Nats dropped four in a row at home—a doubleheader sweep by the Browns on July 16 and a double-header loss to Detroit on July 18—before taking the last two games of the Tigers series, 4–3 and 3–1. After winning the first two games against the visiting Indians, the Nats lost the final three games of the series and the home stand. Washington then lost two of three games in Boston despite Buddy Lewis's arrival. Playing the always-challenging right field at Fenway Park, Lewis misjudged a couple of fly balls but managed hits in two of the three games. The Nats ended July having slipped into third place with a record of 45–41–2, one and a half games behind the Yankees and five and a half games behind the Tigers.

Lewis's misplays at Fenway Park were totally forgotten when the Nats returned to Griffith Stadium to play a twi-night doubleheader on August 1 against their favorite opponent, the Athletics. Connie Mack's outfit was firmly established in its familiar last place, 20½ games off the pace. Griffith dedicated the evening to honor Lewis. In pregame cere-monies, the team gave him a $500 war bond, and Griffith, Mack, and Chandler all lauded his wartime exploits. Mack went so far as to predict that with Lewis back in the lineup, "Washington has a great chance to see a World Series in the fall."[76] Former Nats catcher now Private First Class Jake Early, back on leave from the 87th Infantry Division and battles in France and Germany, also received a warm welcome when he emerged from the dugout to greet Lewis and the crowd. .

Even Lewis's former commander, Major General Elwood Quesada, got into the act. The commanding officer of the IX Tactical Air Com-mand (Ninth Air Force) said, "Buddy flew 368 missions over the hump in India and every man in the Air Force is pulling for him to have [a] .368 average on his return to baseball." In reply, Lewis said simply, "I'm glad to be back. Thank you very much."[77] Unfortunately for everyone, the dampest July in Washington in the 77 years of weather record-keeping—a total of 11.06 inches of rain—truly cast a wet blanket on the festivities. Both games were rained out, forcing the Nats into five straight twi-night doubleheaders in as many days, a stretch that could make or break their chances at a pennant run and further strain Bluege's already taxed pitching staff.

What had happened might rightly be called "the miracle on Georgia Avenue." Through the end of July, the Nats had played 21 doublehead-ers and had managed to sweep both games just six times. But kicking off August at home against the A's, the Nationals put together a streak of

seven wins in a row and nine of the 10 games in those five doubleheaders to boost their record to 54–42–2. The miracle wasn't the winning
streak per se; it was how they did it. What Ossie Bluege had been
fretting about most—Nats' pitching—became their strength just as the
hitting seemed to wilt in the hot, humid Washington summer. Seven
different pitchers started in the seven-game win streak, and each man
pitched a complete game (virtually an impossibility in today's game of
specialist hurlers for the latter innings), yielding a total of just seven
runs, only four of them earned. Among them was one Wally Holborow,
a former semipro hurler making his first start of the season, who allowed the Red Sox just two hits. Overall, Nats pitchers dominated the
A's and Red Sox, who scored a combined total of 7 runs while the Nats
tallied 23 runs in the magnificent seven for an average of 3.29 runs a
game.

The win streak ended in the second game of the August 4 doubleheader against Boston, a 15–4 rout. But the lopsided loss has provided
baseball fans with an intriguing trivia question. Ossie Bluege called on
Cuban pitcher Carlos Santiago "Sandy" Ullrich to start, and he promptly gave up a run in the first and third innings. Then the roof fell in as
Ullrich and reliever Joe Cleary, making his major-league debut, allowed
Boston to score 12 runs in the top of the fourth. Cleary managed to get
just one out while giving up five hits, three walks, and seven earned
runs in just one-third of an inning. The 26-year-old native of Cork,
Ireland, never pitched another inning in the major leagues, so his career earned run average was an astronomical 189, if not an all-time
record then very close to one.

Ceding the game to Boston and trying to save his fatigued pitching
staff, Bluege brought in Bert Shepard with two outs, and for the third
time since his tryout back in April, the one-legged pitcher rose to the
occasion. If the war hero was nervous about appearing in his first regular-season game, he didn't show it. Shepard struck out the first batter he
faced, centerfielder George Metkovich, to retire the side as the 13,035
fans cheered wildly. Shepard went on to pitch the final five innings. His
line score for five and one-third innings was three hits, one walk, one
earned run allowed, and two putouts on grounders back to the mound.
At the plate he went 0–3, with one strikeout and a base on balls. Shepard had indeed realized the dream that had given him a purpose to
survive his German captivity. But with the Nats battling for the pennant

and incurring no further blowout losses, Shepard never took the mound again, ending his brief major-league career with an enviable 1.69 ERA. Thus, the two relief pitchers became the answer to one of the strangest (and more obscure) of all baseball trivia questions: What two team-mates made their major-league debut in the same game when one pitcher replaced the other and neither ever appeared in another major-league game?

The 15–4 Boston blowout aside, Washington pitching dominated the win streak. Led by George Case and George Myatt, the Nats' speed also played an important supporting role. Myatt's hot streak at the plate had boosted his average to .301, which put him on base often enough to run his stolen-base total to 21, tied with teammate and perennial league champion Case. When the Nats headed off to Chicago at the start of their second and final western road swing on August 8, they were just a half game behind league-leading Detroit. They arrived in the Windy City just after the United States dropped the atomic bomb on Hiroshi-ma on August 6. On August 9, when the Nats beat the White Sox, 7–2, a second atomic bomb was dropped on Nagasaki. The emperor, whose voice had never been heard by the ordinary Japanese population, went on the radio on August 15 and announced Japan's surrender. World War II was indeed over.

A week and a half before the Nats reached the Windy City, the Negro Leagues staged their 13th annual East–West classic at Chicago's Comiskey Park on Sunday, July 29. A crowd of 40,000 to 50,000 was expected to attend the tiebreaker as each league had notched six victo-ries in the series with the previous two games having been won by the West. The always-popular Satchel Paige would be there this year, again representing the Kansas City Monarchs; Buck Leonard and pitcher Roy Welmaker would represent the Grays. But Josh Gibson, plagued by mental-health problems and erratic off-field behavior throughout his career, was left off the East squad. The Grays issued a brief statement to the effect that Gibson was in no shape to play either as a catcher or as a batter. Sam Lacy, however, was quick to rally to Gibson's cause. "On a binge or not, Josh is just what I've always considered him. He is a fine batsman but a country cousin in the receiving department. Then why punish him?"[78]

Among the younger All-Stars were Baltimore Elite Giants catcher Roy Campanella on the East squad and Kansas City Monarchs rookie shortstop Jackie Robinson on the West.[79] Although they were originally listed as substitutes, both Campanella and Robinson started and played the entire game. Campanella went two for five and scored one run; Robinson did not get a hit in five plate appearances but caught a hard ground ball behind second base and fired to first to end the game,[80] won by the West, 9–6, its third-straight victory in the series. The day's only disappointment was the attendance. The crowd of 31,714 was far below the expected sellout, and most of the fans were from the Chicago area, the *Chicago Defender* reported,[81] surmising that the government travel restrictions had kept many out-of-towners from attending the game. In his column, *Chicago Defender* sportswriter Fay Young reported that ticket scalpers were "left holding blocks of tickets [at] outlandish prices."[82]

Several weeks later, in mid-August, New York Mayor Fiorello La Guardia announced he was forming a 10-person committee that included Lacy, Rickey, and Yankee president Larry MacPhail to determine "why qualified colored players are denied admission to the organized game."[83] Although the answer to that question was apparent to all and had been for years, the committee was created at the urging of the AFRO publishing group and among those also invited to participate were *New York Times* sports columnist (later sports editor) Arthur Daley and tap dancer Bill "Bojangles" Robinson. Of course, nothing of substance came from the committee because, once again, the two Negro Leagues declined to participate. They and the African American press were still smarting from the sham tryouts in Boston and Bear Mountain in April.

Although the White Sox and Nats had split their early August four-game set at Comiskey Park, the Nats were the bigger loser, having lost George Case for about 10 days when he severely sprained an ankle showing his sliding skills for some motion-picture photographers before the opening game on August 8. Ironically, it was when Case agreed to "one more shot" that his spikes hit the turf and his left ankle turned under him. He was replaced by Mike Kreevich, an outfielder Griffith purchased from the Browns. Kreevich, playing centerfield, promptly added clout at the plate too. Looking ahead to a pennant run, the Old Fox also purchased shortstop Dick Kimble from the Toledo Mud Hens to spell Gil Torres, who'd been playing the position on sore legs and was seeing doctors regularly. Griffith also had shrewdly purchased rookie pitcher Marino Pieretti, who by August 9 was 10–9, though at least four of those six losses could be charged "against his teammates, who have a bizarre habit of bobbling critical plays behind him," Vincent X. Flaherty wrote in the *Sporting News*.[84]

In drafting the five-foot, seven-inch tall Pieretti from the Portland Beavers of the Pacific Coast League (in the off-season the right-hander strengthened his arms by wielding a sledgehammer on cattle in a San Francisco slaughterhouse), Griffith once again lived up to his nickname. As Flaherty reported, the draft rules in place at the time limited each major-league team to signing just one minor leaguer at the minimum $7,500 price. Portland owner Bill Klepper assumed the big leagues would go after one of his outfielders and that Pieretti, who was 26–13 in 1944, would be safe and could be sold later for much more. But the Old Fox crossed up Klepper and chose Pieretti. An angry Klepper said, "Washington grabbed a $75,000 pitcher for $7,500." Griffith no doubt further irked the Portland owner when he acknowledged that he had never even seen Pieretti pitch or even bothered to scout him. "By sin, I don't have to know anything about a feller like that. I'll pay $7,500 for anyone who can win 26 games in a Double-A league."[85] (Pieretti finished the season with a record of 14–13, but earned Bluege's respect and admiration by volunteering for relief duty on days when he wasn't starting. Pieretti pitched for the Nats until 1948, when he was traded to the White Sox. He ended his major-league career as a Cleveland Indian in 1950. Pieretti died in 1981 at age 60.)

Washington, a preseason pick as one of the teams to beat in the AL pennant race, moved on to St. Louis with even less satisfactory results. The Nats won two and lost three games against the sixth-place Browns and fell to three and a half games behind first-place Detroit, their next stop. Despite Detroit having supplanted Washington as the press favorite for the AL flag, it was the Tigers who saved Washington's pennant chances when the Nats won three of four games in the Motor City, an 8–0 opener and 3–1 and 11–5 victories in the final two contests. The Nats then traveled to Cleveland, where they beat the Indians in six of seven games (including three doubleheaders), sweeping the last five to run their record to 67–49–2. But the Yankees promptly cooled their hot streak by sweeping both doubleheaders against the Nats on August 25 and 26 at Yankee Stadium. Clearly, fatigue was taking its toll. Washington rallied to win two of three in Philadelphia and ended its 27-game road trip with a respectable 15–12 record to bring its season record to 69–54–2. And the club did it without Case, who was still recovering from the ankle injury he sustained in Chicago.

Washington was now just one game behind the Tigers with 31 games remaining, 24 of them at Griffith Stadium, including 10 doubleheaders. Under ordinary circumstances, the lopsided home schedule would favor Washington. But the Nats "are so tired most of the regulars are unable to go through both ends of a double-header. And that certainly does not make the ball club look any too good for the rugged home stretch," observed John B. Keller in the *Evening Star.*[86] However, Griffith had little to complain about. The Nats had played better than .500 ball before 354,826 out-of-town crowds during the road trip, which added about $100,000 to his coffers. In Chicago, the Nationals helped the White Sox draw 34,647 fans into Comiskey Park for one game, the second-largest crowd of the season. And in New York, what better way to celebrate the newly won peace than by taking in a Sunday double-header at vast Yankee Stadium? A crowd of 52,797 fans must have thought so, and they saw their Yankees beat the Nats twice on August 26.[87]

In the nation's capital, war-weary workers, many of whom had just gone back to a five-day workweek, set off a mass exodus on Friday, August 31, for the first three-day Labor Day weekend since the war began. As the *Washington Post* reported in its Saturday edition, "Beginning promptly at 5 yesterday cabs, three lanes deep, outside Union Station, disgorged weekend travelers loaded down with luggage, tennis rackets and golf clubs. The crowd was heavier than the normal wartime travel loads, particularly for the trains going to the nearby Maryland beach points and into Pennsylvania." Previously used only sparingly to conserve fuel and tires, so many autos took to the roads in near-perfect weather that Truman himself cautioned extra care. Having just told Congress he considered the $43 billion in lend-lease aid repaid by the Allies' victory, the president now told Americans to "feel a personal responsibility for the preservation of human life by exercising extraordinary caution in operating badly worn cars and tires."[88]

The *New York Times* reported that motorists, returning home on Monday, were "expected to cause a traffic jam of pre-war dimensions," and railroads were "expecting to use every piece of available equipment to take care of the rush. Bus lines also will press into service all their vehicles to handle the crowds that started their exodus Thursday."[89] For servicemen who came to Washington for the Labor Day weekend, hospitality groups set aside 4,300 beds "all amply supplied with clean sheets" for 50 cents a night. The American Women's Volunteer Services made 400 rooms available to service personnel and their families at a daily rate of one to three dollars.[90]

The Nats could have used those accommodations to get some much-needed rest after their long and exhausting road trip. Instead, they carried their fatigue into Griffith Stadium, where sellout crowds were expected for the five holiday weekend games against New York. The Yankees swept the Friday twi-night doubleheader, 3–2 and 3–1, on August 31, and Washington missed a chance to tie the Tigers for the American League lead. The only highlight that day came when General Omar Bradley awarded Bert Shepard the Distinguished Flying Cross. Washington rebounded to win the Saturday game, 3–0. Following the signing of Japan's unconditional surrender aboard the USS *Missouri*, President Truman declared Sunday, September 2, V-J Day and urged Americans to go forward in hope and fraternity toward "a new and better world of peace and international goodwill."[91]

Now that there truly was peace again, a jubilant record crowd of 30,143 at the Sunday doubleheader saw the Nats drop the opening game, 4–2, only to rebound with a 3–0 shutout in the nightcap. Washington, now with a record of 71–57–2, then traveled to Boston, where they split a Labor Day Monday doubleheader with the Red Sox, winning game one, 11–5, and losing the nightcap, 8–4. They then promptly returned to Griffith Stadium for six games against a resurgent St. Louis club. The Browns had just come off a stretch in August of playing .657 baseball, winning 23 of 35 games, one of the best home stands in their history, and they had beaten the Nats 10 of 16 games up to this point in the season. That torrid home stand put the Browns in third place, one and a half games behind the second-place Nationals, who still trailed the league-leading Tigers by two games.

After splitting the first two games, a 2–1 victory followed by a 4–3 loss, Washington beat St. Louis the next three games, all of them by scoring three or fewer runs, 2–0, 3–2, and 3–2. The series finale on September 8 became a footnote in baseball history when a relaxed and victorious Harry S. Truman made the first of his 16 visits to Griffith Stadium during his presidency.[92] One day earlier, Commissioner Happy Chandler had given Truman a gold pass to the upcoming World Series, and the president indicated that he might attend. (If he had, Truman would be the first president to witness the Fall Classic since FDR attended the opening game of the 1933 World Series between Washington and the New York Giants.) *Post* columnist Shirley Povich noted that Truman's gold pass was tax-free because the IRS had exempted all service personnel—and Truman was commander in chief— from paying the 20 percent amusement tax.[93] With 20,000 spectators looking on and in company of first lady Bess Truman, Speaker of the House Rayburn, Fleet Admiral William D. Leahy, and White House press secretary Charlie Ross, the ambidextrous Truman opted to make his first ceremonial toss as a southpaw. A photo of the event also shows the two managers, Ossie Bluege and Luke Sewell, on either side of the president, and although they are smiling, the once close friends had not repaired the rift that began the previous year in St. Louis. In the end, it was Bluege who was smiling last, as his Nats won the finale of the six-game series, 4–1.

The game tested Truman's allegiance as he had rooted for Washington since going to Congress in 1935. But he was born in Lamar, Missouri, and had spent much of his early years as a businessman in Kansas City and followed the St. Louis teams. Truman thus joined the line of chief executives dating back to William Howard Taft who threw out a ceremonial first pitch at Griffith Stadium. As Missouri natives, Griffith and Truman became close friends to the point that both were so at ease in each other's presence that Griffith could call Truman "Harry," rather than the accepted address of Mr. President. (The Old Fox, always a keen judge of talent, correctly predicted in 1948 that Truman would win the presidential election despite all the polls showing him losing badly to two-time Republican nominee Thomas Dewey. In fact, the ever-frugal baseball magnate put his money where his mouth was and contributed to the Truman campaign.)[94] The game also marked the return of third baseman Cecil Travis, who was reunited with Buddy Lewis, the first two Nats to enter the service. While injuries kept Case and Myatt out of the lineup, Lewis's timely hitting gave Washington a more potent offense. Although Travis went hitless in four trips in his return debut, the win evened the season series with St. Louis at 11 games apiece. The Nationals, who were no fans of St. Louis, happily killed any chances the Browns might have had to repeat as the AL pennant winner.

Over the next seven days, the Nats won three of five games against Chicago, including both games of a Sunday doubleheader, 4–2 and 5–4. They followed the Chicago series with a three-game sweep of the Indians during which Walt Masterson pitched a two-hitter to best Bob Feller for a 4–0 win in the second game of the series. The Nats were now just a half game behind Detroit. "With 11 games remaining, the road ahead is rugged, for the pace-setting Detroiters have 14 more engagements on their schedule. Yet should both clubs move along as they have since the Western outfits began their final invasion of the East last week, the Tigers would do no more than tie the Nats for the pennant," observed sportswriter John B. Keller.[95]

Much of that rugged road ahead, however, was caused by Griffith himself. For once, the Old Fox's baseball acumen failed him, and by thinking more of his bottom line than of his baseball fortunes, he committed one of the rare errors in his 50-plus-year career. Based on his club's dismal last-place performance the year before, Griffith had rented his ballpark to the Washington Redskins for the last week in September. So to play the mandatory 77 home games and to make the Redskins deal work, Griffith got the league to agree to a schedule that had the Nats playing 25 doubleheaders at Griffith Stadium, including seven in September, four of which were played on consecutive days, so that the last home game would be on September 18, freeing the ballpark for football. The compacted schedule only further strained Bluege's pitching staff, which was already experiencing the normal fatigue from six months of baseball. As catcher Rick Ferrell told reporters, "If we lose the pennant blame it on double-headers. We're a small club and those double-headers are killing us."[96] When league-leading Detroit followed Cleveland into Griffith Stadium for a crucial five-game series, the Nats' record was 83–61–2. "Anything less than three victories for the Nats in the five games could ultimately cost them the flag," warned Povich.[97]

Despite going with its two best pitchers, Mickey Haefner and Dutch Leonard, Washington promptly lost both games of the Saturday doubleheader to the Tigers, 7–4 and 7–3. The Nats split the Sunday doubleheader, winning 3–2 and then losing the nightcap, 5–4. After an off day Monday, the Nats broke out against Detroit in the finale. By the third inning, Washington led 5–0. Detroit roared back to tie it in the top of the sixth, 5–5, but that was the last of the scoring for the Tigers. The Nats scored four runs in the bottom of the seventh inning and three more in their half of the eighth inning, for seven unanswered runs and a 12–5 victory. So having lost three of the five games that Povich had calculated would doom their chances, the Nats had five games left to play, two in New York and three in Philadelphia. Detroit could ensure a tie for the pennant by winning six of its eight remaining games while Washington needed to run the table and win all of its remaining games.

Washington promptly lost the Thursday game in New York, 6–1, when the Nats' Mickey Haefner was outpitched by another leftie, Joe Page (who later, while still with the Yankees, became one of the earliest specialty relief pitchers), and were outhit when the Yankees amassed 10 base hits, including a double, home run, and single by second baseman George "Snuffy" Stirnweiss. It might have been worse if Joe DiMaggio, who was still in the service, had been in the lineup instead of sitting in the stands as one of the sparse crowd of 6,448.[98] Fortunately for Washington, the Tigers fell to Cleveland, 6–1, but the Nats lost a valuable chance to tie the league leaders, who remained one game up. Bluege called on 42-year-old Johnny Niggeling to pitch the Friday game against Bill Zuber, who'd recently been pitching well and holding teams to just a couple of runs per game.

After just the first inning, Niggeling found himself on the bench and behind New York, 3–0, after Nick Etten hit his 17th homer of the season, with two outs, following walks to outfielders Bud Metheny and Charlie Keller. The Nats scored two runs in the top of the second inning and tied the score with another run in the third, only to see Stirnweiss hit his second home run in two days in the home half of the inning to give New York a 4–3 lead. Zuber pitched a complete game 5–3 victory. Detroit was idle, but the two losses at Yankee Stadium put Washington one and a half games behind the Tigers with three games left to play for the Nats and six for the Tigers. Four wins by the Tigers—even if the Nats swept their perennial patsies, the A's, in the final three games—would give Detroit the American League pennant and a trip to the World Series.

Roger Wolff gained his 20th win of the season in the Saturday opener in Philadelphia pitching a 2–0 shutout over the A's. (The game was actually the 154th for the Nationals. But because the two ties didn't count in the standings, they still had two games remaining.) The Tigers kept their slim lead over Washington, beating the visiting Browns, 9–0, behind a four-hitter thrown by ace Hal Newhouser. Hank Greenberg, playing leftfield with an injured ankle, got two hits, drove in two runs, and scored one. The win meant Detroit could clinch the pennant on Sunday by beating St. Louis if the Nats lost their last two games. In the Sunday do-or-die doubleheader, however, the Nats were their own worst enemy. In game one, Dutch Leonard was pitching a 3–0 shutout into the eighth inning when the usually sure-fielding pair of Cecil Travis and Buddy Lewis made errors in the bottom of the frame, leading to three unearned A's runs. But the worst was yet to come.

Four innings later, with the score still tied, 3–3, centerfielder Bingo Binks went out to his outfield position for the home half of the 12th inning without taking along his sunglasses. With two outs and the bases empty, Ernie Kish lofted a fly ball into centerfield. Binks lost it in the sun, the ball dropped, and Kish ended up on second base with a double. After an intentional pass to Dick Siebert to set up force-outs at the bases, future Hall of Famer George Kell lined the first pitch for a single, scoring Kish and giving the A's a 4–3 win. The Nats, their chances now all but gone, nevertheless gained a half game on Detroit when they managed to win the nightcap behind hurler Marino Pieretti by an identical 4–3 score in eight innings when the game was called because of darkness, while in Detroit, the league-leading Tigers were shut out by Browns pitcher Nelson Potter, 5–0. So Washington's season ended with the Nats trailing Detroit by a single game. The Tigers were 86–64 for a .573 percentage, and the Nationals were at 87–67–2 in the standings for a .565 percentage. Washington's chances for the pennant hung by the barest of threads. The Nationals returned to Washington Sunday evening, September 23, to await their fate and to vote on how to split whatever share of the World Series money they would receive— either some $5,000 a man as pennant winners or considerably less, about $1,200 each, as the second-place finisher.[99]

Detroit needed only to split its remaining four games—two with the Indians at home and the final two against the Browns in St. Louis—to clinch the pennant outright. Only the miracle of twin sweeps by the Indians and Browns would give Washington its fourth pennant. If the Tigers won just one of the four games, Detroit and Washington would meet in a one-game playoff to decide the pennant winner. For once, the Nationals and their fans would be rooting for the despised Browns, their last chance, hoping the Browns would somehow repay Washington for having done them the favor the previous season of knocking off Detroit in the final game to hand the pennant to St. Louis. The Nats' fate was made more suspenseful when Detroit's series opener against visiting Cleveland on Tuesday, September 25, was postponed due to heavy rains. Washington's slim hopes grew slimmer still when the Tigers, again with ace Hal Newhouser on the mound, won the first game of a rescheduled doubleheader on Wednesday, 11–0, assuring Detroit of at least a tie for the pennant. Washington was still alive, however, after Cleveland came back to edge the Tigers, 3–2, in the nightcap, and the Nats gained a half game. But one Tiger win in their final two games in St. Louis would eliminate them.

After a cramped workout at Griffith Stadium where the Nats had to share the facilities with the Redskins, Ossie Bluege planned to take the team to the Bainbridge Naval Station in nearby Port Deposit, Maryland, to practice for the possible playoff game or the World Series if the Tigers lost both games in St Louis. But the odds were not in Washington's favor as Detroit had beaten the Browns in 14 of the 20 games they'd already played. For the Nats, it would be a long four days waiting for the Tigers and Browns to play in St. Louis on Saturday, September 29, and, if need be, on Sunday. With an eye to a possible playoff game against Washington, Tigers manager Steve O'Neill opted to hold Newhouser in reserve and to start Virgil Trucks, who was just discharged from the Navy. Hoping the Browns would prevail in both games, Bluege sent his three top pitchers—Leonard, Wolff, and Haefner—and his two catchers, on to Detroit to be well rested should there be a playoff showdown in the Motor City.

But a 10-day stretch of rain that lingered in the Midwest postponed Saturday's game and set the stage for a definitive doubleheader on Sunday. After rain and then a light drizzle delayed the opener by 50 minutes, the Browns quickly jumped out to a 1–0 lead when leadoff batter Don Gutteridge doubled and Lou Finney singled him home. The Browns held on to their one-run lead into the fifth inning when the Tigers tied the score on a walk and two singles. Detroit took the lead, 2–1, in the following inning, when Paul Richards singled with runners on first and second, scoring Roy Cullenbine. Trucks faltered in the sixth inning, giving up a double to pitcher Nelson Potter and a walk to Don Gutteridge with only one out. O'Neill tossed aside his own game plan and brought in Newhouser to hold the lead, which he did. But the Browns came back with a run in the seventh to tie the game at 2–2 and then went ahead, 3–2, in the home half of the eighth. Then in the top of the ninth with one out, runners on second and third, and Hank Greenberg on deck, Browns manager Luke Sewell ordered Potter to intentionally walk Roger "Doc" Cramer, a .275 hitter to that point in the season, to load the bases and pitch to Greenberg, one of baseball's all-time great sluggers. With one ball and one strike on him, Greenberg deposited Potter's next pitch into the left field stands for a grand-slam home run, a Tigers' 6–3 victory, and a ticket to the World Series. The Nats, sitting on their suitcases at Union Station prepared to travel to Detroit for a tiebreaker, were devastated. "You never saw a sadder bunch," Hillis Layne recalled in an interview years later.[100]

Griffith, Bluege, and the Nats must have been incredulous, unable to fathom Sewell's move. Sewell's stated reasoning to pitch to the slow-footed Greenberg, to try to create a double-play situation at all bases, must rank as one of the most controversial managerial moves in the history of the game. Greenberg, who in truth hadn't yet returned to midseason form after four years in the Army, said afterward that before he went into the service he "could recall each time that American League pitchers intentionally walked the hitter ahead to pitch to me," adding that he "could count on my 10 fingers" the number of times that happened. (Never with the pennant on the line of course.) "But now—well, since I came back in July everybody wants to pitch to me," the future Hall of Famer said.[101] As the *Evening Star*'s Francis E. Stann put it, "prewar strategy would have dictated no such move. Nobody wanted to pitch to Hank in a tight spot before he left for the Army. He was too likely to do what he did last Sunday—break up the ball game with that long hit." However, Shirley Povich accepted Sewell's excuse and noted that "the dissenters won't agree. Never pass anybody [intentionally] to get to Greenberg has been an American League axiom," he wrote.[102]

Even without the advanced sabermetrics of today, Greenberg's statistics overwhelmingly supported that axiom, prewar or postwar: in 1938, the Bronx native hit 58 home runs (2 short of Babe Ruth's record of 60 in 1927) for an average of 1 home run every 9.6 official at bats; in 1940, his last full season before entering the Army, Greenberg again led the league with 41 homers (and 150 RBIs) for a league-best ratio of 1 home run every official 14 at bats. Since coming out of the service in

July, Greenberg had hit 12 homers in just 33 contests, the first of which occurred in his first game back. As any ballplayer or fan will acknowledge, no special speed is needed to trot around the bases after hitting a homer. It would be ludicrous to suggest, even by the big-betting crowd in Detroit, that Sewell's unusual move was actually designed to produce the result it did and thereby thwart his former friend Ossie Bluege's chances of bringing home a pennant to Washington. If anyone did think that, they kept the dark thought to themselves.

For a team that had such a disastrous, historic fall to the bottom of the league the previous season, the Nats' second-place finish, even with the loss of the pennant on the final day of the season, made the 1945 campaign an overwhelming success for Washington. (Sadly, though, for as long as the team remained in the nation's capital, the Washington franchise would never again duplicate or surpass that second-place finish.) The Nationals had come so close to a "last to first" finish. Nevertheless, everyone associated with the team, from Griffith down to the clubhouse manager and the batboys, could only watch as Detroit went on to beat the Chicago Cubs (in the Cubs' last World Series appearance in the 20th century), four games to three. Detroit was led by Newhouser's wins in games five and seven and by Greenberg's series-leading two home runs.

Griffith did fare well, however, when it came to the bottom line. For the season, the Nats had drawn 652,660[103] fans to Griffith Stadium, their best showing of the war years, for a profit of $222,473, narrowly beating the Yankees' $200,957 for tops in the American League. That figure did not include the rental payments Redskins owner George Preston Marshall and Grays co-owner Cum Posey paid Griffith for the use of his stadium. Overall, for the four war years, Washington drew 2,156,082 fans and finished third in total gate receipts with $402,059, behind league-leading Detroit with $532,810, and the surprising St. Louis Browns with $441,716.[104] With peace at hand, an oh-so-close second-place finish, a 20-win season from pitcher Roger Wolff, and with more former players soon to be discharged from the service, Griffith could only be optimistic about the future of his ball club.

The Homestead Grays also had a satisfying if ultimately unfulfilling season. They won both halves of the Negro National League's split season, led by NNL batting-title champion Josh Gibson (.393 and 11 home runs in 44 official games) and teammate Buck Leonard (.375 and

4 home runs), but they failed to win their third-straight world championship.[105] The graying Grays, even with four All-Stars on the team (Leonard, Gibson, Cool Papa Bell, and Jud Wilson) were no match for the first-time Negro American League–champion Cleveland Buckeyes, who had superior youth, speed, and enthusiasm on their side and swept the series, 4–0. The Buckeyes, led by Sam Jethroe, the league batting champion with a .393 average (who along with Robinson had been summarily dismissed after their "tryout" in Boston in April that year), won the first two games at Cleveland's League Park, 2–1 and 4–2. The teams then went to Griffith Stadium, where the Buckeyes shut out the Grays in game three, 4–0, and then wrapped up the series in Philadelphia on September 20, winning the finale, 5–0. The Grays were held to just three runs in the 36 innings of play.[106]

The four games constituted the lowest-scoring, weakest-hitting World Series in Negro Leagues history. The two teams combined for a composite batting average of .195 and a slugging percentage of .222. Cleveland's numbers were 14 runs scored, a team batting average of .220, and hitting the only home run; the Grays managed just three runs, none over the last 22 consecutive innings of the series.[107] The upstart Buckeyes' victory was a cause for celebration among African American baseball fans who saw it as the start of a new era of young black stars as the Gibsons, Leonards, and Paiges were fading from the playing field.

However, a good deal of that new enthusiasm, as well as the widespread hopes that baseball would be integrated in 1946, faded just prior to the Buckeyes' series-clinching victory when Yankees president Larry MacPhail doused any chance of integration any time soon. In a statement, MacPhail publicly affirmed that "the Yankees have no intention of signing Negro players under contract or reservation to Negro clubs." He was responding to a query from the Committee on Unity, the 10-member group New York City Mayor La Guardia had created in August to look into ways to end racial discrimination in the game, the same committee that MacPhail had joined and was boycotted by the Negro Leagues. The Yankees boss charged that unnamed "pressure groups" were behind the move to end discrimination and that there were "few, if any, colored players who could qualify" to play in the major leagues. Further, MacPhail candidly acknowledged that "the big league clubs make too much money off the colored leagues to wreck the relationship," which in the Yankees' case amounted to $100,000 annually for rent and concessions. Then he seemed to close the door by saying, "Under present conditions, I do not believe anything can be accomplished by signing Negro players for small minor league clubs. To give tryouts to players whom you do not intend to employ is sheer hypocrisy." Besides, he said, a major-league player, in addition to talent, "must possess the technique, the co-ordination, the competitive aptitude and the discipline usually acquired after years of training in the smaller leagues," which in the Yankees' case averaged seven years.

MacPhail conveniently discounted the many years black players had toiled in their own leagues, often playing more games per week and under less favorable conditions than their white counterparts in the minor leagues. After adamantly insisting that "unintelligent propaganda will not force major league clubs to employ Negro players," he held out an olive branch and a modicum of hope when he said, "On the other hand, I believe the Negro is entitled to a better deal in baseball and I will favor any practical program to produce this result. If and when the Negro Leagues put their house in order—establish themselves on a sound and ethical operations basis—and conform to the standards of organized baseball—I favor admitting them to organized baseball; and the rights, privileges, and obligations of such membership." If those conditions were met, MacPhail added, he would favor "the adoption of some plan under which a limited number of Negro players, who first establish ability, character, and aptitude in their own leagues, might advance to the majors or big minors of organized baseball."[108]

Among the first to respond to MacPhail's salvo was integration crusader Sam Lacy, also a member of La Guardia's committee. Lacy pulled no punches. He called MacPhail's statement a "flimsy veil with which he covers his reasons" to avoid integration and likened his remarks to Nazi propaganda. Moreover, the black sports columnist charged that the Yankees boss had taken out of context an earlier assessment of Lacy's, that there are "those among our league players who might possibly excel in the matter of hitting or fielding or base-running. But for the most part, the fellows who could hold their own in more than one of these phases of the game are few and far between—perhaps nil." MacPhail, he charged, had emulated Josef Goebbels's "common practice of lifting phrases and half-statements from pronouncements of American and British leaders" to use "as ammunition for the guns of fascism." Lacy said he agreed with MacPhail that the tryouts for some black players earlier in the year by the Dodgers and Red Sox were indeed sheer hypocrisy. "I'm inclined to agree with him for two reasons: (1) he qualifies as a competent judge of hypocrisy, and (2) the two clubs did not have their hearts in the tryouts."[109]

Unbeknownst to Lacy, Smith, and other black sportswriters, as well as to Griffith and the white baseball establishment, a seismic change was coming to baseball sooner than they could possibly have imagined. It began with a scouting trip to the Midwest in August when Dodgers boss Branch Rickey sent his most trusted adviser, Clyde Sukeforth, a baseball lifer with a keen eye for talent, to scout the Negro Leagues. Sukeforth believed he was looking for players to join Rickey's new Brooklyn Brown Dodgers of the USL. Sukeforth was dispatched to Chicago for the specific purpose of assessing one player, Kansas City Monarchs rookie shortstop Jackie Robinson, and to evaluate whether he had the arm strength to throw base runners out from that position. Rickey had already assessed Robinson's character, education, and life-style and found they matched precisely with what he wanted in the man he hoped to employ to break the color barrier. If the Dodgers scout believed Robinson had the arm strength to match his strength of char-acter, Sukeforth was to bring him to Brooklyn.

According to Robinson biographer Jules Tygiel, Sukeforth "realized the magnitude of his journey"[110] when Rickey told him that if Robinson could not make the trip he personally would go there to meet the young black ballplayer. But Robinson had injured his shoulder the previous week, and Sukeforth did not see him play. Nevertheless, when the two men met later in the scout's hotel room in Toledo, where Sukeforth had gone to look over some other minor-league players, the Dodgers scout extended the invitation, and they traveled to Brooklyn together for what became a historic meeting with Branch Rickey[111] on August 28. That meeting in Rickey's office concluded with a $3,500 bonus and contract offer, which Robinson was to sign by November 1. In return, he would play for the Montreal Royals, the Dodgers' top farm club, the following season at $800 a month.[112] Rickey delayed releasing news of the deal until Robinson signed the contract because he was trying to bring into the fold a couple of other Negro League players, namely, catcher Roy Campanella (who initially thought Rickey wanted him to play for the Brown Dodgers) and pitcher Don Newcombe.

Three weeks after the Tigers won the World Series, Rickey and Hector Racine, the owner of the Montreal Royals, called a press conference in Montreal, Quebec, on October 23, to formally announce the signing of Robinson, who would be joining the team for the 1946 season. Black newspapers covered the event with enthusiasm of course, and Robinson responded in kind. "I don't think anybody can make any trouble for me that I can't handle—not here or in Daytona Beach, Florida, at training either," Robinson said in an exclusive interview with Michael Carter of the AFRO newspaper chain. Carter reported that the "tall, dark and handsome young ball player spoke with a great deal of self-assurance but completely without egotism" when Robinson said (in unusually stilted language that sounded more like a press release than the actual words of the always clear and articulate Robinson), "I know that my position was obtained only through the constant pressure of my people and their press. It's a press victory, you might say." Robinson knew too that if he flopped or conducted himself poorly, "I'll set this advancement back a hundred years."[113]

Although Robinson was still the property of the Kansas City club, Monarchs co-owners Tom Baird and J. L. Wilkinson altruistically agreed not to stand in the way of the deal. "For many years we have urged Organized Ball to accept Negro players. Whether we get any recompense for Robinson may be considered beside the point. We want Jackie to have a chance," Baird said, according to Dan Daniel's column in the *Sporting News*.[114] (In an accompanying sidebar story written for the baseball journal by *Durham Morning Herald* reporter Jack Horner, Judge W. G. Bramham, president of the minor-league National Association, said that when the Robinson contract reached his desk for approval, "it will be promulgated just as any other contract.")[115] When Daniel, in a brief question-and-answer session, asked Rickey why Robinson was signed by Montreal, the Dodgers' boss explained, "He is not now major league stuff and there is not a single Negro player in this country who could qualify for the National or American leagues." When a reporter pressed Rickey further, he replied, "He is not Dodger quality. Not yet. Usually you send a player of his rating to a Class B or C club. But Robinson is 26, and I did not want to throw him in with a lot of kids."[116]

As always, Rickey had chosen his words carefully, especially when he said Robinson "is not now major league stuff" and "there is not a single

Negro player in this country who could qualify for the National or American leagues." The latter part of that observation was true, of course, since the only true qualification besides outstanding baseball skills was white skin. As for Robinson not being of major-league caliber at the moment, that was true as well. But as for Rickey not wanting him to start in the lower minors "with a lot of kids," there was only a grain of truth to that. The average age of the Class AAA Montreal Royals of the International League in 1946 was 27.4 years,[117] precisely Robinson's age. By the same token, the average age of Griffith's Double-A Chattanooga Lookouts of the Southern Association in 1946 was older, 28.1 years.[118]

It was common in that era for players to start at the lower levels, Class C or D, and spend four, five, or more years moving about the minor leagues before being called up, if at all, to the majors in their late 20s or even early 30s. If Robinson's playing skills were at the Class B or C level at the moment and he needed a few seasons at that level, he would not have stood out as an older player. So why burden him with having to prove himself right off the bat at the top level, Triple A, if he wasn't ready yet? If Rickey truly believed his own words, he would have started Robinson at a lower minor-league level, kids or no kids as his teammates. The Dodgers boss knew precisely what he was doing. In his attempt to keep the bigots of baseball at bay for the moment, Rickey's plan was to introduce a black ballplayer in two stages—first "off Broadway" in Montreal before taking center stage in New York at Brooklyn's Ebbets Field. Rickey had confidence not only in Robinson's abilities on and off the field but also in his own ability to judge major-league talent and the fortitude of men. Rickey, whose nickname was "the Deacon," had the wisdom and the patience to wait, certain that God would favor his endeavor.

To his credit, the new baseball commissioner did not interfere. While on a visit to Washington, Chandler was asked about the signing by the *Chicago Defender*. He explained that neither Robinson's Kansas City Monarchs nor the Negro American League had protested it. "Until he gets such a protest," the paper reported, "Chandler will not act."[119] As commissioner, Chandler was required to sign off on all player contracts, but his role in the Robinson story remains somewhat of an enigma. When he was elected to the Hall of Fame in 1982, Chandler offered this explanation for his actions in 1946 and 1947: "I figured that someday I'd have to meet my Maker and he'd ask me why I didn't let that boy play. I was afraid that if I told him it was because he was black, that wouldn't be sufficient. I told Rickey to bring him on."[120] When stacked up against Chandler's record in Congress as a supporter of the segregationist Dixiecrats and his attempt to run as the vice-presidential candidate on arch-segregationist George Wallace's third-party ticket in 1968, those last two sentences appear to be an embellishment of the truth. Nevertheless, as governor, Chandler used National Guard troops to enforce school integration, and he did warn the Louisville Colonels, the Royals' opponents in the 1946 minor-league championship series, that he would not tolerate any racial protests during the series.

As usual, Clark Griffith also came in for black-press scrutiny and criticism over the Robinson signing. An unsigned commentary distributed by the National Newspaper Publishers Association, NNPA (also known as the Black Press of America), and published in the *Amsterdam News* a week after the Robinson signing, claimed that Griffith, "a shrewd business man," praised the Negro National League as being well established (that is, a legal entity that could challenge the Robinson and other black signings in court) because he didn't want the major leagues to raid its players. "If colored players become accepted in the major leagues and are seen in action at Griffith Stadium the attendance at Homestead Grays' games may drop. That would mean less revenue for Griff," the article claimed. But Griffith "has had no qualms about raiding Cuban ball clubs and Cuban leagues and signing any likely-looking Latin American player who would accept his terms," it continued. "Only when the Nationals are in the first division do they draw well. Through the thin years colored baseball fans have been the backbone of their support. Be it said to Griff's credit, however, he has had the decency not to attempt any race segregation of fans." (Indeed, Washington's black community enjoyed better—and less restrictive—quasi-segregated seating at Griffith Stadium than anywhere in the South.) Griffith's response was that he wasn't criticizing the Robinson signing per se, he was merely commenting on "the ethics in the method of obtaining the player. I have always believed that contracts and players under reservation with any recognized and established baseball organization should be respected, regardless how they are organized."[121]

When the baseball moguls convened for their annual winter meetings in Chicago on December 10, the owners had more important issues to discuss than that of a black ballplayer signing a minor-league
contract for a team not based in the United States. Among the main
issues were clearly delineating the limits of Chandler's authority as
commissioner, whether the Pacific Coast League was ready to be a
major league (it was not), and what to do about the wartime novelty of
night baseball now that hostilities were over. (Griffith wanted to play 33
home night games in 1946.) Chandler came into the meetings after
being roughed up at the minor-league owners' gathering in Columbus a
week earlier. There, the owners rebuffed Chandler's ability to legislate
or to interject his authority into anything he deemed detrimental to
baseball. Although the major-league owners planned to do precisely the
same thing, in the end Chandler prevailed when the owners granted
him the same powers that his predecessor had.

For Griffith was a big winner too. He returned from Chicago with one
solid victory, one that he hoped would be felt in his cash register. When
the two leagues could not agree on how many postwar night games each
team could play, Chandler sided with the National League's position of
lifting virtually all restrictions, and the owners voted for unlimited night
baseball (except on Sundays and holidays) with the agreement of the
visiting club.[122] The leagues also agreed to guarantee players returning
from the service a 30-day tryout and 15 days of pay if they applied
within 90 days of their discharge.[123]

For Nationals fans, however, the big news came just after the Chicago meetings when Griffith traded George Case to Cleveland for mal-
content power-hitting outfielder Jeff Heath, a move Ossie Bluege
wanted so he could add real power to his lineup.[124] But, for once, the
Old Fox's wheeling and dealing did not work out. Heath hit just four
home runs in 166 official at-bats over 48 games for Washington in 1946,
and in June he was shipped to the St. Louis Browns. (After one season
in Cleveland, Case returned to Washington and played there for part of
the 1947 season before retiring at age 31.)[125]

Sadly, too, Griffith's optimism about the future of his beloved team
was misplaced. The Nats finished fourth in 1946, but over the next 14
years, they never rose out of the second division. In 1956, the year
following Griffith's death on October 27, 1955, the franchise officially
became the Washington Senators again, reverting to the nickname it

had when the team joined the new American League in 1901. This time, the name change did not result in a league or world championship as it had in the 1920s. The Senators would not be a pennant contender again until the franchise moved to Minneapolis–St. Paul for the 1961 American League season and became the Minnesota Twins. By that time, Griffith had been dead for almost six years. A plaque and monument were later erected at Griffith's beloved spring-training site at Tinker Field in Orlando. The bronze plaque read in part: "Clark Griffith gave the national pastime great dignity and respect . . . truly one of its finest benefactors, the image of baseball is exemplified by the immortal 'Old Fox.'" Sometime in early 2014, the plaque was stolen.

6

1946 AND BEYOND

Extra Innings

Branch Rickey's interest in and support of the new Negro United States League in 1945 was not to build a roster for his Brooklyn Brown Dodgers or to expand opportunities for African Americans to play segregated baseball. His participation in the new USL, which so rankled his old manager Clark Griffith, was a smoke screen behind which he could scrutinize black talent with a view to signing the one African American equipped with precisely the right tools Rickey believed were needed on the field, and even more so off the field, to play for the Brooklyn Dodgers. And of course, Rickey pulled it off with the perfect candidate. In his only season in the minor leagues, Jackie Robinson put up some eye-popping numbers, including a batting average of .349 in 124 of the 154-game season. He had 155 hits, 113 runs scored, 66 RBIs, 25 doubles, eight triples, three home runs, and an on-base percentage of .468.[1]

If any of the major-league owners were worried about what effect the Robinson signing might have on the game's popularity, they needn't have. Major-league attendance, which had fallen to a wartime low of 7.5 million in 1943, promptly rose to 18.5 million in 1946,[2] the first full postwar year, as many of the stars returned the major-league diamonds. (Joe DiMaggio returned to the Yankees in 1946, although he had what for him was a subpar season, batting .290, with 25 home runs and a respectable 95 RBIs. Also in 1946, Ted Williams rejoined the Red Sox and earned his first Most Valuable Player award while leading the league with an on-base percentage of .497, 343 total bases, and 142 runs scored. Led by Williams, the Red Sox played in their first World Series since 1918.) Two year later, major-league-baseball attendance passed 20 million.[3]

After only one year in a Royals uniform, Robinson made his Brooklyn Dodgers' debut on April 15, 1947, and he and Branch Rickey promptly went into the history books. Later that same year, on July 5, Larry Doby played his first game for Cleveland, integrating the Indians and the American League. Interestingly, the third team to integrate was the overtly racist St. Louis Browns, who had taunted the Nats' Cubans so mercilessly that it destroyed the long-standing friendship between the two managers, Ossie Bluege and Luke Sewell. The Browns signed free agent Hank Thompson on July 17, less than two weeks after Doby's debut. Hank Thompson played in only 27 games that season, mostly at second base, before St. Louis released him. (Less than two years later, Thompson began an eight-year stint with the New York Giants, where he earned the singular distinction of having integrated not one but two major-league teams and was a teammate of Willie Mays until Thompson retired after the 1956 season. Thompson also was one-third of the first all–African American major-league outfield when he, Monte Irvin, and Mays took the field against the Yankees in the 1951 World Series.)[4] Times indeed were changing for major-league baseball.

Griffith, having missed numerous opportunities to improve his team with the addition of gifted Negro League players, was devoid of excuses by the late 1940s and early 1950s. Nevertheless, for whatever reasons, he remained steadfastly on the wrong side of the color line until 1954. Then another Cuban, this one with a decidedly darker complexion than any of his predecessor countrymen teammates, outfielder Carlos Paula, joined the Nats on September 6, the last full month of the season. Sports historians generally consider Paula to be Washington's first black player although he could not be called African American. Paula played parts of three seasons for the Nats, from 1954 to 1956. With the signing of Paula, Washington became the 12th team to integrate, solidly among the second-division holdouts of the 16 clubs.[5] (Somewhat appropriate for a team that, after finishing fourth in 1946, never again climbed out of the second division until the franchise's second year in Minneapolis in 1962.) Paula's only full season with Washington came in 1955, when he batted .299 over 115 games with 105 hits, six home runs, seven triples, and 45 RBIs. However, his 10 errors as the Nats right fielder led the league that year.[6]

Washington's first African American ballplayer arrived one year after Paula had departed, when Plainfield, New Jersey, native Joe Black joined the club late in the 1957 season after three and a half years with the Dodgers and a brief stop in Cincinnati. Black had appeared in two World Series for Brooklyn, becoming the first African American to win a World Series game when he pitched a complete game to beat the Yankees, 4–2, on October 15, 1952, in the series opener at Ebbets Field. But Black appeared in only seven games for Washington in 1957, yielding 10 earned runs over 12⅔ innings for a whopping 7.11 ERA. Black, then 33, was released after the season, and he retired from baseball. He died in Scottsdale, Arizona, on May 17, 2002, at age 78. Clark Griffith died on October 27, 1955, of pneumonia while battling a gastric hemorrhage. The Old Fox would have been 86 in November. Among his pallbearers were Ossie Bluege and George Case. Other baseball dignitaries in attendance included Joe Cronin, Bucky Harris, Branch Rickey, along with Walter O'Malley and Horace Stoneham, owners of the Dodgers and Giants, respectively. Griffith was buried in the family crypt at Fort Lincoln Cemetery in Brentwood, Maryland.

Clark Griffith was elected to the Baseball Hall of Fame in 1946, by the Veterans Committee, the same committee that would elect Rickey in 1967. Rickey's plaque at Cooperstown lauds him as having created major-league baseball's farm system for assessing and improving baseball talent and for his many years as a baseball executive. The last line of Rickey's plaque simply reads, "Brought Jackie Robinson to Brooklyn in 1947."[7] No further explanation is needed. Griffith's Washington franchise was still devoid of African Americans when he died on October 27, 1955, prompting some baseball historians to judge him more harshly than they might otherwise have done.

Griffith's "resistance to change, his position with Connie Mack as the leaders of baseball's traditionalist old guard, and his southern clientele in Washington made his stance about more than just dollars and cents. During the late 1940s and early 1950s, Griffith's economic rationale no longer made sense," judges author Brad Snyder. "By that time, the Grays drew meager crowds at Griffith Stadium and then disbanded. Meanwhile, Griffith saw firsthand how [Satchel] Paige and Doby [both were with the Cleveland Indians in 1948] brought out the city's black fans en masse. By finding a few black players of his own, Griffith could have cultivated sellout crowds every night."[8]

But Griffith biographer Ted Leavengood sees it differently. He says, "The tragedy for the elderly Griffith was how poorly he understood the way in which his actions on the issue of race would diminish his reputation in later years. . . . Most came to believe that when Jackie Robinson broke the color barrier, the gritty competitor known in his best days as the Old Fox had lost that fiery edge that had made him a legend within the game. After the end of World War II, Clark Griffith was barely hanging on as his moment in history passed him by."[9] Griffith's Hall of Fame plaque duly acknowledges his "more than 50 years as a pitcher, manager and executive" and his more than "200 victories as a pitcher, manager of the Cincinnati N.L. and Chicago, New York and Washington A.L. teams for 20 years."[10] Had he been brave enough to buck the strong tide of segregation and heed the many pleas of the likes of Sam Lacy, Ric Roberts, and even Paul Robeson, Cooperstown might also have remembered him as the man who brought integration to Washington and the national pastime.

NOTES

PREFACE

1. Richard Goldstein, *Spartan Seasons*, 4.
2. Gary Bedingfield, Baseball in Wartime, "Baseball in World War II," http://www.baseballinwartime.com/baseball_in_wwii/baseball_in_wwii.htm.
3. Philip J. Lowry, *Green Cathedrals*, 243.
4. "Washington Nationals," Sports E-cyclopedia, http://www.sportsecyclopedia.com/al/wasdc/nats.html.

1. 1941

1. Ted Leavengood, *Clark Griffith*, 8.
2. Ibid., 11.
3. "Old Hoss Radbourn,"Baseball-Reference.com, http://www.baseball-reference.com/players/r/radboch01.shtml.
4. Leavengood, *Clark Griffith*, 13.
5. Mark Grahek, "Clark Griffith," SABR, http://sabr.org/bioproj/person/96624988.
6. Leavengood, *Clark Griffith*, 34.
7. Ibid., 32.
8. Grahek, "Clark Griffith."
9. Leavengood, *Clark Griffith*, 44.
10. Leavengood, *Clark Griffith*, 44, 57.
11. Lowry, *Green Cathedrals*, 101.

12. Roger Rubin, "In 1944, the Dodgers, Yankees and Giants Faced Off in a Single Nine-Inning Game to Support the War Effort," *New York Daily News*, May 10, 2014, http://www.nydailynews.com/sports/baseball/yankees/1944-ny-baseball-teams-faced-support-war-effort-article-1.1787483

13. Shirley Povich, *The Washington Senators*, xiii.

14. Tom Deveaux, *The Washington Senators*, 49–50.

15. Leavengood, *Clark Griffith*.

16. S. L. Price, "The Second World War Kinks [*sic*] Off," *Sports Illustrated*, November 29, 1999, http://157.166.246.201/vault/article/magazine/MAG1017830/index.htm.

17. "Army, Navy Call Key Personnel," *Washington Post*, December 8, 1941, 16.

18. Peter Jennings and Todd Brewster, *The Century*, 230.

19. Price, "Second World War."

20. Dave Anderson, "The Infamous Day That Colonel Donovan Was Paged," *New York Times*, December 1, 1991, S10.

21. Robert Wernick, *Blitzkrieg*, 138.

22. U.S. Department of State, Office of the Historian, "The Neutrality Acts, 1930s," http://history.state.gov/milestones/1921-1936/Neutrality_acts.

23. *Pan-Americanism and the Pan-American Conferences*, Portland State University, 8, http://www.upa.pdx.edu/IMS/currentprojects/TAHv3/Content/PDFs/PanAmericanism.pdf.

24. *Congressional Digest*, August–September 1941, 216, 218.

25. Joseph E. Persico, "The Day When We Almost Lost the Army," *American Heritage* 62, no. 1 (Spring 2012), http://www.americanheritage.com/content/day-when-we-almost-lost-army?page=show.

26. Wernick, *Blitzkrieg*, 138.

27. "Induction Statistics," Selective Service System, http://www.selectiveservice.us/military-draft/8-induction.shtml.

28. Goldstein, *Spartan Seasons*, 3.

29. "Induction Statistics," Selective Service System, http://www.sss.gov/induct.htm.

30. Robert C. Albright, "Nation, Led by President, Embarks on Course of 'All-Out' Industrial Aid to Great Britain," *Washington Post*, January 5, 1941, B1.

31. Dr. George Gallup, "The Gallup Poll: Public Believes U.S. Safety Depends on British Victory," *Washington Post*, January 3, 1941, 1.

32. Albright, "The State of the Union," *Washington Post*, January 7, 1941, 1.

33. "Pacifist Group Stages March to White House," *Washington Post*, January 5, 1941, 5.

34. "D.C. Shouts Old Year Out, Gayly Greets 1941," *Washington Post*, January 1, 1941, 1.

35. Joseph Alsop and Robert Kintner, "Roosevelt—Man of the Year," The Capital Parade, *Washington Post*, January 1, 1941, 7.

36. Ernest K. Lindley, "Die-Hard Isolationists," *Washington Post*, January 1, 1941, 7.

37. Michael Seidel, *Streak, Joe DiMaggio and the Summer of '41*, 171.

38. William B. Mead, *Baseball Goes to War*, 29.

39. Ibid., 25.

40. William B. Mead and Paul Dickson, *Baseball: The Presidents' Game*, 71.

41. Goldstein, *Spartan Seasons*, 4.

42. Deveaux, *The Washington Senators*, 47.

43. Povich, This Morning, *Washington Post*, December 9, 1941, 26.

44. Mead and Dickson, *Baseball*, 76.

45. According to the 22nd Amendment, only a person who succeeds to the presidency with less than two full years remaining in the previous president's term would be eligible to serve as president for another two full terms and thus could break Roosevelt's eight successive years of throwing out the ceremonial first pitch on opening day.

46. Justine Lorelle LoMonaco , "Rare Film Shows FDR Walking," Bio, http://www.biography.com/news/fdr-walking-video-footage#awesm=~oEwXuC4kg7ALlr.

47. Povich, This Morning, *Washington Post*, November 4, 1941, 20.

48. Benjamin G. Rader, *Baseball*, 138.

49. Brad Snyder, *Beyond the Shadow of the Senators*, 57.

50. Frederic J. Frommer, *The Washington Nationals,* 99.

51. David Nemec and Saul Wisnia, *100 Years of Major League Baseball*, 185.

52. Frommer, *Washington Nationals*, 99.

53. Povich, This Morning, *Washington Post*, November 4, 1941, 20.

54. By contrast, the federal government fined General Motors Corp. a record $35 million in 2014, which would have been the equivalent of about $840 million in 1907, for delays in recalling a number of vehicle models with faulty ignition switches that were linked to 13 deaths. Jim Puzzangher, "GM Fined $35 Million for Faulty Ignition Switch Recall Delays," *Los Angeles Times*, May 16, 2014, http://www.latimes.com/business/autos/la-fi-gm-recall-ignition-switch-20140516-story.html.

55. Rader, *Baseball*, 105.

56. John Drebinger, "Baseball Men Advised to Move Cautiously in Gearing Game to War Conditions," *New York Times*, December 9, 1941, 49.

57. Judson Bailey, "Baseball Heads Pause to Ponder War News," *Washington Post*, December 9, 1941, 26.

58. Povich, This Morning, *Washington Post*, December 9, 1941, 26.

59. Ibid.

60. Mead, *Baseball Goes to War*, 25.

61. Ibid., 26, 27.

62. Matt Schudel , "Buddy Lewis, Nats Star and WWII Pilot, Dies at 94," *Washington Post*, February 26, 2011, http://www.washingtonpost.com/wp-dyn/content/article/2011/02/26/AR2011022604207.html.

63. Author David E. Hubler interview with Charles "Chuck" Taylor, recorded on October 5, 2013.

64. Rob Kirkpatrick, "Cecil Travis," SABR, http://sabr.org/bioproj/person/4d5ab420.

65. "Cecil Travis Stats," Baseball Almanac, http://www.baseball-almanac.com/players/player.php?p=travice01.

66. Drebinger, "Baseball Men Advised to Move Cautiously in Gearing Game to War Conditions," *New York Times*, December 9, 1941, 49.

67. United Press, "Sports Prepared to Carry On; Government Attitude Awaited," *New York Times*, December 9, 1941, 49.

68. Drebinger, "Baseball Men Advised to Move Cautiously," 49.

69. Robert W. Creamer, *Baseball in '41*, 213.

70. Seidel, *Streak, Joe DiMaggio and the Summer of '41*, 158–59.

71. Ibid., 161.

72. In 1939, for example, Washington ranked last in gross operating income, earning just $215,292 at Griffith Stadium, $116,422 on the road, and a mere $20,429 from concession sales. Jeff Obermeyer, *Baseball and the Bottom Line in World War II*, Kindle edition, location 2439.

73. Snyder, *Beyond the Shadow*, 33, 87.

74. Ibid., 34, 36, 38.

75. Ibid., 11.

76. Ibid., 88–89.

77. "Griffith Again Serving Nation and Game," *Sporting News*, January 8, 1942, 4.

78. Thomas Gilbert, *Baseball at War, World War II and the Fall of the Color Line*, 55.

79. Mead, *Baseball Goes to War*, 34.

2. 1942

1. "1942 the Home Grown Champions," This Great Game, http://www.thisgreatgame.com/1942-baseball-history.html.

2. Will Harridge, "Harridge Defines Baseball's Role," *New York Times*, January 8, 1942, 30.

3. Goldstein, *Spartan Seasons*, 33.

4. "U.S. Provoked War, Nye Says," *Washington Post*, December 8, 1941, 8.

5. "January 1942," Franklin D. Roosevelt Presidential Library and Museum, Hyde Park, NY, http://www.fdrlibrary.marist.edu/daybyday/resource/january-1942-2/.

6. Gerald Bazer and Steven Culbertson, "When FDR Said 'Play Ball': President Called Baseball a Wartime Morale Booster," *Prologue* 34, no. 1 (Spring 2002), National Archives, http://www.archives.gov/publications/prologue/2002/spring/greenlight.html.

7. "January 1942," Franklin D. Roosevelt Presidential Library and Museum, http://www.fdrlibrary.marist.edu/daybyday/resource/january-1942-2/ .

8. Leavengood, *Clark Griffith*, 259.

9. Mead, *Even the Browns*, 36.

10. Goldstein, *Spartan Seasons*, 22–23.

11. Lewis Wood, "Army Gets Power to Move Citizens or Aliens Inland," *New York Times*, February 21, 1942, 1.

12. "Washington Roster Swept by Turnover," *Sporting News*, January 8, 1942, 5.

13. "American League Loses 29 to Services, National Only 18," *Washington Post*, January 24, 1942, 19.

14. "Elmer Gedeon," Baseball-Reference.com, http://www.baseball-reference.com/players/g/gedeoel01.shtml.

15. Goldstein, *Spartan Seasons*, 248–49.

16. "History of the Washington Navy Yard," Naval History and Heritage Command, http://www.history.navy.mil/faqs/faq52-1.htm.

17. Leavengood, *Clark Griffith*, 260.

18. Jim Vankoski, email correspondence with author David E. Hubler, September 25, 2013.

19. Goldstein, *Spartan Seasons*, 56.

20. Bedingfield, " Gary Bedingfield's Biography," Baseball in Wartime, www.baseballinwartime.com/about/my_bio.htm.

21. Lowry, *Green Cathedrals*, 139.

22. Rader, *Baseball*, 138.

23. "Cubs Timeline," Chicago Cubs Major League Baseball, http://chicago.cubs.mlb.com/chc/history/timeline10.jsp.

24. Drebinger, "Majors Raise Limit of Home Night Games to 14, Except for 21 at Washington," *New York Times*, February 4, 1942, 24.

25. Ibid.

26. Goldstein, *Spartan Seasons*, 124–25.

27. Drebinger, "Big Leagues Decide on Two All-Star Games but Deadlock on Night Baseball," *New York Times*, February 3, 1942, 25.

28. George Case Jr., narrator, *Ballfield to Battlefield and Back: From FDR to JFK*, DVD, personal home movies and recollections of George Case Jr. and Mickey Vernon.

29. The trio gained immortal fame in a short poem written in 1910 by Franklin P. Adams, a *New York Evening Mail* columnist.

> *These are the saddest of possible words:*
> *"Tinker to Evers to Chance."*
> *Trio of bear cubs, and fleeter than birds,*
> *Tinker and Evers and Chance.*
> *Ruthlessly pricking our gonfalon bubble,*
> *Making a Giant hit into a double—*
> *Words that are heavy with nothing but trouble:*
> *"Tinker to Evers to Chance."*

30. Author David E. Hubler's personal inspection of Tinker Field, Orlando, Florida, May 2, 2013.

31. Povich, This Morning, *Washington Post*, March 19, 1942, 21.

32. "Evans, Nats' Catcher, Gets 1A Draft Rating," *Washington Post*, March 15, 1942, 28.

33. Povich, "Leonard Again Rejects Terms Offered by Nats," *Washington Post*, February 26, 1942, 18.

34. Povich, This Morning, *Washington Post*, March 28, 1942, 17.

35. "Bobo Newsom," Baseball-Reference.com, http://www.baseball-reference.com/players/n/newsobo01.shtml.

36. Povich, This Morning, *Washington Post*, April 2, 1942, 24.

37. George Case III, telephone interview with author David E. Hubler, October 15, 2013.

38. Ed Butka, telephone interview with author David E. Hubler, January 7, 1992, on his 76th birthday. Butka played in only 18 games for Washington in his two-year major-league career. The birthday call came as something of a gift, he said, because he was happy just to be remembered. Butka died in 2005 at age 89.

39. Povich, This Morning, *Washington Post*, April 9, 1942, 22.

40. George Case Jr., narrator, *Ballfield to Battlefield and Back: From FDR to JFK*, DVD.

41. "April 1939," Roosevelt cable to Hitler, April 15, 1939, Franklin D. Roosevelt Presidential Library and Museum, http://www.fdrlibrary.marist.edu/daybyday/event/april-15-1939/.

42. Merrill W. Whittlesey, "Now Pitching for White House—Vice President Wallace!" *Washington Post*, April 15, 1942, 24.

43. Charles Glass, *Americans in Paris*, 226.

44. Ibid., 227.

45. Franklin D. Roosevelt Presidential Library and Museum, http://www.fdrlibrary.marist.edu/archives/significant.html.

46. "The Doolittle Raid (CV-8)," USS *Hornet* Museum, http://www.uss-hornet.org/history/wwii/doolittle_4.shtml.

47. Whittlesey, "Now Pitching for White House," *Washington Post*, April 15, 1942, 24.

48. Mead and Dickson, *Baseball*, 23–24.

49. Ibid., 24, 25, 28.

50. Ibid., 27.

51. Ibid., 158.

52. "This Week in Washington," *Cambridge* [MD] *Tribune*, May 1, 1942, 3.

53. Alfred Friendly, "Cost of Millions of Articles Are Put at Highest Figure in March," *Washington Post*, April 29, 1942, 1.

54. *Congressional Digest* 20, no. 10 (October 1941): 227–28.

55. Walter Lippmann, Today and Tomorrow, *Washington Post*, April 30, 1942, 19.

56. "Press Comment on President's Plan," *New York Times*, April 28, 1942, 12.

57. "Rented Homes Must Be Listed with OPA," *Washington Post*, April 30, 1942, 14.

58. Bill Gilbert, *They Also Served*, 69.

59. Goldstein, *Spartan Seasons*, 40.

60. Lieutenant General Jonathan Wainwright report to Army Chief of Staff General George C. Marshal, Franklin D. Roosevelt Presidential Library and Museum, declassified War Department document, May 4, 1942.

61. FDR response to Lieutenant General Wainwright, Franklin D. Roosevelt Presidential Library and Museum, declassified War Department document, May 5, 1942.

62. Povich, This Morning, *Washington Post*, June 1, 1942, 16.

63. "Calvin Griffith Biography," The Baseball Page.com, http://www.thebaseballpage.com/history/calvin-griffith-biography-baseball-page.

64. Furman Bisher, "Everything Jake with Jacobs Who Develops Fastball at 28," *Sporting News*, August 13, 1942, 10.

65. Goldstein, "Calvin Griffith, 87, Is Dead; Tight-Fisted Baseball Owner," *New York Times*, October 21, 1999, http://www.nytimes.com/1999/10/21/sports/calvin-griffith-87-is-dead-tight-fisted-baseball-owner.html.

66. "The Obit for Calvin Griffith," The Deadball Era, http://www.thedeadballera.com/Obits/Owners/Griffith.Calvin.Obit.html.

67. "Play for Army and Navy," *Sporting News*, May 7, 1942, 10.

68. Rader, *Baseball*, 145.

69. "Big Guns Set for All-Star Pitchers," *Washington Afro-American*, May 30, 1942, 25.

70. "Grays Battle All-Stars in Griffith Stadium Tilt," *Washington Afro-American*, May 30, 1942, 27.

71. Ric Roberts, "22,000 See Paige and Grays Rout Dean Stars 8–1," *Washington Afro-American*, June 6, 1942, 26.

72. Roberts, "All Up in Washington," *Baltimore Afro-American*, June 2, 1942, 22.

73. Rob Kirkpatrick, "Cecil Travis," SABR, http://sabr.org/bioproj/person/4d5ab420.

74. Gary Obermeyer, *Baseball and the Bottom Line*, Kindle edition, location 2186.

75. "Grays Take 2 from Yanks to Maintain League Lead," *Washington Afro-American*, May 16, 1942, 28.

76. "Landis Outlaws Non-Relief Exhibition Games," *Washington Post*, June 5, 1942, 22.

77. Ibid., 22.

78. Snyder, *Beyond the Shadow*, 118.

79. Ibid., 119.

80. Ibid., 120.

81. Ibid., 2.

82. Michael Tomasky, "The Racist Redskins," *Daily Beast*, http://www.thedailybeast.com/articles/2013/06/01/the-racist-redskins.html.

83. Povich, *The Washington Senators*, 209–210.

84. Snyder, *Beyond the Shadow*, 166.

85. Ibid.

86. "Landis on Negro Players," *Sporting News*, July 23, 1942, 11.

87. Snyder, *Beyond the Shadow*, 283.

88. Lowry, *Green Cathedrals*, 244.

89. Snyder, *Beyond the Shadow*, 286.

90. Author David E. Hubler interview with Charles "Chuck" Taylor, Mickey Vernon's longtime friend and agent, October 4, 2013.

91. Roberts, "All Up in Washington," *Baltimore Afro-American*, May 16, 1942, 26.

92. Obermeyer, *Baseball and the Bottom Line*, Kindle edition, location 1697.

93. "Battle of the Coral Sea, 7–8 May 1942: Overview and Special Image Selection," Naval History and Heritage Command, http://www.history.navy.mil/photos/events/wwii-pac/coralsea/coralsea.htm.

94. "The Battle of the Coral Sea," Naval History and Heritage Command, http://www.history.navy.mil/history/CoralSea.htm.

95. Stanley Johnston, "Witness of Coral Sea Battle Gives Picture from Carrier," *New York Times*, June 13, 1942, 1.

96. Thomas J. Hamilton, "President Directs Listing of Holders of Gasoline Cars," *New York Times*, May 16, 1942, 1.

97. "Baruch Returns 'X' Card for Gas, Takes 'A' Instead," *Washington Post*, May 15, 1942, 8.

98. Roland Nicholson, "Holders of 'X' Cards Will Be Made Public, Senators Keep Theirs: All Registration Data Except That of Military Forces Will Be Disclosed," *Washington Post*, May 16, 1942, 1.

99. Charles E. Egan, "Rationing of Gas Goes into Effect on National Scale," *New York Times*, December 1, 1942, 1.

100. Ben W. Gilbert, "Nation-Wide Gas Rationing Held Necessary," *Washington Post*, July 30, 1942, 1.

101. "Nats Return Home Tonight with Browns," *Washington Post*, June 2, 1942, 19.

102. Ed Butka, telephone interview with author David E. Hubler, April 21, 1992.

103. Povich, This Morning, *Washington Post*, June 10, 1942, 22.

104. Povich, This Morning, *Washington Post*, June 12, 1942, 23.

105. Charles Hurd, "Gen. Eisenhower Takes Up Headquarters in London," *New York Times*, June 26, 1942, 1.

106. Michael R. Beschloss, *Eisenhower*, 37–38.

107. Ibid., 40.

108. George Case Jr., narrator, *Ballfield to Battlefield and Back*, DVD.

109. "Battle of Midway, 4–7 June 1942: Overview and Special Image Selection," Naval History and Heritage Command, http://www.history.navy.mil/photos/events/wwii-pac/midway/midway.htm.

110. "Battle of Midway: 4–7 June 1942," Naval History and Heritage Command, http://www.history.navy.mil/Midway/Battle-of-Midway-Overview.html.

111. Jack Munhall, "Feller, Tars Wins, 5–2, over Soldier Nine," *Washington Post*, June 22, 1942, 16.

112. Roberts, "28,000 See Grays Nip Monarchs, 2–1, in First Night Game under Major League Arc Lights in Washington," *Washington Afro-American*, June 27, 1942, 26.

113. Snyder, *Beyond the Shadow*, 136.

114. Roberts, "Grays Outdraw All Sports Events at Griff Stadium; Battle Newark Sunday," *Washington Afro-American*, June 23, 1942, 25.

115. Povich, "It's Wynn Who Wins as Other Nats Fail," *Sporting News*, July 9, 1942, 3.

116. Povich, "Nats Decide to Sink or Swim with Sullivan at Shortstop," *Washington Post*, June 24, 1942, 23.

117. George Case III, email correspondence with author David E. Hubler, October 28, 2013.

118. Daniel M. Daniel, "World Series War Aid Plans Laid by Majors," *Sporting News*, July 9, 1942, 1.

119. Povich, "Defiant Griff Turns to 'Twi-Night' Ball," *Sporting News*, July 16, 1942, 1.

120. Ibid.

121. Ibid.

122. Povich, "It's Wynn Who Wins as Other Nats Fail," *Sporting News*, July 9, 1942, 3.

123. Associated Press, "Baseball Men against World Series 'On Tour,'" *Washington Post*, June 30, 1942, 18.

124. "Zeller Modifies Short-Season Plan to Provide for 140 Games," *Sporting News*, July 9, 1942, 3.

125. Bailey, Associated Press, "Jack Zeller of Detroit Criticized," *Washington Post*, July 1, 1942, 23.

126. Richard Ben Cramer, *Joe DiMaggio*, 221.

127. Bailey, Associated Press, "Future of All-Star Service Game Doubted," *Washington Post*, July 9, 1942, 20.

128. Ibid.

129. Povich, This Morning, *Washington Post*, July 2, 1942, 24.

130. "Dodger-Giant Net for Army $80,000," *New York Times*, August 4, 1942, 1.

131. "Senate Group Approves Medal for FBI Chief," *Washington Post*, July 9, 1942, 5.

132. "Conserve Tea! Skip a Spoon for the Pot," *Washington Post*, July 9, 1942, 4.

133. Will Swift, *Pat and Dick*, 76.

134. Thomas F. Hawkins, Associated Press, "Nazis Parade So-Called 'Best' Troops in Paris; Goebbels Dares Us to Invade," *Washington Post*, July 30, 1942, 2.

135. The nearest an enemy German sub came to the Chesapeake was U-701. It torpedoed the 7,000-ton tanker *British Freedom* near the Chesapeake Lightship. The tanker limped into Norfolk for repairs. "Later, while laying mines near the Bay mouth in 1942, the U-boat was sunk off Hatteras." Kent Mountford, "Bay's Subs Have Run the Gamut from Military Games to Diving Sites, Races," *Bay Journal*, June 1, 2010, http://www.bayjournal.com/article/bays_subs_have_run_the_gamut_from_military_games_to_diving_sites_races.

136. Dillard Stokes, "Justices Question Plea 8 Took Role of Spies to Escape from Nazis," *Washington Post*, July 30, 1942, 1.

137. Library of Congress, legal citation: *Ex parte Quirin*, 317 U.S. 1, 30–31 (U.S. 1942), http://www.loc.gov/rr/frd/Military_Law/pdf/Supreme-Court-1942.pdf.

138. "George John Dasch and the Nazi Saboteurs," Federal Bureau of Investigation, http://www.fbi.gov/about-us/history/famous-cases/nazi-saboteurs.

139. Povich, This Morning, *Washington Post*, July 30, 1942, 20.

140. Povich, "Scatter-Arms Make Vaulter of Vernon," *Sporting News*, August 6, 1942, 5.

141. "'Double Duty' Radcliffe Dies at 103," ESPN Classic, http://espn.go.com/classic/obit/s/2005/0811/2131415.html.

142. "No Good from Raising Race Issue," *Sporting News*, August 6, 1942, 4.

143. Bob Considine, "On the Line," *Washington Post*, August 15, 1942, 15.

144. Snyder, *Beyond the Shadow*, 168–69.

145. Povich, "All Rivals Look Alike to Griffs as They Grab 14 of 21 Games," *Sporting News*, August 13, 1942, 1.

146. Povich, *Washington Senators*, 207.

147. Povich, "Newsom Sale Price More Than $25,000," *Sporting News*, September 3, 1942, 2.

148. Povich, *Washington Senators*, 213.

149. Ibid., 214.

150. Snyder, *Beyond the Shadow*, 140.

151. George Lyle Jr., "Monarchs Trip Grays, 9–5, to Clinch World Series," *Washington Afro-American*, October 3, 1942, 27.

152. Snyder, *Beyond the Shadow*, 144–47.

153. Obermeyer, *Baseball and the Bottom Line*, Kindle edition, table 8, location 2506.

154. Daniel, "What? No Fish Sandwiches!" *Sporting News*, August 27, 1942, 12.

155. *Congressional Digest* 21, no. 12 (December 1942): 289–90.

156. "Press Comment on the Election," *New York Times*, November 5, 1942, 31.

157. The full text of Roosevelt's speech can be found at http://www.ibiblio.
org/pha/policy/1942/421107c.html.

158. Edward T. Folliard, "Lands from Atlantic, Mediterranean to Block Axis
Move against Americas," *Washington Post*, November 8, 1942, 1–2.

159. John Gordon IV, "Joint Power Projection: Operation Torch," *Joint Force
Quarterly* (Spring 1994): 63–64, http://www.dtic.mil/dtic/tr/fulltext/u2/
a528962.pdf.

160. Goldstein, *Spartan Seasons*, 99.

161. Ibid.

3. 1943

1. According to Gary Bedingfield, "World War II Timeline," Baseball in
Wartime, www.baseballinwartime.com, there were 195 major leaguers serving
in the military at the start of 1943, and at least 19 former minor-league players
had lost their life in military service since 1940.

2. Obermeyer, *Baseball and the Bottom Line*, Kindle edition, location
2510.

3. "Peter Seitz," Baseball-Reference.com, http://www.baseball-reference.
com/bullpen/Peter_Seitz.

4. "Reserve Clause," Baseball-Reference.com, http://www.baseball-
reference.com/bullpen/reserve_clause.

5. Leavengood, *Clark Griffith*, 260.

6. Goldstein, *Spartan Seasons*, 100.

7. "Value of One-Man Leadership Again Proved," *Sporting News*, January
7, 1943, 4.

8. Daniel, "Action Hailed as Salutory," *Sporting News*, January 14, 1943, 7.

9. "Two Manpower Rulings on the Game," *Sporting News*, January 14,
1943, 4.

10. Povich, "Proselyting? Senators Get Three College Bids," *Sporting News*,
January 14, 1943, 2.

11. Povich, "Nats Go Collegiate, Frat Houses'n All," *Sporting News*, January 28, 1943, 5.

12. Ibid.

13. "Dutch Leonard 1942 Game by Game Hitting Logs," Baseball Almanac,
http://www.baseball-almanac.com/players/pitchinglogs.php?p=leonadu02&y=
1942.

14. Povich, "Nats Go Collegiate, Frat Houses'n All," *Sporting News*, January 28, 1943, 5.

15. Povich, "Nats Hope to Meet Rivals Comin' Down," *Sporting News*, January 7, 1943, 7.

16. "Baseball Leagues Face Blackout by ODT Bus Ban," *Washington Afro-American*, March 13, 1943, 27.

17. Ibid.

18. "Negro League History 101," Negro League Baseball, http://www.negroleaguebaseball.com/history101.html.

19. Art Carter, "ODT Bus Ban Forces Clubs to Use Trains," *Washington Afro-American*, April 3, 1943, 22.

20. Ibid.

21. Carter, "Help Baseball ODT Order May [*sic*],"*Washington Afro-American*, April 10, 1943, 24.

22. Ibid.

23. Harold Jackson, On the Sports Front, *Washington Afro-American*, April 10, 1943, 25.

24. Snyder, *Beyond the Shadow*, 165.

25. Carter, "ODT Bus Ban Forces Clubs to Use Trains," *Baltimore Afro-American*, April 3, 1943, 22.

26. "Pre–Negro Leagues Candidate Profile: James Allen "Candy Jim" Taylor," National Baseball Hall of Fame and Museum, http://web.archive.org/web/20060522232748/http://www.baseballhalloffame.org/hofers_and_honorees/taylor_candy_jim.htm.

27. "Veterans Await Opening of Grays' Camp at Akron," *Washington Afro-American*, April 10, 1943, 25.

28. Nelson B. Bell, "It May Have Been Luck, or Merely Nice Planning," *Washington Post*, February 8, 1943, 11.

29. "Washington Club Makes Trip by Boat," *Washington Post*, February 21, 1943, R6.

30. "AL's Big Mileage Cut," *Sporting News*, March 18, 1943, 4.

31. Author David E. Hubler interview with Shirley Povich at Povich's home in Washington, DC, November 4, 1992.

32. "Youth Latest of Cambria's Mound Finds," *Washington Post*, March 17, 1943, 16.

33. Gilbert, *They Also Served*, 100.

34. "Bob Johnson," Baseball-Reference.com, http://www.baseball-reference.com/players/j/johnsbo01.shtml.

35. "Johnson Joins Nats; Glad to Escape Macks," *Washington Post*, March 28, 1943, R3.

36. "Bob Johnson," Baseball-Reference.com, http://www.baseball-reference.com/players/j/johnsbo01.shtml.

37. Scribbled by Scribes, "Pride Led Johnson from A's," *Sporting News*, April 1, 1943, 4.

38. Smith was the only sportswriter to win the Pulitzer Prize for Distinguished Commentary. He also was the recipient of the J. G. Taylor Spink Award from the Baseball Hall of Fame in 1976, baseball's highest honor for print journalists.

39. Povich, "Bluege Goes All Out on Nats' Outfield," *Sporting News*, April 1, 1943, 3.

40. Dick Farrington, "'Keep the Game Going!' Landslide Opinion Voiced," *Sporting News*, April 1, 1943, 7. The *Sporting News* ballot asked readers their attitude toward continuing the deferment of players classified as 3-A and thus keeping the sport going during the war. By a 40:1 ratio, the poll found overwhelming support for the game. But when the balloting was criticized as inherently biased because only baseball fans would be reading the baseball newspaper, a second poll was taken of travelers passing through Union Station in St. Louis without mentioning the 3-A classification. That travelers' poll confirmed the initial 40:1 ratio of Americans who wanted baseball to continue.

41. Charles "Chuck" Taylor, personal interview with author David E. Hubler, November 14, 2013. Taylor, Vernon's close friend, said that, like most players of that era, Vernon had to negotiate his salary for the following season in a face-to-face meeting with Griffith as soon as the previous season was over. Rarely did any of the players win concessions from management. "It was take it, or I'll send you back to the minors next year," Taylor said.

42. "Nats Call Up Prout, Chattanooga 1st Sacker, Army Status of Vernon Is Doubtful," *Washington Post*, March 20, 1943, 10.

43. Noel Hynd, "The Inside Story about Baseball in 1943 Was Less Bounce to the Ounce," *Sports Illustrated*, May 13, 1985, http://sportsillustrated.cnn.com/vault/article/magazine/MAG1119464/3/index.htm.

44. "Players Crowding Bases for Uncle Sam," *Sporting News*, April 1, 1943, 6.

45. "No Soft Berths for Managers in '43," *Sporting News*, January 7, 1943, 4.

46. Goldstein, *Spartan Seasons*, 134.

47. Ibid., 135.

48. George Case III, personal email correspondence with author David E. Hubler, December 3, 2013.

49. "Training Gets Under Way in Strange Circumstances," Editorial, *Sporting News*, March 18, 1943, 4.

50. Povich, This Morning, *Washington Post*, March 18, 1943, 12.

51. "Spring Comes with Wet Snow and Accidents," *Washington Post*, March 22, 1943, 1.

52. Mead, *Baseball Goes to War*, 76.

53. Goldstein, *Spartan Seasons*, 119–20.

54. Carter, "Fans Hold Keys to Major League Baseball Doors," From the Bench, *Baltimore Afro-American*, March 27, 1943, 26.

55. Hawkins, "The Nationals Are Learning of Navy Life," *Washington Star*, April 2, 1943, C-1.

56. Povich, "Nat Infield Status Clarified by Clary," *Sporting News*, April 8, 1943, 2.

57. "Milk Price Boosted; Retain Ceiling to Come," *Washington Post*, April 6, 1943, 3.

58. "What People Say about Meat Rationing in Washington," *Washington Afro-American*, April 3, 1943, 24.

59. Gilbert, *They Also Served*, 80.

60. Ibid., 85.

61. Albert Zan, "Quonset Huts—A Brief History," EzineArticles.com, http://ezinearticles.com/?Quonset-Huts---A-Brief-History&id=1884016.

62. "Glen Echo Park Inaugural Set for April 10," *Washington Post*, March 28, 1943, L2.

63. Brigid Schulte, "Protest on a Sculpted Horse," *Washington Post*, June 29, 2004, B01.

64. Snyder, *Beyond the Shadow*, 168–69.

65. "Nats Told Baseball Is a War 'Must,'" *Washington Post*, April 15, 1943, 14.

66. Hawkins, "Win, Lose or Draw," *Washington Evening Star*, April 13, 1943, A14.

67. "Nats Told Baseball Is a War 'Must,'" *Washington Post*, April 15, 1943, 14.

68. "Opening Day," Baseball Almanac, http://www.baseball-almanac.com/opening_day/opening_day.shtml.

69. Associated Press, "Who's Chief with Roosevelt, Wallace Away?" *Washington Post*, April 21, 1943, 5. Under the rules of succession at the time, cabinet officers, in the order of their departments' creation beginning with the secretary of state, would have succeeded to the presidency. On July 18, 1947, President Harry Truman signed the Presidential Succession Act placing the Speaker of the House and the Senate president pro tempore, as elected officials, at the head of the line of succession.

70. "Text of War Department's Statement on Tokyo Raid," *Washington Post*, April 21, 1943, 1.

71. "Connie Mack Biography," Biography Base, http://www.biographybase.com/biography/Mack_Connie.html. In 1901, when Mack took ownership of the new American League Philadelphia Athletics, New York Giants manager

John McGraw called the Athletics "a white elephant nobody wanted." Mack adopted a white elephant as the team's logo, which the Athletics, throughout their franchise moves from Philadelphia to Kansas City to Oakland, have used off and on ever since.

72. Povich, This Morning, *Washington Post*, April 22, 1943, 16.

73. Orlo Robertson, Associated Press, "Majors to Get Livelier Ball in Two Weeks," *Washington Post*, April 24, 1943, 8.

74. Associated Press, "New 'Bouncy' Balls Ready for 2 Leagues," *Washington Post*, May 5, 1943, 21.

75. Milton Eisenhower letter to President Roosevelt, April 22, 1943, Franklin D. Roosevelt Presidential Library and Museum, http://www.fdrlibrary.marist.edu/archives/significant-findingaid.html.

76. "Miners Played Part in Strike 40,000 of Our[*sic*]," *Baltimore Afro-American*, May 8, 1943, 5.

77. Associated Press, "President's Telegram," *New York Times*, April 30, 1943, 10.

78. Leavengood, *Clark Griffith*, 268.

79. "League History," All-American Girls Professional Baseball League, http://www.aagpbl.org/index.cfm/pages/league/12/league-history.

80. W. H. Lawrence, "Invasion One Topic: Prime Minister's Party Includes High Army and Navy," *New York Times*, May 12, 1943, 1.

81. Josef Stalin letter to President Roosevelt, June 11, 1943, Franklin D. Roosevelt Presidential Library and Museum, www.fdrlibrary.marist.edu/archives/significant-findingaid.html.

82. Lawrence, "Church Pledges Japan's Ruin, but Reaffirms Nazis Come First; Junction on Attu Corners Enemy," *New York Times*, May 20, 1943, 1.

83. "Norfolk Sailor Nine Best Conditioned Team in U.S.," *Washington Post*, April 30, 1943, 17.

84. Hutchinson, a much-beloved ballplayer, managed the Tigers, Cardinals, and Reds in the 1950s and early 1960s. A heavy smoker from his Navy days, he died at the age of 45 on November 12, 1964, from inoperable lung cancer. The Hutchinson Cancer Research Center in Seattle opened in 1975 with Joe DiMaggio and President Gerald Ford on hand as guests.

85. Folliard, "Wounded Army Flier Hurls First Ball at War Bond Game," *Washington Post*, May 25, 1943, 13. Beginning in 1969 through the mid-1970s, Kate Smith's rendition of "God Bless America" was played before home games of the National Hockey League's Philadelphia Flyers. It became the team's good-luck charm, especially after she performed it live before game six of the NHL finals in 1974 when the Flyers won the Stanley Cup championship.

86. Al Costello, "Griffith Urges All Clubs to Stage War Bonds Games," *Washington Post*, May 25, 1943, 13.

87. Povich, This Morning, *Washington Post*, May 25, 1943, 13.

88. In an April 25, 2014, telephone conversation between author David E. Hubler and Stengel's grand-niece, Toni Mollett, she explained that Stengel's leg had been seriously injured when he was struck by a taxicab. Because he was a proud man, he refused to return to the game walking with a cane. So he created his own physical-therapy regimen by walking backward up and down from his hillside home to strengthen his leg muscles.

89. Povich, "Nats Make Capital out of Rise, Swing for Mark at Gate," *Sporting News*, June 10, 1943, 1.

90. Snyder, *Beyond the Shadow*, 165–66.

91. Actually, Clark Griffith did not have much leeway in his payroll, which came under the wartime price and wage controls. "Under Treasury Department regulations enacted prior to the 1943 season and in effect throughout the war, no ballplayer could make more money than the top salary paid by his club during the 1942 season unless special permission was obtained." Goldstein, *Spartan Seasons*, 146.

92. Alvin Moses, "Baseball Magnates Blind to Value of Colored Players," *Baltimore Afro-American*, May 22, 1943, 24.

93. Leavengood, *Clark Griffith*, 267.

94. Carter, "Player War Shows Urgent Need for Baseball Czar," From the Bench, *Washington Afro-American*, May 8, 1943, 24.

95. Founded as the Miami Ethiopian Clowns in the late 1930s by showman and promoter Syd Pollock, an early proponent of baseball integration, the clowning team barnstormed across the United States playing more than 100 games a season; they also changed their hometown affiliation on several occasions. The team was renamed the Cincinnati Ethiopian Clowns when it joined other black teams in founding the Negro American League in 1942. "The Indianapolis Clowns—Baseball's Entertainers," *Monarchs to Grays to Crawfords*, official blog of the Negro Leagues Baseball Museum, http://nlbm.mlblogs.com/2013/10/16/the-indianapolis-clowns-baseballs-entertainers/comment-page-1.

96. Raymond A. Mohl, "Clowning Around: The Miami Ethiopian Clowns and Culture Conflict in Black Baseball," *Tequesta*, February 2002, http://digitalcollections.fiu.edu/tequesta/files/2002/02_1_02.pdf.

97. Ibid.

98. "No Joint Agreement between Leagues—Posey," *Washington Afro-American*, May 8, 1943, 25.

99. "Roy Campanella," Baseball-Reference.com, http://www.baseball-reference.com/bullpen/Roy_Campanella#Suspension_and_flight_to_Mexico.

100. Ibid.

101. Carter, "Baseball Makes Mistake in Dealing with the Press," From the Bench, *Washington Afro-American*, June 12, 1943, 24.

102. "'Gosh!' Says Roosevelt on Death of Yamamoto," *New York Times*, May 22, 1943, 5.

103. "General Staff for the Home Front," *New York Times*, May 30, 1943, E1.

104. "40,000 Are on Strike in Rubber Plants; Auto Men Stay Out," *New York Times*, May 23, 1943, 1.

105. Lewis Stark, "Coal Miners Resume Strike with Conferees Deadlocked; Contract Ended at Midnight," *New York Times*, June 1, 1943, 1.

106. United Press, "Strikes at Record since Pearl Harbor," *New York Times*, June 2, 1943, 1.

107. Stark, "WLB Kept in Power," *New York Times*, June 4, 1943, 1.

108. Associated Press, "Mine Strikes Cost 2,000,000 Man-Days," *New York Times*, June 9, 1943, 34.

109. International News Service, "Col. Roosevelt Survivor of Crash Landing," *Washington Post*, June 6, 1943, M16.

110. "Trouble in Detroit," The Nation, *New York Times*, June 27, 1943, E2.

111. "Detroit Riot Inquiry Discounts Migration: Sociologist Finds Influx from South Not a Factor," *New York Times*, June 27, 1943, 13.

112. Associated Press, "Army Patrols End Detroit Rioting; Death Toll at 29," *New York Times*, June 23, 1943, 1.

113. "Trouble in Detroit," The Nation, *New York Times*, June 27, 1943, E2.

114. Rev. Anson Phelps Stokes, letter to President Roosevelt, June 26, 1943, President's Official File 93-C: Detroit Race Riots, Franklin D. Roosevelt Presidential Library and Museum, Hyde Park, NY.

115. Bob Clark, supervisory archivist at the Franklin D. Roosevelt Presidential Library and Museum, email exchange with author Joshua H. Drazen on January 8, 2014, wrote: "FDR was publicly silent on the Detroit race riots. At the very end of a press conference held on July 25, 1943, a reporter asked FDR if he had heard Vice President Wallace's speech in Detroit, and President Roosevelt's simple reply was that he 'liked it very much.' The press conference then ended."

116. Franklin D. Roosevelt letter to Rev. Anson Phelps Stokes, July 1, 1943, President's Official File 93-C: Detroit Race Riots, Franklin D. Roosevelt Presidential Library and Museum, Hyde Park, NY.

117. Email reply to author Joshua H. Drazen from Bob Clark, supervisory archivist Franklin D. Roosevelt Presidential Library and Museum, Hyde Park, NY, January 8, 2014.

118. "V. President Wallace Wants Vote for All," *Baltimore Afro-American*, July 24, 1943, 8.

119. "Gillette Airs All-Star," *Sporting News*, June 10, 1943, 4. A post–All-Star-Game report, however, put the broadcast licensing fee at $50,000.

120. Povich, This Morning, July 3, 1943, 10. From the inception of the All-Star Game in 1933 through 1946, the players were selected by the managers of the two league teams. Beginning in 1947, fans selected the rosters by submitting ballots, but when Cincinnati fans "stuffed the ballot box" in 1957 and elected eight Reds as the NL starters, MLB returned the balloting by the managers, the players, and the coaches. Fans regained the right to vote in 1970 and have done so ever since.

121. Gilbert, *They Also Served*, 100.

122. Povich, This Morning, *Washington Post*, July 3, 1943, 10.

123. "No Yankees Used in Dream Contest," *New York Times*, July 14, 1943, 24.

124. Drebinger, "Cooper, Beaten All-Star Pitcher, Retains Confidence of Manager," *New York Times*, July 15, 1943, 26.

125. Mead, *Baseball Goes to War*, 119.

126. James P. Dawson, "$115,174 Realized for Bat-Ball Fund," *New York Times*, July 14, 1943, 24.

127. Franklin D. Roosevelt, "Letter to Henry A. Wallace and Jesse H. Jones on Economic Warfare," July 15, 1943, The American Presidency Project, http://www.presidency.ucsb.edu/ws/?pid=16429.

128. Franklin D. Roosevelt: "Executive Order 9361 Establishing the Office of Economic Warfare," July 15, 1943, The American Presidency Project, http://www.presidency.ucsb.edu/ws/?pid=16431.

129. International News Service, "Col. Elliott Roosevelt Here, Praises Precision Bombing," *Washington Post*, July 25, 1943, M5. Upon his return to Washington in late July, Colonel Roosevelt shed some light on the quick victory in Sicily when he told the press, "For a week before the attack our forces systematically bombed the Sicilian airfields so that they were no longer of any value. We even hit enemy planes in revetments (a form of shelter)." Parentheses as published. Roosevelt had taken part in the Allied aerial photo-reconnaissance missions over Sicily that had prepared the way for the bombings.

130. "Eisenhower's Plea," *Washington Post*, July 30, 1943, 8.

131. "Jake Powell Played in 3 World Series," *Washington Post*, November 5, 1948, B5.

132. Povich, This Morning, *Washington Post*, August 7, 1943, 8.

133. Steve Wulf, "Bigot Unwittingly Sparked Change," ESPN, http://m.espn.go.com/mlb/story?storyId=10496417. Powell likely was lying about his winter job. Wulf reports that Powell was never a member of the Dayton Police Department. "He had applied for a job in the department but was never hired." But Wulf's premise (and the article's title) is misleading. The Powell incident

of 1938 did provoke outrage and wide condemnation among the black communities nationwide, but in actuality, it did little if anything to "pave the way for baseball's integration," which did not happen for another nine years. Powell played two more seasons for the Yankees after the incident before going into the service and then returning to the diamond in Washington in 1943.

134. Snyder, *Beyond the Shadow*, 77.

135. Ibid., 79.

136. Povich, This Morning, *Washington Post*, August 7, 1943, 8. In his column, Povich rendered the offensive passage as: "I'm a cop, in Dayton, Ohio, in the winter," said Jake forthrightly, "and I spend the offseason clubbing citizens over the head." It was very weak choice of word substitution from such a talented wordsmith, no doubt, but Povich never would have used Powell's choice of words in a "family newspaper." The incident happened years before the *Post* adapted a rule that quotes had to be rendered as spoken and the euphemism "the N word" had not became the widely accepted alternative to the much-despised epithet.

137. Snyder, *Beyond the Shadow*, 170. On November 4, 1948, Powell shot and killed himself in a DC police station after being arrested on an outstanding warrant for passing bad checks in Florida. He was 40 years old.

138. Marcus Hayes, "'The Mecca of Black Baseball' in Negro Leagues, the All-Star Game Was Bigger Event Than World Series," *Philadelphia Daily News*, July 2, 1996, Philly.com, http://articles.philly.com/1996-07-02/sports/ 25621333_1_kansas-city-monarchs-east-west-josh-gibson.

139. Jackson, On the Sports Front, *Washington Afro-American*, July 31, 1943, 26.

140. Jackson, "Gibson and Suttles Hit Long Home Runs," *Washington Afro-American*, August 14, 1943, 27. Jackson was probably exaggerating somewhat because in 1943 the deepest part of centerfield at Griffith Stadium measured 420 feet, according to Philip J. Lowry's history of baseball parks, *Green Cathedrals*.

141. "Bobo Newsom," Baseball-Reference.com, http://www.baseball-reference.com/players/n/newsobo01.shtml.

142. Povich, "Nats Regain Newsom for Waiver Price," *Washington Post*, September 1, 1943, 16. Newsom had a record of three wins and three losses for the Nationals and an ERA of 3.83 in his two months with Washington. Griffith traded him to the Athletics in December for pitcher Roger Wolff.

143. C. Peter Chen, "Quadrant Conference," World War II Database, http:// ww2db.com/battle_spec.php?battle_id=67.

144. Povich, *Washington Senators*, 207.

145. "1943 American League Attendance and Miscellaneous," Baseball-Reference.com, http://www.baseball-reference.com/leagues/AL/1943-misc.shtml.

146. Obermeyer, *Baseball and the Bottom Line*, Kindle edition, table 8, location 2506.

147. Snyder, *Beyond the Shadow*, 172.

148. "Predicts Negroes in Major Baseball Leagues by 1945," *New York Amsterdam News*, September 4, 1943, 17.

149. Jon Meacham, "The Winding Road to D-Day," *Time*, June 18, 2014, 25.

150. Franklin D. Roosevelt, "Executive Order 9412—Seizure and Operation of the Railroads," The American Presidency Project, http://www.presidency.ucsb.edu/ws/index.php?pid=16357.

151. Paul Dickson, *Bill Veeck: Baseball's Greatest Maverick*, 90. In writing this award-winning biography, Dickson was able to access the transcript of the minutes of the December 3, 1943, meeting thanks to Jim Gates at the National Baseball Library and Archives. According to Dickson, this appears to have been the first public airing of the full transcript, which had been kept as a confidential document for more than 60 years.

152. Snyder, *Beyond the Shadow*, 180.

153. Dickson, *Bill Veeck*, 91.

154. Ralph Matthews, "Clark Griffith Won't Budge on Use of Colored Players," *Baltimore Afro-American*, December 11, 1943, 1.

155. Sam Lacy, Looking 'Em Over, *Washington Afro-American*, January 8, 1944, 17.

156. Daniel, "'Football Jeopardizes Baseball's Hold upon U.S.,' Rickey Warns," *Sporting News*, January 6, 1944, 1.

157. "End the NFL's Tax Free Status? Why Is the NFL Tax Free?" Democratic Underground, http://www.democraticunderground.com/10024390747. According to the site, the last time the NFL League Office paid taxes was in 1966. Congress then expanded the definition of 501(c)6 not-for-profit organizations in the tax code to include professional football leagues, one of the greatest lobbying successes ever. The NFL also was granted antitrust exemption (like baseball), which has given the league a monopoly in TV revenue. The 1966 law also gave the NFL an uncommon antitrust exemption allowing it to create a monopoly to negotiate TV rights at the same time, the site reports.

4. 1944

1. "Congress Attacks Big Issues Today," *Washington Post*, January 10, 1944, 1.

2. According to a story by David Camelon in the February 1969 issue of the *American Legion Magazine*, Gibson was away from Washington as the conference committee was about to vote on the bill's stumbling block to ap-

proval, Title IV, the veterans' job-placement section. The Senate version left unemployment matters with the U.S. Employment Service while the House wanted such matters to be overseen by the Veterans Administration. Gibson earlier had voted by proxy for the latter, but his vote inexplicably wasn't counted. So a mad scramble ensued to find the Georgia legislator involving the Georgia State Police, local radio stations, and Eastern Airlines. Gibson was finally located at about 11 p.m. as he was arriving at his home in Douglas, Georgia, and he promptly agreed to get to Capitol Hill as quickly as possible. Officials at Eastern Airlines, then headed by World War I ace Eddie Rickenbacker, held up a flight leaving Jacksonville, Florida, so that Gibson could make the 130-mile trip to get onboard. Gibson was met at Washington's National Airport at 6:37 a.m. and was sped to the Capitol in time for the 10 a.m. conference committee vote. "With the deadlock broken, the three negative votes from the House gave up and made it unanimous. The long seven months [*sic*] fight was won." Roosevelt signed the historic bill into law on June 22. David Camelon, "How the First GI Bill Was Written (Part II)," *American Legion Magazine*, February 1969, http://www.legion.org/documents/legion/pdf/gibillpitkinpt2.pdf.

3. "Servicemen's Readjustment Act (G.I. Bill)," NOLO,http://www.nolo.com/legal-encyclopedia/content/gi-bill-act.html. In the GI Bill's peak year of 1947, armed with funding provided by the bill, veterans accounted for 49 percent of all college admissions, according to the VA, which also noted that from 1944 to 1952 the law backed almost 2.4 million home loans. Colmery lived long enough to witness the fruits of his labor. He died in 1979 at age 88.

4. Mark Sullivan, "Chaos at Home," *Washington Post*, January 10, 1944, 10.

5. Franklin D. Roosevelt, "State of the Union Message to Congress," January 11, 1944. The American Presidency Project, http://www.presidency.ucsb.edu/ws/?pid=16518.

6. "FDR and the Holocaust," Franklin D. Roosevelt Library and Museum, http://www.fdrlibrary.marist.edu/archives/pdfs/holocaust.pdf.

7. J. A. Fox, "President Names Special Board to Rescue European Refugees," *Sunday Star*, January 23, 1944, 1.

8. Gould Lincoln, "Party Leaders Back 4th Term for Roosevelt," *Sunday Star*, January 23, 1944, 1.

9. Jackson, On the Sports Front, *Washington Afro-American*, January 8, 1944, 18.

10. Lacy, "Mystery Shrouds NNL Baseball Meeting in N.Y.," *Washington Afro-American*, January 8, 1944, 18.

11. Ibid. In an effort to bring Negro League baseball more in line with a professional-sports business, the black owners did agree on four recommenda-

tions from NAL president Dr. J. B. Martin. Lacy reported that the owners would "give serious consideration" to hiring a statistician to keep playing records, no games would be played as exhibitions in the coming season, the teams would not borrow or lend players "regardless of the condition of the club making the request," and "the world series playoff will be limited to a first-four-out-of-seven basis." The owners tabled a fifth recommendation that the series would be limited to the home cities of the two teams.

12. Povich, "Griffith's Club Just One Big Happy Family," *Sporting News*, January 6, 1944, 2. According to Povich, Griffith plowed the profits into ball-park improvements and the small farm system he maintained. The sportswriter put the Nats capitalization at a mere $200,000.

13. Frank Graham Jr., "When Baseball Went to War," SI Vault, *Sports Illustrated*, http://sportsillustrated.cnn.com/vault/article/magazine/MAG1079753.

14. "To Be or Not to Be 2-B," *The Sporting News*, March 16, 1944, 10.

15. "A Country That Found Itself at War," Baseball and Other Contact Sports,http://www.jcs-group.com/sports/baseball/wwii2.html.

16. Ibid. With the help of his father-in-law, Browns' manager William De-Witt, Laabs was transferred to St. Louis, where he made pipes that were later used in the Oak Ridge, Tennessee, facility where the first atomic bombs were constructed. Laabs, who was available for home games and weekend trips to other midwestern cities, hit two home runs against the Yankees to clinch the pennant for St. Louis on the final day of the season. But in game two of the World Series, he made two errors and was almost charged with a third if the base runner had chosen to take another base on Laabs' errant throw.

17. Graham Jr., "When Baseball Went to War," SI Vault, *Sports Illustrated*, http://sportsillustrated.cnn.com/vault/article/magazine/MAG1079753.

18. Grantland Rice, "Win, Lose or Draw," *Washington Evening Star*, March 16, 1944, A-14.

19. "GIs Critical of Ballplayer Holdouts for Big Dough," *Washington Post*, March 15, 1944, 10.

20. Snyder, *Beyond the Shadow*, 181.

21. Ibid., 194–96. According to Snyder, Lacy also aimed his poison pen at Shirley Povich after the *Post* sportswriter in 1939 reported comments that Walter Johnson made to him while they watched a game at Tinker Field in April of that year between the Grays and the Newark Eagles. Johnson praised the play of Josh Gibson and called him better than Yankees backstop Bill Dickey. "Too bad this Gibson is a colored fellow," Povich quoted Johnson as saying. "The column cast Povich in the vanguard of white sportswriters promoting integration. It also drew Lacy's ire," Snyder said, no doubt for stealing some of Lacy's integration thunder and also because of several factual errors in

the column that indicated to Lacy that Povich didn't know much about the Negro Leagues or their players. Lacy's "tremendous enmity toward Povich" lasted for many years as evidenced during Snyder's interview with Lacy in 1992, when "the mere mention of Povich's name caused Lacy to erupt."

22. Lacy, Looking 'Em Over, *Washington Afro-American*, March 4, 1944, 18.

23. Povich, "Our Spring Puts the Freeze on Griff, Yearning for Dixie," *Washington Post*, April 6, 1944, 12.

24. Rick Ferrell ended his career in 1947, catching his final game with Washington on September 14. He was a month shy of turning 42.

25. Rick Ferrell, personal telephone interview with author David E. Hubler, December 10, 1992. At the time, Ferrell was an executive consultant for the Detroit Tigers. Ferrell died on July 27, 1995.

26. Povich, "Nats Outfield Crippled by Forced Deal," *Washington Post*, March 29, 1944. 12. The trade was a lucky break for Moore, who played in his only World Series as a member of the Browns.

27. Povich, "Mike Guerra Pushes Rick Ferrell for Job?" *Washington Post*, April 5, 1944, 10.

28. "Return of Campanella, Butts Lifts Elite Hopes," *Washington Afro-American*, April 22, 1944, 18.

29. "Grays Meet Newark in D.C. Exhibition, Sunday," *Washington Afro-American*, April 22, 1944, 18.

30. Mead, *Even the Browns*, 134.

31. Povich, This Morning, *Washington Post*, April 19, 1944, 12.

32. Wallace's tenure as the 33rd vice president was notable for other aspects besides his throwing arm. He first served in Roosevelt's cabinet as secretary of agriculture between 1933 and 1940; after being dropped from the number-two spot on the Democratic ticket in 1944 in favor of Truman, he returned to the cabinet as secretary of commerce from 1945 to 1946.

33. "Grays Meet Newark in D.C. Exhibition, Sunday," *Washington Afro-American*, April 22, 1944, 18.

34. Lacy, Looking 'Em Over, *Washington Afro-American*, May 13, 1944, 18.

35. Ibid.

36. Shirley Povich in-person interview with author David E. Hubler, November 4, 1992.

37. Jack Hand, "229,821 Keep Griffs' Till Ringing," *Washington Post*, May 23, 1944, 13. The largest single-game attendance to that point was 54,725 at Yankee Stadium on May 21 to watch New York sweep a doubleheader from St. Louis. By contrast, the Browns also racked up the smallest single-game attendance when just 758 patrons showed up at Sportsman's Park on May 3 for a

game against the visiting Tigers. "1944 St. Louis Browns," Baseball-Reference.com, http://www.baseball-reference.com/teams/SLB/1944-schedule-scores.shtml.

38. "Grays Tackle Stars in First Arc Game," *Washington Afro-American*, May 20, 1944, 18.

39. "Griff Honor Guest at Touchdown Club," *Washington Post*, May 21, 1944, M6. Griffith was voted into the Hall of Fame at Cooperstown, NY, by the Veterans Committee, as a pioneer/executive in 1946. His induction ceremony was held in 1947.

40. Rick Ferrell, telephone interview with author David E. Hubler, December 10, 1992.

41. Memorial Day, May 30, was permanently moved to the last Monday in the month by the Uniform Monday Holiday Act of 1971, which was signed into law on June 28, 1968, and took effect on January 1, 1971.

42. "1944 Washington Senators Schedule," Box Scores and Splits, Baseball Almanac, http://www.baseball-almanac.com/teamstats/schedule.php?y=1944&t=WS1.

43. "8,000 Watch as Elites Break Even with Grays," *Washington Afro-American*, May 20, 1944, 18.

44. "General Dwight D. Eisenhower (Ike) D-Day Message," Kansas Heritage Group, http://www.kansasheritage.org/abilene/ikespeech.html.

45. In *Even the Browns*, 136, author William B. Mead points out that no one in St. Louis, including the press and the players, had any notion that the Browns could be a contender not only in 1944 but ever. He quotes former Browns infielder Don Gutteridge as saying, "They had some pretty good ballplayers but they had a defeatist attitude. They didn't think they could do it; they didn't have the confidence. They said, 'Oh, what the hell, we're going to lose anyway.' And that attitude was eating up the Browns, really, year after year."

46. Povich, "Bluege Installs Joe Vosmik as Nats' Regular Rightfielder," *Washington Post*, June 20, 1944, 8.

47. Joe Vosmik appeared in only 14 games for the Nats in 1944, batting an anemic .194. Following another Nats' Sunday doubleheader loss to the Indians on July 23, Vosmik's major-league career ended, conveniently for him in his hometown of Cleveland.

48. Povich, *Washington Post*, June 20, 1944, 8.

49. Povich, "Bluege Still Expresses Faith in Nats despite Post in Cellar," *Washington Post*, June 25, 1944, M6.

50. Bell's speed was so legendary his teammates often said he could turn out the light in the room and be in bed before the room got dark. Bell was elected

to the Baseball Hall of Fame by the Negro Leagues Committee in 1974. He died March 7, 1991, in St. Louis.

51. Snyder, *Beyond the Shadow*, 185.

52. Nicholas Dawidoff, ed., *Baseball*, excerpt from Donald Honig, *Baseball When the Grass Was Real*, 139.

53. "Two Gray Stars Arouse Bosses' Ire; One Ousted," *Washington Afro-American*, May 27, 1944, 18.

54. Carter, "Joltin' Josh Helps Grays Hit the Jackpot," *Washington Afro-American*, July 24, 1943, 26.

55. "Fisticuffs Enliven Gray-Baron Twin Bill," *Washington Afro-American*, June 17, 1944, 18.

56. "NNL Wars on Saperstein, Raps American League," *Washington Afro-American*, July 1, 1944, 26.

57. Ibid.

58. "Elmer Gedeon," Baseball's Greatest Sacrifice, http://www.baseballsgreatestsacrifice.com/biographies/gedeon_elmer.html.

59. "Harry O'Neill," Baseball's Greatest Sacrifice, http://www.baseballsgreatestsacrifice.com/biographies/oneill_harry.html.

60. By that time, Johnson was a resident of Germantown, Maryland, where he had served as a Montgomery County commissioner in 1938. Urged by his father-in-law, Republican representative Edwin Roberts, in 1940, Johnson ran unsuccessfully for a congressional seat in Maryland's 6th district. Two years after his appearance on War Relief Night, Johnson died of a brain tumor, on December 10, 1946, one month after his 59th birthday. He was buried in Union Cemetery in nearby Rockville, Maryland.

61. Povich, This Morning, *Washington Post*, July 12, 1944, 8. Povich also reported that "Tom Yawkey, at Boston, and William Wrigley, at Chicago, former die-hard opponents of night ball, are beginning to weaken on their ideas." Here, Povich is either referring to William Wrigley Jr., the chewing gum magnate who purchased the Cubs in 1921 and who died in 1932, (although the first night game wasn't played until 1935 in Cincinnati) or he inadvertently confused him with Wrigley Jr.'s son, Philip K. Wrigley, who succeeded his father. P. K. Wrigley's son, William Wrigley III, became Cubs president in 1977. Nevertheless, it wasn't until 1988, when the Cubs, then owned by the Chicago Tribune Company, and the last holdout against night baseball, finally installed lights at Wrigley Field.

62. "Army Draft Hits Nats' Four Latins," *Washington Post*, July 16, 1944, M6.

63. Ibid. (In 1992, before beginning this history, David E. Hubler, was preparing to write a novel about the wartime Nationals. He contacted several former Nats to interview. He also attempted to get in touch with catcher Mike

Guerra, whose nine-year baseball career had ended in 1951 with Washington. Several letters to Guerra's home in Miami, Florida, went unanswered, but just as he was beginning an early draft of the book that November, he received a short note from Mrs. Carmen Guerra. She wrote to say that Mike had recently died after a long battle with heart disease, two days before what would have been his 80th birthday on October 11, 1992. She said Mike knew of the book project and closed with "I thank you so much for the kind words. They meant a lot to him.")

64. Povich, This Morning, *Washington Post*, August 24, 1944, 16.

65. "Joltin' Josh Helps Grays Hit the Jackpot," *Washington Afro-American*, July 24, 1944, 26.

66. "A Peek into the Future, Connie Mack Sees Baseball as 'Exciting Postwar Game,'" *Washington Post*, August 1, 1944, 8.

67. Jackson, On the Sports Front, *Washington Afro-American*, July 31, 1943, 26.

68. Staff Correspondent, "Can Satchel Paige Stop the East–West Classic?" *Washington Afro-American*, August 12, 1944, 26.

69. Jackson, "46,000 See West Win All-Star Classic, 7–4," *Baltimore Afro-American*, August 19, 1944, 18.

70. John B. Keller, "Nationals, Flag-Hopeless, Home for 20 Games; Poor Feeling Anchors Club; Split with Bosox," *Evening Star*, August 7, 1944, 8.

71. "Ed Boland," Baseball-Reference.com, http://www.baseball-reference.com/players/b/bolaned01.shtml#trans.

72. Keller, "Nationals, Flag-Hopeless, Home for 20 Games; Poor Feeling Anchors Club; Split with Bosox," *Evening Star*, August 7, 1944, 8.

73. "Early Wynn," Baseball in Wartime, http://www.baseballinwartime.com/player_biographies/wynn_early.htm.

74. The bigotry was not limited to the Browns. Their cotenant at Sportsman's Park, the Cardinals, were reportedly prepared to strike if Brooklyn's Jackie Robinson took the field against them in 1947. Although in later years Cardinal players on that team denied the published reports of the threat to walk off the field, Robinson biographer Jules Tygiel writes that "the strike saga amounts to somewhat more than the denials of the players, but quite a bit less than [*New York Herald Tribune* sports editor Stanley] Woodward's allegations implied. Robinson's promotion [to the major-league club] undeniably aroused considerable discontent among the Cardinals and other teams. The idea of organizing a strike probably surfaced."

75. Mead, *Baseball Goes to War*, 133. The wire screen that had been installed in 1929 finally was taken down before the 1955 season (the second season that the Cardinals occupied Sportsman's Park alone, the Browns having relocated to Baltimore following the 1953 season and renamed the Orioles).

The screen was not removed to make it easier for African Americans to watch the game, however. "Cards manager Eddie Stanky and General Manager Dick Meyer thought that the Cards would benefit [with more home runs] with their predominantly left-handed batting lineup." Lowry, *Green Cathedrals*, 231.

76. Povich, This Morning, *Washington Post*, August 24, 1944, 8.

77. "Aug 20, 1944, Browns and Senators Box Score and Play by Play," Baseball-Reference.com, http://www.baseball-reference.com/boxes/WS1/WS1194408202.shtml.

78. Ibid.

79. Povich, This Morning, *Washington Post*, August 24, 1944, 8.

80. "Leyte," U.S. Army Center of Military History, http://www.history.army.mil/brochures/leyte/leyte.htm.

81. Meacham, *Franklin and Winston*, 298. Meacham reports that instead of going directly to Hyde Park to pick up the first lady, FDR's train first stopped in New Jersey for him to visit Lucy Rutherford at her late husband's estate, tour the grounds, and have a somewhat formal lunch. Meacham writes: "It was a remarkable scene: a wartime president of the United States, en route to a conference with the prime minister of Great Britain, stealing a few hours to lunch with a long-ago love, surrounded by the titled guests and extended relatives, all discreet enough to know that the whereabouts of this most public of men were to be guarded with tact."

82. During the next six months, the Germans launched 1,400 V-2s at Britain. "September 1944," Franklin D. Roosevelt Presidential Library and Museum, http://www.fdrlibrary.marist.edu/daybyday/event/september-1944-8/.

83. Mead, *Even the Browns*, 165.

84. Lowry, *Green Cathedrals*, 40.

85. "No Scandal in Brownies, Bill Stern Says," *Sporting News*, September 21, 1944, 4.

86. Red Smith, "Blows Fly as Browns Play Nats," *Sporting News*, September 28, 1944, 1.

87. Povich, This Morning, *Washington Post*, September 23, 1944, 10. Povich reported the events from Chicago, where the Nationals had gone to open a series against the White Sox.

88. Ibid. Writing for a "family newspaper," Povich surely cleaned up the language Bluege used in his instructions to his team just as he had when he reported Jake Powell's offensive remark about African Americans.

89. "Sep 26, 1944, Red Sox at Browns Box Score and Play by Play," Baseball-Reference.com, http://www.baseball-reference.com/boxes/SLA/SLA194409260.shtml.

90. Mead, *Even the Browns*, 176.

91. Ibid.

92. Ibid.

93. Ibid.

94. Ibid., 178.

95. Graham Jr., "When Baseball Went to War," SI Vault, *Sports Illustrated*, April 17, 1967, http://sportsillustrated.cnn.com/vault/article/magazine/ MAG1079753/index.htm.

96. Ibid. Managing from the first- or third-base coaching box was not exclusive to Sewell. Leo Durocher, who managed both the Dodgers and the Giants, was fond of running his club from the third-base coaching box, where his first rite always was to erase the chalk line around it with his spikes.

97. Mead, *Even the Browns*, 179.

98. Ibid., 187.

99. Gilbert, *They Also Served*, 155.

100. Obermeyer, *Baseball and the Bottom Line*, Kindle edition, table 8, location 2506.

101. Dryden also coined a similar and equally unflattering comment about the Browns: "First in shoes, first in booze, last in the American League." Paul Dickson, *Baseball's Greatest Quotations*, 117.

102. "Auto Crash Weakens Barons for Series Opener," *Washington Afro-American*, September 16, 1944, 30.

103. "Pittsburgh Crawfords of 1935," Black Baseball's Negro Baseball Leagues, http://blackbaseball.com/2010/12/pittsburgh-crawfords-of-1935/.

104. Don De Leighbur, "Greenlee Throws Scare into Baseball; Players Benefit," *Baltimore Afro-American*, September 9, 1944, 18.

105. Wallace missed becoming the 33rd president of the United States by just 82 days. After his second cabinet appointment as commerce secretary, Wallace became the editor of the *New Republic* magazine in 1946, on whose pages he often vociferously criticized Truman's foreign policy, especially toward the Soviet Union. In 1947, Wallace predicted the Truman Doctrine, which aimed at thwarting growing Soviet influence in Europe, would mark the beginning of "a century of fear." In 1948, Wallace ran for president on the Progressive Party ticket, advocating friendly relations with the Soviet Union, an end to the growing Cold War and racial segregation, and demanding full voting rights for African Americans. If anyone could dream up a less popular platform than that, no one ever came forward with one. During the campaign, he refused to appear before segregated audiences; neither would he eat or stay in segregated restaurants and hotels. With endorsements from the Communist Party of the United States and the American Labor Party of New York State, Wallace won about one million popular votes nationally but not a single electoral vote. He died in 1965 at age 77.

106. Turner Catledge, "2D Ballot Decides, Wallace, Leading 429½ to 319½ on First, Is Crushed 1,100 to 66," *New York Times*, July 22, 1944, 1.

107. Catledge, "Michigan's 19 Put Roosevelt's Total of Electors at 432," *New York Times*, November 10, 1944, 1.

108. John H. Crider, "President Says That Election Shows 'Reviving Democracy,'" *New York Times*, November 9, 1944, 1.

109. "Judge Landis Dies; Baseball Czar, 78," *New York Times*, November 26, 1944, 56.

110. "Landis' Body Cremated," *New York Times*, November 27, 1944, 23.

111. Povich, "Indispensable List Includes but Six Griffs," *Sporting News*, December 14, 1944, 16.

112. Edgar G. Brands, "Player Deals Slowed by Manpower Order," *Sporting News*, December 14, 1944, 1.

113. The night before, American bandleader Glen Miller and his British pilot, Flight Officer John R. S. Morgan, took off from an airfield near Cambridge, England, to organize a Christmas show for troops in Paris. They were never seen again, and it's presumed their plane went down—either from enemy fire or from mechanical problems—somewhere in the North Sea.

114. "President Has Hankering," *Sporting News*, December 16, 1944, 16.

5. 1945

1. Bedingfield, *Baseball in Wartime*, newsletter, vol. 4, no. 28 (January 2010), http://www.baseballinwartime.com/BIWNewsletterVol4No28January2010.pdf.

2. "New Baseball League of Six Clubs Formed," *Chicago Defender*, January 6, 1945, 7.

3. "Fourth Inaugural Address of the President," Franklin D. Roosevelt Presidential Library and Museum, http://www.fdrlibrary.marist.edu/aboutfdr/pdfs/inaug_45address.pdf.

4. When Stalin reneged on the Yalta agreement, specifically with regard to the makeup of postwar Europe, Roosevelt came in for considerable criticism for having "given away" Eastern Europe to the Soviet Union.

5. Goldstein, *Spartan Seasons*, 211.

6. "President Gives Baseball Hope as Nat Boss Presents Passes," *Evening Star*, March 13, 1945, A-10.

7. Keller, Win, Lose or Draw, *Evening Star*, March 13, 1945, A-10.

8. Ibid.

9. About the same time, troops from the 1st Army were preparing to cross the Rhine River at Remagen on a pontoon bridge built by the 276th Engineer

Combat Battalion; among them was Warren Spahn, a young former Boston Braves pitcher, who had survived the collapse of the Ludendorff Bridge there on March 17 that killed more than 30 Army engineers. Bedingfield, *Baseball in Wartime*, newsletter, vol. 4, no. 28 (January 2010), http://www.baseballinwartime.com/BIWNewsletterVol4No28January2010.pdf.

10. Walter Haight, "Pieces of Haight," *Washington Post*, March 15, 1945, 10. After covering the Washington Nationals every year since the 1920s, Shirley Povich went into the service in 1945 as a war correspondent in the Pacific, where he reported on the battles of Iwo Jima and Okinawa with the First Marine Division.

11. Gilbert, *They Also Served*, 170.

12. Bus Ham, "Majors Propose Cut in Exhibition Season," *Washington Post*, March 16, 1945, 12.

13. "Ken Keltner Leaves War Job to Report to Indian Camp," *Washington Post*, March 15, 1945, 10.

14. Dan Burley, "Confidentially Yours," *New York Amsterdam News*, January 6, 1945, B6.

15. "Ken Keltner Leaves War Job to Report to Indian Camp," *Washington Post*, March 15, 1945, 10. In 1944, when Keltner reported for spring training, he was reclassified 1-A and was accepted into the Navy after passing a physical. When he wasn't called up, he was reclassified to 2-A, which was again changed when he went back to his defense job in Milwaukee after the baseball season.

16. Had Ken Keltner gone into the service when the draft was first instituted, Joe DiMaggio's epic 56-game hit streak in 1941 might have been extended. It was Keltner, playing third base for the Cleveland Indians, who made two brilliant putouts of balls hit by DiMaggio down the third-base line to end the streak on July 17. DiMaggio promptly started a 16-game hit streak one game later.

17. Ham, "McNutt Clears Baseball Players of Job Jumping; Edict Assures Game Enough Manpower," *Washington Post*, March 22, 1945, 8.

18. One local official who objected to hiring Powell in that position was Montgomery County councilman Walter Johnson, the Nats' Hall of Fame pitcher. Steve Wulf, "Bigot Unwittingly Sparks Change," ESPN, http://m.espn.go.com/mlb/story?storyId=10496417.

19. Haight, "Griff Raves as Shepard Drills with Yanks," *Washington Post*, March 19, 1945, 10.

20. "Shepard, Hero Pitcher, Works with Yankees; Griffith Raves," *Washington Post*, March 19, 1945, 1.

21. Former A's outfielder Hal Peck, who accidently shot off two toes on his left foot, was called up to the Philadelphia A's that year after Connie Mack shelled out $20,000 and four minor leaguers to the Milwaukee Brewers of the

American Association for him. With a specially designed shoe, Peck was the fastest player in the Frederick, Maryland, camp. "Special Shoe Gets Rookie A's Contract," *Washington Post*, March 21, 1945, 12. He played in 112 games that year and hit .276. with five home runs.

22. "Survey Shows Majors Lost 79.2% of 1941 Performers," *Washington Post*, April 15, 1945, M6.

23. "In the Service," *Sporting News*, May 10, 1945, 12.

24. In a letter dated October 18, 1963, to Louis Reed, a former senatorial aide, Truman recounted how he learned of Roosevelt's death and why he failed to say anything to Reed when he encountered him in the Capitol: "In reply to yours of the 14th, when I saw you I was on my way to see Sam Rayburn, where I was instructed to go to the White House. When I arrived at the White House I was informed of the President's death, and was sworn in as President of the United States about 7 p.m. At the time I saw you I didn't know President Roosevelt was dead anymore than you did. It was just as much of a surprise to me as it was to anyone else." "Harry Truman Tells How He Learned He Became the President: FDR's Death, He Says, Was a Complete Surprise," Shapell Manuscript Foundation, http://www.shapell.org/manuscript.aspx?truman-fdr-presidency-death.

25. David McCullough, *Truman*, 341–42.

26. Ibid., 346.

27. Frank L. Kluckhohn, "States His Policy: President Pledges U.S. to Work for World Security League," *New York Times*, April 17, 1945, 1.

28. "Same-Day Harry Truman Letter Written as Vice-President—But Signed as President with 'Terrible Responsibilities,'" Shapell Manuscript Foundation, http://www.shapell.org/manuscript.aspx?170253 . As far as we can ascertain, this is the first mention of the Truman note to Clark Griffith. When we emailed a scan of it to the Franklin D. Roosevelt Library and Museum in Hyde Park, NY, an official there said they did not have that particular original communication on file but the signature appeared to be authentic.

29. Snyder, *Beyond the Shadow*, 214–15.

30. Lacy, Looking 'Em Over, *Baltimore Afro-American*, January 20, 1945, 23.

31. "Branch Rickey Biography," Bio, http://www.biography.com/people/branch-rickey-9458118.

32. Lacy, Looking 'Em Over, *Baltimore Afro-American*, April 7, 1945, 22.

33. "Terris McDuffie," Pitch Black Baseball, http://www.pitchblackbaseball.com/nlotmterris.html. According to the site, Branch Rickey deemed both men too old to make it in the major leagues. McDuffie was in his mid-30s at the time of the "tryout" and Dave "Showboat" Thomas was 40.

34. "Red Sox Tryouts Given Trio of Colored Players," *Baltimore Afro-American*, April 21, 1945, 22.

35. Snyder, *Beyond the Shadow*, 222.

36. Will Harridge, "A.L. to Rank as Most Notable in Game's History," *Washington Post*, April 15, 1945, M6.

37. According to a published report by AP sportswriter Bus Ham, citing Yankees president Larry MacPhail, Chandler endeared himself to the baseball owners and went to the top of the candidates' list after Chandler and a friend, Colonel John Gottlieb, a member of the general staff of the War Department in Washington, were driving to a meeting with Secretary of State Cordell Hull at the State Department. When Chandler saw a sandlot baseball game in progress on the National Mall, he told Gottlieb to stop the car, and he watched the game so long that he was a half-hour late for his meeting with Hull, who apparently wasn't angry. MacPhail revealed that the incident convinced the owners that anyone who'd keep the secretary of state waiting 30 minutes to watch a baseball game "unquestionably was profoundly interested in the sport." Bus Ham, "Keeping Secretary of State Waiting 30 Minutes to Watch Sandlot Game Won Commissioner's Job for 'Happy,'" *Washington Post*, May 6, 1945, M6.

38. "Senator Chandler Gets Baseball Post," *New York Times*, April 25, 1945, 28.

39. Povich, This Morning, *Washington Post*, July 11, 1945, 14.

40. "Nats to Dedicate Opening Game to Roosevelt," *Washington Post*, April 14, 1945, 8.

41. Truman's position was that the people should decide the selection of such a high public official, not the president. In a letter to Congress in June, Truman urged revising the existing law, enacted in 1886, under which members of the cabinet would succeed to the presidency in the order in which they were created, starting with the secretary of state, then the secretary of the Treasury, and so forth. Truman recommended a succession order of elected officials beginning with the Speaker of the House, as it was the body closest to the people. In 1967, the 25th Amendment to the Constitution was enacted and provided for such a line of succession. When he ran for election in his own right in 1948, Truman chose Kentucky Senator Alben Barkley as his vice president. Interestingly, Barkley's primary opponent in 1938 was A. B. "Happy" Chandler, now the baseball commissioner.

42. Lewis F. Atchison, "Win, Lose or Draw," *Evening Star*, April 21, 1945, A-12.

43. Binks had a three-year career with Washington. He then went to the Athletics for two seasons and concluded his brief five-year career with the

Browns in 1948, at age 34. When he died at age 96 on November 13, 2010, he was among the 100 longest-living ballplayers.

44. "Chandler Visits with Truman, Says President Is Great Fan," *Washington Post*, April 29, 1945, M6.

45. "President Truman to Look into Matter, Says Baseball Boss," *Washington Post*, May 2, 1945, 10.

46. "Chandler to Move Baseball Headquarters to Cincinnati," *Washington Post*, May 4, 1945, 10.

47. Ham, "Keeping Secretary of State Waiting 30 Minutes to Watch Sandlot Game Won Commissioner's Job for 'Happy,'" *Washington Post*, May 6, 1945, M6.

48. James E. Chinn, "No Separate Peace, Reply of Truman to 1st Nazi Bid," *Washington Post*, April 29, 1945, M1.

49. "Richey [*sic*] Reveals Formation of Negro League," *Washington Post*, May 8, 1945, 8.

50. Jules Tygiel, *Baseball's Great Experiment*, 47.

51. Lacy, Looking 'Em Over, *Baltimore Afro-American*, May 19, 1945, 18.

52. "AFRO Leads Move to Abolish Major League Baseball Discrimination," *Baltimore Afro-American*, June 16, 1945, 18.

53. Paul Dickson, "The Importance of Oscar Charleston," National Pastime Museum, http://www.thenationalpastimemuseum.com/article/importance-oscar-charleston.

54. Fay Young, Through the Years, *Chicago Defender*, March 10, 1945, 7.

55. "Richey [*sic*] Reveals Formation of Negro League," *Washington Post*, May 8, 1945, 8.

56. "United States Baseball League (Negro) Encyclopedia and History," Baseball-Reference.com, http://www.baseball-reference.com/nlb/league.cgi?code=USBL&class=Neg.

57. Tygiel, *Baseball's Great Experiment*, 47–48.

58. Lacy, Looking 'Em Over, *Baltimore Afro-American*, June 2, 1945, 22.

59. Ibid.

60. Fay Young, Through the Years, *Chicago Defender*, May 26, 1945, 7.

61. "V-E Day Proclamation Text," *Evening Star*, May 8, 1945, 1.

62. "Browns, Mound City Fans Allergic to Nats' Cubans," *Washington Post*, May 10, 1945, 10.

63. The 1945 season was Zardon's only year in the big leagues. He appeared in 54 games for Washington and hit a very respectable .290 with 38 hits including three triples and 13 RBIs.

64. Mead, *Even the Browns*, 220–21.

65. Povich, This Morning, *Washington Post*, June 10, 1945, 10.

66. Joseph Young, "20,000 a Month Facing Loss of Federal Jobs," *Evening Star*, June 4, 1945, 1.

67. Surprisingly, the Brooklyn Dodgers, playing in a ballpark that held only 34,000, led the majors in attendance at midseason (about 100,000 better than the same time in 1944). The Nats had drawn 235,700 fans. Overall, more than 5.75 million paying customers had visited the 16 ballparks. "Dodgers' 715,465 Customers Tops Attendance in Majors," *Washington Post*, July 10, 1945, 10.

68. Jerry Links, "Six Night, One Day Game Scheduled for Tomorrow, Tuesday," *Washington Post*, July 8, 19445, M6.

69. "One-Legged Shepard Placed on Nats' Active Player List," *Washington Post*, July 20, 1945, 10.

70. Churchill had to be called home in the middle of the conference after his Tory Party was defeated in a national election and Clement Attlee replaced him as prime minister, joining Truman and Stalin in Potsdam on July 26.

71. "Notes by Harry S. Truman on the Potsdam Conference, July 17–30, 1945," Harry S. Truman Library and Museum, http://www.trumanlibrary.org/whistlestop/study_collections/bomb/large/documents/index.php?pagenumber=2&documentid=63&documentdate=1945-07-17&studycollectionid=abomb&groupid.

72. Povich, This Morning, *Washington Post*, July 11, 1945, 14.

73. Ibid.

74. Povich, "Happy Given Final Word, Fund Control," *Washington Post*, July 13, 1945, 8–9.

75. "Of all the supplies delivered to China from 1942 through 1945, 81 percent came by air over the Hump. Chinese forces tying up one million Japanese troops meant that the Japanese Imperial Army had far fewer resources to oppose the amphibious landings and other island campaigns mounted by America and its allies in the fighting throughout the Pacific. Airlift thus emerged as a significant new military consideration in future applications of air power." "Flying the Hump," The United States Army Air Forces in World War II, http://www.usaaf.net/ww2/airlift/airliftpg7.htm.

76. "Lewis May Bring Flag to Griffs, Connie Declares in Tribute," *Evening Star*, August 1, 1945, A-14.

77. "Nats Honor Buddy Lewis in Ceremony," *Washington Post*, August 1, 1945, 8.

78. Lacy, Looking 'Em Over, *Baltimore Afro-American*, August 18, 1945, 23.

79. Jackie Robinson became the only player in MLB history to have played in the Rose Bowl (while at UCLA), the World Series, the major-league All-Star Game, and the Negro League East–West game.

80. Young, Through the Years, *Chicago Defender*, August 4, 1945, 7.

81. "West Takes All-Star Classic 9 To 6," *Chicago Defender*, August 4, 1945, 7.

82. Young, Through the Years, *Chicago Defender*, August 4, 1945, 7.

83. "Mayor La Guardia Takes Up Afro Study Idea in Move to Erase Baseball JC," *Baltimore Afro-American*, August 18, 1945, 23.

84. Vincent X. Flaherty, "Conking Cattle with Sledge-Hammer Produced Pieretti's Pitching Power," *Sporting News*, August 9, 1945, 5.

85. Ibid.

86. Keller, "Pennant Hopes Dim Despite 24 of 31 Games on Home Lot," *Evening Star*, August 30, 1945, A-16.

87. Keller, Win, Lose or Draw, *Evening Star*, August 30, 1945, A-16.

88. "Happy Throngs Start Exodus for Holidays," *Washington Post*, September 1, 1945, 1.

89. "Vast Traffic Jam Expected Tonight as Holiday Ends," *New York Times*, September 3, 1945, 1.

90. "Happy Throngs Start Exodus for Holidays," *Washington Post*, September 1, 1945, 1.

91. William S. White, "Hails Era of Peace," *New York Times*, September 2, 1945, 1.

92. Mead and Dickson, *Baseball*, 83.

93. Povich, This Morning, *Washington Post*, September 13, 1945, 10.

94. Mead and Dickson, *Baseball*, 85.

95. Keller, "Rampaging Nats Can't Win the Flag in Series Here, Say Tigers," *Evening Star*, September 14, 1945, A-8.

96. "If We Lose, Blame Twin Bills, Says Ferrell," *Washington Post*, September 6, 1945, 10.

97. Povich, This Morning, *Washington Post*, September 15, 1945, 6.

98. Drebinger, "Yankees Topple Senators, 6–1, with Page Outpitching Haefner," *New York Times*, September 21, 1945, 24.

99. "Griffs Await Outcome of Tigers-Indians Series," *Washington Post*, September 25, 1945, 12.

100. Hillis Layne telephone interview with author David E. Hubler, December 20, 1992.

101. Francis E. Stann, Win, Lose or Draw, *Evening Star*, October 2, 1945, A-12.

102. Povich, This Morning, *Washington Post*, October 1, 1945, 10.

103. "1940–1949 Attendance," Ballparks of Baseball, http://www.ballparksofbaseball.com/1940-49attendance.htm.

104. Obermeyer, *Baseball and the Bottom Line*, Kindle edition, table 8, location 2506.

105. "Josh Gibson Wins NNL Batting Title," *Baltimore Afro-American*, September 22, 1945, 22.

106. "Cleveland Captures 1945 World Baseball Crown," *Baltimore Afro-American*, September 29, 1945, 23.

107. "1945 Negro World Series—BR Bullpen," Baseball-Reference.com, http://www.baseball-reference.com/bullpen/1945_Negro_World_Series.

108. "No Colored Players to Be Hired by Yankees Declares McPhail [*sic*]," *Baltimore Afro-American*, September 22, 1945, 22.

109. Lacy, Looking 'Em Over, *Baltimore Afro-American*, September 29, 1945, 29.

110. Tygiel, *Baseball's Great Experiment*, 65.

111. Tygiel suggests that Rickey could have been drawn to Robinson as "the perfect candidate to cross the color line" from a preseason article in a black sports magazine coauthored by Wendell Smith and Sam Lacy. For one, having played sports at UCLA, Robinson was used to integrated competition. Tygiel, *Baseball's Great Experiment*, 63–64.

112. Ibid., 67.

113. Carter, "It's a Press Victory, Says Jackie Robinson," *Baltimore Afro-American*, November 3, 1945, 1.

114. Daniel, "Negro Player Issue Heads for Showdown," *Sporting News*, November 1, 1945, 4.

115. Jack Horner, "Bramham Scores 'Raid' Against Negro Loops," *Sporting News*, November 1, 1945, 4.

116. Daniel, "Negro Player Issue Heads for Showdown," *Sporting News*, November 1, 1945, 4.

117. "1946 Montreal Royals," Baseball-Reference.com, http://www.baseball-reference.com/minors/team.cgi?id=7d25f8c5.

118. "1946 Chattanooga Lookouts," Baseball-Reference.com, http://www.baseball-reference.com/minors/team.cgi?id=5ab7b46c.

119. "Chandler Gets No Protest: Can't Act," *Chicago Defender*, November 3, 1945, 9.

120. Ira Berkow, "Sports of the Times; Where Did Happy Stand on Jackie?" *New York Times*, June 29, 1991, http://www.nytimes.com/1991/06/29/sports/sports-of-the-times-where-did-happy-stand-on-jackie.html. Berkow says when asked years later what Chandler did about the Robinson signing, Hall of Famer Ralph Kiner, who played for Pittsburgh in 1947, said, "As far as I know, not a thing."

121. "Griffith Gets a Big Rakeoff," *Amsterdam News*, November 10, 1945, 13.

122. Brands, "Majors Back Chandler's Authority over Game," *Sporting News*, December 20, 1945, 4.

123. Povich, "Minor Veto Amendment Squelched," *Washington Post*, December 13, 1945, 12.

124. Speaking of the potential trade, Bluege said, "This is our only chance to get that long-hit ball that we've needed ever since I became manager. They say Heath is temperamental and that he's a headache to manage, but I'm willing to put in a supply of aspirin and risk any headaches if he will hit .300 for us and bang our right field fence occasionally." Povich, This Morning, *Washington Post*, December 13, 1945, 12.

125. In an email to the authors, George Case Jr.'s son, George Case III, explained the reasoning for the trade: "Washington was looking for more power in the line-up. My dad had come off a pretty good season in 1945—batting .294 with 30 stolen bases but only 1 home run as a right-handed hitter with the left field line at Griffith Stadium 405 feet. Jeff Heath had a good year for Cleveland hitting .305 with 15 home runs as a left-handed hitter. Griffith Stadium during that era was much 'friendlier' to left-handed batters. So, on paper, the trade made sense. However it did not work out that way and for the 1947 season, Mr. Griffith traded knuckleball pitcher, Roger Wolff to Cleveland in exchange for my father, who had not had a good year in Cleveland—many injuries, hitting .225 with a league leading 28 stolen bases. Roger Wolff was coming off a 5-8 season (following a 20-win season in 1945) so my dad's trade value and Wolff's trade value had diminished quite a bit by 1947. Mr. Griffith did tell my father (my dad had been one of Mr. Griffith's favorite players), 'I'm bringing you home, George.'"

6. 1946 AND BEYOND

1. "1946 Montreal Royals," Baseball-Reference.com, http://www.baseball-reference.com/minors/team.cgi?id=7d25f8c5.

2. Obermeyer, *Baseball and the Bottom Line in World War II*, Kindle edition, location 3495.

3. "From the Ballfields to the Battlfields, 1940–1952," The National Pastime Museum, http://www.thenationalpastimemuseum.com/exhibition/ballfields_to_battlefields.

4. Darren Sands, "On the Anniversary of Historic Jackie Robinson Deal, the Braves Have an All-Black Outfield," Black Enterprise, http://www.blackenterprise.com/functional/braves-all-black-outfield-upton-trade-signing/. Sands, the author, makes one mistake in his write-up, misnaming Thompson's 1951 team as the San Francisco Giants. The franchise did not move to that West Coast city until after the 1956 season.

5. Steven Goldman, "Breaking the Barrier: Integrating the Major Leagues One Team at a Time 1947–1959," SB Nation, http://www.sbnation.com/mlb/2013/4/11/4190990/jackie-robinson-42-integration-baseball-pumpsie-green.

6. According to an online posting by Jim Vankoski, a close friend of Mickey Vernon's, the Nats first baseman told a funny story about Carlos Paula's fielding talents or lack thereof. Paula was playing left field in Fenway Park once when a hard-hit ball went right through his legs. When he turned to chase it down, the ball hit the Green Monster and rolled through his legs a second time, now going in the opposite direction. Mark Hornbaker, "Looking Back on Jackie Robinson Day—Washington Senators Were Behind the Times," D.C. Baseball History, http://dcbaseballhistory.com/2014/04/looking-back-on-jackie-robinson-day-washington-senators-were-behind-the-times/. In a follow-up query to Vankoski, he told the authors that Vernon never said whether Paula was charged with one or two errors on the play.

7. "Branch Rickey," National Baseball Hall of Fame and Museum, http://baseballhall.org/hof/rickey-branch.

8. Snyder, *Beyond the Shadow*, 284.

9. Leavengood, *Clark Griffith*, 272.

10. "Clark Griffith," National Baseball Hall of Fame and Museum, http://baseballhall.org/hof/griffith-clark.

BIBLIOGRAPHY

BOOKS AND ARTICLES

Beschloss, Michael R. *Eisenhower: A Centennial Life*. New York: HarperCollins, 1990.

Camelon, David. "How the First GI Bill Was Written (Part II)." *American Legion Magazine*, February 1969. http://www.legion.org/documents/legion/pdf/gibillpitkinpt2.pdf.

Cramer, Richard Ben. *Joe DiMaggio: The Hero's Life*. New York: Touchstone, 2000.

Creamer, Robert W. *Baseball in '41: A Celebration of the "Best Baseball Season Ever"—in the Year America Went to War*. New York: Penguin Books, 1991.

Daniel, Clifton, ed. *Chronicle of America*. Mount Kisco, NY: Chronicle, 1992.

———, ed. *Chronicle of the 20th Century*. Mount Kisco, NY: Chronicle, 1988.

Dawidoff, Nicholas, ed. *Baseball: A Literary Anthology*. New York: Library of America, 2002.

———, ed. *The Catcher Was a Spy: The Mysterious Life of Moe Berg*. New York: Pantheon Books, 1994.

Deveaux, Tom. *The Washington Senators: 1901–1971*. Jefferson, NC: McFarland, 2001.

Dewey, Donald, and Nicholas Acocella. *Encyclopedia of Major League Baseball Teams: Every Franchise, Past and Present, Officially Recognized by Major League Baseball*. New York: HarperCollins, 1993.

Dickson, Paul. *Baseball's Greatest Quotations*. New York: HarperCollins, 1991.

———. *Bill Veeck: Baseball's Greatest Maverick*. New York: Walker, 2012.

Frommer, Frederic J. *The Washington Nationals 1859 to Today*. Lanham, MD: Taylor Trade, 2006.

Giamatti, A. Bartlett. *Take Time for Paradise: Americans and Their Games*. New York: Summit Books, 1989.

Gilbert, Bill. *They Also Served: Baseball and the Home Front, 1941–1945*. New York: Crown, 1992.

Gilbert, Thomas. *Baseball at War: World War II and the Fall of the Color Line*. New York: Franklin Watts, 1997.

Glass, Charles. *Americans in Paris: Life and Death under Nazi Occupation*. New York: Penguin Books, 2011.

Goldstein, Richard. *Spartan Seasons: How Baseball Survived the Second World War*. New York: MacMillan, 1980.

Gordon, John, IV. "Joint Power Projection: Operation Torch," *Joint Force Quarterly* (Spring 1994): 63–64, http://www.dtic.mil/dtic/tr/fulltext/u2/a528962.pdf.

Graham, Frank, Jr. "When Baseball Went to War." SI Vault, *Sports Illustrated*, April 17, 1967. http://sportsillustrated.cnn.com/vault/article/magazine/MAG1079753/8/index.htm.

Grahek, Mark. "Clark Griffith." SABR. http://sabr.org/bioproj/person/96624988.

Jennings, Peter, and Todd Brewster. *The Century*. New York: Doubleday, 1998.

Leavengood, Ted. *Clark Griffith: The Old Fox of Washington Baseball*. Jefferson, NC: McFarland, 2011.

Lowry, Philip J. *Green Cathedrals: The Ultimate Celebration of All 271 Major League and Negro League Ballparks Past and Present*. Reading, MA: Addison-Wesley, 1986.

McCullough, David. *Truman*. New York: Simon and Schuster, 1992.

Meacham, Jon. *Franklin and Winston: An Intimate Portrait of an Epic Friendship*, New York: Random House Trade Paperback, 2004.

Mead, William B. *Baseball Goes to War: Stars Don Khaki, 4-Fs Vie for Pennant*. Washington, DC: Farragut, 1985.

———. *Even the Browns: The Zany, True Story of Baseball in the Early Forties*. Chicago: Contemporary Books, 1978.

Mead, William B., and Paul Dickson. *Baseball: The Presidents' Game*. Washington, DC: Farragut, 1993.

Mohl, Raymond A. "Clowning Around: The Miami Ethiopian Clowns and Culture Conflict in Black Baseball." *Tequesta*, February 2002. http://digitalcollections.fiu.edu/tequesta/files/2002/02_1_02.pdf.

Nemec, David, and Saul Wisnia. *100 Years of Major League Baseball: American and National Leagues, 1901–2000*. Lincolnwood, IL: Publications International, 2000.

Obermeyer, Jeff. *Baseball and the Bottom Line in World War II: Gunning for Profits on the Homefront*. Jefferson, NC: McFarland, 2013. Kindle edition.

Pan-Americanism and the Pan-American Conferences. Portland State University. http://www.upa.pdx.edu/IMS/currentprojects/TAHv3/Content/PDFs/PanAmericanism.pdf.

Persico, Joseph E. "The Day When We Almost Lost the Army," *American Heritage* 62, no. 1 (Spring 2012). http://www.americanheritage.com/content/day-when-we-almost-lost-army.

Povich, Shirley. *The Washington Senators*. Kent, OH: Kent State Press, 2010.

Price, S. L. "The Second World War Kinks [*sic*] Off." *Sports Illustrated*, November 29, 1999. http://157.166.246.201/vault/article/magazine/MAG1017830/index.htm.

Rader, Benjamin G. *Baseball: A History of America's Game*. Urbana: University of Illinois Press, 1992.

Rubin, Roger. "In 1944, the Dodgers, Yankees and Giants Faced Off in a Single Nine-Inning Game to Support the War Effort." *New York Daily News*, May 10, 2014. http://www.nydailynews.com/sports/baseball/yankees/1944-ny-baseball-teams-faced-support-war-effort-article-1.1787483.

Seidel, Michael. *Streak, Joe DiMaggio and the Summer of '41*. New York: McGraw-Hill, 1988.

Snyder, Brad. *Beyond the Shadow of the Senators: The Untold Story of the Homestead Grays and the Integration of Baseball*. Chicago: Contemporary Books, 2003.

Swift, Will. *Pat and Dick*. New York: Threshold Editions, 2014.

Tygiel, Jules. *Baseball's Great Experiment: Jackie Robinson and His Legacy*. Exp. ed. New York: Oxford University, 1997.

U.S. Department of State, Office of the Historian. "The Neutrality Acts, 1930s." http://history.state.gov/milestones/1921-1936/neutrality-acts.

Wernick, Robert. *Blitzkrieg*. World War II. New York: TimeLife Books, 1977.

Wilson, Andrew. *Shadow of the Titanic: The Extraordinary Stories of Those Who Survived*. London: Simon and Schuster, 2011.

WEBSITES

www.aagpbl.org: Official website of the AAGPBL (All-American Girls Professional Baseball League Players Association). Includes articles, photographs, interviews, and statistics about the women who played professional baseball from 1943 through 1954 and who were the inspiration for the film *A League of Their Own.*

www.americanheritage.com: The American Heritage portal provides articles and information on 4,000 historical sites, including online access to digital images and descriptions of millions of artifacts in American museums, historical societies, national parks, and other institutions across the country.

www.archives.gov: The Internet portal to the National Archives based in Washington, DC. The National Archives and Records Administration (NARA) is the nation's record keeper. Of all documents and materials created in the course of business conducted by the United States federal government, only 1 percent to 3 percent are so important for legal or historical reasons that they are kept by the National Archives forever. Those valuable records are preserved and are available to the public, whether the subject contains clues about a family's history, there is a need to prove a veteran's military service, or there is a need to research a historical topic.

www.ballparksofbaseball.com: Ballparks of Baseball offers information on past, present, and even possible future stadiums of Major League Baseball teams. The site contains videos, pictures, renderings, statistics, and news about stadiums of Major League Baseball.

www.baseball-almanac.com: Baseball Almanac has more than 500,000 pages of baseball history, more than 1,500,000 fast facts, original research from recognized experts, and information including, but not limited to, player stats and biographies, team histories, game results, stadium information, and attendance figures.

www.baseballhall.org: The official site of the National Baseball Hall of Fame and Museum in Cooperstown, New York. The site offers information about the museum and its inductees. Included on the site are biographies and pictures of people (and their plaques) inducted into the Hall of Fame.

www.baseballinwartime.com: Gary Bedingfield's Baseball in Wartime is dedicated to preserving the memories of all baseball players (major league, Negro League, minor league, semipro, college, amateur, and high school) who served with the military between 1940 and 1946. It includes articles about baseball during WWII and biographies about those who served.

www.baseball-reference.com: Baseball-Reference.com is a comprehensive source offering information from the late 1800s through the present on a variety of baseball leagues, including the major leagues. The database includes, but it not limited to, major-league baseball player and manager bios, including birth dates, birthplaces, death dates (when applicable), death places (when applicable), career stats, league leaders, player salaries and transactions, teams played for or managed. The site also includes complete franchise histories and encyclopedias comprised of, but not limited to, statistics including yearly team records, standings, franchise relocations, box scores, records, attendance, home ballparks, playoff and World Series statistics, and final results. The site also includes a sizeable database of minor-league teams, players, statistics, and results. There also is some information about the Negro Leagues and their players.

www.baseballsgreatestsacrifice.com: Gary Bedingfield's Baseball's Greatest Sacrifice is dedicated to players who lost their lives in military service. Whether they were killed in action, died from wounds, illness, or accident, detailed biographies of these men are included. There are currently 523 names listed on the Website with 487 individual biographies available.

www.bayjournal.com: The *Bay Journal* is published by Chesapeake Media Service, a 501(c)3 nonprofit, to inform the public about issues and events that affect the Chesapeake Bay. With a print circulation of 50,000, the *Bay Journal* is published monthly except for midsummer and midwinter and is distributed free of charge.

www.biography.com: The Website companion to the A&E television network's series on famous people. With more than 7,000 biographies and daily features that highlight newsworthy, compelling, and surprising points of view, it is a digital source for true stories about noteworthy people.

www.biographybase.com: Biography Base offers a wide selection of biographies and related resources. The site's collection currently contains 5,485 biographies.

www.blackbaseball.com: Edited by James A. Riley, a foremost authority on the history of baseball's Negro Leagues and a past director of research at the Negro Leagues Baseball Museum in Kansas City, Missouri. Blackbaseball.com includes articles, information about books, photos, videos, and a basic history of the teams and players of the Negro Leagues.

www.chicago.cubs.mlb.com: The official site of the Chicago Cubs on Major League Baseball's official Website. Includes scores, stats, the team roster, pictures, articles, and many other items about the Chicago Cubs baseball franchise.

www.cslib.org/iconnsitemap/staff/AboutiCONNOneSearchPublic.htm: Portal from the Connecticut Public Library system (East Haven, CT: Hagaman Memorial Library portal) to iCONN's research site used to access a variety of documents utilized for background information and for directly cited material from *Congressional Digest*.

www.dcbaseballhistory.com: A site dedicated to the history of major-league baseball teams that have called Washington, DC, home, including the Nationals, Senators, and the National Association's Washington Olympics. There are articles, stats, records, photos, and videos about the history of professional baseball in Washington, DC.

www.democraticunderground.com: Democratic Underground is an online community where politically liberal people interact with like-minded people, share news and information free from the corporate-media filter, and participate in discussions. It has no affiliation with the Democratic Party, although one of its stated goals is to elect more Democrats to public office. The site also contains links to articles on current events on its home page.

http://digitalcollections.fiu.edu/tequesta/: *Tequesta* is the scholarly journal of the Historical Association of Southern Florida, which has been published annually since 1941.

www.dtic.mil: Portal to the Defense Technical Information Center (DTIC), which has served the information needs of the defense community for more than 65 years. DTIC reports to the assistant secretary of defense for research and engineering, ASD(RE).

www.espn.go.com: The official Website of the ESPN cable sports network. Information from most major sports leagues can be found, along with articles, opinion pieces, statistics, photos, and videos.

www.ezinearticles.com: A searchable database of hundreds of thousands of quality original articles, posted by expert authors and writers.

www.fbi.gov: The official Website of the Federal Bureau of Investigation. Includes information about the FBI, as well as bureau news, press releases, and research databases.

www.fdrlibrary.marist.edu: The official site of the Franklin D. Roosevelt Presidential Library and Museum located in Hyde Park, New York. The site offers information about the museum; archives, including documents from President Roosevelt's life, personal life, and presidency; photos; biographies; and a searchable day-by-day calendar of events during Roosevelt's presidency.

www.history.army.mil: Site for the U.S. Army Center of Military History. The Center of Military History (CMH), which reports to the administrative assistant to the secretary of the army, is responsible for the appropriate use of history throughout the United States Army. Traditionally, this mission has meant recording the official history of the army in both peace and war, while advising the army staff on historical matters. CMH online is an outreach service provided by the U.S. Army Center of Military History. Its mission is to establish a global forum for the Center of Military History to distribute historical information and products to inform, educate, and professionally develop the soldiers and leadership of the U.S. Army.

www.history.navy.mil: Site of the (U.S.) Naval History and Heritage Command (NHHC). Whether visiting one of the official U.S. Navy museums, taking advantage of public programs and publications, or seeking knowledge through the artifacts, documents, images, and artwork available at the NHHC, this is where the history, legacy, and traditions of the United States Navy come alive.

www.history.state.gov: The U.S. Department of State, Office of the Historian, provides historic documents, foreign policy texts, department histories, biographies, and key milestones in American diplomacy.

www.ibiblio.org: Home to one of the largest "collections of collections" on the Internet, ibiblio.org is an online public library with freely available software and information, for topics such as music, literature, art, history, science, politics, and cultural studies.

www.kansasheritage.org: The Kansas Heritage Group history archives are devoted to digitally preserving Kansas's past, giving future generations the opportunity to learn from family and local Kansas history online.

www.latimes.com: Portal for the *Los Angeles Times*.

www.legion.org: The official website of the American Legion. Focusing on service to veterans, service members, and communities, the American Legion currently has about 2.4 million members in 14,000 posts worldwide.

www.loc.gov: Official website of the Library of Congress in Washington, DC. The Library of Congress is the nation's oldest federal cultural institution and serves as the research arm of Congress. It is also the largest library in the world, with millions of books, recordings, photographs, maps, and manuscripts in its collections. The library's mission is to support the Congress in fulfilling its constitutional duties and to further the progress of knowledge and creativity for the benefit of the American people.

www.mlb.com: The official site of Major League Baseball. Includes team and player statistics, articles, photos, and videos.

www.negroleaguebaseball.com: Includes articles, histories, team and player information, and timelines related to Negro League baseball.

www.nlbm.mlblogs.com: *Monarchs to Grays to Crawfords*: The Official Blog of the Negro Leagues Baseball Museum.

www.nolo.com: NOLO Law for All states its mission as trying to help consumers and small businesses find answers to their everyday legal and business questions. NOLO began publishing do-it-yourself legal guides in 1971. With more than 50 web properties, the NOLO network is one of the web's largest libraries of consumer-friendly legal information—all available for free.

www.nydailynews.com: Portal for the *New York Daily News*.

www.nytimes.com: Portal for *The New York Times*.

www.philly.com: Portal for news from the Philadelphia, Pennsylvania, metro area. Includes stories from the *Philadelphia Inquirer* and the *Philadelphia Daily News*.

www.pitchblackbaseball.com: Site managed by Kyle McNary, dedicated to the Negro Leagues and includes in-depth biographies of players.

www.presidency.ucsb.edu: Website of the American Presidency Project at the University of California, Santa Barbara. The American Presidency Project (americanpresidency.org) was established in 1999 as a collaboration between John T. Woolley and Gerhard Peters at the University of California, Santa Barbara. The archives hold 107,266 documents related to the study of the presidency. The site also provides data on elections, an audio/video archive containing speeches and appearances by various presidents, and statistics related to the presidency.

www.sabr.org: The official site of the Society for American Baseball Research provides online links to historic newspaper collections and information on major- and minor-league baseball officials, broadcasters, and writers, as well as numerous former players. Includes biographies and statistics of past and present ballplayers.

www.search.proquest.com/hnpnewyorktimes/barcode?accountid=34227&groupid=72504: Portal from the Fairfax County, Virginia, Public Library to Proquest's research site used to access directly cited material from the *New York Times*.

www.search.proquest.com/hnpwashingtonpost/barcode?accountid=34227&groupid=72504: Portal from the Fairfax County, Virginia, Public Library to Proquest's research site used to access directly cited material from the *Washington Post*.

www.selectiveservice.us: Offers information about Selective Service process and the history of Selective Service in the United States.

www.shapell.org: The official website of the Shapell Manuscript Foundation, an independent educational organization dedicated to the collection and research of original manuscripts and historical documents of the United States and the Holy Land, with emphasis on the 19th and 20th centuries.

www.si.com/VAULT: The official site of *Sports Illustrated*'s magazine archive, which includes the publication's articles and photographs on U.S. and international sporting events and personalities.

www.sportsecyclopedia.com: Includes team histories in the four major sports of MLB, NFL, NBA, and NHL, including a history through pictures. The pages are updated periodically through the season and annually prior to each new season.

www.sss.gov: The official U.S. government website for the Selective Service System. Includes information about the process of registering for Selective Service, as well as history and records, such as the number of people inducted into the armed services at certain points in U.S. history.

www.thebaseballpage.com: The Baseball Page states its goal as helping users experience baseball through all mediums—articles, blogs, pictures, videos, and interactive community. The page includes the stories of the game, whether they happened yesterday or 140 years ago.

www.thedailybeast.com: The *Daily Beast* offers original reporting and sharp opinion in the arenas of politics, pop culture, world news, and more. Fiercely independent and armed with irreverent intelligence, the *Daily Beast* now reaches more than 17 million readers per month.

www.thedeadballera.com: The Deadball Era, created by Frank Russo, is a site dedicated primarily to deceased major-league baseball players. It includes biographies, causes of death, and burial sites of former major-league players. It also lists baseball players who served in the military and contains photos, audio, and video of players from the past.

www.thenationalpastimemuseum.com: The National Pastime Museum's mission is to educate the public about the history of baseball and the people who influenced the game by using a collection of baseball artifacts, artworks, literature, photographs, memorabilia, and articles in a fun and creative way. The National Pastime Museum is an online museum based on a private collection of baseball artifacts. The love of the game and its history prompted the creation of this site. It serves as a way to share this significant collection with the public and to facilitate a conversation about the role baseball continues to play in our lives and in our nation's history.

www.thisgreatgame.com: This Great Game, created by Ed Attanasio (a copywriter and member of SABR) and Eric Gouldsberry (a graphic designer) is a comprehensive and mostly oral history of major-league baseball from 1900 to the present. The heart of the site is the "Yearly Reader" section, which represents every year in modern major-league history by including a central oral summary; final standings; the "It Happened In . . ." section, featuring capsulated reviews of the year's list of firsts, records, and oddities; the "They Were There" interviews with players who bore witness or took part in baseball's memorable moments; and the "Leaders and Numbers" page, an oral and statistical overview of the year's best hitters and pitchers.

www.trumanlibrary.org: The official website of the Harry S. Truman Library and Museum, which is located in Independence, Missouri. The site includes numerous documents, articles, photos, and educational materials about Harry S. Truman's life and presidency.

www.upa.pdx.edu: The site of Portland State University's current projects includes documents on Pan-Americanism and the Pan-American Conferences.

www.usaaf.net: The United States Army Air Forces in World War II website offers in-depth articles by various authors on U.S. Army Air Force operations during World War II.

www.uss-hornet.org: Aircraft Carrier Hornet Foundation preserves and honors the legacy of the USS *Hornet*, a national historic landmark, and its role in naval aviation, the defense of our country, the Apollo Program, and exploration of space. The USS *Hornet* Museum connects the greatest generation of Americans with future generations, educating and inspiring them to meet their challenges. The website includes the history of the USS *Hornet*, photos, and information about the museum.

www.washingtonpost.com: Portal for the *Washington Post*.

INDEX

A.G. Spalding and Brothers Co., 98, 108

A's. *See* Athletics

Aaron, Henry, 118

ABCs, 93

African Americans in baseball, 29, 30 56, 57, 59–64, 71, 79–80, 91–93, 101, 104, 116, 131, 140, 144, 157, 196–97, 202–04, 215, 226–29, 231, 232, 235–37

African campaign of WWII, 76, 84, 110–11, 112, 119–21

Albright, Robert C., 15

All-American Girls Professional Softball League, 110

All-Star Game, 19, 20, 25, 31, 42, 57, 58, 72, 74–75, 85, 91, 118, 122, 123, 124, 128, 130, 151, 159, 160, 161, 165, 209, 214, 226. *See also* East–West game

Allison, Bob, xviii

Alsop, Joseph, 16

Altrock, Nick, 67

America First, 14

American Association, xvi, 4

American Giants, 93

American Heritage (Persico), 14

American League, xiii–xix, 1, 3–9, 18, 20, 27, 28, 33, 46, 50, 63, 69, 72–75, 80, 81, 85, 94, 98, 108, 111, 113, 114, 117, 123, 124, 142, 152, 164, 170, 171, 172, 176, 181, 182, 190, 193, 198, 201, 216, 223, 225, 230, 233, 236

American League Park I, xvii, 29

American League Park II, xvii

American Legion, 135

American Peace Mobilization, 15

American Women's Volunteer Services, 218

Anderson, Dave, 10

Angels, xviii

Anglo-German Naval Agreement, 47

Anson, Cap, 4

Archie, George, 37

Arhens, Richard, 95

Army vs. Navy exhibition game (1942), 70

Army/Navy relief fund games, 56–57, 59–60, 73–76

Atchison, Lewis F., 200

Athletics, xvii, xviii, 38, 68, 72, 78, 80, 85, 87, 90, 96, 106–08, 122, 129, 142, 149, 151, 153, 158, 161, 169, 177, 193, 199, 206, 208, 209, 212, 216–17, 221, 222

Atlanta Black Crackers, 185

Atlantic Charter, 65

Atlantic City Bacharach Giants, 29

Atomic bomb, xv, 210, 214

Attlee, Clement, 210

Aunt Addie. *See* Griffith, Ann

Bader Field, 192

Bailey, Judson, 23, 75

Bainbridge Naval Station training, 223

Baird, Tom, 229

Baker, Abram, 104

Baker, Newton, 19
Baker, Samuel, 104
balata baseballs, 97–98, 108
Ball Players Protective Association
    (BPPA), 4–5
Ball, Philip, 22, 176
Baltimore Elite Giants, 39, 82, 93,
    114–15, 118, 148, 152, 177, 214
Baltimore Orioles, 6, 51, 105, 190
Baltimore Stars, 29
Barbary, Donald Odell, 82
Barkley (U.S. Senator), 148
Barkley, Alben W., 106
Barnes, Donald, 23, 31, 72
Barnhill, Dave, 128
Barrow, Ed, 41, 142, 143
Baruch, Bernard, 66, 112
Basca, Nick, 10
baseball, construction, 97–98, 108
*Baseball and the Bottom Line in World
    War II* (Obermeyer), 58
baseball cards, 5
Baseball Hall of Fame, 3, 5, 26, 30, 31, 43,
    64, 102, 113, 118, 127, 131, 151, 160,
    162, 167, 181, 222, 224, 230, 237, 238
Baseball in 41 (Creamer), 28
Baseball Writers' Association, 31
Baseball: The President's Game (Mead/
    Dickson), 49
Bassett, Lloyd "Pepper," 178
Bat and Ball Fund, 43, 85
Bataan death march, 54
bats, construction of, 98–99
Battle of Britain, 15
Battle of the Bulge, 182, 188
Baugh, Sammy, 10
Bauman, Bob, 174
Bears, 105
Bell, James "Cool Papa," 155–56, 157, 226
Bell, Nelson, 94
Benjamin, Jerry, 155, 157
Benny, Jack, 94
Benswanger, William, 110
Berg, Moe, xiv–xv, 11
Bergman, Ingrid, 94
Bevil, Lou, 82
Beyond the Shadow of the Senators
    (Snyder), 71
Biddle, Francis, 37

"Big Train" Johnson. *See* Johnson, Walter
    "Big Train"
Binks, George "Bingo," 200, 206, 222
Birmingham Black Barons, 79, 93, 131,
    157, 177–78
Bisher, Furman, 56
Black Barons, 79, 93, 131, 157, 177–78
Black Crackers, Atlanta, 185
Black Senators, 63
Black Sox scandal, 22, 211
Black Yankees, 58, 93, 150, 202–03
Black, Joe, 237
Bloodworth, Jimmy, 37
Bloom, Sol, 183
Blue Jays, xix
Bluege, Ossie, 67, 72, 82, 90, 93, 95, 97,
    103, 105, 107, 126, 141, 145–47, 153,
    155, 159, 160, 162, 170, 173, 174, 181,
    182, 191, 192, 200, 209, 212, 213,
    219–21, 223, 225, 232, 236, 237
Bogart, Humphrey, 94
Boland, Ed, 163–64, 166
Bombers, 185
Bonham, Ernie "Tiny," 124
Bostic, Joe, 79, 197
Boston Braves, 45, 113, 118, 190, 193,
    198, 209
Boston Red Sox, 7, 21, 25, 28, 37, 44, 66,
    76, 78, 101, 108, 113, 125, 126, 128,
    130, 149, 154, 163, 169, 170, 177, 190,
    198, 202, 208, 209, 213, 218, 228,
    235–36
Boudreau, Lou, 159
boycott, African-American boycott of
    MLB, 195–96
Bradley, Alva, 41, 75
Bradley, John, 200
Bradley, Omar, 218
Brady, Jim, 177
Bramham, W. G., 229
Braves, 29, 45, 113, 118, 190, 193, 198,
    209
Braves Field, 40
Breaking Bad (TV show), xv
Brewer, Forrest Vernon "Lefty," 38
Brewers, 3, 200
Briggs Stadium, 40, 171, 175
Britton, Johnny, 178
Bronson Bombers, 149

Brooklyn Brown Dodgers, 203–04, 228

Brooklyn Dodgers, 7, 10, 27, 32, 41, 56–57, 61–63, 73, 76, 81, 90, 94, 101, 102, 118, 123, 129, 134, 142, 182, 188, 196–98, 203–05, 209–11, 228, 230, 235, 237

Brown Bombers, 185

Brown Dodgers, 203–04, 228

Brown, Prentiss, 84

Brown, Ray, 155, 202

Browns, 1, 3, 18, 22, 23, 28, 31, 41, 51, 72, 80, 83, 88, 96, 112, 122, 125, 128, 130, 142, 145–46, 150–52, 154, 159, 161, 162, 167–73, 175, 176, 193, 196, 201, 206–08, 212, 215, 216, 218–23, 225, 232, 236

Buckeyes, 93, 118, 198, 226

Buford, Don, 79

Bunnell, John, 95

Burke, Edward, 13

Burke-Wadsworth Bill, 13

Burley, Dan, 190, 197

Butka, Ed, 45–46, 67, 163, 168

Butt, Archibald, 50

Butts, Tommy, 147

Byrd Stadium, 146

Byrd, Harry Clifton, 100

Byrnes, James F., 119, 125, 182, 190, 201

California League, 4

Calvin Griffith Park, 56. *See also* Griffith Stadium

Cambria, Joe, 61, 95, 145

Camden Yards, 6

Campanella, Roy, 118, 147, 178, 214–18, 228

Campbell, Bruce, 37

Candini, Milo, 96, 113, 123, 149, 155

Cantor, Eddie, 186

Cardinals, 4, 5, 32, 41, 53, 81, 88, 112, 162, 176, 196

Carrasquel, Alex, 61, 80, 113, 147, 148

Carter, Art, 92, 101, 117, 144, 156, 157

Carter, Gary, xix

Carter, Jimmy, 50–51

Carter, Michael, 229

Casablanca (movie), 94

Case, George III, 72, 99

Case, George Jr., 36, 37, 43, 45–46, 72, 78, 80, 97, 98, 102, 107, 112, 123, 124, 126, 130, 145, 150–54, 158–59, 163, 168, 173, 174, 181, 188, 193, 206, 214, 215, 219, 232, 237

Casey, Hugh, 102

Catholic University, 89

Chamberlain, Neville, 47

Chandler, Albert B. "Happy,", 105, 191, 199, 201–02, 211, 212, 218–19, 230–32

Chandler, Spud, 124

Chapman, Ben, 37

Charleston, Oscar, 30, 203–04

Charlotte Hornets, 38, 55–56

Chattanooga Lookouts, 230

Chicago American Giants, 29, 93

Chicago Black Sox scandal, 22, 211

Chicago Brown Bombers, 185

Chicago Colts, 4

Chicago Cubs, 22, 29, 38, 40, 43, 44, 59, 62, 73, 78, 79, 101, 109, 182, 209, 225

Chicago Orphans, 4

Chicago Whales, 22

Chicago White Sox, xvii, 22, 23, 51, 55, 61, 64, 101, 111, 112, 114, 122, 125, 126, 151–53, 159, 162, 167, 170, 171, 173, 177, 201, 207–09, 211, 214–17, 220

Chicago White Stockings, 5, 6

Churchill, Clementine, 169

Churchill, Winston, 64, 68, 94, 106, 111, 129, 132, 169–70, 180, 186, 210

Cincinnati Buckeyes, 118

Cincinnati Clowns, 93, 118, 157

Cincinnati Reds, 7, 20, 29, 40, 76, 98, 112, 162, 196, 209, 237

Citizens Committee for National War Service, 13

Citrus Bowl, 43–44

Civil War, 2, 22, 49, 180

Clark, Grenville, 13

Clary, Ellis, 78, 103, 107, 172, 176

Cleary, Joe, 213

Cleveland Buckeyes, 93, 118, 198, 226

Cleveland Indians, xiv, 41, 44, 51, 54, 63, 64, 75, 101, 110–13, 122, 123, 125, 130, 151, 152, 158, 162, 166–67, 173, 177, 190–91, 207, 209, 216, 221, 223, 232, 236, 238

Clift, Harlond, 154, 159, 160, 162, 163

Clowns, Cincinnati, 93, 118, 157
Clowns, Miami Ethiopian, 117–18
Cobb, Ty, 204
Cochrane, Mickey, 75
Coleman, Lou, 108
College Park training field, 89–90
Collins, Eddie, 101
Colmery, Harry W., 137–38
Colonels, 231
Colts, 4
Comiskey Park, 42, 127, 165, 209, 214, 215, 216, 217
Comiskey, Charlie, xvii, 3–5, 8
Committee on the Negro American in Defense Industries, 121–22
Committee on Unity, 226–27
Congress of Industrial Organizations (CIO), 119
Considine, Bob, 35, 80
Coogan's Bluff, 6
Coolidge, Calvin, 183
Cooper, Gary, 17
Corregidor, 54
Cozzi, Sam, 70
Crackers, 185
Cramer, Roger "Doc," 37, 224
Crawfords, 179, 185, 197, 205
Creamer, Robert W., 28
Cronin, Jim, 21
Cronin, Joe, 149, 198, 237
Crosby, Bing, 94, 112
Crosetti, Frankie, 21
Crosley Field, 20, 40
Crosley, Lewis, 29, 40
Crosley, Powel Jr., 29, 40
Croucher, Frank, 37
Cuban players, 60–61, 93, 116, 128, 145, 161–63, 167, 168, 172, 189, 206, 207, 213, 231, 236
Cubans (New York ball team), 197
Cubs, 22, 29, 38, 40, 43, 44, 59, 62, 73, 78, 79, 101, 109, 182, 209, 225
Cullenbine, Roy, 78, 81, 223
Curtis Bay Naval Station exhibition game, 193

D.C. Stadium, xix
D-Day/Operation Overlord, 111, 153
Daley, Arthur, 215

Dandridge, Ray, 148
Daniel, Dan, 83, 88, 229
Darlan, Jean-Francois, 47
Davis, Bette, 94
Davis, Slats, 157
Dawson, Andre, xix
de Gaulle, Charles, 169, 180
De Leighbur, Don, 179
Dean, Dizzy, 53, 57, 158
deferments for players during World War II, 24–25, 89, 142, 190–91. *See also* Selective Service
DeShong, Jimmie, 20
Detroit race riots (1943), 109–10, 121
Detroit Tigers, 37, 44, 54, 64, 74, 81, 95, 102, 111–13, 122, 125, 127, 130, 151, 152, 158, 162, 166, 170, 173, 175, 201, 207, 209, 212, 214, 216–18, 220–25, 229
Deveaux, Tom, 8
Dewey, Thomas E., 170, 180, 219
Dickey, Bill, 124
Dickson, Paul, 49, 204
DiMaggio, Dom, 28, 102
DiMaggio, Joe, 17, 21, 26, 28–29, 33, 57, 71, 75, 81, 124, 221, 235
Dixon, Alan, 177
Dizzy Dean's All-Stars, 58–59
Doby, Larry, 63–64, 236, 237–38
Dodgers, 7, 10, 27, 32, 41, 56–57, 61–63, 73, 76, 81, 90, 94, 101, 102, 118, 123, 129, 134, 142, 182, 188, 196–98, 203–05, 209–11, 228, 230, 235, 237. *See also* Brown Dodgers
Dodgers, Manila, 167
Dog House, xvii
Donovan, William J., 10–11, 10
Doolittle, James H. "Jimmie," xiv, 48, 107
Doolittle Raid on Tokyo, xiv, 48, 53, 107
Doubleday, Abner, 49, 143
draft. *See* Selective Service
Drebinger, John, 23, 41, 43, 124
Dreyfuss, Barney, 110
Dryden, Charles, xvii, 177
Duffy, Hugh, 198
Durocher, Leo, 61–62, 209

Eagles, 9, 82, 93, 109, 114, 118, 128, 132, 141, 147, 156, 164, 178, 197

Early, Jake, 80, 107,123, 145, 212
Early, Steve, 148, 193
East-West game, 58, 91, 127–28, 165,
    179, 185–86, 214
Eastern Colored League, 63
Eastern League, xvi
Eastman, Joseph, 85, 88, 91–92
Eastman-Landis Line, 88
Ebbets Field, 42, 57, 156, 204, 230, 237
Eckstein, Billy, 131
Eden, Anthony, 186, 194
Eisenhower, Dwight D., 26, 37, 68–69,
    120, 125–26, 129, 153
Eisenhower, Milton, 37, 108–09
Elite Giants, 63, 82, 93, 114–15, 118, 148,
    152, 177, 214
Emil Verban Memorial Society, 177
Estalella, Roberto, 60–61, 62, 96
Ethiopian Clowns, 117–18
Etten, Nick, 221
European theatre of WWII, 68–69,
    76–77, 84, 111, 132, 153, 168, 169,
    182, 188, 193, 206, 208, 210
Evans, Al, 102, 163
Even the Browns (Mead), 35
exhibition games, 58–59, 73, 75, 101, 102,
    146–47, 193, 209–10
Expos, xix
Eynon, Edward B., 141

Farley, James A., 34
FDR. *See* Roosevelt, Franklin D.
Federal League, 22
Fell, Jesse, 3
Feller, Bob, 17, 33–34, 57, 70, 71, 75,
    93–94, 102, 220
Fellowship of Reconciliation, 13
Fenway Park, 40, 126, 149, 198, 209, 212
Ferrell, Rick, 145–47, 151–54, 160, 163,
    175, 188, 220
Finley, Charles, 87
Finney, Lou, 223
Flaherty, Vincent X., 61, 216
Flood, Curt, 4
Florida State League, 43
Forbes Field, 30, 83, 110, 179
Foreman, Chester, 95
Foster, Rube, 29
Foxx, Jimmie, xiv, 61, 156

Franklin, Murray, 102
Frick, Ford C., 27, 42, 98, 181, 190
Friendly, Alfred, 51
Frisch, Frankie, 188
Frommer, Frederic J., 21

G-girls, 103
Gagnon, Rene, 200
Galehouse, Denny, 142, 174
Garlington, S. W., 197
gas rationing during WWII, 65–67, 85
Gedeon, Elmer, xv–xvi, 38
Gehrig, Lou, xiv, 17
George Washington Slept Here (movie),
    94
Georgetown University training camp, 89,
    190
Georgia Sports Hall of Fame, 26
Georgia-Florida League, 95
GI Bill, 138, 208
Giants (New York), 6, 7, 8, 10, 32, 41, 57,
    76, 81, 101, 105, 142, 162, 188, 190,
    236, 237
Giants (Atlantic City), 29
Giants (Chicago American), 29, 93
Giants, Baltimore Elite, 39, 82, 93,
    114–15, 118, 148, 152, 177, 214
Giants, Washington Elite, 63
Gibson, John (congressman), 138
Gibson, Josh, 30, 58, 61, 62, 83, 93, 104,
    114, 115, 128, 130, 155–57, 166, 178,
    202, 214, 225–26
Gilbert, Ben W., 66
Gilbert, Bill, 53, 103, 177, 189
Gilbert, Thomas, 31
Giles, Warren, 98
Gillette (U.S. Senator), 148
Giuliani, Angelo "Tony," 146
Glen Echo Park, 104
Goebbels, Josef, 77, 227
Goldstein, Richard, xiii, 36, 39, 99
Gomez, Lefty, xiv, 113–14, 123, 154
Gomez, Preston, 161, 163
Gordon, Joe, 124
Grapefruit League, 46
Gray, Pete, 193, 197
Grays, 3, 29–31, 57–59, 61, 63, 64, 70, 71,
    78, 80, 82, 83, 91–93, 104, 109, 110,
    114–18, 127, 128, 130–32, 147,

150–52, 155–57, 164, 165, 177, 178, 185, 186, 193, 202–04, 215, 225, 226, 231, 237

Great Depression, 21

Great War. *See* World War I

Green Cathedrals (Lowry), xvii

"green light letter," 34–36, 39, 72

Green, Pumpsie, 198

Greenberg, Henry "Hank," 17, 34, 127, 207, 222–25

Greenfield, Eggie, 157

Greenlee, Gus, 91, 178, 179, 185, 186, 197, 203, 205

Gresham, Walter, 22

Griffith Days, 19

Griffith Stadium, xviii, 8, 9, 19–21, 25, 28, 30, 38, 41, 46, 49, 50, 57, 59, 67, 70, 77–80, 83, 92, 100, 104, 109, 111, 114, 115, 127, 128, 130, 131, 147, 150, 151, 156, 159, 164, 166, 167, 179, 199, 209, 212, 217, 218, 220, 223, 225, 226, 231, 237

Griffith, Ann, 55

Griffith, Calvin Robertson, 36, 55, 60

Griffith, Clark, xiii–xvii, 1–9, 18–21, 23–26, 29–31, 35, 36, 38–40, 44, 45, 48, 49, 54, 56, 60–63, 65, 67, 72, 73, 78–81, 85, 87–90, 94, 100, 101, 104, 105, 107, 110, 112, 114, 123, 130, 134, 141, 144, 145, 147, 148, 150, 151, 154, 159, 177, 181, 182, 187, 188, 190–92, 195, 196, 198, 200, 209, 211, 216, 219, 224, 225, 230–38

Griffith, Isaiah, 2

Griffith, Sarah Anne, 2

Griffith, Thelma Robertson, 55

Guerra, Mike, 146, 159, 161, 163, 172, 181

Gutteridge, Don, 168, 176, 223–24

Haefner, Mickey, 145, 147, 153, 181, 191, 220, 221

Hafey, Chick, 162

Hafey, Tom, 162

Haight, Walter, 189

Hall of Fame. *See* Baseball Hall of Fame

Halsey, William F. "Bull," 169

Ham, Bus, 190

Harder, Mel, 152

Harlem Globetrotters, 117, 157

Harridge, Will, 27, 31, 33–34, 98, 181, 190, 198–99, 201

Harris, Bucky, 1, 8, 44–46, 54, 61, 67, 72, 82, 105, 237

Harris, Lum, 108

Harris, Vic, 63, 93

Harvey, Bob, 178

Hawkins, Burton, 102, 105

Hayes, Ira, 200

Haynes, Joe, 55

Heath, Jeff, 54, 232

Heisenberg, Werner, xv

Henderson, Leon, 51, 66

Henreid, Paul, 94

Henrich, Tommy, 81, 124

Hershey, Lewis B., 24–25, 39, 147, 161, 182

Highlanders, 6, 7, 141, 204

Hilltop Park, 6

Hiroshima, 214

history of leagues, xvi–xvii

history of team name, xvi–xvii

Hitler, 12, 15, 47, 111, 139, 168, 170

Hobby, Oveta Culp, 69

Hoffman, Ray, 82

Hoffman, Trevor, 123

Holborrow, Wally, 213

Holman, Joe, 30

Holocaust, 139

Holway, John, 115

Homestead Grays, 3, 29–31, 57–59, 61, 63, 64, 70, 71, 78, 80, 82, 83, 91–93, 104, 109, 110, 114–18, 127, 128, 130–32, 147, 150–52, 155–57, 164, 165, 177, 178, 185, 186, 193, 202–04, 215, 225, 226, 231, 237

Hoover, J. Edgar, 76, 191

Hope, Bob, 94

Hopkins, Harry, 48

Horner, Jack, 229

Hornets, Charlotte, 38, 55–56

Hostetler, Charlie, 175

housing shortages during WWII, 103–04

Howard University, 104

Hudson, Sid, 45, 67, 71, 74–75, 80

Hunter, Jim "Catfish," 87

Hutchinson, Fred, 101, 112

Hynd, Noel, 98

Indiana University, 106
Indianapolis ABCs, 93
Indians, xiv, 41, 44, 51, 54, 63, 64, 75, 101,
    110–13, 122, 123, 125, 130, 151, 152,
    158, 162, 166–67, 173, 177, 190–91,
    207, 209, 216, 221, 223, 232, 236, 238
integration. *See* African Americans in
    baseball
Irvin, Monte, 236
Ismay, J. Bruce, 50
Iwo Jima, 200

Jackson (U.S. Senator), 148
Jackson, Harold, 92, 128, 140, 165, 166
Jackson, Rufus "Sonnyman," 91, 150
Jackson, "Shoeless Joe," 23
Jakucki, Sigmund, 173–74, 176
Japan, xiii–xiv 1, 48, 107
Japanese American internment camps,
    37, 109
Jethroe, Sam, 198, 226
Jewish Holocaust, 139
Johnson, Ban, xvii, 4, 50
Johnson, Bob, 96–97, 106, 107, 112, 123
Johnson, J. Monroe, 190
Johnson, Judy, 30
Johnson, Walter "Big Train," 8, 21, 50, 61,
    67, 160, 200
Johnston, Stanley, 65
Jones, Jesse H., 124
Judge, Joe, 67

Kampouris, Alex, 126
Kansas City Athletics, xviii
Kansas City Monarchs, 39, 57, 63, 70, 83,
    93, 118, 128, 165, 198, 214, 228, 229,
    230
Keeler, Wee Willie, 28
Kell, George, 222
Keller, Charlie, 124, 221
Keller, John B., 166, 217, 220
Kelly, Charles "Commando," 160
Kelly, Harry F., 121
Keltner, Ken, 159, 190–91
Kennedy, Joseph, 11
Killebrew, Harmon, xviii
Kimble, Dick, 215
King, Mackenzie, 12, 129
Kintner, Robert, 16

Kish, Ernie, 222
Klepper, Bill, 216
Knox, Frank, 112, 119
knuckleball, 146
Knudsen, William S., 51
Kramer, Jack, 167, 174
Kreevich, Mike, 215
Kuhel, Joe, 147, 153, 181, 193, 200
Kuhn, Bowie, 51

La Guardia, Fiorella, 149, 164, 215,
    226–27
Laabs, Chet, 142, 176
Lacy, Sam, 29, 115, 132–34, 140–41, 144,
    145, 150, 156, 178, 195–97, 203–05,
    214, 215, 227–28, 238
Ladd, Bruce, 177
Lajoie, Napoleon, 5
Lamour, Dorothy, 94
Landis, Abraham Hoch, 22
Landis, Kenesaw Mountain, 22, 23,
    34–35, 36, 39, 41, 59, 60–62, 72, 73,
    86, 87, 88, 94, 97–98, 114, 132–34,
    146, 160, 181, 195, 199, 201, 210, 211
Landis, Mary Kumler, 22
Langer, William "Wild Bill," 208
Lary, Lyn, 21
Laval, Pierre, 47
Lawson, F. J., 208
Layne, Hillis, 37, 224
League of Their Own, A (movie), 110
League Park, Cleveland, 226
leagues, history of, xvi–xvii
Leahy, William D., 47, 170, 219
Leavengood, Ted, 2–3, 4, 9, 116, 238
LeFebvre, Bill, 126, 145, 166
Leonard, Buck, 58, 62, 83, 93, 104,
    115–16, 130–31, 155, 157, 181, 202,
    214, 225–26
Leonard, Dutch, 44, 45, 90, 102, 107, 123,
    124, 145, 147, 160, 174, 175, 187–88,
    191, 193, 207, 220, 222, 223
Lerner ownership group, xix, 6
Lewis, John Kelly "Buddy," 24–25, 37, 39,
    44, 78, 90, 209, 211, 212, 219, 222
Lewis, John L., 109, 120
lights. *See* night games
Lincoln, Abraham, 180

Lindbergh, Charles, 15
Lindell, Johnny, 124
Lindley, Ernest K., 17
Lippmann, Walter, 53
Lookouts, 55, 230
Lopat, Eddie, 153
Los Angeles Angels, xviii
Los Angeles Dodgers, 32
Louisville Colonels, 231
Lowry, Philip J., xvii
Lucas (U.S. Senator), 148

MacArthur, Douglas, 48, 169
Mack, Connie, 4, 8, 68, 83, 96, 107,
    164–65, 195, 199, 212, 237
MacPhail, Larry, 27, 40, 41, 73–74, 81,
    191, 192, 203, 215, 226–28
Major League Baseball, xix
Mancuso, Frank, 142, 159
Manhattan Project, 210
Manila Dodgers, 167
Manley, Effa, 141
Manning, Jimmy, 6
March of Dimes, 186
Marion, Marty, 176
Marshall, George C. (general), 53, 68–69,
    138
Marshall, George Preston, 9, 60, 225
Martin Bombers, 146–47
Martin, Glenn, 98–99
Martin, J. B., 91, 158, 165, 166, 185–86
Martin, Mike, 123, 141
Maryland Terrapins (Terps), 89
Masterson, Walter, 101, 220
Mayor's Trophy, 7
Mays, Willie, 30, 204, 236
McAleer, Jimmy, 7
McCarthy, Joe, 49, 124, 200
McClure, H. A., 101
McCullough, David, 193
McDuffie, Terris "the Great," 197
McElwain, Bill, 144–45
McGraw, John, 6–8, 204
McKellar (U.S. Senator), 148
McNutt, Paul V., 106, 143, 191
Meacham, Jon, 132
Mead, William B., 18, 24, 25, 32, 35, 49,
    167, 174, 176
Meade (U.S. Senator), 148

Memorial Stadium, 51
Memphis Red Sox, 93
Metheny, Bud, 221
Metkovich, George, 213
Metropolitan Civilian Defense, 70
Mets, 40
Mexican League, 30–31, 118, 148, 179
Mexican players, 147
Miami Ethiopian Clowns, 117–18
Mickey Vernon Sports Museum, 38
Midway, Battle of, 69–70
Milan, Clyde, 55, 174, 200
Military Training Camps Association, 13
Millers, 126
Milwaukee Brewers, 3, 200
miners' strike (1943), 109
Minneapolis Millers, 126
Minnesota Twins, xviii, 233
Mohl, Raymond, 117
Molotov, Vyacheslav, 186
Monarchs, 39, 57, 63, 70, 83, 93, 118, 128,
    165, 198, 214, 228, 229, 230
Monterrey Industrials, 118
Montreal Expos, xix
Montreal Royals, 228–30, 236
Moore, Gene, 126, 146
Moreland, Nate, 61
Morgenthau, Henry Jr., 140, 170
Morrissey, John, 141
Moses, Wally, 126, 130
Most Valuable Player awards, 29, 33, 176,
    236
Mountbatten, Louis, 129
Mud Hens, 162, 215
Mulcahy, Hugh, 17–18
Municipal Stadium, 42, 75, 209
Murphy, Howard H., 133
Murrow, Edward R., 10
Musso, Marius, 124
Mussolini, Benito, 125
Myatt, George, 103, 181, 149, 153, 154,
    214, 219

Nagasaki, 214
national anthem played before games, 53
National Association, xvi, 229
National Football League, 134
National League, xvi–xix, 3–5, 7, 20, 21,
    32, 38, 40, 51, 72, 75, 81, 85, 94, 98,

113, 114, 117, 123, 160, 176, 181, 230, 232

National Security Training Commission, 13

National War Labor Board, 109

Nationals, xiii–xx, 1, 3, 6, 8, 9, 11, 20–26, 29–31, 33, 37, 38, 40, 44–46, 49–51, 55–57, 59–62, 64, 66, 67, 69–76, 78–83, 85, 89, 90, 93, 95–98, 100–06, 108, 110–14, 116, 122, 123, 125–31, 141, 144–47, 149–56, 158–64, 166–75, 177, 182, 187–93, 195, 198–200, 202, 204, 207, 208–09, 211–25, 231, 232, 236, 237

Nationals Park, xvi, 38, 180

National Foundation for Infantile Paralysis, 186

Naval Training Station exhibition games, 70, 94, 101–03, 111, 141, 193

Nazis, xv, 11, 12, 47, 77, 139, 182

Negro American League, 39, 58, 79, 82, 91, 93, 117, 127, 128, 157–58, 165, 185, 186, 203, 226, 230

Negro Leagues, 29, 30, 39, 59, 63, 64, 71, 79, 80, 91–93, 101, 116–18, 127, 128, 131–32, 140, 144, 147, 148, 155–58, 164, 178, 185, 190, 197, 198, 203–05, 214, 215, 226, 228, 229, 235, 236

Negro National League, 30, 57, 58, 63, 80, 82, 91, 93, 117, 127, 128, 141, 148, 157–58, 165, 177, 178, 185, 186, 203, 225, 231

Negro United States League, 235

Negro World Series, 178

Neutrality Act, 11

New Deal, 10, 35

New York Black Yankees, 58, 93, 150, 202–03

New York Cubans, 93, 128, 197

New York Giants, 6, 7, 8, 10, 32, 41, 57, 76, 81, 101, 105, 142, 162, 188, 190, 236, 237

New York Highlanders, 6, 7, 141, 204

New York Yankees, xix, 7, 18, 21, 28–29, 41, 44, 46, 49, 57–59, 66, 71, 72, 80–83, 85, 87, 90, 94, 96, 101, 108, 113–14, 123, 124, 126, 129, 142, 143, 149, 152, 154, 165, 168, 169, 173, 175, 176, 190–92, 199, 201, 203, 215–18,

221, 225–27, 235, 236

Newark Bears, 105

Newark Eagles, 82, 93, 109, 114, 118, 128, 132, 141, 147, 156, 164, 178, 197

Newcombe, Don, 228

Newhouser, Hal, 173, 222–25

Newsom, Buck/Bobo, 45, 54–55, 67, 71, 80–81, 123, 129, 130

Niggeling, Johnny, 145, 147, 149, 152, 181, 221

night games, 20–24, 27, 35–42, 44, 53, 63, 72, 73, 85, 91, 104, 110–11, 114, 125, 142, 150–52, 160, 164–64, 187, 232

Nixon, Richard Milhous, 76

Now Voyager (movie), 94

Noyes, Thomas C., 49–50

Nye (U.S. Senator), 148

Nye, Gerald, 34

O'Brien, Pat, 9

O'Connor, Leslie M., 181, 201–02

O'Mahoney (U.S. Senator), 148

O'Malley, Walter, 237

O'Neill, Harry, 38, 158

O'Neill, Steve, 175, 223–24

Oakland Athletics, 87

Oakland Colts, 4

Obama, Barack, 51

Obermeyer, Jeff, 58, 64

Office of Defense Transportation (ODT), 81–83, 91. *See also* travel restrictions during WWII

Office of Economic Warfare, 125

Office of Price Administration (OPA), 51

Office of Strategic Services (OSS), xiv–xv, 11

Old Fox, the, 3. *See also* Griffith, Clark

Old Hoss, 3. *See also* Radbourn, Charles

Old Timers Committee, 31

Olympic Grounds, xvi

Olympics, the, xvi

opening pitch, xiii, 19, 46, 49–51, 106, 148, 200, 219

Operation Overlord/D-day, 111, 153

Operation Torch. *See* African campaign of WWII

Oriole Park, 6

Orioles, 6, 51, 105, 190

Orlando, Florida, 43

Orphans, 4
Ortiz, Roberto, 61, 155, 161–63, 168, 172
Ott, Mel, 188

Pacific Coast League, 31, 216, 232
Pacific theater of WWII, 46, 48, 53–54,
    65, 68–70, 107, 119, 129, 169, 214,
    218, 231
Page, Joe, 221
Paige, Satchel, 57–59, 70, 79, 80, 83, 118,
    128, 130, 165–66, 178, 179, 214, 226,
    237
Pan American Union, 12
Partlow, Roy, 64, 70–71
Patterson, Robert, 187, 189
Patton, George C., 125
Paula, Carlos, 236–37
Pearl Harbor, xiii, 1, 9, 10, 14, 19, 23, 24,
    27, 33, 34, 39, 51, 70. *See also* Pacific
    theater of WWII
Penn State, 30
Pepper, Claude, 14
Persico, Joseph E., 14
Petain, Henri-Philippe, 47
Phelps Stokes Fund, 121–22
Philadelphia Athletics, xvii, xviii, 38, 68,
    72, 78, 80, 85, 87, 90, 96, 106–08, 122,
    129, 142, 149, 151, 153, 158, 161, 169,
    177, 193, 199, 206, 208, 209, 212,
    216–17, 221, 222
Philadelphia Eagles, 9
Philadelphia Phillies, 5, 17–18, 40, 51, 57,
    73, 76, 82, 105, 108, 147, 163, 190, 209
Philadelphia Stars, 82, 93, 114, 118, 151,
    178, 198
Phillies, 5, 17–18, 40, 51, 57, 73, 76, 82,
    105, 108, 147, 163, 190, 209
Piedmont League, xv, 55–56
Pieretti, Marino, 216, 222
Pirates, 9, 30, 51, 57, 101, 110, 151, 179,
    188, 198, 209
Pittsburgh Crawfords, 179, 185, 197, 205
Pittsburgh Pirates, 9, 30, 51, 57, 101, 110,
    151, 179, 188, 198, 209
Pofahl, Jimmy, 96
Pohlad, Carl, 56
Pollock, Syd, 117–18
Polo Grounds, 6, 10, 41, 42, 72, 74, 76, 81,
    105, 209

Posey, Cumberland "Cum," 30, 83, 91,
    117, 150, 157–58, 165, 166, 186, 203,
    225
Potomacs, 29, 63
Potter, Nelson, 168, 222, 223
Povich, Shirley, 8, 19, 20, 24, 35, 44, 45,
    49, 54, 61, 67, 71, 76, 78, 95, 100, 108,
    112–14, 123, 126, 127, 148, 151, 160,
    168, 199, 208, 219, 221, 224
Powell, Adam Clayton Jr., 197
Powell, C. B., 133
Powell, Jake, 126–27, 147, 154, 155, 175,
    191, 196, 207–08
price freeze. *See* Salary caps and price
    controls
Price, S. L., 9
Priddy, Jerry, 96, 103, 106, 107, 141
Pride of the Yankees, The (movie), 17
Prout, Bill, 97
Providence Grays, 3

Quebec Conference, 180
Quesada, Elwood, 212

racial unrest/riots (1943), 121
Racine, Hector, 229
Radbourn, Charles, 3
Radcliffe, Ted "Double Duty," 79, 204
Rader, Benjamin G., 20, 40, 57
radio broadcast of games, 123
railroad strike (1943), 132
Rangers, xix
"Rapid Robert.". *See* Feller, Bob
rationing during WWII, 65–67, 76, 85, 97,
    103, 119
Rayburn, Sam, 193, 200, 219
Reagan, Ronald, 37, 177
Red Sox, 7, 21, 25, 28, 37, 44, 66, 76, 78,
    101, 108, 113, 125, 126, 128, 130, 149,
    154, 163, 169, 170, 177, 190, 198, 202,
    208, 209, 213, 218, 228, 235–36
Red Sox, Memphis, 93
Reds, 7, 20, 29, 40, 76, 98, 112, 162, 196,
    209, 237
Redskins, 9, 10, 60, 220, 223, 225
Reese, Pee Wee, 102
Reid, Warren, 95
Reiser, Pete, 94
reparations to Japanese Americans, 37

Repass, Bob, 37, 44, 72
Reynolds, Allie, 152
Rhines, John T., 150
Rice, Grantland, 50, 143, 204
Richards, Paul, 146, 223
Richardson, George, 141
Richardson, William M., 8, 67–68, 141
Rickey, Branch, 134, 142, 185, 196–97, 203, 205, 215, 228–30, 235, 237
Ring of Stars, 26
Ritchie Stadium/Coliseum, 89, 145
Rivera, Mariano, 123
Rizzuto, Phil, 94, 102, 124
Road to Morocco (movie), 94
Robert F. Kennedy Memorial Stadium, xix, 26, 79
Roberts, Ric, 62, 64, 71, 115, 238
Robertson, John, 55
Robeson, Paul, 133, 134, 140, 147, 238
Robinson, Bill "Bojangles," 215
Robinson, Frank, xix
Robinson, Jackie, 60, 61, 63, 198, 215, 226, 228–31, 235, 236, 237
Rockefeller, John D., 22
Rommel, Ed, 172
Rommel, Erwin, 76
Roosevelt, Eleanor, 19, 66, 170, 194, 202
Roosevelt, Elliott, 120
Roosevelt, Franklin D., xiii 10–11, 12, 14–19, 34–40, 44, 46–48, 51, 53, 64, 65, 67, 68, 72, 77, 84, 105, 106, 108–09, 118–22, 124–25, 129, 132, 137–39, 148, 169–70, 180, 182, 186, 187, 190, 193, 195, 198, 199, 201
Roosevelt, James, 186
Roosevelt, Theodore, 22
Ross, Charlie, 219
Royals, 228–30, 236
rubber workers strike (1943), 119
Ruel, Muddy, 160
Ruffing, Red, 124
Ruppert, Jacob Jr., 29
Rutgers University, 133
Ruth, Babe, xiv, 21, 112, 156, 224

Saints, 126
salary caps and price controls, 5, 42, 51–53, 65–67, 76, 103
Sampson, Tommy, 178

San Francisco Giants, 32
Sanford, Jack, 70
Saperstein, Abe, 117, 157–58, 166, 179
Sayre, John Nevin, 13
Scarborough, Ray, 141
Seargeant York, 17
Seidel, Michael, 17, 28
Seitz, Peter, 87–88
Selective Service, 12–14, 17, 147, 161–62, 182, 190–91, 199, 201
Selkirk, George, 21
Senators, xiii–xix, 6, 38, 41, 71, 93, 115, 116, 144, 155, 172, 232–33
Sengstacke, John Herman Henry, 132–33
Severeid, Eric, 10
Sewell, Luke, 25, 168, 171, 172, 176, 219, 224, 236
Seybold, "Socks," xvii
Shackelford, John, 185, 203, 204
Shepard, Bert, 187, 189–92, 197, 210, 213–14, 218
Sheridan, Ann, 94
Shibe Park, 83, 85, 122, 124, 150, 153, 199, 209
Shipstead (U.S. Senator), 148
Shively, Jacob Chester, 112
Short, Bob, xix
Siebert, Dick, 222
Silver Slugger award, 69
Simmons, R. S., 93
Sisler, George, 28
Smith, Kate, 112
Smith, Red, 96–97, 171–72
Smith, Wendell, 178, 198
Snyder, Brad, 30, 59, 63, 71, 80, 83, 93, 104, 115, 127, 130–31, 155, 195
softball league, 110
Somers, Charles, 4
Southern Association, 55, 230
Spartan Seasons (Goldstein), xiii, 39
Spence, Stan, 28, 37, 74–75, 78, 80, 97, 112, 126, 128, 145, 153, 154, 160, 175, 181, 188, 191
Sportsman's Park, 32, 41, 129, 152, 162, 167, 171, 172, 175, 201, 209
spring training restrictions, 88, 99–101
Spy Museum, Washington, DC, xv
St. Louis Browns, 1, 3, 18, 22, 23, 28, 31, 41, 51, 72, 80, 83, 88, 96, 112, 122,

125, 128, 130, 142, 145–46, 150–52, 154, 159, 161, 162, 167–73, 175, 176, 193, 196, 201, 206–08, 212, 215, 216, 218–23, 225, 232, 236

St. Louis Cardinals, 4, 5, 32, 41, 53, 81, 88, 112, 162, 176, 196

St. Louis Stars, 93, 158, 185

St. Louis Terriers, 22

St. Paul Saints, 126

Stalin, Josef, 68, 111, 132, 180, 186, 210

Stann, Francis E., 224

Stars, Phil, 29, 82, 93, 114, 118, 151, 178, 198

Stars, St. Louis, 93, 158, 185

Statesmen, the, xvi

Stengel, Casey, xiv, 113–14

Stephens, Vern, 171, 176

Stern, Bill, 170–71

Stettinius, Edward, 186

Stimson, Henry L., 119, 121

Stirnweiss, George "Snuffy," 221

Stokes, Anson Phelps, 121–22

Stone, Chief Justice, 194

Stone, Harlan, 186

Stoneham, Horace, 237

strikes, general industry (1943), 119–21, 132, 138–39

Suarez, Luis, 154

Sukeforth, Clyde, 228

Sullivan, John, 72, 78, 102, 107, 181, 191

Super Bowl, 134–35

Swampoodle Grounds, xvi

Sweeney, Martin, 14

Taft (U.S. Senator), 148

Taft, William Howard Taft, 49–50, 219

Tatum, Art, 131

Taylor, Candy Jim, 93, 150

Taylor, Zack, 174

team names, history of, xvi–xvii

Tehran Conference, 132

Terriers, 22

Texas Rangers, xix

They Also Served (Gilbert), 53

Thomas (U.S. Senator), 148

Thomas, Dave "Showboat," 197

Thompson, Hank, 236

Thomson, Bobby, 81

Thunder Twins.". *See* Gibson, Josh; Leonard, Buck

Tigers, 37, 44, 54, 64, 74, 81, 95, 102, 111–13, 122, 125, 127, 130, 151, 152, 158, 162, 166, 170, 173, 175, 201, 207, 209, 212, 214, 216–18, 220–25, 229

Tinker Field, 43, 86, 145, 233

Tinker, Joe, 43

Tito, Josip Broz, xiv

Toledo Mud Hens, 162, 215

Toronto Blue Jays, xix

Torres, Gilberto "Gil," 161–63, 168, 181, 215

Touchdown club, 151

training camps, 43, 145, 146, 187, 188

travel restrictions during WWII, 85, 88, 81, 92–95, 119–20

Travis, Cecil, 24–26, 29, 33–34, 37, 39, 44, 57–59, 78, 90, 182, 219, 222

Trimble, Jim, 38

Trout, Dizzy, 175

Trucks, Virgil, 223

Truman, Bess, 194, 219

Truman, Harry S., 78, 106, 148, 180, 186, 193, 194, 195, 199, 200, 201, 202, 206, 210, 218, 219

Truman, Margaret, 194

Turner, Tom, 172

Tuskegee Airmen, 144

twilighters, 151

Twins, xviii, 233

Tygiel, Jules, 203, 205, 228

Uhle, George, 163

Uline Arena, 14

Ullrich, Carlos Santiago "Sandy," 213

Union Association, xvi

United Mine Workers of America, 109, 120, 138

United Nations, 179, 187

United States Negro Baseball League, 185, 197, 203–05, 228, 235

University of Maryland training center, 89, 95, 100–01, 145, 187

University of Virginia, 89

USO baseball tour (1945), 187–88

V-2 attacks, 170

V-E day, 206

V-J day, 214, 218
Valentine, Lewis, 42
Vandenberg (U.S. Senator), 148
Vankoski, Jim, 38
Vaughn, Fred, 168, 175
Veeck, Bill, 178
Verban, Emil, 176–77
Vernon, Mickey, 37–39, 44, 64, 69, 78, 80, 90, 97, 107, 112, 141
Veterans Administration, 137
Vichy government in France, 47
Villard, Oswald Garrison, 14
Vincent, Beverly, 14
Vinson, Fred M., 119
von Choltitz, Dietrich, 168
Vosmik, Joe, 154–55

Wadsworth, James, 13
Wagner, Charlie, 101
Wagner, Honus, 5
Wainwright, Jonathan, 48, 53
Wallace, George, 231
Wallace, Henry, 49, 106, 122, 148, 180
Walters, Bucky, 188
War Labor Board, 119
War Manpower Commission (WMC), 87, 89, 106, 190, 199
War Mobilization Commission, 182
War Powers Act, 109
War Production Board, 119
War Refugee Board, 140
War Relief Night, 159
Washington Baseball Club, 104
Washington Black Senators, 63
Washington Braves, 29
Washington Elite Giants, 63
Washington Nationals, xiii–xx, 1, 3, 6, 8, 9, 11, 20–26, 29–31, 33, 37, 38, 40, 44–46, 49–51, 55–57, 59–62, 64, 66, 67, 69–76, 78–83, 85, 89, 90, 93, 95–98, 100–06, 108, 110–14, 116, 122, 123, 125–31, 141, 144–47, 149–56, 158–64, 166–75, 177, 182, 187–93, 195, 198–200, 202, 204, 207, 208–09, 211–25, 231, 232, 236, 237
Washington Nationals 1859 to Today (Frommer), 21
Washington Potomacs, 29, 63

Washington Redskins, 9, 10, 60, 220, 223, 225
Washington Senators, xiii–xix, 6, 38, 41, 71, 93, 115, 116, 144, 155, 172, 232–33
Washingtons, xvi
Wavell, Sir Archibald, 112
Weeghman, Charles "Lucky," 22
Wells, Willie, 148
Welmaker, Roy, 202, 214
Western Association, 3
Western League, 4
Whales, 22
Wheeler, Burton K., 11, 15–17
White (U.S. Senator), 148
White Sox, xvii, 22, 23, 51, 55, 61, 64, 101, 111, 112, 114, 122, 125, 126, 151–53, 159, 162, 167, 170, 171, 173, 177, 201, 207–09, 211, 214–17, 220
White Stockings, 5, 6
Wilkinson, J. L., 229
Will, George, 177
Williams, Dick, xix
Williams, Marvin, 198
Williams, Ted, 26, 28, 33, 57, 75, 149, 235–36
Willkie, Wendell, 16
Wilson, Art, 178
Wilson, Jack, 81
Wilson, Jud, 71, 226
Wilson, Tom, 158, 185–86
Wolff, Roger, 145, 147, 153, 166, 171, 210, 221–23, 225
Women Accepted for Voluntary Emergency Service (WAVES), 69
Women's Army Auxiliary Corps (WAAC), 69
Women's Auxiliary Ferrying Squadron (WAFS), 69
Wood, Phil, xviii
Woodall, Larry, 198
World Series, 5, 8, 9, 46, 51, 81, 93, 95, 96, 107, 113, 123, 160, 175, 178, 209, 211
World Series (1919), 170
World Series (1941), 28, 46
World Series (1942), 73
World Series (1943), 176
World Series (1944), 141, 173

World Series (1945), 199, 219, 221, 223, 224, 229
World Series (1946), 236
World Series (1951), 236
World Series (1952), 237
World Series, Negro League, 127
Wright, John, 202
Wrigley Field, 40, 57, 59, 109
Wrigley, Philip K, 29, 109–10
Wynn, Early, 45, 67, 71, 106, 111, 113, 126, 141, 145, 149, 150, 152, 154, 155, 159, 160, 167, 188

Yalta conference, 186–87
Yankee Clipper, 23. *See also* DiMaggio, Joe
Yankee Stadium, 40, 57, 83, 149, 156, 171, 200, 202, 216, 217, 221

Yankees, xix, 7, 18, 21, 28–29, 41, 44, 46, 49, 57–59, 66, 71, 72, 80–83, 85, 87, 90, 94, 96, 101, 108, 113–14, 123, 124, 126, 129, 142, 143, 149, 152, 154, 165, 168, 169, 173, 175, 176, 190–92, 199, 201, 203, 215–18, 221, 225–27, 235, 236
Yeager, Joe, 196
York, Alvin, 17
Young, Cy, 5
Young, Fay, 204, 206, 215
Young, Frank A., 178

Zardon, Jose, 206, 207
Zarilla, Al, 176
Zeller, Jack, 74
Zuber, Bill, 96, 221

ABOUT THE AUTHORS

David E. Hubler is the author of three previously published books. This is his first sports-history volume. A graduate of New York University and the University of New Hampshire, Hubler has taught high-school and college English courses. He also has had a lengthy career as a journalist writing and editing for such organizations as the Washington Post Company, United Press International, and Voice of America, where he served as literary editor for a decade. Raised in the shadow of Yankee Stadium, he is a lifelong Yankees fan. Hubler lives in northern Virginia with his wife Rebecca and their two dogs, Phil (after Rizzuto) and Flora.

Joshua H. Drazen is a graduate of the University of Pennsylvania where he earned a BA in history with a special focus on 20th century and Middle Eastern studies. He later received an MSJ from Northwestern University's Medill School of Journalism and a JD from the University of Connecticut School of Law. Prior to attending Medill, where he was a reporter in Chicago and on Capitol Hill for a variety of news outlets, Drazen worked as advertising copywriter in New York City. Like Hubler, he is a lifelong Yankees fan. A licensed attorney, Drazen lives in southern Connecticut, where his golden retriever, Yogi (after Berra and Bear), kept him company as he worked on what is his first sports-history volume. Drazen is currently working on a thriller based on contemporary geopolitical events.